WHAT REVIEWERS HAVE SAID ABOUT *Strange Fatality...*

"The bloody night that saved Canada. Elliott has succeeded marvellously
in turning a military history into a real cliff-hanger."
**Hans Werner, *Toronto Star***

"Detailed battle accounts are notoriously difficult to write. Elliott is
thorough, accurate, evenhanded and vivid. Strange Fatality reads like
a novel ... good, gory, realistic stuff which accurately depicts the most
unpopular conflict in U.S. history before Vietnam."
**William David Barry, *Portland Press Herald***

"A nail-biting, flesh-and-blood showdown that feels like it took place
last week. In almost any other country this would be a movie and a
prominent piece of the national mythology."
**Gord Henderson, *Windsor Star***

"A gripping account of an import'
soldiers from the poseurs ... spar
**Geoff Heinricks, (**

"Welcome and much-needed analys.                    ...₋₋₄₅ ₁ong been
worthy of an exceptional book of this calibre ... impressive research
and writing. Lively and reader-friendly ... meticulous and well-
illustrated. His portrayals of the human dimensions of the
struggle and its aftermath are gripping."
**Gord McNulty, *Hamilton Spectator***

"Elliott relates the details of this little-known but thrilling nighttime
clash with the panache of a good novelist. Strange Fatality is history, to
be sure, but it's also a page turner."
**Dan Morley, *Erie Times-News***

"One can smell the gun smoke and feel the f...
**Chris Raible, *OHS Bulletin***

"An electric shock. An exquisitely detailed yarn that never drags or descends into academic torpor. Highly recommended."
**David Young, *Hamilton Magazine***

"Brings to life a tale of courage and incompetence … about a little-known battle that changed the course of the war. A superb job of integrating contemporary sources into a fascinating narrative."
**Robert Burnham, *War of 1812 Magazine***

"Exhaustive primary research, a master story-teller's turn of phrase and a reporter's nose for human interest and quest for truth."
**Michael McAllister, *Fife and Drum***

"A terrifying tale … a must read."
**Annette Hamm, *CHCH TV***

"Sheds light on a battle too often misunderstood … had [it] turned out differently the Stars and Stripes might now be adorning flagpoles throughout southwestern Ontario."
**Don Glynn, *Niagara Gazette***

"Explains how much we have to learn about this conflict that defined Canada. Well-researched and full of illustrations."
**J. L. Granatstein, *Legion Magazine***

"A compelling account and a meticulous marshalling of facts … that takes the reader through the actions of real-life characters."
**Michael-Alan Marion, *Brantford Expositor***

"An excellent job. Brisk and engaging. Enjoyable for casual readers of military history and useful to scholars."
**Tim Compeau, *The Beaver: Canada's History Magazine***

# STRANGE FATALITY

## THE BATTLE OF
## STONEY CREEK, 1813

James E. Elliott

*M*aps by Nicko Elliott

ROBIN BRASS STUDIO

Published 2009 by Robin Brass Studio Inc.
www.rbstudiobooks.com

Website for this book: www.strangefatality.com

ISBN-13: 978-1-896941-58-5
ISBN-10: 1-896941-58-3

Reprinted 2009, 2010

Printed and bound in Canada by Marquis Imprimeur Inc., Cap-Saint-Ignace, Quebec


**Library and Archives Canada Cataloguing in Publication**

Elliott, James, 1945-

    Strange fatality : the Battle of Stoney Creek, 1813 / James E. Elliott.

Includes bibliographical references and index.
ISBN 978-1-896941-58-5

1. Stoney Creek (Ont.), Battle of, 1813. 2. Canada – History – War of 1812 – Campaigns. I. Title.

FC446.S75E45 2009    971.03'4    C2009-901078-X

# Contents

# Preface

This a book about the Battle of Stoney Creek. An obscure action in an obscure war that remains largely ignored by the two main antagonists, the British and the Americans. Only the Canadians, upon whose estate most of the action took place, saw much worth remembering of a conflict historian Arthur Lower characterized as "a succession of timorous advances and hasty retreats, of muddle-headed planning and incompetent generalship, interspersed with a few sharp actions and adroit manoeuvres which reflected credit on a few individuals and discredit on many."

Nearly two centuries after the last musket was fired in the War of 1812, a close look at Stoney Creek reveals a narrative that encompasses all of Lower's essential 1812 ingredients – a confused and timorous advance directed by incompetent generals leading to a very sharp action followed by a hasty retreat. A microcosm of the War of 1812. And it all occurred over the space of 10 days in the spring of 1813 as an American army quickly won, then just as quickly lost, the coveted Niagara Peninsula. The fulcrum of this stunning reversal of fortune was a confusing night action in a boggy meadow which both sides lost, one worse than the other. This is the story of a campaign designed to redress the humiliations of the war's first year for one side, and the other side's equally-determined effort to keep the King's colour flying over Upper Canada. It was a campaign that began with brilliant promise for one side and bleak prospect for the other. And it ended in the dark at Stoney Creek. Although the war continued on for another 18 months and Niagara was invaded again, Stoney Creek would remain the high-water mark. No American army would ever get that far again.

For clarity, American regiments are rendered in words (e.g., Sixteenth Infantry) while their British counterparts are designated in numbers (e.g., 49th Regiment). All times cited in the book, although drawn from primary sources, are approximate. Seventy-two years before the implementation of Standard Time and 82 years before DST, watches were set according to a locally agreed time based on the noon-hour sun.

I owe a debt of gratitude to a number of individuals and an organization who assisted me materially and spiritually during the writing of this book, which turned out to be a much more protracted process than I ever imagined.

First among equals is John C. Fredriksen, military historian and War of 1812 biographer, who responded to all queries with grace and humour, generously shared sources that only decades of research can uncover and constructively vetted an early manuscript. The Stoney Creek Historical Society, which takes its mandate seriously, for coming on board early with a generous grant. Peter Rindlisbacher, who used his considerable talent to pick up where C.W. Jeffreys left off and produced a compelling cover that captures the primal ferocity of a bayonet charge. Margaret Houghton, the archivist at Hamilton Public Library, who greeted my numerous, and often arcane, early history enquiries with enthusiasm and invariably had, or quickly found, the information.

Jack Bilow of Plattsburgh, New York, for sharing his comprehensive files on American War of 1812 casualties. Robin Brass, who edited judiciously and deftly wove a mound of drawings, paintings, maps and photographs into the manuscript to produce this handsome work.

My cartographer, Nicko Elliott, who used his illustration skills to draft a series of lucid and informative maps.

René Chartrand, whose knowledge of 1812 uniforms and material culture is unparalleled, cheerfully provided the disparate coat and trouser colours worn by American troops in 1813 and served as a guide to the plumage of rank.

Pat Kavanaugh, the Buffalo historian who shared pertinent files and microfilm from his personal collection. Pennsylvania writer and researcher Mark Painter, who shared his files on the Twenty-Second Infantry, including the soldier's will James Crawford wrote before going into battle. Eric E. Johnson of Avon Lake, Ohio, for access to his detailed research into the United States Army, particularly the U.S. Voluntary Corps during the War of 1812. The four readers who fearlessly tackled a raw manuscript – Gary Gibson, the late Robert Malcomson, Stuart Sutherland and Tessa Ryan-Lipp – saved me from several embarrassing lapses and substantially improved the book. Craig Williams for his line drawings of the 49th Regiment and access to files on the same regiment, Peter Twist for his painting of the 8th Foot and Scott Paterson for his drawing of the Twenty-Second Infantry. Ray Hobbs of Hamilton for information on the 41st Regiment and Thomas Taylor. Irene Spence of Perth, Ontario, for sharing her research on Alexander Fraser. Susan Ramsay, curator of Battlefield House Museum, for access to files on the Women's Wentworth Historical Society.

And lastly to my wife, Irene, for her unquestioning support. Loyalty forever.

JAMES E. ELLIOTT
*South Stipeley*
*28 April 2009*

# **1** "Perhaps the last time I will write."[1]

Long before dawn the American camp was awake and in motion.

In the darkness, a dripping wet mist obscured every sign of the sky. Over-hanging trees wept onto tent canvas. Musicians stripped linen jackets from their drums, firmed up tension ropes, and on the cue of the duty drummer, raised fifes and bugles to their lips, drumsticks to their eyebrows and unleashed a shrill, raucous refrain that rolled down the tent lines, gathering strength as the various unit drummers joined in turn.

In tents along the Lake Ontario shoreline at the mouth of Four Mile Creek, officers belted swords while other ranks shouldered cartridge boxes and bayo-nets and thumbed musket flints. And men, in the manner of warriors since the beginning of time, shared the same unspoken dread that precedes battle.

Fifty-four years earlier a British army had landed at this creek en route to wresting control of Fort Niagara and much of the Upper Great Lakes from the French Crown. On this day an American army was embarking from the creek on an equally ambitious quest to strip the British Crown of what remained of that territory. Four miles down the lakeshore, contesting the mouth of the Ni-agara River, was the objective: the stronghold of Fort George, gateway to Upper Canada. To carry that prize, more than 5,000 men – the largest army of regular troops fielded by either side in the war so far – had assembled in the still chill air. Farm boys from the frontiers, cobblers and cordwainers, cooks and coopers, and a dozen other trades, including butchers, masons, wheelwrights and labourers, all had recently downed tools and taken up arms. Despite widespread opposi-tion to the war, they represented every state from the Carolinas in the south to New Hampshire in the north. Men who, the night before, had talked loud and late, were now alone with their thoughts as they shuffled in the near-dark to the waiting boats. Assembling with the advance force – the shock troops who would be first ashore – was a rangy, fair-skinned sergeant who shepherded his section to one of the scores of flat-bottomed bateaux drawn up on the beach.[2]

Whatever thoughts occupied 23-year-old James Crawford that morning, getting his affairs in order was not among them. Recruited from western Pennsylvania a year earlier, the only son in a family of seven, James Crawford had already reflected on his mortality. He was literate, a distinct advantage in an army drawn from the lower segments of society and likely the reason he advanced to sergeant. Two days before, when the prospect of action became certain, Crawford, along with many of his comrades, had penned a soldier's will. His began: "*My father, perhaps the last time I will write to you. Should I be kild in action I write these few lines to be sent to you after my death. I expect to go in to action…. I go with a heart undaunted and Regardless of Death, with a conscience clear of gilt Either to God or man.*"[3]

In a more worldly vein, he also directed disposal of his estate, which consisted of $112 in back pay due from the army, $16.20 of due bills on soldiers and a collection of books. The letter was addressed to his best friend in Mercer, Pennsylvania, requesting – in the event of his death – delivery to his father.

By 3:30 a.m. the troops were fully embarked and the first signs of nautical dawn appeared. From the nearby woods a ponderous general officer and his staff emerged on horseback. A splendid uniform – gold-laced coat with silver stars on the epaulets, red leather sword belt and high boots with gilt spurs – could not conceal the fact Major General Henry Dearborn was not well. Cumbrous on his feet, unsteady of gait, he showed the continuing effects of a fortnight-long fever. One of the staff officers thought the Revolutionary War veteran looked like an invalid. Helped from his horse, the 62-year-old commander braced himself with a pinch of snuff while he surveyed the boats stuffed with men, bristling with bayonets. Then, steadied by staff, he boarded the

**Sergeant, Twenty-Second U.S. Infantry.** A senior non-commissioned officer of the regiment as he might have appeared on the morning of 27 May 1813 when Sergeant James Crawford helped load the men of McFarland's company into bateaux for the assault on Fort George. In this illustration by Scott Paterson his rank is denoted by the white epaulets and the short, curved sword. (Scott Paterson)

commodore's barge, which after a few oar strokes disappeared into the fog.[4]

Crawford and the 15 other men in his boat from Captain Daniel McFarland's company of the Twenty-Second Infantry were part of the 600-strong advance or "forlorn hope" under the command of an ambitious young Virginian, Winfield Scott, Dearborn's chief of staff. Scott – always keen for action – had sought permission to lead the advance and had collected the best light troops in Dearborn's army. To accompany him he had gunners and dragoons, both acting as infantry – two companies of rifles as well as two companies from the Twenty-Second Infantry and one from the Twenty-Third.[5] Commanding the Twenty-Third's detachment was a 35-year-old captain, Drake Peter Mills, who had been commissioned 14 months earlier near Albany, New York. Although a new regiment, less than a year old, the Twenty-Third had been blooded at Queenston Heights and Frenchman's Creek in the fall of 1812 and Scott had chosen Mills's light company as part of the advance – a post of honour.

Ordered to carry only muskets, ammunition, blankets and one day's ration, ready-cooked, many of the men dug into their haversacks and ate whatever they had – perhaps a heel of bread, a slab of pease porridge or smoked bacon. Dressed for the expected warmth of a late-spring day in coats now clammy in the cold mist, many soldiers felt, and stifled, the urge to shiver.

A gun boomed in from the fog to signify that the fleet was under way and at least 12 dozen small craft began leaving the beach, led by the advance and followed by three more waves at 20-minute intervals. After some initial confusion in the fog, they organized into divisions with the advance leading in an open column, four boats wide, followed by the three brigades at intervals of two to three hundred yards. Boats carrying brigadier generals bore a large green bough in the prow, and those with unit commanders on board displayed their dark-blue regimental standard.[6]

Pulling out into the lake and skirting across the mouth of the Niagara River, the boats of the advance, carrying infantrymen like Mills and Crawford as well as cavalry troopers, artillery gunners and riflemen, made for the Canadian side. Some two miles from shore they were ordered to lie upon their oars while three armed schooners took position. As the descent resumed, the fog began to dissolve. The musicians, concentrated in one boat, struck up *Yankee Doodle*[7] and the invaders caught their first glimpse of the steeply banked shoreline where the British army waited.

James Crawford, Peter Mills and more than 5,000 other uninvited guests, poised to make their first extended visit to Canada, murmured simple prayers for life and honour.

# 2 Modern Times

### THE QUICKENING OF A NEW ORDER

In the spring of 1813, the salons of Regency London were captivated by the astonishing mathematical prowess of a nine-year-old boy from the American backwoods. Zerah Colburn, the son of a New England joiner, had astonished educators and scientists in America with his ability to do complex calculations in his head.

In 1810 when he was six, the editors of the influential Boston monthly *Anthology* had declared him "the most astonishing instance of premature skill in arithmetical combinations that the world ever saw."[1] Taken to England by a father keen to cash in on his unusual gift, Zerah lived up to his advance billing. In audiences with royalty and intellectuals, in exhibitions for industrialists and scientists, the lad calmly and quickly calculated, in his head, the answers to random questions that would stress even an accomplished mathematician using pencil and paper.

The number of days and hours in 1,811 years was answered correctly in 20 seconds. The number of 3-foot steps necessary to cover 65 miles took 10 seconds to compute. Asked to square 888.888, the boy gave the correct result in 12 figures. Luminaries of the day, including the Duke of York, Princess Charlotte, the Bishop of Oxford, French mathematician Pierre-Simon LaPlace, chemist Humphry Davy and physicist Michael Faraday, came to marvel at an unschooled child capable of performing such prodigious feats of computation.[2]

The fascination with the learned innocent was symptomatic of the age. Math-

ematics is the language of science and science was the new religion. The modern age, conceived in the 1780s at the beginning of the Industrial Revolution, was rapidly approaching full term in 1813, and the world was experiencing the first quickening of a new order that would profoundly affect politics, science, economics and the arts.

**Zerah Colburn (1804-1840).** At the age of nine, the largely untutored son of a Vermont woodworker was the toast of two continents for his extraordinary prowess as a math prodigy. In 1813 he was giving exhibitions in England for the cream of society, including the Duke of York, chemist Humphry Davy and physicist Michael Faraday. (Engraving from a drawing by T. Hull. Science & Society Picture Library)

Politically, the winds of radical change were stirring all over the globe in 1813. Napoleon, still reeling from his disastrous 1812 foray into Russia, was gradually losing his iron grip on Europe. By the end of the year after a costly defeat at the hands of a massive allied army at Leipzig, *L'Empereur* would be on the ropes. The military resources of Great Britain though, after more than two decades of nearly continuous war with the French, were perilously close to the breaking point.

In Mexico, the revolt against Spanish rule started three years earlier by the *criollo* priest Miguel Hidalgo had reached the point where a hastily convened congress had issued a premature declaration of independence. The actual realization was still eight bloody years away, but the die was cast.

In Venezuela, Simón Bolivar captured Caracas from the Spanish as part of his continental liberation campaign that would, within a decade, divest Spain of Bolivia, Panama, Colombia, Ecuador, Peru and Venezuela.

In industry, steam power was ascendant. In London, John Walker, publisher of *The Times,* had placed an order for two of Friedrich Koenig's revolutionary printing presses. Within a year *The Times* would be the first newspaper in the world printed on a high-speed, steam-driven press. Capable of 1,100 copies an hour, the new press quadrupled the output of a comparable hand-powered press.

Steamboats already carried mail and passengers, the first primitive railroad locomotives were in service, the London firm of Donkin, Hall and Gamble – the first commercial "preservatory" in the world – had just begun to supply the army and the Royal Navy with preserved food,

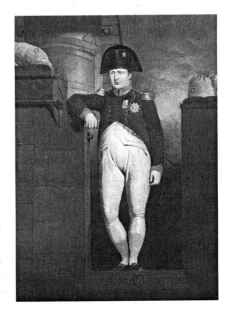

**Napoleon (1769-1821).** Imperial sunset. After nearly 20 years of military success that propelled him from little corporal to *L'Empereur* of Europe, Napoleon was tasting defeat. The disastrous invasion of Russia in 1812 emboldened some of his major allies to throw off the yoke and defect to the British. By the end of 1813, after the decisive Battle of Leipzig, Napoleon would be in retreat. He is shown here on his way to exile on HMS *Bellerophon* in 1815. (Engraving by Charles Turner after painting by Charles Eastlake. Library of Congress)

vacuum sealed in tin-lined canisters, or cans. Humphry Davy, the pioneering chemist who invented the first electric light in 1809, was building a giant 2,000-plate battery in the basement of the Royal Society to test his theories of electrolysis. By New Year's Eve 1813, coal-gas lanterns would illuminate Westminster Bridge.

Innovation, more often than not springing from the brains of uneducated mechanics and tinkerers, wrought deep changes on industry and society, not all of them positive. The most extreme response to industrialization came in Yorkshire, where traditional craftsmen, calling themselves Luddites,[3] tried to halt mechanization of the textile industry by smashing the mechanical looms used to weave stockings. The movement was serious enough that the government deployed the army and made the crime of loom-smashing punishable by death. In January 1813, 17 Luddites were hanged in York.

In the same month, the London house of Thomas Egerton published an anonymous comedy of manners about provincial middle-class life. The only clue to the author's identity was the notation that it was "By the author of *Sense and Sensibility*," which Egerton had successfully published two years earlier. The new novel, entitled *Pride and Prejudice*, had an initial print run of 1,500 copies, which sold out in six months. The author, Jane Austen, had previously sold Egerton the copyright for £110.

In Germany, a pair of sibling academics, Wilhelm and Jacob Grimm, published the first volume of *Kinder und Hausmärchen*, a collection of folk tales that included Snow White, Cinderella and Little Red Riding Hood. The first English translation of what would be known as *Grimm's Fairy Tales* followed in 1823.

In Rome, Antonio Canova, the greatest sculptor of his time, was beginning work on a commission for the Duke of

**Jane Austen (1775-1817),** widely regarded as the originator of the modern novel, was still largely unknown in 1813 when she published *Pride and Prejudice* with an initial print run of 1,500. Nearly two centuries later the novel is available in 130 editions, which regularly sell more than 100,000 copies a year. (Steel engraving from Duyckinick's *Portrait Gallery of Eminent Men and Women.* James Smith Noel Collection)

Bedford. *The Three Graces,* representing splendour, peace and happiness, would become one of his most famous masterworks.

In Milan and Venice, opera composer Gioacchino Rossini was becoming the prototype for the modern pop superstar. In 1813, the 22-year-old, who had already been composing for half his life, had four operas premiere, and two of them, *Tancredi* and *L'Italiana in Algeri,* were smash hits. The outrageously gifted Rossini, already a master of the dazzling, carefully orchestrated crescendo that would characterize his comic operas, composed *L'Italiana* in just 18 days.

Rossini's literary counterpart in unfettered, extravagant genius was the English poet Lord Byron. Characterized by one of his many lovers as "mad, bad and dangerous to know," Byron had just published the first two cantos of *Childe Harold's Pilgrimage,* a satire of the Establishment that made him the darling of London society. "I awoke one morning and found myself famous," he quipped

**Gioacchino Rossini (1792-1868).** The most popular opera composer of his time, "Signor Crescendo" was also one of the most prolific, premiering no less than four operas in 1813, two of which – *Tancredi* and *L'Italiana in Algeri* – were smash hits. Drawing on a seemingly inexhaustible supply of melodies, he was able to produce arias in a matter of minutes and once claimed he would happily set a laundry list to music. (Engraving by Henri Grevedon, 1828. Archiva Teatro Napoli, Collezione Ragni)

**Lord Byron (1788-1824).** George Noel Gordon, 6th Baron Byron, was as famous for being infamous as he was for his poetry. Sexually ambivalent, openly dissolute and "mad, bad and dangerous to know," he was also the leading poet of the 19th-century English Romantic movement. *The Bride of Abydos,* published in 1813, sold 6,000 copies in the first month, and the following year *The Corsair* would sell 10,000 copies on the day of publication. (Steel engraving from Duyckinick's *Portrait Gallery of Eminent Men and Women.* James Smith Noel Collection)

famously. A rake, rebel, atheist and defender of the Luddites, Byron published two more poems in 1813, both Oriental romances and both wildly successful. *The Giaour*, one of the first examples of vampire fiction, went through seven editions in six months, while *The Bride of Abydos* sold 6,000 copies in the first month. A lifestyle that was profligate in the extreme brought him notoriety and, within three years, permanent exile from England.

> For the sword outwears its sheath
> And the soul wears out the breast.[4]

At the same time Byron was scandalizing the drawing rooms of London, a new dance, fast-paced and intimate, was scandalizing the ballrooms of London. "The indecent foreign dance called the Waltz," sputtered *The Times,* was an assault on national virtue. "So long as this obscene display was confined to prostitutes and adulteresses, we did not think it deserving of notice; but now that is attempted to be forced on the respectable classes of society by the evil examples of their superiors, we feel it a duty to warn every parent against exposing his daughter to so fatal a contagion."[5]

In Vienna, the other outrageous genius of the age, Beethoven, arguably the mostly profoundly innovative composer of all time, was reaching the peak of his popularity. In 1813, he would premiere several new works, including the Seventh Symphony and the Battle Symphony, conducting an all-star orchestra at the University Hall in Vienna. The concert was a resounding success, both critical and popular. The nearly deaf Beethoven, in all his truculent brilliance, had become as venerated as the old Christian saints. Indeed, as his health failed and his behaviour became more irrational, Beethoven became the prototype of the divine madman, a martyr to his art. In Europe,

**Ludwig van Beethoven (1770-1827).** Perhaps the greatest composer of all time, Beethoven in 1813, although nearly deaf, was at the height of his Romantic period and wildly popular, premiering several works, including the Seventh Symphony and the Battle Symphony. Unheard in America, it would be 1817 before any of his symphonic works were played in the United States. (Portrait by Carl Jaeger. Library of Congress)

Germaine de Stäel, den mother of the Romantic poets, would champion the concept of architecture as frozen music.

The growing emergence of music as a mass market phenomenon, with its attendant and increasingly profitable ancillaries of concerts and publishing, would be underscored by the founding of the Philharmonic Society of London in 1813. Celebrated town planner John Nash's grand vision for Regent's Park and Regent Street included a purpose-designed music centre encompassing an academy, music library, music printing and publishing centre. The society was formed by a group of professional musicians at a time when there were no permanent London orchestras. Propelled by the burgeoning local music publishing industry, the Philharmonic Society of London would soon become a giant in the music world. Beethoven, in return for a £50 fee, wrote his Ninth Symphony on a commission from the society.

Across the ocean in the salons of Philadelphia and New York, where Beethoven's monumental symphonic works had yet to be heard,[6] conversation regularly centred on a war the woefully-unprepared young republic had declared on Great Britain the previous year. It was a conflict that might have been averted but for the bitter ideological residue of the American Revolution that afflicted the governments of both countries. In Washington the ruling Republicans resented the British for their arrogance and condescension,[7] while Conservative government ministers in London regarded American republicanism as a dangerous political virus. Out of that mutual antagonism grew the obscure, ostensibly mercantile and marine impetus to war. British insistence on the right to search American shipping for Royal Navy deserters and American territorial ambitions on Indian and Crown land further fuelled the animosity.

U.S. war strategy was predicated on the belief that Britain, locked in a life-death struggle with Napoleon that required all its resources, would forgo any serious defence of Canada. The planned conquest, however, had so far turned out to be little more than a farce, with a string of humiliating defeats at Detroit, Queenston Heights, Michilimackinac, Fort Dearborn, Ogdensburg and the River Raisin. Indeed, instead of adding territory, the war had so far cost America control of the vast Michigan Territory encompassing present-day Michigan, Wisconsin and part of Minnesota. Able to report nothing but catastrophes, the outspoken American press was increasingly restive. After just two months of war the *Federal Republican* in Washington declared: "Disgrace has been brought upon the American arms and the character of the nation is tarnished."[8]

In Congress the Federalist opposition pilloried the government. "Our Northern & Western Armies," wrote the distinguished Revolutionary war veteran and congressman Benjamin Tallmadge, "seem to be doomed to misfortune and Disgrace." At the beginning of the new year a Connecticut paper rolled out an epic satire in rhyme that included this cheeky doggerel: "The nation, pillag'd of its fame / Is sunk in infamy and shame / 'Six months' are past and yet the foe, / Laughs at our force and scorns the blow."[9]

And at sea the powerful Royal Navy had begun closing America's seaports to commerce in what would become a massive naval blockade. The U.S. Navy, still in its infancy, could not break the blockade although its frigates were winning impressive one-on-one battles and the visionary inventor Robert Fulton was birthing a concept that would eventually revolutionize naval warfare. In 1813 he travelled to the new national capital, still a swampy backwater, to present President James Madison with plans for a steam-powered warship specifically designed to break the Royal Navy blockade.

*Demologos*, Voice of the People, was conceived as a catamaran with the twin hulls protecting a paddle wheel in the centre and the whole vessel surrounded by a 5-foot-thick timber belt enlarged to 11 feet around the engine. Fulton called his battleship a "floating steam battery" and so it was, with twenty-four 32-pdr guns capable of firing red-hot shot. Designed to make 3 to 4 knots against the wind, such a vessel could wreak havoc on a becalmed fleet. And for good measure, *Demologos* could also carry another Fulton invention – a massive 100-pdr. gun designed to be fired underwater.[10]

Before travelling to Washington, Fulton had further enhanced his position

as America's pre-eminent engineer and inventor by exposing a scientific charlatan operating in New York City. Charles

**James Madison (1751-1836),** fourth president of the United States and one of the Founding Fathers, was pressured into declaring war on Great Britain in 1812 in the belief the conquest of Canada would be "a mere matter of marching." Saddled with a military reduced to near-token status by his predecessor, Thomas Jefferson, and in poor health, Madison struggled to prosecute the war. (Print after portrait by Gilbert Stuart. Library of Congress)

Redheffer, a Pennsylvania mechanic, was charging the public a dollar to see his perpetual motion machine in operation. Redheffer's apparatus had originally surfaced in Philadelphia in 1812, attracting considerable interest in the press and some notable champions, including journalist William Duane, who also happened to be adjutant general of the army. A debate raged on whether Redheffer's wheeled and geared apparatus could actually generate power without fuel but there was no question that it did generate money – up to $100 a day. And stoking the interest were press reports that Redheffer had refused a $200,000 offer for patent rights. On New Year's Eve, Redheffer relocated his exhibition to Manhattan, where one of the early visitors was Fulton. Observing the device in operation, he noted that it wobbled and the speed varied. Confronting Redheffer, the angry Fulton, encouraged by the crowd, knocked away some boards from a wall beside the machine and uncovered a catgut belt which he traced to an upper room where an old man sat turning a crank. Enraged by the hoax, the crowd smashed the machine and its inventor fled.[11]

Also in January 1813 the eastern newspapers carried accounts of the army's latest abortive attempt to invade Canada in which a newly-minted brigadier general, John Chandler, had his first taste of combat command.

In 1813 Congress passed the first public health program in U.S. history, An Act to Encourage Vaccination. Inspired by the crusading Baltimore physician James Smith, Congress authorized the subsidized distribution of smallpox vaccine to any citizen in the country by providing free postage. The 1798 discovery of a smallpox vaccination was heralded as a miraculous cure at a time when the disease killed 400,000 a year in Europe alone.[12]

**Robert Fulton (1765-1815).** A brilliant American engineer who developed the first practical steamboat, Fulton also designed and built the first successful submarine. In 1813 he unveiled plans for a steam-powered warship designed to break the Royal Navy's blockade on eastern ports. The ship, *Fulton the First*, the first of its kind in the world, was launched in 1814. (Library of Congress)

By 1813 the 18 states had a total population of close to eight million. New York City with 123,000 people was the largest city, followed by Philadelphia at 100,000 and Baltimore at half that.[13] The republic was still overwhelmingly agrarian and rural, less than one in 12 living in cities. Uncle Sam, as the personification of the American government, made his first appearance in 1813 in the pages of an upper New York State newspaper. Enemy or not, the booksellers of Boston, New York and Philadelphia were hawking the latest titles from England including Byron's romaunt *Childe Harold's Pilgrimage* at 75 cents a copy; theatres offered English drama with English stars; and merchants advertised the best English Casimeres and Kerseymeres and the finest Suwarrow boots.[14]

Along the republic's northern boundary the remaining British colonies in North America were, by comparison, sparsely populated and undeveloped; they were thinly garrisoned and irresistibly tempting to the promoters of a philosophical notion that 30 years on would become known as *Manifest Destiny*. The two most accessible prizes were the adjoining colonies of Upper and Lower Canada. Detailed articles on both provinces were widely circulated in the American press as virtual catalogues for the next proprietor. Potential visitors to Upper Canada were assured: "Inhabitants are well-disposed towards the United States and are intimately related to them by consanguinity, customs, language and interest." Nearly every newspaper carried prominent advertisements for maps of Upper and Lower Canada, pre-eminent among which was Scottish-American cartographer John Melish's coloured *Seat of the War* which sold for $1.[15]

The longer-settled and largely French-speaking Lower Canada was the more coveted, with Quebec and Montreal as the prime military targets. Montreal, in 1813 already 171 years old, was a commercial and industrial centre of about 16,000 with a public library and a newspaper older than *The Times*. Brewing pioneer John Molson had two steamboats operating on the St. Lawrence River, and Scottish trader and politician James McGill, one of the wealthiest men in Montreal when he died unexpectedly in 1813, bequeathed £10,000 and his 46-acre estate at the foot of Mount Royal to establish the university that would bear his name.[16]

Upper Canada, hived off from the vast Quebec territory 22 years earlier as Britain's Anglo enclave in the heart of North America, was little more than an embryo struggling to survive. The first significant influx of Europeans had been the American Loyalists, exiled after the Revolution for their allegiance to the British Crown. To the politicians in Washington, the colony must have seemed virtually uninhabited. Although extensive on paper, Upper Canada, in reality, was a precariously thin strip of settlement along the Lower Great Lakes. "All frontier and nothing else," Wellington said. The total population, no more than 80,000, was less than two-thirds that of New York City; Kingston the largest town, had 1,000 people; the capital York, "a dirty straggling village" according to one British army officer, had 600 people living in 60 mostly wood-frame houses.[17]

In an effort to boost the population of the fledgling colony, the Crown offered free land to anyone who would take an oath of allegiance, and thousands of Americans, including some who had borne arms against Britain during the Revolution, took up the offer. By 1813 a sizeable proportion of the population, at least a third, were recent arrivals from the United States whose loyalty to the Crown was questionable at best.

As early as 1800, fears were raised that American settlers would become "a nest of vipers in the bosom that fosters them." One American newcomer said he came to Upper Canada before the war "in order to obtain land upon easy terms (as did most of the inhabitants now there) and for no other reason."[18]

**"Seat of the War."** A detail from Melish's map published in the United States in 1813. (Library and Archives Canada, NMC-6760)

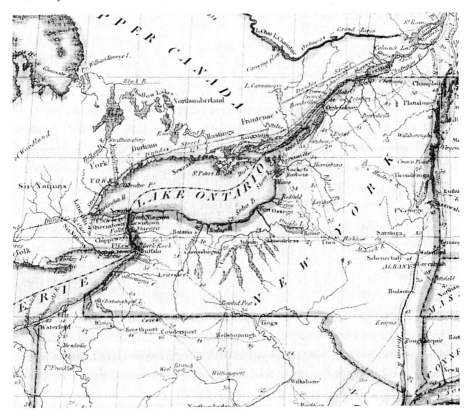

Ninety-five per cent of the population lived on subsistence farms; only Kingston, York and Newark could support a newspaper; there was no public school system and little in the way of a common identity. For most inhabitants, active involvement in politics was a luxury still to be attained. Of much more immediate concern was the success or failure of the crops in the ground, usually wheat or rye. So perilous was the food supply that in March 1813 the legislative council in York instituted the first prohibition in Canadian history, banning production of whisky from grain to conserve supplies.[19]

The number of British troops had increased somewhat since the beginning of the war, when there were barely 1,800 regulars in Upper Canada, but still fell far short of what was necessary to effectively defend some 400 miles of border.

The militia numbered 12,000 men but were of such dubious quality that the governor-in-chief, Sir George Prevost, deemed it unsafe to arm more than 4,000. And for their part, a significant proportion of militia had no desire to be armed. A farmer on the militia rolls as a private earned the equivalent of 10 cents a day while the same farmer on contract to transport supplies for the army could make the equivalent of $4 a day. Even a day labourer could make up to $2 a day working for the Crown as a civilian.[20]

The most highly developed area in Upper Canada was the Niagara Peninsula with 12,000 inhabitants in 20 townships from Ancaster to Wainfleet. Situated between Lake Ontario and Lake Erie and bounded on the east by the Niagara River, Niagara – or Lincoln County as it was officially known – was still heavily timbered with white pine, black walnut, hickory, oak and beech. The central town and former capital, Newark or Niagara,[21] was a handsome borough of 500 with two churches, a jail, an academy, six taverns and 20 shops.

Newark prospered as garrison town for the rickety bastion, Fort George, which guarded the western mouth of the Niagara River. Twelve hundred yards across the river in New York State stood Fort Niagara. In November 1812 the two forts had exchanged over 2,000 rounds in a prolonged but inconclusive artillery duel. Thirty-five miles south, opposite the town of Buffalo, the British controlled the Lake Erie entrance to the river from Fort Erie. And just above the mighty falls of Niagara a small British detachment was posted at the village of Chippawa.

The Niagara Peninsula's chief geographical feature is a steep limestone escarpment that extends like a crooked spine to the Head of the Lake before veering north. Beneath this cliff the Canadians called the Mountain, fruit flourished, including apples, pears, peaches, melons, nectarines, apricots, plums, cherries and grapes. Not surprisingly, bees to pollinate the fruit trees and provide honey abounded as well. The average farm could harvest between 16 and 24 bushels of wheat per acre, as well as flax, Indian corn and potatoes. In Grantham township, now the site of St. Catharines, a well-kept "milch" cow pastured on white clover and timothy could produce 12 quarts of milk a day, enough to make two pounds of cheese.[22]

In Barton Township, where the expansive bay that defined the township's northern boundary had been declared "as beautiful and romantic a situation as any in interior America," land that sold for the equivalent of 25 cents an acre in 1792 was now selling for $6 an acre. For all of that though, the settlement that would eventually become the city of Hamilton could muster little more than 100 inhabitants.[23] In adjoining Saltfleet Township, which included the hamlet of Stoney Creek, superior grazing land produced some of the best butter in the entire colony.[24]

For defensive purposes, Lincoln County mustered five numbered battalions of the Lincoln Militia with a total strength of about 1,500, of whom the majority were Loyalists. However, apart from the flank companies, which had been reasonably well trained, the militia was not well regarded by the British army. And, for their part, many of the militia strongly suspected that if push came to shove, the army was prepared to abandon most of Upper Canada.

The American settler and itinerant Baptist preacher Michael Smith said in 1813 "it is now generally expected that the province will fall into the hands of the American government," and "the opinion of many in Canada now is that the province ought now to be conquered for the good of the inhabitants on both sides."[25]

After visiting Upper Canada in 1811, John Melish said that "were 5000 men to be sent into the province with a proclamation of independence, the great mass of the people would join the American government."[26]

One of the popular American almanacs published that year matter-of-factly concluded a capsule description of Canada, Upper and Lower, with: "This is the country which the government of the United States has undertaken to conquer."[27]

## 3 "So unequal a contest."[1]

### YANKEE DOODLE COME TO TOWN

In the beginning there was fog. A thick, heavy cloud that cloaked the lake like a shroud.[2] Fifty yards off shore the bottle-green lake simply disappeared. And stare as they might, the party of British officers beside the stone lighthouse could discern nothing but an opaque wall of mist.

Voices could be heard and the splash of oars but there was nothing to be seen. For three days the British had been bracing for the invasion – there could hardly have been a soul on either side of the Niagara River that did not know it was coming. The softening-up process had begun two days earlier with a destructive bombardment of Fort George. Clearly the moment of invasion was at hand. Much less certain, however, was where the landing would take place.[3]

With only 1,000 regular troops and 300 militia to oppose an invasion force at least four times bigger along an 11-mile front extending the length of the Niagara River from Newark to the village of Queenston, the best Brigadier General John Vincent could hope for was to disrupt the initial landing. The Anglo-Irish officer had seen action in Haiti, Holland and Denmark but had been on garrison duty in Canada since 1802 and had not been in combat for 12 years. Quite possibly he reflected for a moment on a plan he had proposed a month earlier that could have forestalled this invasion by seizing Fort Niagara when it was garrisoned by only a few hundred troops.[4]

Now, the opportunity for pre-emptive strikes long-since squandered, Vincent faced the prospect of confronting an opponent that dwarfed his little force. Certainly when the fog, like the curtain on a grand theatrical production, began to lift at 6 a.m.[5] the enormity of the task he faced rapidly became apparent.

Facing him in an extended half-circle of more than two miles was a vast flotilla beyond anything ever seen on the lake. A corvette, a brig and eight schooners – 16 armed vessels in all – and scores of Durham boats, scows, bateaux, whalers, long boats, skiffs and launches, all tightly packed with troops and

**Brigadier General John Vincent (1764-1848).** With 32 years of service, the Irish-born Vincent was considered a competent officer. Earlier in his career he had seen action in Haiti, Holland and Denmark but he had been on garrison duty in Canada since 1802. He was in charge of Kingston in November 1812 when an American squadron under Commodore Isaac Chauncey aggressively engaged shore batteries and the *Royal George* in an intense two-hour gun battle. (Trustees of Muckross House, Killarney)

artillery, hovered off shore.[6] To the defenders on the Canadian side, most of whom had slept only sporadically over the previous three days, it was a daunting sight.

A Canadian militia officer said the fog had allowed the Americans to "place every vessel and boat exactly where they wished without our being able to annoy them in the least or even knowing where they were. When the weather cleared up we found ourselves surrounded with boats and vessels on every side." An American staff officer said the fog lifted just enough to allow the flotilla to manoeuvre yet "at the same time [we] were as much concealed from the enemy's observation as if we had been approaching in a squadron of diving bells."[7]

And yet, despite the vast force arrayed against them, British morale was high – the regulars were in good spirits and the militia, notwithstanding their inexperience, eager for action. Vincent's second-in-command, Colonel Christopher Myers, who had little respect for his adversary's military prowess, was impatient to punish what he regarded as American arrogance.[8]

From the American side of the Niagara River the vast flotilla presented a unique and grand spectacle. Indeed, for some the harmony of light and water momentarily transcended the lethal intent. In the eyes of one American officer,

**Battle of Fort George, 27 May 1813.** In this contemporary depiction of the combined naval and military operation, the divisions of small boats can be seen threading their way through Chauncey's squadron as they make for their landing point to the right of the lighthouse. A heavy early-morning fog had enabled the Americans to place all their vessels virtually undetected. (Archives of Ontario, S1439)

"the ascending vapours, gilt by the bright sun, floating above – the lofty fleet and bannered boats moving below – together formed a scene at once imposing and beautiful."[9]

On the signal of a rocket fired from Fort Niagara, the guns of that fortification and five land batteries opened a furious 30-minute barrage on Fort George and the adjoining town of Newark. Fort George, which had been hammered during the two previous days' bombardments, did not respond. When the firing ceased, Scott's advance could be seen pulling for the mouth of Two Mile Creek to the west of the lighthouse. The common adjoining that landmark stone structure had been an obvious landing site but memories of the disastrous magazine explosion at Fort York exactly a month earlier had convinced the American leadership to give the stone lighthouse a wide berth.[10] As the advance made for shore, the schooners of Commodore Isaac Chauncey's fleet took marked positions and with a variety of ordnance ranging from 4 pdrs. to 32 pdrs. engaged the British shore batteries. Across the river, the guns at Fort Niagara weighed in and drove in all British pickets along the shoreline between Fort George and the lighthouse.

From Fort Niagara and its five adjacent batteries, the Americans brought 25 guns and mortars to bear on the Canadian shore. Another 51 guns on the fleet completed the crossfire position. In response the British, working from Fort George and five adjacent batteries, could bring only 16 guns and mortars into action[11] and the majority of those only temporarily.

West of the lighthouse three American schooners, including the *Scourge*, were directed to anchor and cover a particular piece of shoreline. The owner of the property, James Crooks, a prominent merchant who commanded a company of the 1st Lincoln Militia waiting on shore, certainly would have recognized one of the vessels manoeuvring through the smoke and fog to enfilade his farm.

Indeed, the 50-ton topsail schooner, with the likeness of Britain's most famous naval hero on the bow, had been built at Newark two years earlier by James Crooks and his brother William for the transport of military provisions, grain and potash across Lake Ontario. Originally named *Lord Nelson*, the vessel was seized by the U.S. Navy in 1812 and fitted with ten guns. In an ironic twist, Crooks' merchantman, renamed *Scourge*, was about to riddle the property of her legal owner with a lethal combination of grape and canister shot.[12]

As the American boats approached Crooks' property, a single-gun battery near the mouth of Two Mile Creek, probably an 18-pdr. carronade, fired on the schooners, missed and sent its shot skipping menacingly towards the advance. In the stern of a skiff behind the advance, a young staff officer watched the shot as it ploughed to a halt and sank: "The compliment was soon returned by the schooners, whose long toms being trained so as to cross their lines of fire just behind and over the battery, threw in a brace of spherules, which intersecting each other at the battery, furrowed and tore things pretty much to pieces there, and then bounding off through the woods in opposite direction, felled more branches in a few moments, than a good axeman could lop off in as many days."[13]

While the naval and land artillery bombarded the shoreline from Fort George in the east to Two Mile Creek in the west, the flotilla of landing craft swept for the shore, heartened by cheering spectators on the American bank and a spirited rendition of *Yankee Doodle* from the amalgamated fife and drum, all stuffed into one boat.[14]

On the receiving end of the artillery, a British staff officer, Captain George Fowler, was astonished at the intensity of the barrage by which "a great extent of ground was plainly brought under the fire of an amazing quantity of ordnance, a great part of which was of large calibre."[15]

**"With equal obstinacy on both sides."** When Colonel Winfield Scott led the American advance ashore near Two Mile Creek, he was met by the resolute bayonets of the Glengarry Light Infantry, the Royal Newfoundland Regiment, Runchey's Coloured Corps and the 1st Lincoln Militia. The two sides pounded each other in a fierce, 15-minute fire fight before the British withdrew in the face of superior numbers. (Detail of a painting by Peter Rindlisbacher. Parks Canada, Fort George National Historic Site)

Even the old hands on the British line were impressed. Lieutenant Colonel John Harvey had been a soldier for 19 of his 35 years and seen extensive action in Europe, Africa and Asia. Deputy adjutant general, and Vincent's chief of staff, he was arguably the most able field-grade officer in the entire Canadian command. Standing with the reserves in the rear, Harvey reported "the most complete cross fire I ever witnessed. The whole plain of Fort George was plowed & intersected in the most extraordinary manner & you perpetually found shots passing you from Front & Rear at the same moment, added to this an armed schooner took her station on each street of the Town for the purpose of scouring it when any of our men showed themselves." After the battle, British prisoners acknowledged they had never seen more accurate artillery fire.[16]

In a thicket near the mouth of Two Mile Creek, Captain John Norton, the Cherokee-Scot war chief, could see the unnerving effect naval firepower and superior numbers were having on his band of 60 Grand River warriors. Crouched in a shallow ravine as Chauncey's guns ranged the wooded shoreline, Norton could only watch helplessly as two-thirds of his force calculated the odds and slipped away.[17]

However, as the boats carrying the advance passed between the schooners and the shore, the naval guns were momentarily checked. This delay allowed the British to form on the shore and unleash at least two concentrated volleys at the approaching troops, inflicting some casualties and silencing the musicians. To the troops confined in open boats, particularly those working the oars with their backs to the shore, the opening riposte was especially harrowing.

Having split his force in three parts, Vincent had only about 250 men to oppose the initial landing – two under-strength companies of the Glengarry Light Infantry, one of the Royal Newfoundland Fencibles, a small detachment of Runchey's

**Lieutenant Colonel John Harvey (1778-1852).** One of the ablest British officers in North America with extensive combat experience in Europe, Africa and Asia, Harvey was so keen to reach his posting at Niagara that he travelled 1,400 miles overland from Halifax, part of the way on snowshoes, in February 1813. Had the Americans been prompt in their pursuit after Fort George, the British army, Harvey said, would have been "caught under a circumstance of every possible disadvantage." (Library and Archives Canada, C2733)

Coloured Corps and about 100 men of the 1st Lincoln Militia.[18] A hodgepodge of unequal units to be sure, but still effective enough in concert to lay down an impressive fusillade. American troops reported a massive discharge of musketry.[19]

Brigadier General John Parker Boyd, commanding the brigade immediately behind the advance, said the concentrated fire whipped the lake into a foam. One of his staff officers reported the opening volley burst like a moving flame along the bank. Another officer said that for 15 minutes the fire was incessant and the bullets fell like hail on the water. A company commander of the Sixteenth Infantry, writing to a friend in Baltimore two days later, made it sound like a rousing adventure: "Our men landed under a tremendous fire of grape, cannister, musket and buck shot, which whistled round my ears most musically – but neither balls, British nor Indians could damp the ardor and gallantry of our troops."[20]

A young staff officer watched his orderly take a hit and tumble into the lake: "It was no time for sympathy or delay and we passed over his body, which sunk without a struggle as if it had been a stone thrown overboard."[21] Still American casualties in the landing craft were surprisingly light, prompting the same officer to credit poor British marksmanship. "If … he had fired at us with his eyes shut, scarcely a bullet could have failed to violate the sixth commandment. Nothing but Providence and exceedingly bad shooting permitted so many of us to live and fight another day."[22]

The Second Artillery, led by the towering figure of Winfield Scott, was the first unit to hit the narrow beach, debark and quickly form up under the steep ten-foot banks. Scott, Dearborn's chief of staff, was considered by the old revolutionary to be the most promising officer in the northern army.[23] On Scott's right flank were

**John Norton, Teyoninhokarawen, Mohawk war chief (1770-ca.1825)** was one of the most intriguing characters of the War of 1812. The son of a Cherokee father and a Scottish mother, he was educated in Scotland before coming to America, where he was successively a soldier, schoolteacher, fur trader and interpreter for the Indian Department. Under Joseph Brant's sponsorship he was appointed the Mohawks' war chief and at Queenston Heights his warriors played a significant part in the British victory. (Watercolour by Mary Ann Knight. Library and Archives Canada)

Benjamin Forsyth's riflemen and on his left, under Lieutenant Colonel George McFeely, were Milliken's and McFarland's companies from the Twenty-Second Infantry, Mills' company from the Twenty-Third Infantry and a company of rifles. Scott, in the centre, had Nicholas's and Biddle's companies from the Second Artillery, Stockton's company of the Third Artillery and a detachment of the Second Light Dragoons.

Scott and Captain Jacob Hindman, both five-year veterans of an army still composed largely of novices, stepped ashore to face the resolute bayonets of British infantry. From the viewpoint of the next brigade about to come ashore, the way ahead appeared "as red with the enemy as if a fire were spreading through the underbrush." Confronted with this, the artillerymen faltered briefly, regrouped and then, with the rest of the advance, engaged the British troops, now reinforced by five companies of the 8th Regiment – in total about 560 men of which 440 were regulars.

Scott's advance had equal numbers and a fierce, close-range fire fight commenced "with equal obstinacy on both sides." For 15 minutes they whaled away at each other from 20 to 30 feet, neither side giving an inch, both knowing the success of the entire operation hung in the balance right there.[24] But as Boyd was able to bring more and more of his brigade of 1,300 into action, sheer numbers began to tell and the British were forced back.[25]

So intense was the initial clash that U.S. surgeon James Mann counted 391 casualties in an area barely 200 yards long and 15 yards wide. British resistance had been stiff, and it cost the redcoats dearly. Official returns acknowledge only 52 regulars killed but other sources indicate the actual figure may have been two or even three times higher. A young American staff officer recoiled

**Colonel Winfield Scott (1786-1866).**
Perhaps the ablest young field officer in the American command, Scott, ignoring orders to the contrary, aggressively pursued and nearly overtook the retreating British army in the hours after the fall of Fort George. His commanding officer, Henry Dearborn, said, "No officer in the Northern Army … possesses the necessary requisite for forming a great officer, in so eminent a degree as Col. Scott." (*Portfolio Magazine*, 1816)

from the carnage – "one could hardly take a step without running the hazard of stumbling over the corpse of some soldier." Three brigades had followed Scott's advance guard ashore, the first commanded by a former soldier of fortune, John Parker Boyd, the second by a Baltimore lawyer, William Henry Winder, and the third by a one-time blacksmith and tavern keeper, John Chandler.[26]

Throughout the entire action Scott's combined light companies were the sharp end of the stick and paid the steepest price. The advance, 600-strong, took 89 casualties including 23 killed. Sergeant James Crawford of the Twenty-Second and Captain Peter Mills of the Twenty-Third, however, were unscathed. Boyd's brigade, at nearly three times the size of the advance, had 55 casualties. Winder's brigade had six and Chandler's none. The commanding officer, Henry Dearborn, largely debilitated by illness, had to be carried on board the American flagship, *Madison,* and never landed at all, witnessing the entire battle from the lake.[27]

Shortly past noon it was over.[28] Overwhelmed by numbers and outgunned by artillery that gutted Fort George and cut huge swaths through his infantry, Vin-

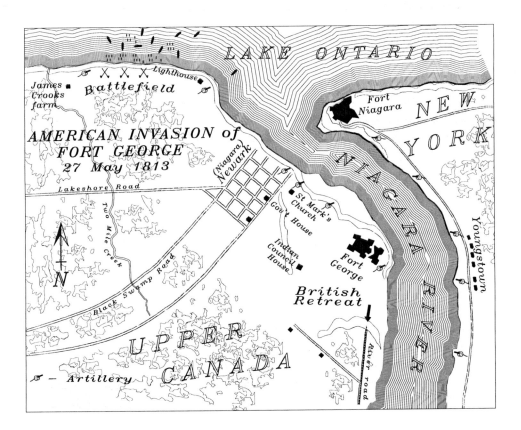

cent had little choice but to gather his dwindling forces and retreat south along the Niagara River towards Queenston. "I could not consider myself as justified," he wrote, "in continuing so unequal a contest."[29] Among the 14 officer casualties was the would-be chastiser, Colonel Christopher Myers, who was wounded five times and captured.

In advance of his retreat, Vincent sent a courier from the provincial dragoons to Fort Erie ordering Lieutenant Colonel Cecil Bisshopp to withdraw all his regular troops and field guns along the Niagara River. To the west along Lake Ontario, he sent another dragoon, 19-year-old W. Hamilton Merritt, to intercept two companies of the King's Regiment and a small Royal Navy detachment under Commander Robert Barclay at Twenty Mile Creek, where they had arrived by boat from the Head of the Lake.[30]

When Scott tore down the King's colour from the Fort George staff, spectators on the American side of the river cheered and the army as a whole rejoiced. "One of the handsomest spectacles I ever beheld," an American officer crowed. "The cannonading of the navy and batteries, the musquetry from the bank, the shots and shells which filled the air, the calm sunshine of the day, and finally the velocity of the flying enemy, altogether formed a scene sublime beyond description."[31]

At last the Americans had achieved what for them was an extreme rarity so far in the war – a decisive victory. No generals killed, as Pike had been at York. No generals captured, as Winchester had been at the River Raisin and Hull at Detroit. The army and the navy had acted in concert to execute a textbook-worthy amphibious landing – unlike the army's disaster at Queenston Heights. They had beaten and dispersed some of the best infantry in the world. The Bulwark of Upper Canada had fallen.[32] Could the rest of the upper province be far behind?

An officer who witnessed the invasion from an artillery battery reflected the growing confidence of the American army: "Our flag waves triumphant over Fort George, the strongest place in Upper Canada. We shall do well this campaign, whatever they may say about our former misfortunes. Our cause draws down the blessings of heaven."[33]

## 4  "We ought to have pursued the enemy night and day."[1]

### CARRYING OFF THE KERNEL, LEAVING THE SHELL.

Carried into what was left of Fort George, the ailing Revolutionary, Henry Dearborn, penned a brief report to Secretary of War John Armstrong commending the infantry, the navy and the artillery for routing the enemy. "Our light troops pursued them several miles," he noted, "but having been under arms from one

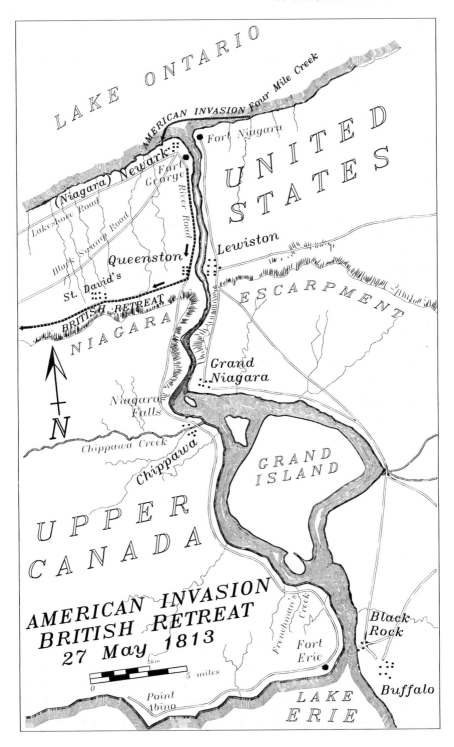

LAKE ONTARIO

AMERICAN INVASION Four Mile Creek

Fort Niagara

UNITED STATES

(Niagara) Newark
Fort George
River Road

Lakeshore Road
Black Swamp Road

Queenston
St. David's

Lewiston

BRITISH RETREAT

NIAGARA

ESCARPMENT

Grand Niagara

Niagara Falls

Chippawa Creek

Chippawa

GRAND ISLAND

UPPER CANADA

Black Rock

AMERICAN INVASION
BRITISH RETREAT
27 May 1813

Frenchman's Creek

Fort Erie

Buffalo

0   5 km   5 miles

Point Abino

LAKE ERIE

o'clock in the morning were too much exhausted for any further pursuit ... tomorrow we shall proceed further on."[2]

Certainly it was an improvement on Dearborn's first invasion of Canada in 1775, when as part of the disastrous Montgomery/Arnold expedition, the young company commander had been taken prisoner at Quebec.[3]

He concluded his report to the secretary with a woefully-inaccurate casualty report – 17 killed and 45 wounded.[4] The actual numbers were at least two and half times higher. It would not be the last time the major general would release spurious casualty figures. He did not tell the secretary of war that the only American officer killed, Lieutenant Henry Hobart, was also his grandson.

The brevity of his report certainly had much to do with Dearborn's health. A physician by training, the 62-year-old had been battling a chronic fever for two weeks before the invasion. Against the advice of his surgeons he accompanied the expedition but was so feeble he could barely stand and had to be helped on and off boats and horses. Most of the day would be spent on board ship.[5]

In his youth Henry Dearborn had a distinguished career. The prominent Republican politician Charles Ingersoll said: "He was early and active, brave and exemplary in the field, from first to last in the war of the Revolution ... on all occasions a meritorious officer when young." Thirty years later however, "there appeared ... a want of alacrity, of activity, a torpor about Dearborn's movements."[6] For the second consecutive action, the highest-ranking officer in the American army witnessed a land battle from his naval transport. Although the descent on York

**Major General Henry Dearborn (1751-1829).** An active officer who fought at Bunker Hill, Quebec, Ticonderoga, Monmouth and Saratoga during the American Revolution, Dearborn was well past his best-before date in 1813. As the ranking officer for the first year of the war, his record was dismal with only meaningless victories at York and Fort George against a litany of failures from Lacolle to Queenston Heights. (Engraving by K.H. Burn. Library of Congress)

had been a success, little of the credit reflected on Dearborn. From the American camp at Four Mile Creek one of his subordinates noted: "The officers are all disgusted with the ignorance and foolish conduct of Gen. Dearborn. Indeed, I wish we had a single man here qualified to command a regiment."[7]

Effective command of the invading army at Newark fell to Major General Morgan Lewis, former governor of New York, whose campaign experience was largely limited to the electoral variety. Described by one of his contemporaries as "a Major General who could not execute the duties of Quarter Master," Lewis was a cautious man, a characteristic he displayed at Fort George.[8]

For all the planning and preparation that went into the descent on Fort George – it was the best joint-forces effort by the Americans in the entire war – there was a lapse in forethought when it came to actually finishing off the British army.[9] With Vincent in retreat – his troops through the woods, his artillery and baggage on the Queenston road – the intrepid Winfield Scott seems to have been the only senior officer to grasp what was happening: a beaten army was being allowed to escape. Scott sent the bulk of his vanguard – light companies and riflemen – after the British while he and Hindman stormed into the ruins of Fort George.

Undeterred by a collarbone broken by flying timber when one of the powder magazines exploded, Scott – on Colonel Myers' horse with the King's colour from the fort draped over the saddle – caught up with the advanced guard just outside the village of Newark. The artillery, being drawn by hand, soon fell hopelessly behind.[10] Authorized to take orders from major generals only, Scott had received several orders to halt, "but as these did not come thro' the proper channels, I pursued my march."[11]

Across the river from Five Mile Meadow, Scott halted while the Second U.S. Regiment of Light Dragoons under Colonel James Burn landed to join the chase with a loud fanfare of bugles. The original plan had been for the dragoons to be ferried across the river to cut off Vincent's retreat but the cavalry had been delayed by fire from a pair of field guns at de Puisaye's house and the opportunity lost. Another presented itself, however, because the dragoons gave Scott the ideal weapon for running down a fleeing army.[12]

Although entitled to command by seniority, Burn deferred to the hard-charging Scott. The cavalry colonel, born in South Carolina and educated in Europe, was considered a brave soldier but lacked the brash certainty that drove Scott.[13] It was not the last time Burn would balk at the prospect of command.

With Queenston in sight, an express arrived, bearing a direct order from Lewis to end the pursuit. Scott had pushed his initiative as far as he dared. Not only had Lewis sent the order to halt, he also reprimanded him for having gone so far.[14] The advance guard – supported by fresh cavalry, reinforced by Boyd's brigade and only a few miles behind the British – was halted and led back to the battered village of Newark.

Who actually ordered the recall of the pursuit remains contentious. Dearborn said he had issued no orders from the ship and maintained that Lewis, being on shore, had immediate command.[15] Lewis, for his part, said he was given a direct order by Dearborn to halt the pursuit.[16] To an ailing Henry Dearborn, unable to remain upright more than a quarter of an hour, it may have seemed a minor disappointment at the end of an otherwise highly successful day.[17] But he had been warned about allowing the British army to escape only a few days earlier by the secretary of war.[18] And among the officers and men of the advance there were ominous grumblings about timid generals – Dearborn's nickname was "Granny"[19] – and lost opportunities.

A young artillery officer from Philadelphia, Patrick McDonough, wrote to his parents that "we might have taken them all prisoners were it not that our Generals advanced too cautiously."[20]

Lieutenant Colonel George McFeely, who commanded four companies of light troops in the advance, felt the same way: "We returned with reluctance from the pursuit. This was in my opinion highly censurable on our generals. We ought to have pursued the enemy night and day while they were under panic. We could have captured all their stores and baggage that evening and a greater number of their army…. Our Generals appeared to act as if Canada were conquered."[21]

Colonel James Miller, who landed the Sixth Infantry as part of Boyd's brigade, said that if the initial successes had been properly followed up "it would [have] been one of the first and most brilliant achievements during the war."[22] Even the rank and file were mystified. A private in the volunteer Baltimore Blues who came ashore with Boyd's brigade wrote home: "I can hardly tell how we let the enemy off so easy here. We had five men to their one."[23]

Morgan Lewis, well known for his love of comfort on campaign, was likely the target of an infantry captain who complained, "there was no necessity for stopping at Newark except the Generals having been hungry…. I suppose they thought they had glory enough for one day without following up the enemy."[24]

Lewis, however, would remain adamant – his army, despite two brigades that had hardly fired a shot, was spent. "Infantry, after eleven hours severe duty, unaided by cavalry, and destitute of the means of moving artillery," his reasoning went, "have little chance of overtaking in a hostile country, a flying enemy much less fatigued than his pursuers."[25]

Meanwhile, the "flying enemy," in reality badly-mauled and reeling from heavy losses – 350 regular casualties and 85 militia killed and wounded – could hardly credit its good fortune, having been allowed to escape "this disastrous day."[26] John Harvey, Vincent's second in command, knew that the British had been let off the mat at the very moment they were most vulnerable. "The troops continued their retreat towards Queenston Mountain in perfect order without the slightest molestation from the enemy," he wrote. "Of the Field Guns not only, not one of any description but not a Tumbril or a single article of their equipment fell into his hands. He gained nothing but the smoking ruins of the fort & the possession of a deserted village."[27]

This was precisely the scenario – carrying off the kernel and leaving the shell – the secretary of war had cautioned Dearborn to avoid just days before the invasion. "In the affair before you," John Armstrong wrote, "nothing will, I hope, be omitted, nor anything misunderstood, and that with regard to the garrison in particular it will not be permitted to escape to-day that it may fight tomorrow."[28]

But for all his bravado, Harvey had no illusions about what was at risk if the remaining British force were cornered and defeated by the enemy: "The Niagara, the finest, the most populous, the richest & the most desirable angle of the Province, would fall into his possession & the whole be thrown open to his victorious career."[29] The remnants of Vincent's army may have lived to fight another day, but the former capital, and its fort, believed "the strongest place in Upper Canada," were now in American hands along with 2,000 barrels of flour, 150 barrels of pork and 20 barrels of whisky.[30]

While Dearborn's troops were fighting their way ashore at Newark, a naval reconnaissance mission with profound implications for his Niagara campaign was underway at the other end of Lake Ontario.

One hundred and fifty miles to the east, just off the American naval base at Sackets Harbor, the crew of a small Royal Navy vessel, perhaps a gig or a cutter, was carefully counting masts and campfires. Within an hour the vessel would be scurrying back to Kingston with the news the American fleet and most of the troops stationed there were gone.[31] The first-hand information, gathered by the newly arrived Lake Ontario commodore, Sir James Yeo, confirmed what an American spy had reported earlier.[32]

In Kingston, governor and military chief of British North America Sir George

Prevost was about to make an uncharacteristically bold move, one that would directly affect American war strategy.[33] Prevost, constrained by shortages of manpower and material from the very beginning of the war, invariably proceeded according to one principle – prudence. "Act with such caution as would enable you to husband your resources for future exertion"[34] was advice he issued repeatedly to subordinates throughout the war. Yet, the situation on and around Lake Ontario was rapidly deteriorating and caution, even in the eyes of Prevost, was becoming a liability.

The larger and better-armed American fleet had the upper hand on the lake and roamed freely. That superiority was already responsible for the first American victory of the war. The attack on York on 27 April cost the British not only crucial manpower and supplies but also a new 32-gun frigate[35] they were forced to burn before retreating. The Americans had not been able to add the vessel to their fleet as they hoped but with the new 26-gun frigate on the stocks at Sackets Harbor, the balance of power was poised to swing even more decisively to their side.

The British, for their part, had a dynamic and experienced naval commander in Yeo. His early career was the stuff of legend – "one of those salt-water Hotspurs." When he won his first command at the age of 23, he was already a 13-year veteran with active service in the Atlantic, the Caribbean, the Mediterranean and the Adriatic. Five years later he was knighted – by two countries – for taking French Guiana with only 400 men.[36]

**Lieutenant General Sir George Prevost (1767-1816)** was commissioned an ensign in his father's regiment at the age of 11 and was a major by the time he was 23. An accomplished soldier in his youth, he saw action in the West Indies before his appointment as commander-in-chief, British North America. An able administrator, he was hamstrung in his prosecution of the war by a chronic lack of men and resources. (Library and Archives Canada, C-6152)

Yeo had arrived at Kingston earlier in the month, bringing with him a large detachment of experienced Royal Navy officers, seamen and considerable expectations. "This most seasonable reinforcement," Prevost wrote, "will I hope enable us to regain an ascendancy upon Lake Ontario."[37]

In the meantime though, that ascendancy was still a ways off and Prevost had a crisis on his hands. Aware that Fort George had been bombarded, he knew "this miserable stockade"[38] was by no means secure and could fall to superior numbers. A strong invasion force supported by the American fleet could quickly cut the upper province in half.

The American focus on Fort George, however, had left Sackets Harbor temptingly vulnerable. With Chauncey's fleet at Niagara, along with several thousand troops, the naval base had only a small garrison to protect the new ship on the stocks. If the British could mount a surprise attack and destroy the naval base, including the new vessel, the balance of power would swing back to the British side. Additionally, the loss of Sackets Harbor would deprive the American fleet of its only safe harbour on the entire lake.[39] Faced with the tantalizing prospect of landing the sort of decisive blow that could cripple American naval power on Lake Ontario, and moreover, perhaps end the war, even the habitually tentative Prevost was prodded into action.

"The situation of Upper Canada becoming extremely critical," the American-born governor general reasoned,[40] "I determined in attempting a diversion in Col. Vincent's favor."[41]

**Commodore Sir James Lucas Yeo, RN (1782-1818).** Every inch a sailor, the Royal Navy's Great Lakes commodore had been at sea since the age of 10 with active service in the Atlantic, the Caribbean, the Mediterranean and the Adriatic and had been knighted twice. A bold and original talent, Yeo chafed under Prevost's cautious direction but without him the 1813 Niagara campaign would have had a completely different ending. (Engraving after a painting by A. Buck. Toronto Reference Library)

# **5** "A flying enemy much less fatigued than his pursuers."[1]

### VINCENT ABANDONS THE NIAGARA.

Late in the afternoon of 27 May a lone dragoon reined up his lathered mount inside the stone and log fortification guarding the Lake Erie end of the Niagara River and delivered the bad news to the garrison commander, Lieutenant Colonel Cecil Bisshopp.[2]

Fort George, the linchpin in the Crown's Niagara defences, had fallen and Bisshopp was ordered to withdraw all his regular forces along the river, destroy all the works, including Fort Erie, and join the main body of the retreating army. Within hours, all of Bisshopp's command was on the march. To forestall pursuit and any immediate occupation of the works by Americans from across the river, he left a detachment of the Lincoln Militia behind to bombard the American shore with the artillery.[3]

Vincent's orders to level the fortification at the southern end of the Niagara River represented a complete turnabout in strategy. His original intent was to retreat to Fort Erie and make a stand there. Nothing appears in official documents of the abortive plan but it is described in some detail in an 1817 memo written by Robert Nichol, who, as quarter master general of militia, was retreating with Vincent.[4]

A Brock appointee, the abrasive but talented Scot saw nothing but bad tidings in the strategy. Vincent, he said, "proposed falling back on Fort Erie, taking with him different detachments stationed along the Line of the Niagara towards Fort Erie – Adding that he would order brigadier Procter to destroy Detroit and Amherstburg and join him with the force under his command at that place."[5] In other words, according to Nichol, Vincent intended to abandon all that Brock

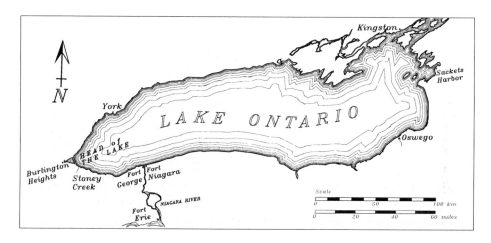

had won at Detroit, plus the southwestern part of the colony, and collapse all British forces on the old and largely inadequate Fort Erie.[6]

Such a move, Nichol warned, was pure folly. Fort Erie had no supplies to support his army and locating there would sever communications with Prevost in Kingston, leave Vincent trapped and imperil the entire upper province. "He would go into a *Trou de Loup*," Nichol said, "from which no talent or bravery could extricate him, and that the effect of this movement would be to compromise the safety of the whole division as well as the whole of the province above Kingston." In the face of additional opposition from Harvey and one of Prevost's aides-de-camp,[7] Vincent jettisoned the plan.

Although a few stragglers were picked off the end of the column, the British troops were able to retire in good order and by 3 o'clock had reached Queenston Heights, overlooking the Niagara River, where Vincent again considered making a stand. The heavy guns on the heights, however, had – on the order of a nervous staff officer – been spiked and the ammunition dumped, rendering the position, which included barracks, indefensible. The distressed Vincent, expecting the American army to appear any minute, had no alternative but to continue the retreat another ten miles to an area of ponds and marsh on the escarpment called Beaver Dams.[8] That move, hastily conceived and undoubtedly cursed by the exhausted troops, probably saved the British army from destruction.

**DeCew House.** The house of militia captain John DeCew on the escarpment was Brigadier General John Vincent's first stop after retreating from Fort George. Near the present site of Thorold, it served throughout the war as a supply depot and advanced picket for the British army. This photo dates from the early 1890s. The house was destroyed by fire in 1950. (*A Veteran of 1812*)

With the rearguard dragging field guns and what little baggage had been saved from Fort George, the main body struggled on to reach by nightfall the substantial stone house of militia captain John DeCew, where Vincent had wisely cached a modest supply of ammunition and three days' provisions.[9] For troops that had been under arms for 24 hours, fought a pitched battle, retreated 17 miles and not eaten all day, the rest and food would have been especially welcome.

Just a few miles below at Shipman's Corners[10] on the same Twelve Mile Creek that drained Beaver Dams, John Norton and his small party met nearly 200 Grand River warriors who had been on their way to Fort George. Instead of continuing and joining Vincent on the Mountain, Norton stayed put as an advanced picket in case of American incursion.[11]

No Americans were in pursuit that night but the Natives did encounter the two companies of the 8th Regiment, Barclay's Royal Navy detachment and their dragoon guide, Captain Merritt, before sending them through the woods up the escarpment to DeCew's.[12]

At midnight Harvey arrived at DeCew's house with the rearguard and, shortly after, Bisshopp's various detachments from along the Niagara began to arrive – principally the 41st Regiment with smaller details of the 8th and 49th, the latter detachment commanded by a 33-year-old Irish lieutenant, James FitzGibbon.

Although the British had lost 350 men earlier in the day, the various reinforcements more than replaced those numbers and Vincent's little army had grown to a respectable force of 1,600 men with 11 pieces of artillery.[13]

Back in Fort Erie, some 30 militiamen from the 2nd and 3rd Lincoln, aided by a few regulars from the 41st, spent the night serving the aged iron guns of the garrison and the adjacent batteries, initiating an artillery duel that raged sporadically through the night with Black Rock across the one-and-a-half-mile-wide river.[14]

**William Hamilton Merritt, Upper Canada Militia (1793-1862),** commanding officer of the Niagara Provincial Light Dragoons at the age of 19, was on almost continual service through the first two years of the war and saw action at Queenston Heights, Fort George, Stoney Creek and Lundy's Lane, where he was captured. In his postwar career as politician and promoter, he was instrumental in the building of the Welland Canal between Lake Erie and Lake Ontario. (Lossing, *Pictorial Field-Book of the War of 1812*)

"Not a person was injured at the Rock during the whole cannonade," the *Buffalo Gazette* reported, though "the barracks and several private buildings received a few shot."[15]

At dawn the Canadian gunners deliberately burst their guns, blew up the magazines, burned barracks and stores and evacuated the fort, retreating with some of the wives from the 41st Regiment[16] along the Lake Erie shoreline towards the Grand River.[17] Shortly after the dust settled, the Twelfth U.S. Infantry crossed the river and occupied the dismantled works.

At the other end of the river, Thomas Clark,[18] a prominent local merchant and commanding officer of the 2nd Lincoln Militia, led a small party of his men to Queenston Heights just after dawn to destroy stores hastily abandoned there the day before on Vincent's retreat.

At Beaver Dams, Vincent's army rested only a few hours before they were roused in the dark to begin their descent to the plains bordering Lake Ontario below. The general, once again prodded by Robert Nichol, had now set his sights on Burlington Heights at the Head of the Lake as his defensive position.[19]

The American high command blamed troop fatigue for not immediately pursuing the retreating British army – Morgan Lewis's "flying enemy"[20] – yet they could hardly have been more tired than their British counterparts.

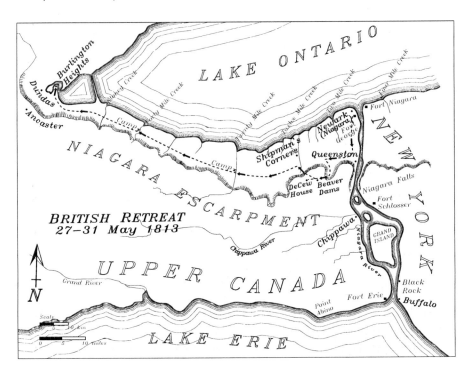

Vincent's second in command, John Harvey, was no stranger to hard service. He had cut his teeth in wars on three different continents and had a well earned reputation as a tough and decisive officer. With the St. Lawrence blocked by ice when he arrived in Halifax, the newly appointed deputy adjutant general for Canada, keen to gain his station, covered 1,400 miles – 160 of them on snowshoes – to reach Niagara overland in 28 days by the end of February 1813.[21] And from the moment he arrived, the small British force was on high alert for the expected invasion.

Given responsibility for the entire frontier between Lake Ontario and Lake Erie, Harvey said "the most unremitting vigilance was indispensably necessary…. For three months I scarce ever had my clothes off."[22]

The provincial dragoons captain Hamilton Merritt, who often rode night patrols with Harvey, routinely went consecutive days without sleep, and his troopers, as vedettes and express riders, were on service for weeks at a time. "It was impossible for the duty to be more severe," he said.[23]

For at least a week prior to the actual invasion, troops along the Canadian side of the river had been turned out every night at 2 a.m. and remained under arms until daylight, catching whatever sleep they could during the day.[24]

# 6 "The continual wavering of the commanding General."[1]

### NOW IS THE SUMMER OF OUR DISCONTENT.

When the sickly and fevered Dearborn returned to his bed in Fort George on the night of 27 May, he had assured the secretary of war in Washington that American forces would be in hot pursuit of the British the following day. True, Vincent's army by all accounts was in disarray and probably ripe for the picking. But did the commander in chief know where to find him?

Dearborn's intelligence was poor and his relationship with second in command Morgan Lewis even worse. Appointed senior commander of the armed forces by President James Madison in January 1812, Dearborn found himself increasingly undermined by the presidential ambitions of the secretary of war, John Armstrong. Another Revolutionary War veteran, Armstrong fancied himself commander-in-chief of the army and he had little but contempt for Dearborn. Morgan Lewis was Armstrong's brother-in-law.

The result was a subversive war-within-a-war that pitted Lewis and his minions against Dearborn and his underlings. Lewis, according to Dearborn, was slow to follow orders, timid and derelict in his duty. During the descent on Fort George, he said, the former New York governor had to be ordered to leave the

*Madison* and only joined the troops on shore after the battle.[2] Lewis, for his part was miffed because he had been denied overall command of the operation – "placed in an equivocal, subordinate position" where Dearborn would get all the credit and Lewis all the blame.[3]

Both denied responsibility for recalling the pursuit, each blaming the other for issuing the order. "The whole British force might have been captured," Dearborn said, "but for his total negligence and inefficiency." He met Lewis late in the day, "expressed his disapprobation" and ordered him to be on the road after the British by 5:00 the next morning.[4]

Lewis said the orders were not received until 10 o'clock the next day. He was to assemble Chandler's and Winder's brigades, Porter's artillery, including some heavy, siege-calibre ordnance, a detachment of light dragoons and several light companies – in total about 3,000 troops – "to march without delay [and] ... by all the means in your power, defeat and capture the enemy." As well, Lewis was directed to take possession of all enemy posts and garrisons, including Fort Erie.[5]

Dearborn's directives, however, like Stephen Leacock's description of Lord Ronald, who "flung himself on his horse and rode madly off in all directions,"[6] gave Lewis no comfort.

Missing from the orders were any directions. Was the force to follow the river road south to Queenston? Or the lake road west toward Burlington Heights? Lewis requested clarification from the commander in chief, pointing out the British were thought to be at Beaver Dams. Taking the

**Major General Morgan Lewis (1754-1844).** No model of military prowess, the former New York State governor was 30 years removed from his last military service when he parlayed political and family connections into a major general's commission in the regular army. His immediate superior, Henry Dearborn, considered him "totally destitute of any practical qualifications necessary for an officer of his rank." (New York State Office of Parks, Recreation and Historic Preservation, Mills Museum Historic Site)

lake road, Lewis reasoned, would either put the Americans between Vincent and the Head of the Lake or close on their rear. To be sure of cutting off their retreat, Lewis suggested the immediate dispatch of 1,500 troops to the Head of the Lake by ship.[7]

Major Christopher Van De Venter, Lewis's quarter master of division, supported the plan, urging prompt pursuit by land and sea to put Vincent's troops between two forces. "The British army must have inevitably fallen under any tolerable execution of this plan,"[8] he argued. With Van De Venter as witness, Lewis made his case to the commanding general and a heated discussion took place. But in the end Dearborn would have none of Lewis's plan and ordered him to march to Beaver Dams via Queenston[9]

Lewis then asked about supplies for the division, pointing out that ammunition was running low and some of the troops had been without food more than 24 hours.[10] Again, Dearborn was adamant and as soon as Porter's artillery and horses had crossed the river, Lewis's brigade prepared to head south towards Queenston."[11]

It was now near one o'clock on Thursday, 28 May, a full day since the battle. Lewis was mounting his horse when a staff officer reported that Vincent's army had left Beaver Dams at dawn and his force included the garrisons from the now-abandoned positions at Chippawa and Fort Erie. Once again, Dearborn remained unconvinced. "Though his information was derived from an indubitable source," Van Deventer said, "and the author introduced to the general, it was pronounced by gen. Dearborn, to be a lie, to deceive him; he was positive in the reiteration of the order to move on to the Dams."[12] These orders to Lewis call into question the calibre of intelligence Dearborn was rely-

**Secretary of War John Armstrong (1758-1843).** A veteran of the Revolution and a former ambassador to France, Armstrong was well connected politically through his wife's family. Capable but encumbered by presidential ambitions and his open contempt of cabinet colleagues, he tried to conduct the war as if he were still in uniform and ultimately failed. (National Portrait Gallery)

ing on, not to mention his grasp of the local geography[13] and his relationship with senior officers.

While Lewis and other officers knew the British had retreated from Beaver Dams, Dearborn had yet to be apprised of the fact, and when he was, refused to believe it.[14] What he did believe was that the British had sent a preposterously large reinforcement, 2,500 troops, from Kingston, which had landed and made its way to Beaver Dams. As well, the militia had been called in, and together, this force, well over 4,000 troops by Dearborn's math, was preparing to make a stand against the Americans.[15]

Finally, at four o'clock, just as it began to rain, Lewis's division began trudging up the river road towards Queenston. Although Lewis may have known the position there had long since been abandoned by the British, some of his officers at least were surprised at what they found. Or rather did not find.

Winfield Scott, once more in command of the advance, put it succinctly: "On arriving at Queenston we found the bird had flown."[16] Darby Noon, a major in the Albany Volunteers, arrived hoping for some action, "but to our astonishment the enemy evacuated this place and also Fort Erie, taking with them all the stores they could and destroying the remainder."[17]

A young artillery officer in Winfield Scott's regiment was equally taken aback. "On the 28th we proceeded on our march towards Fort Erie thinking they would make a stand there," wrote Lieutenant Patrick McDonough, "but on our arrival at Queenstown found that they had taken a different route, blown up their fort and were drawing their forces towards York."[18] Similarly a company commander of the Sixth Infantry confirmed "an immense quantity of provisions and military stores of all kinds" but no opposition.[19]

Compounding American discomfiture was the quality of their senior commanders. As shaky as Dearborn's leadership skills were, Lewis, 30 years removed from his last military service, was no model of martial prowess either. A graduate of Princeton who married into the influential Livingston family, he had parlayed his connections into a 25-year career in politics that included terms as governor and attorney general of New York. A personal friend of President James Madison and brother-in-law of the secretary of war, John Armstrong, he secured a major-general's commission in the wartime army.

That high rank however, could not guarantee him respect. One of his senior commanders, Colonel James Burn, said he was "a pleasant gentleman, but as an officer he was laughed at by all."[20]

Militia general Peter Porter said the former governor, while brave and capable, believed in campaign comfort: "His own baggage moves in two stately waggons, one drawn by two & and the other by 4 horses carrying the various furniture of a Secretary of State's office, a lady's dressing chamber, an alderman's dining room & contents of a grocer's shop."[21]

Dearborn regarded the former governor as a pompous object of ridicule, "totally destitute of any practical qualifications necessary for an officer of his rank," and beyond hope of "ever making an officer of any worth or use to the army."[22]

Despite the positive start to the 1813 campaign, dissension was widespread in Dearborn's leadership corps. Indeed, even the overwhelming success of American arms at Fort George had done little to calm what was already a viper's nest of malcontents. Jealousy and discontent in the high command spawned an astonishing amount of recrimination and backbiting in the subordinate ranks. The command structure was rife with politics and many officers spent more energy plotting and infighting with their fellow officers than they did fighting the British. "We cannot," lamented the *Albany Argus*, "but express our regret at the feuds and cabals which exist among the officers of the army."[23]

In Washington, the army's inspector general, Charles K. Gardner, complained that the camp at Niagara was "rent with quarrels, petty jealousies and plots among its own officers." Some of these quarrels escalated into duels. Ten days before the invasion, James Bronaugh of Virginia, surgeon of the Twelfth Infantry, shot fellow Virginian Major John Stanard of the Twentieth Infantry in the thigh. A few days after the invasion, Winfield Scott called the commanding officer of the Fifth Infantry, Homer Virgil Milton, a coward but declined Milton's challenge to a duel.[24]

The unrest percolated all the way to the top and at least one of Dearborn's senior officers privately questioned his capabilities. "He ought to give up the command," wrote Lieutenant Colonel Alexander Macomb of the Third Artillery, "he is so exceedingly cross that is difficult to be near him without receiving some very unpleasant language... This conduct had caused considerable dissatisfaction among the officers."[25] Even his chief of staff, Scott, who was generally sympathetic, admitted "nature never designed him for a great General."[26]

Certainly Dearborn's lack of resolution was alarming his subordinates. The deputy quarter master general, Major Christopher Van De Venter, went straight to Armstrong with his concerns. "The opinion is also prevalent with the best officers," Van De Venter wrote to the secretary of war, "that no conquest of character will be made if your plans be subject to the continual wavering of the commanding General."[27]

Others charged the old general with cronyism. Captain John Walworth of the Sixth Infantry complained privately that Dearborn "seldom rewards those most entitled to it. He has his particular favourites in whom he places implicit confidence, and they will undoubtedly tell a good story for themselves – it is sufficient to say that he is the most unpopular man with that part of the army that I know."[28]

Ironically, in December 1812 after his timorous attempt to invade Montreal from Plattsburgh, New York, had petered out, Dearborn had offered his resignation. "A general who becomes unpopular," he wrote to the secretary of war, "either by conduct, deficiency of the necessary qualifications, misfortune, or accident, ought not to be continued to command."[29]

But William Eustis, in one of his final acts before retiring, refused the resignation, telling Dearborn, "fortunately for you the want of success which has attended the campaign will be attributed to the Secretary of War." Three months later Dearborn had again offered to step aside, telling Madison, "I have no desire for any particular command."[30]

After almost a full year of war the United States Army was still struggling to field an effective fighting force. Amateur officers begat amateur troops. Poorly trained, poorly equipped and fighting in an often-hostile climate against a thoroughly professional enemy, they were, more often than not, overmatched.

## **7** "The total want of Enterprise."[1]

### VINCENT GAINS SOME BREATHING ROOM.

While Dearborn and Lewis quarrelled over the whereabouts of the British, Vincent's army was completing an arduous descent from Beaver Dams.

The dozens of creeks and streams that spill over the Niagara Escarpment have scoured deep ravines into the rock and numerous defiles into the plain below. Vincent's path of descent almost certainly paralleled Twelve Mile Creek as it flows to Lake Ontario. Given the high volume of rain in the spring of 1813 – "a most extraordinary wet season," one Upper Canadian noted – transport in Niagara was a nightmare. Swollen creeks and dirt tracks knee-deep in mud rendered the passage of each gun carriage and baggage wagon a backbreaking exercise for both man and beast. Vincent's artillery train included five brass 6-pdrs., one iron 6 pdr., four brass 3 pdrs. and a brass 5½-inch howitzer. A single brass 6-pdr. with carriage and limber weighed 3,080 pounds and normally required a minimum of four horses for transport. Such was the determination to avoid being cut off by the enemy that the army still managed a respectable mile-an-hour average on the descent.[2]

After "considerable difficulty in getting the baggage & Guns through 7 or

8 miles of Mountainous Roads," Vincent's second in command, John Harvey, was justifiably relieved when they gained the great road west towards Burlington Heights.[3] Given Lewis's intelligence and inclination to pursue directly to Twelve Mile Creek that very morning, Harvey's apprehension was warranted. "Had the enemy moved a sufficient Corps to this point even on the Morning of the 28th," he said, "we must have been intercepted & if not compelled to surrender, at least fight in a situation where our artillery would have been no service to us – in short caught under a circumstance of every possible disadvantage."[4]

Although the British army was undeniably in flight after a major defeat, Harvey sensed in the indecision of his American pursuers the first stirrings of a revival in Crown fortunes. "This display of the total want of Enterprise in the Enemy's Generals gave me a most encouraging impression of their talents &

**British field artillery, 1813.** On the retreat from Fort George, Major William Holcroft, RA, had an 11-piece artillery train that included an iron 6-pdr. similar to this reproduction. On the descent from the DeCew House, horses, artillery drivers and infantrymen struggled mightily to keep the guns moving. A single brass 6-pdr. with carriage and limber weighed more than 3,000 pounds. (Friends of Fort George)

inspired the first feelings of that confidence in myself which every subsequent operation in this Campaign tended to augment."[5]

That glowing ember of confidence, however, did not extend to the hundreds of militia who joined the column expecting Vincent to make a stand at the Beaver Dams. But the brigadier had no particular use for the militia, which he regarded as unreliable amateurs largely indifferent to the British cause.[6] Of course militia officers like Thomas Clark were useful when he needed to borrow money to feed his troops, Merritt's dragoons were necessary as express riders and Runchey's Coloured Corps as artificers but he and many of his fellow officers shared a professional disdain for the colony's citizen soldiers[7]

In his District General Order, Vincent was contemptuous in his dismissal of the militia: "It is not by joining up as a military body that our cause can, at this moment, be best advanced."[8] Certainly his treatment of the Lincoln Militia, who left their farms and presented themselves ready for duty, did little to encourage loyalty.[9] Or foster confidence in the British army's commitment to defend the Niagara Peninsula

"To our great surprise and annoyance," Merritt observed, orders were issued for the army to retreat to the Forty, while the militia, almost as an afterthought,

could go or stay. To their credit most opted to stay with the army. Merritt, like many of his fellow militia, feared the worst: "I strongly suspected, from the indifferent manner the Militia were treated, that the Upper Province was to be abandoned."[10]

**Upper Canada militia, 1813.**
Among the approximately 30 militia at Stoney Creek – including all five Lincoln regiments, the 1st and 2nd York and the 1st Oxford – most of the rank and file were without uniforms, going to battle in their civilian clothes equipped with military cartridge box, bayonet belt and musket. (Parks Canada)

For most of Lewis's brigade of infantry, artillery, dragoons and rifles, the rain that pelted them as they slogged up the river road towards Queenston was just the latest seasonal insult in a spring that had been miserably cold and wet.

In 1813, spring came late, or perhaps not at all. Lake Ontario harbours were still full of ice in the third week in April. When the ice cleared, the weather did not. Through late April and May it was cold and stormy. For an army on the offensive such weather rendered life miserable.

Ensign Joseph Dwight kept a diary of his two years in the Thirteenth Infantry. His entries were brief and sharply observed. Before and after the invasion of York on 27 April he recorded a litany of weather woes – from wind delays in port to heavy swells and violent storms on the lake – all while the troops were packed on board the fleet, most crowded together on open decks.[11]

Army surgeon James Mann, a progressive, energetic physician, knew only too well that foul weather could easily cause as much damage as any enemy. During their passage to York, Mann said, "they were night and day unavoidably exposed to the weather, and so much crowded on board the transports, that little opportunity was had for repose. After the attack upon Little York, and when the army had re-embarked, the troops were exposed a number of days on the decks of the vessels to a violent storm during which period they were constantly soaked with rain."[12]

And when the victorious army finally sailed to Niagara, Dwight recorded, the troops "lay all night on the beach in a cold rain storm without tents, blankets or fire."[13]

The wounded brought to Fort Niagara on 5 May fared little better. "They were put into the large mess house which had no roof," regimental commander George McFeeley wrote, "the rain fell in torrents and the poor fellows lying cold and wet with their broken legs and arms undressed since they were wounded."[14]

Eight days later, on May 13 the temperature plummeted and, while McFeeley could at least report no rain, conditions hardly improved. "Lay on the ground without tents," he wrote, "this night cold and a heavy white frost."

Then the rain came again and an American officer wrote home to Baltimore: "The season is uncommonly wet. Old inhabitants say they have not seen so rainy a summer for twenty-five years. I dread the consequences to the health of our army."[5]

# 8 "Disappointed & dispirited."[1]

## RECALLING THE PURSUIT

Having marched seven miles and run out of daylight, Lewis ordered a halt at the village of Queenston for the night. In case there were still British troops in the area, the former New York governor ordered Winder's brigade westward three miles to the hamlet of St. David's just below the escarpment. Chandler, however, insisted the advance posting was his by right of seniority. Lewis conceded, and Chandler, a close friend of Dearborn, went forward. Vedettes of light dragoons were posted to the south and the west within five miles of Beaver Dams. The provisions Dearborn promised had not arrived and so Lewis ordered out foraging parties in Queenston to look for cattle: "A few meager beasts were found," to be slaughtered the following morning.[2] Both Lewis and Chandler were reported to have found shelter in civilian homes overnight. The troops, without tents or rations, were left, once again, to fend for themselves in the rain.

Back at Fort George, Dearborn, living up to his reputation for indecision and beset with second thoughts about his original strategy, issued new orders, which reached Lewis just past midnight. What the commander in chief had declared a lie only eight hours earlier had suddenly gained credence. In the first of what would become an increasingly confusing series of orders over the next ten days, Lewis was ordered to send half his force, Chandler's brigade, back to Fort George and then, with the remaining half, pursue a British army newly reinforced with the garrisons from Fort Erie and Chippawa

"If you are fully satisfied that the enemy has left the Beaver Dams," Dearborn wrote, "and is on his way for the head of the lake, as I am induced from the latest information to believe is the fact, you will give such directions for pursuit directly."[3] Nearly a day and a half after the last positive sighting of the British army, Dearborn, perhaps experiencing the first belated tinge of urgency, felt compelled to end his orders with the admonition: "No time should be lost."[4]

Five hours later, at dawn on the 29th, Lewis sent an express to Chandler with the news. The rider, on his way to St. David's, likely passed another rider going in the opposition direction. Brigadier Chandler had just dispatched an express to Lewis requesting permission to return to Fort George because his troops had no food.[5]

While his cooks slaughtered and roasted the few head of cattle brought in the night before, Lewis sent word to Dearborn confirming that the British army, including the Chippawa and Fort Erie garrisons, had indeed departed from Beaver Dams 20 hours earlier, and his brigade would move in pursuit, as soon as the troops were fed. He ordered the dragoons, supported by the light troops under Scott and backed by Winder's brigade, to advance "with all possible celerity."[6]

The rain slackened off and the brigade was formed and prepared to move out when yet another express rider galloped up from Fort George headquarters with a whole new set of directions. Lewis was told to post 500 troops and a company of artillery at Queenston and send detachments of infantry and artillery to secure Fort Erie. In the meantime, he was instructed, "you will give the necessary orders for the return of the remainder of the troops to this place, as speedily as possible."[7]

Thus terminated the first American pursuit of Vincent's army. No contact, no combat, but not without casualties, namely "a considerable addition to the sick list from fatigue, starvation and exposure, for twenty hours, to incessant rain without any shelter of any description." Winfield Scott, who led the advance on this fruitless, wet expedition, could not hide his frustration at once more failing to track down the British. "We again came back to this place, disappointed & dispirited."[8]

At army headquarters, bad news was compounding for Henry Dearborn. Writing to the secretary of war, he explained that he initially believed the British, reinforced by troops from Kingston and local militia, would make a stand at Beaver Dams, thereby allowing the Lewis brigade to cut off his line of retreat.

"I have been disappointed," the old general wrote, "he broke up yesterday precipitately, continued his route along the mountain and will reach the head of the lake by that route."[9]

An alternate plan beckoned – transporting troops down the lake by sail. "We may yet cut off the enemy's retreat at York, but unfortunately we have plenty of rain but no wind; it may, however, change for the better in a few hours."[10]

But Commodore Chauncey, aware that his new ship on the stocks was vulnerable now that his Royal Navy counterpart, Sir James Yeo, was on the lake, grew restive. "He is very anxious to return to Sackett's Harbor,"[11] Dearborn lamented.

## 9 "A scandalously managed affair."[1]

### THE SACKETS HARBOR RAID, 29 MAY 1813

Commodore Isaac Chauncey, a 41-year-old career naval officer, had good reason to be anxious about his prolonged absence from Sackets Harbor. Indeed, if he was in any way an intuitive man, he would have been positively agitated. While his fleet sat anchored at the mouth of the Niagara River on 29 May, waiting for the rain to stop and wind to start, his crucial naval base, some 150 miles to the northeast, was in a desperate fight for its life.

Tantalized by the prospect of a pre-emptive strike to destroy the Americans' 26-gun frigate before it could be launched, as well as to afford Vincent's army some breathing room in the Niagara Peninsula, Governor Prevost cobbled together 800 regulars and a small party of natives[2] while Yeo assembled a squadron of seven armed vessels and 33 bateaux.

With luck and resolve, Prevost stood a good chance of landing the sort of body blow that could alter the face of the war – the loss of Sackets Harbor as a secure naval base would effectively cripple any campaign against Upper Canada. However, like so many actions in the war, the British thrust went awry early and often. Beset by adverse weather and top-level indecision after anchoring off Sackets Harbor, the British delayed the landing for a day, wasting the element of surprise and ensuring a much warmer welcome when they finally put ashore.

The land fighting was fierce, the Royal Navy was never able to bring its guns to bear and the British lost more than a third of their force, killed, wounded or missing. The Americans lost similar numbers and a significant quantity of naval stores but won the day because the British were repulsed and the future *General Pike* was saved.

**Sackets Harbor, the American navy's Lake Ontario base,** was established in 1810 and became a major naval and military centre in the war. The deep and accessible harbour provided shelter for the squadron and by the spring of 1813 there were upwards of 4,000 troops stationed there under command of Brigadier General John Chandler. When the troops and the naval squadron left to attack York and Fort George, the base was left in a vulnerable position. (U.S. Naval Historical Center, NH-1696)

There was considerable recrimination, much of it directed towards Prevost, when the British withdrew. One British officer called it "a scandalously managed affair. We gained a surprise and threw it away." The relationship between Prevost and Yeo would never recover from this misadventure. A golden opportunity was lost. British control of Sackets would have swept the American fleet from Lake Ontario and probably forestalled their efforts to build a fleet on Lake Erie.[3]

The Americans could rightfully claim a victory but in the end it was only tactical. The British, though few cared to at the time, could claim a strategic victory of sorts, for all the blood and blunder of Sackets Harbor had purchased at least one positive result – Chauncey, when he finally heard details of the raid and realized how close he had come to losing his naval base, would not venture on the lake again until his new warship was ready for service.

Dearborn would order a *feu de joie* to mark "the brilliant success of American arms in repelling and defeating the British General,"[4] but the absence of the American navy severely restricted his offensive options. The loss of marine troop transport effectively killed any hope of cutting off Vincent's retreat. He would have to be pursued and, if possible, brought to battle.

However, on the day Sackets Harbor was attacked, the increasingly anxious Chauncey, still anchored at the mouth of the Niagara, could only wait impatiently for the weather to allow his squadron back on the lake. In the meantime there were practical measures at hand such as liberating the naval flotilla at Black Rock.

The previous fall, naval Lieutenant Jesse Elliott had led boarding parties that captured two British brigs anchored off Fort Erie. One was subsequently

**Commodore Isaac Chauncey, USN (1772-1840).** The American naval commander on the Great Lakes was a vital part of the first two American victories of the war – the invasion of York and the fall of Fort George. His enthusiasm, however, was curbed by the near-capture of his base at Sackett's Harbour and he would not venture on the lake again until his 26-gun corvette *General Pike* was ready at the end of July. (Portrait by Gilbert Stuart, 1818. Naval Historical Center)

lost but the other, *Caledonia*, was brought intact to Elliott's fledgling naval base at Black Rock, three miles north of Buffalo on the Niagara River. Four commercial schooners and a sloop had been converted into gunboats and together with the *Caledonia* were intended to become part of the embryonic U.S. Navy squadron on Lake Erie. Provided of course, they could gain entry into the lake.

Given the seven-knot current of the upper Niagara River the vessels could only be towed into the lake, making them ideal targets for the guns of Fort Erie and adjacent batteries. By April the *Buffalo Gazette* reported plans to get the vessels into the lake had been abandoned, "it being considered almost impossible to tow them up the rapids while the enemy were in possession of the opposite shore."[5]

With the fall of Fort George and with both sides of the Niagara under American control, the equation changed and the open waters of the lake beckoned. Master Commandant Oliver Hazard Perry, with 35 carpenters and 55 seamen from Sackets Harbor, quickly had the vessels fitted out and ready to sail. Bucking the strong Niagara current and contrary winds, 200 soldiers, along with the carpenters and seaman and aided by a few teams of oxen, spent a week, beginning the 30th of May, warping the five vessels up the river and safely into the lake. Perry would report "incredible fatigue both to officers and men."[6]

Their safe delivery to Lake Erie would have a profound effect on the balance of power in the Great Lakes by summer's end.[7]

## 10 "The roads, they say, are very bad."[1]

### RETREAT IN THE RAIN

As night fell on 28 May, there was no letup in the heavy rain that had been falling since mid-afternoon. The main body of Vincent's army halted two miles west of Twenty Mile Pond on the farm of James Henry, formerly of Butler's Rangers. The advanced guard, including Vincent, reached the edge of Forty Mile Creek. The rear brigade, under Harvey, which included the baggage and the artillery, halted before Twenty Mile Creek, about three miles from the lake on the high ground above Twenty Mile Pond.[2]

The British troops, like their American counterparts in the field, enjoyed little in the way of shelter. Most had lost all their personal belongings and clothing at Fort George and Vincent had petitioned Kingston for replacements: "We want everything – shoes, stockings, blankets, tents and shirts." The 49th were particularly destitute and everyone needed boots. "We are more in want of them than any other article," Vincent implored.[3] Shoeless, shirtless, shelterless and fatigued from shouldering baggage wagons and 11 pieces of artillery through muddy defiles and swollen creeks in the rain, Harvey's rear brigade halted for the night on the edge of Twenty Mile Creek.

Near midnight a civilian rider emerged from the rain with a note for Harvey from "a friend to the British in Fort George" warning that the whole of the American army, estimated at 10,000 men, was in close pursuit.[4]

Harvey and Bisshopp reacted immediately. Harvey's brief description gives a vivid sense of the desperation driving the British retreat: "Although the troops were exhausted, the Artillery horses scarce able to move & those of the Baggage Waggons in a still worse state & the night was extremely dark and pouring with rain (as indeed it had been during the whole of the latter part of the preceding day) it was nevertheless determined that the Troops should move on."[5]

While the weary men were being roused and horses put in harness, a detachment under a field officer demolished the bridge over Twenty Mile Creek and felled trees across the road to delay any pursuit.

Heading west on the Queenston road, Harvey discovered a good deal of the main army's baggage had been abandoned in the haste of retreat. Sending out parties to farms in the adjoining countryside to impress wagons for transport, he was able to salvage much of the deserted baggage.[6]

The rearguard was demolishing a bridge and dumping ammunition in the water when they were overtaken by Norton's party of warriors. The Mohawk war chief told them they were wasting their time – the midnight message had been a false alarm. "For all the injury that they did the Roads, the Enemy could repair while the horses were taking breath, and what they did with the ammunition was uselessly distressing themselves – for that the Enemy was lying still at Fort George."[7] Harvey stayed with the rearguard until noon the following day, and with no sign of pursuit, deemed it safe to push on to Forty Mile Creek.

The enemy was indeed nowhere in sight because the American high command had abandoned the idea of pursuit in favour of interception. Continuing his erratic course, Dearborn ordered most of Lewis's brigade to sail to York and cut off the British retreat, which he was now convinced would not end until Kingston. He did not, however, think much of Lewis's chances.[8]

The weather system that had harried the retreating British now kept the U.S. Navy off the lake.

At dawn on 30 May, the troops were embarked on Chauncey's vessels and stuffed into smaller Durham boats. But, once again Dearborn changed plans. The winds were high and unfavourable. And that evening Chauncey heard the British fleet was on the lake and menacing Sackets Harbor.[9]

After three false starts and three days wasted in dawdling, the American commander was back at his starting point – pursuit of the British army by the most direct route – along the lakeshore.

The troops were disembarked and artillery officer Patrick McDonough wrote his parents in Philadelphia: "We were all embarked this morning at daylight but the wind being very high and against us, the General countermanded the order.... We are to march around by land tomorrow – or next at farthest. The roads, they say, are very bad"[10]

## 11 "They also talk of following us in force."[1]

### VINCENT LOOKS OVER HIS SHOULDER, 29 MAY 1813.

Forty miles to the west, where the logically-named Forty Mile Creek empties into the lake, Vincent's troops were enjoying their first downtime in nearly a week, drying out uniforms, cleaning weapons and eating cooked food. Their situation, for the moment, was relatively secure and the closest American force on the road behind them was a small party of light dragoons near Twelve Mile Creek.[2]

For the first time since leaving Fort George the British were in a position they could defend with some confidence. On their right they would have the Mountain, cut by a steep, inaccessible ravine, surrounded by thick forest, and on their left the lake. In between ran Forty Mile Creek, in front of which the ground had been cleared, giving artillery a clear field of fire. Two roads terminated at the creek and then diverged again on the other side, affording abundant means of retreat.

The Mohawk war chief Norton, who had a sharp eye for terrain, thought the position offered "the most flattering prospect of glorious Issue to a contest ... while our flank was secure they never could penetrate our Line in front."[3] Harvey concurred and told Vincent as much but as a relative newcomer was ignored.[4]

The militia who had accompanied the army thus far knew it as well, and they had stayed because they believed Vincent would make a stand at the Forty.[5] William Claus, colonel of the 1st Lincoln and an Indian Department official, was mystified when orders were issued to move out: "Why we left this position, God knows, it was the best we could take up."[6] But the Irish-born brigadier had decided to push on to Burlington Heights[7] at the western end of Lake Ontario known as the Head of the Lake. The militia was given no encouragement to accompany the army, whose ultimate destination was Kingston.[8]

Vincent, when he sat down to write a report on the previous week's events to Prevost, did not sound like a man of resolve. Yes, he would halt at Burlington Heights, but only while anxiously awaiting instructions. The American force, he believed, was 10,000 men and growing daily. There was no mention of any strategy for holding the heights, only an urgent request for lake transport "in the event of it becoming necessary that I should fall back upon York."[9]

In a brief separate report, Harvey, citing intelligence from a paroled militia officer, confirmed the American occupation of Queenston, Chippawa and Fort Erie, adding, "they also talk of following us in force."[10]

If Vincent's intelligence was accurate, he had ample reason to be apprehensive. To oppose a force he believed was approaching 10,000, Vincent had but 1,792 officers and men, including the last Fort Erie detachment that had just arrived that afternoon. The infantry regulars comprised 632 of the 49th Regiment, 425 of the 41st and 382 of the King's or 8th Regiment. The fencibles included two under-strength companies of the Royal Newfoundland Regiment, totalling 71 men, and the remnants of three companies of the Glengarry Light Infantry, amounting to only 68 men. The provincial units were the Niagara Provincial Light Dragoons with 41 men and Runchey's Corps of Artificers with 30 officers and men. The sedentary militia counted 52 total all ranks.[11]

To service and transport the 11 guns in the train of artillery – six 6-pdrs., four 3-pdrs. and one 5½-inch howitzer – the Royal Artillery had 99 men, including gunners and artillery drivers.

The point Vincent had selected for his next stopover was the 950-acre homestead of prominent politician, Indian trader and merchant Richard Beasley on Burlington Heights overlooking the western end of Lake Ontario. Pointing north like an outstretched finger between the marshland of Coote's Paradise to the west and Little Lake – now Hamilton Harbour – to the east, Burlington Heights was the prehistoric shoreline of a much-deeper glacial lake that preceded Lake Ontario. A peninsula nearly three miles long and barely 100 yards wide at its narrowest point, it rises steeply 100 feet above the lake. In 1813 this position could only be approached on a narrow front from the south and was otherwise surrounded by water. Communications were reasonable with roads to York in the north via a ferry off the northern tip and to Lake Erie in the south and the lake off Joseph Brant's house, which offered a good anchorage.[12] Little Lake was separated from Lake Ontario by a shifting sandbar cut by a narrow, shallow opening that restricted passage to small craft. In short it was a strategic position but given its size, one that was defensible only with considerably more troops than Vincent had at his command.

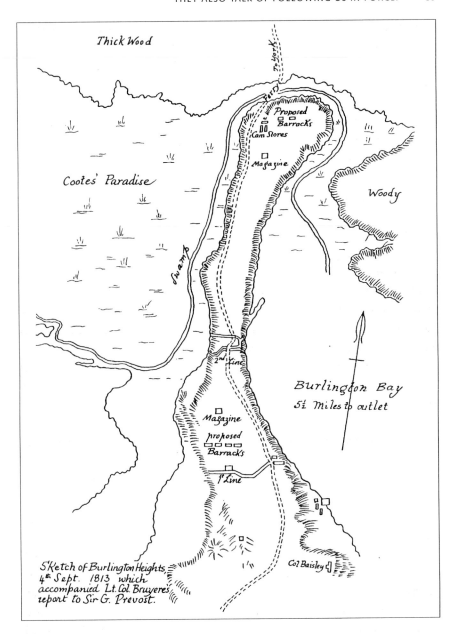

The labels visible within the map include:

Thick Wood

To York

Proposed Barracks

Com Stores

Magazine

Cootes' Paradise

Woody

Swamp

2nd Line

Burlington Bay
5½ Miles to outlet

Magazine

proposed Barracks

1st Line

Sketch of Burlington Heights
4th Sept. 1813 which
accompanied Lt. Col. Bruyeres'
report to Sir G. Prevost.

Col Baisley

**Burlington Heights.** This map, after one sketched by Lieutenant Colonel Ralph Bruyeres of the Royal Engineers in September 1813, shows some proposed changes to the defensive position but does not show the defensive line that was hastily thrown up by Vincent in early June. Richard Beasley's house, the site of Dundurn Castle today, is in the lower right corner as "Col Baisley." Remnants of the "1st Line" can still be seen today in Hamilton Cemetery. (Hamilton Military Museum)

The heights, long a native campground before Beasley arrived, had impressed Elizabeth Simcoe 17 years earlier. "When we had near crossed the bay," the lieutenant governor's wife recorded, "Beasley's house became a very pretty object. We landed at it, and walked up the hill, from whence is a beautiful view of the lake, with wooded points breaking the line of shore and Flamborough in the background. The hill is quite like a park, with large oak trees dispersed, but no underwood."[13]

By 1813 Beasley had cleared and fenced 160 acres on which he cultivated buckwheat and rye and tended an extensive 200-tree apple orchard. His holdings included a Georgian brick house, barn, storehouse and out-buildings, a garden with a number of choice fruit trees and an apple tree nursery

In the evening of 31 May the British army arrived at Burlington Heights, commandeered the property and evicted the Beasley family, including eight children and servants. Beasley's family home became the quarters for Vincent and his staff, his fence rails quickly disappeared into cooking fires, his wheat and rye stocks were fed to the Royal Artillery horses, his hogs fed the troops, and his barn became a makeshift barracks.[14]

There is no surviving documentary evidence that Vincent constructed de-

**King's Head Inn.** Also known as the Government House, the inn built on the southerly end of Burlington Beach near the basin of Big Creek in 1794 was used as a depot for public stores. On 11 May 1813, two U.S. Navy schooners landed 100 troops of the Twelfth Infantry, who, after chasing off the militia guard, looted and burned the inn. (Drawing by Elizabeth Simcoe. The Diary of Mrs. Simcoe)

fensive fieldworks in the days immediately following his arrival on the heights, but given his own determination – "I ... have taken up a strong position that I propose keeping"[15] – it is difficult to imagine that some sort of makeshift works would not have been completed. There is archaeological evidence a natural rise extending west from Beasley's house to the York road was enlarged by trenching in front and a gun position established. The work was likely supervised by Lieutenant James Robertson, who commanded the all-black provincial unit, Runchey's Corps of Artificers. Hastily built, it fell below Royal Engineer standards for a defensive work but afforded the encampment some protection at least.[16]

Blossoms were still on Beasley's apple orchard when the trees were put to the axe to give artillery a clear field of fire and deny cover to advancing infantry. Some of his big oaks probably fell to the axe as well, their branches sharpened to provide abatis in front of the earthwork to obstruct any direct assault.

Certainly the threat of attack was not new. The American army had already been to the Head of the Lake. Three weeks earlier, on 11 May, two armed schooners from Chauncey's squadron anchored off the King's Head Inn on Burlington Beach that separated Lake Ontario from Little Lake. Protected by the nine guns of the *Conquest* and *Governor Tompkins,* 100 troops of the Twelfth Infantry under Captain Willoughby Morgan, son of Revolutionary hero Daniel Morgan, came ashore.[17]

Protecting the property was a mixed company of 5th Lincoln and 2nd York under Captain Samuel Hatt and Lieutenant Robert Land that numbered 63 men, including Abraham Markle of Ancaster and William Green of Stoney Creek. Confronted by the American force, they abandoned the post. Captain Morgan landed his troops and after carrying off the public stores – primarily gifts intended for the Crown's Indian allies – burned the inn and its out-buildings. The party then rowed to the other end of Burlington Beach and broke the windows of Joseph Brant's house. The militia, now reinforced, returned and Morgan ordered his men back to the ships without any casualties. Vincent, alarmed at the incursion and angry over the destruction of public property, called the raiding party marauders while a militia officer from the Western District decried the wanton destruction of an inn with no strategic value whatsoever.[18]

Digging in on Beasley's farm, Vincent had drawn a line in the sandy soil of Burlington Heights, the retreat – for the moment at least – was over. One of his officers, with a hint of prescience, reflected the pride of an army anxious to redeem itself: "The enemy have spread a report of ... intercepting us. If he attempts it here he will perhaps catch a Tartar. His Ship Guns will avail him nothing against our bayonets."[19]

# 🔢 "Some extraordinary delusion."[1]

### THE PURSUIT RESUMES, 1 JUNE 1813.

On the 31 May the American high command at Newark, alarmed by reports Brigadier General Henry Procter had left Fort Malden to join forces with Vincent, pushed forward a flag party under three officers, one of them the son of the American secretary of war, John Armstrong.[2] Ostensibly they were bearing a message regarding the families of officers left behind at Newark, but in reality it was a reconnaissance mission to determine British strength and position.

The flag party was met at the Forty by dragoon captain Hamilton Merritt and detained overnight. The following morning the three officers and escort had barely departed before Merritt received word that a detachment of American light dragoons had approached the Twenty. After several false starts – on land and sea – the pursuit in force was finally about to begin.

This time, an ambitious 38-year-old Baltimore lawyer was getting his chance to do something that so far had eluded the Americans – bring the British army to a decisive action. Thin, fair-haired and quick-tempered, William Henry Winder had been a soldier for almost 15 months when he boldly sought, and received, command of the pursuit brigade. One of Baltimore's most successful barristers and a staunch Federalist – his uncle Levin Winder was the Federalist governor of Maryland – he had defected to the ruling Republicans in early 1812 and been rewarded with command of the newly-formed Fourteenth Infantry recruited in Maryland and Virginia.

Promoted full colonel in July 1812, the handsome and voluble Winder delivered an Independence Day speech in Washington that was more mitigating than militant: "Let us cautiously avoid undervaluing the power, resources and character of our adversary; we wage war with a great, gallant and powerful nation; the struggle requires that we bring to the contest our united will and power."[3]

His military career however, had not begun well. Camped at Buffalo in the fall of 1812, the Fourteenth Infantry, commanded by Winder, was accorded the most humiliating assessment imaginable for a professional soldier when the army inspector wrote of his troops: "They are mere militia, and if possible, even worse, and if taken into action in their present state will prove more dangerous to themselves than to their enemy."[4]

A month later, in November Winder got his first taste of combat when he led 250 troops across the upper Niagara River from Black Rock, in the campaign's second ill-fated invasion of Canada. He had landed only a portion of his troops at Frenchmen's Creek when a superior British force arrived with a field gun and forced him to withdraw after taking 28 casualties, including six killed. A contemporary observer referred to Winder's sortie as "this worse than useless expedition." Five days later Winder requested the Fourteenth be relieved of frontier duty because "the last eight or ten days have so shattered the regiment, both officers and men, that repose and comfort are absolutely necessary to them." The 1812 Niagara campaign then ended – not with a decisive battle against the British but with a bloodless duel between the American commander, Alexander Smyth, and militia general officer Peter Porter over a cowardice charge. After both officers missed their opening shot, Winder, who was Smyth's second, effected a retraction of the insult and the two sides were reconciled. In keeping with the farcical tone, one newspaper said, "It is generally believed that their pistols were as empty of solid matter as their heads."[5]

Despite the fiasco of that offensive – termed a "discreditable abortion" by one influential congressman – Winder was still held in some regard for he was summoned to Washington during the winter to consult on the upcoming 1813 campaign. The plain-spoken Peter Porter thought him intelligent, zealous and brave. Another observer wrote: "Colonel Winder is here, a kind of Secretary of War, and like a Bonaparte, has a room full of maps, roads, &c. &c., enveloped in which you can just see his little head above them – and of that head much is expected." One of the influential Washington newspapers, the *Federal Republican*, found him "sleek and courtly."[6]

In March 1813, still riding a wave of expectation, he was promoted brigadier general, despite being less than universally admired. William Duane, the army's acid-tongued adjutant general, said that prior to his appointment Winder "knew no more of Military affairs than his horse; and I am satisfied he could not put a company in motion." A fellow officer at Niagara was more charitable: "If he had one or two years experience in the field as a platoon or field officer he might then have made a tolerable good General."[7]

Dragoon colonel James Burn struck a balance of sorts, describing Winder as brusque to the point of rudeness but keen and able. Winder had complained openly about the quality of generalship at the capture of Fort George and had lobbied hard for command of the pursuit brigade.[8]

Of the generals Dearborn had available, Winder, green as he was, was probably not a bad choice, but the decision to send him off with a single brigade underscores Dearborn's incompetence. By 31 May, when Winder's marching orders were issued, the commander-in-chief should have had a reasonably accurate estimate of Vincent's army. The absurd earlier rumour of a 2,500-man reinforcement from Kingston had been shrunk to a more realistic, though still inaccurate, estimate of 300.[9] There was no authentic intelligence Procter was on his way from Fort Malden.

On 28 May Dearborn had despatched Morgan Lewis with two brigades containing approximately 3,000 troops, heavy artillery and cavalry to confront the British. Yet, three days later, he considered a single brigade sufficient to do the job.

Winder's force was a patchwork brigade of under-strength regiments and piecemeal detachments from other units. Officially his brigade contained the Fifth, Thirteenth, Fourteenth and Sixteenth regiments of infantry, two companies of the Second Artillery, a partial company of riflemen and a detachment of light dragoons. In all about 1,400 men.[10] Unofficially, there were small groups from several other units as well, including two companies of the Twenty-Second Infantry, a third and fourth company of Second Artillery and smaller detachments from the Twentieth and Twenty-First Infantry.[11]

As American regiments during the War of 1812 were rarely up to authorized strength of 900 troops,[12] units that made up Winder's brigade would seldom field more than 500 effectives and often considerably less. Still, even after allowing for a higher than normal number of sick, the numbers suggest a brigade strength somewhat higher than 1,400.

Taking into account the extra Second Artillery companies, the Twenty-Second companies and whatever orphan companies were pressed into service, the real figure had to be at least 1,700.[13] Other sources, put Winder's brigade at 2,000, and, according to one of his company commanders, even 3,000 troops,[14] although the latter figure seems unlikely.

**Brigadier General William Henry Winder (1775-1824).** A prominent Baltimore lawyer when he was given command of the Fourteenth Infantry, Winder was ambitious but lacking in military experience. In the fall of 1812 his regiment was adjudged "more dangerous to themselves than to their enemy." Still he was not without supporters, including Winfield Scott and Peter Porter. Even after Winder orchestrated the disastrous defence of Washington in 1814, Scott believed him more unlucky than unable. (Library of Congress)

Whatever the actual brigade strength, what is known is that core regiments were anything but uniform in strength. A detachment of the Fourteenth had been assigned to Fort Schlosser. The Sixteenth marched out without a single field officer. Its colonel, Cromwell Pearce, was ill, its lieutenant colonel, after spending only a few days at the front, was on leave, as were two majors and two captains. Regimental command fell to a tall 28-year-old Virginian, Captain George Steele, who was still recovering from a gunshot wound at Fort George.[15]

If the figure of 1,700 is used, then Winder's army was approximately the same size as Vincent's force. Given that Vincent's troops were all well seasoned and fighting on friendly ground, the young American general was already at a disadvantage. Winder was apparently a favourite of Dearborn's, yet he was dispatched without an adequate force.[16]

In keeping with Dearborn's increasingly erratic and indecisive directives, the departure on 1 June was predictably muddled. It began at 3:30 in the morning at Queenston. Morgan Lewis, posted there with the Thirteenth Infantry, was informed by express that a squadron of dragoons, travelling via the Black Swamp road, were to escort the Thirteenth back to Fort George so it could join Winder's brigade on the march to Twelve Mile Creek.[17]

The directions once more raise questions about the high command's curious grasp of local geography. The Black Swamp road ran west from Niagara towards Twelve Mile Creek, *away* from Queenston. Travelling on the swamp road, the dragoons would never have intercepted the Thirteenth. Furthermore, why would a regiment already at Queenston – which was roughly 12 miles from Twelve Mile Creek – march seven miles back to Fort George and then turn around and march a dozen miles to Twelve Mile Creek?

Lewis, with some delicacy, managed to point that out by proposing the Thirteenth be ordered directly to Twelve Mile Creek.[18] The suggestion was accepted and the Thirteenth was spared a seven-mile march by proceeding straight to Twelve Mile Creek from Queenston.

Considering the directions the secretary of war had given Dearborn on how best to vanquish the small British forces in Upper Canada – "send therefore a force that shall overwhelm them, that shall leave nothing to chance.... Double the number you propose sending"[19] – and considering the old general's own overly-cautious nature and the obvious success of overwhelmingly superior numbers at Fort George, it is difficult to imagine what Dearborn was thinking in sending a small brigade under a rookie brigadier in pursuit of a professional army of equal or greater numbers.

General Dearborn, in failing to recognize these apparent truths, was "under some extraordinary delusion," the secretary of war said, and perhaps he was.[20] Certainly he was under the weather. And heavy weather it was.

In 1775 at Quebec, as a 24-year-old major serving under Benedict Arnold, Dearborn had nearly died from pneumonia on that ill-fated campaign to conquer Canada. And now, nearly four decades later, here he was again – once more invading Canada from his sick bed, his physician fearful for his life. Having relinquished field command to subordinates, he retreated even further from active command in the days following the invasion and was rarely seen by his troops.[21] Most in need of strength and resolution from its leadership, the American army instead got age and infirmity in the form of a superannuated revolutionary.[22]

Meanwhile, Dearborn's equally apprehensive naval counterpart, Isaac Chauncey, had sailed his squadron across the lake from Niagara to cruise the waters off York and Kingston in hope of encountering Yeo's squadron. Only when he reached Sackets Harbor on 1 June did he finally realize that the British had indeed attacked and come perilously close to destroying his new ship on the stocks. Although the attack had failed, Chauncey was shaken.

"I have determined," he wrote the secretary of the navy, William Jones, "to remain at this place and preserve the new ship at all hazards.[23] And so he did. It would be the last week of July before the full squadron, led by the 26-gun frigate *General Pike*, would return to the lake to challenge the British. In the interim the Royal Navy squadron would have free rein on the lake and make good use of it.

Henry Dearborn, who began the Niagara campaign with an impressive amphibious assault on Fort George, now found himself bereft of naval support and wholly dependant on the most pedestrian form of transport.

# **13** "'Tis the eye of childhood that fears a painted devil."[1]

## THE CROWN'S NATIVE ALLIES

On the evening of the 1 June, the advanced element of Winder's brigade – three companies of the Second Artillery, riflemen and dragoons – arrived at Fifteen Mile Creek, while the main body halted at Twelve Mile Creek, where it was joined by the Thirteenth Infantry. Although unencumbered by baggage – it was to follow the brigade by bateaux along the lake as sufficient horses could not be found – progress was slow. The creeks were flooded and the British rearguard had destroyed bridges as well as felling trees across the muddy track as they retreated west.[2]

Winder, who was well regarded by Armstrong, might have reflected on the advice the secretary of war had issued to young generals the year before.

Offensive movements must be promptly taken and more rapid than the enemy, Armstrong cautioned: "Give him time to *breathe* – above all give him time to *rest* and your project is blasted; his forages will be completed and his magazines filled and secured – the roads of approach will be obstructed, bridges destroyed and strong points everywhere, taken and defended."[3]

Navigating a battery of one-ton iron guns through the quagmire ravines was slow and heavy work. A single 6-pdr., normally pulled by four or six horses, required eight or more to get through some of the gorges. The same applied to the few baggage wagons that accompanied the brigade. And when the advance was not putting its shoulders to the wheel, it was keeping an eye out for the enemy. The adjutant reported almost hourly contact and skirmishes with vedettes and pickets.[4]

The next morning, 2 June, a flag party pushed forward to pass another letter from Dearborn to Vincent, this time concerning prisoners and, of course, to discover what, if any, forward defence positions the British had established. Shortly after, Merritt's vedette at Twenty Mile Creek was driven in by the light troops of Winder's advance. The talk of following in force that Harvey had noticed three days earlier had finally turned to action. As had the weather, lurching from cold and wet to hot and humid as an intense June sun began to steam moisture from the sodden ground.[5]

As the distance between the two forces steadily diminished, Vincent and his staff pondered their prospects for success. Estimates of the size of the American force approaching had shrunk to more realistic numbers, but Vincent, unaware Chauncey had fled to Sackets Harbor, still believed he would be assailed by land and sea. His intelligence put Winder's brigade at 2,100 and he expected another large force to be landed from the lake side to cut off his retreat.[6] At least one of his company officers was convinced a third force, approaching from the Mountain, was descending on them as well.[7]

Harvey, having surveyed the army's position on Burlington Heights – "if position it can be called" – was not optimistic about the chances of mounting a successful defence. He outlined the dilemma facing the British force: "It will be obvious at the slightest glance at the plan that an open position of near three miles in extent was not to be defended by 1400 men against three times their numbers, nevertheless this appeared to be the only alternative as retreat to York & from thence to Kingston (220 miles) was utterly impossible from the state of the roads."[8]

Further complicating Vincent's rock-and-a-hard-place circumstance was the behaviour of the Crown's Indian allies. The practice of using native auxiliaries was well established in the British army at this time. Manpower was short in Canada. And the Grand River warriors, for their part, had a deep-seated enmity towards Americans stretching back to the Revolution, when they were driven from their ancestral lands in upper New York. With their superb fieldcraft they made excellent guides and skirmishers, though discipline was a constant concern.

William Claus, the deputy superintendent of the Indian Department, outlined the fundamental cultural disconnect when he complained about English officers who expected Indians "to obey orders the same as soldiers & because they did not, they and their officers were a set of damned useless people."[9]

Isaac Brock, who handled natives as well as any British officer, understood there was always an element of uncertainty, that native warriors could not be expected to act like regulars, that their loyalty was usually trumped by self-interest and they had a profoundly different concept of war than the Europeans. Clearly they vexed him, for he called them "fickle and degenerate" but at the same time acknowledged the psychological fear factor they brought to any conflict.[10]

The writer John Howison, who travelled Upper Canada just after the war, neatly summed up British ambivalence: "The Indians are feeble and useless allies, but dangerous enemies ... had they been hostile to us, they might have done incalculable mischief; for their intimate knowledge of the woods, their talents for ambuscade, and the unerring fire of their rifles, would enable them to harass and weaken an enemy, without incurring almost any risk themselves."[11]

Whatever qualms the British had, there was no denying the Natives' psychological weight in any conflict. Contemporary American historian Charles Ingersoll said, "Dread of the scalping knife and tomahawk did more to save Canada for England, than the equivocal loyalty of her Canadian subjects, [and] the skill, valour and admirable tactics of her best officers and soldiers.... Dread of the Indians multiplied their numbers and powers so fearfully to American recollections that Indian barbarities were by far the most formidable of English means of hostility against the United States."[12]

Captain Robert McDouall, Prevost's aide-de-camp, who was on his way to join Vincent at Burlington Heights, cynically understood the powerful fears Indian warfare aroused in the American psyche. "Our Indians prove themselves right worthy and right useful auxiliaries," he wrote. "Macbeth says ''tis the eye of childhood that fears a painted devil.' But it is so far lucky that our opponents are mere infants in the sublime science of war."[13]

Any reservations Vincent might have had about employing Indians had clearly been resolved. After the fall of York he had sent a desperate appeal to Procter in Amherstburg to forward him 500 Indians by ship "with as great expedition as possible."[14]

The 200 Grand River warriors that joined Norton after the fall of Fort George had returned home when Vincent retired from the Forty to Burlington Heights. The loss of Fort George and the Niagara Peninsula had left their settlement vulnerable to attack by the American army. Many of the Six Nation warriors were old enough to remember the 1779 Sullivan Expedition during the Revolution that plundered and burned their ancestral homeland in upper New York. Quite possibly they also knew that one of Sullivan's regimental commanders on the expedition was a 28-year-old lieutenant colonel, Henry Dearborn.[15]

Along with the militia, the Iroquois strongly suspected the British were poised to abandon most of the upper province, and if that was so, then they were rethinking their traditional allegiance to the Crown. Certainly complete withdrawal was an option fraught with peril. William Nichol, the militia quarter master, believed the Grand River warriors, "seeing themselves abandoned after all our protestations would in all probability purchase peace of the Enemy by the Massacre of the population."[16]

Dearborn knew the Iroquois were fearful of a repeat of 1779 and some had even initiated contact with the American camp. Norton, well aware of this growing tension, and its implication, was distressed by his waning influence and subsequent inability to field more warriors.[17]

As the storm clouds gathered the Grand River warriors opted to sit on their hands and see what developed.

In the afternoon of 2 June, the advance of Winder's brigade pushed a section of dragoons forward to the Forty Mile Creek, forcing Merritt to retire on the forward British post at Stoney Creek. His small company of provincial dragoons, 41 in

**Grand River warrior.** Although largely absent for most of the 1813 Niagara campaign, the warriors of the Six Nations played a significant role nonetheless, inspiring fear and dread in the Americans and in their allies, the British. This painting by G.A. Embleton depicts a chief in a characteristic mix of native and European dress. (Parks Canada)

total, had been on duty around the clock for six days and both men and horses were approaching exhaustion.[18]

Merritt's first contact with the American force, the advance guard, likely gave the dragoon captain little cause for optimism. The core of the advance was three companies of Winfield Scott's Second Artillery, the shock troops at Fort George. Although designated and trained as artillery, the Second was equally adept as light infantry and represented the cream of the American army. The advance also had a partial or full company of another elite unit – riflemen, either the First Regiment of U.S. Rifles or a comparable company of U.S. Volunteers. For speed and communication there was also a detachment, perhaps 100 troopers, of the Second Light Dragoons. The whole advance guard was under command of a 24-year-old Marylander, Captain Jacob Hindman, an accomplished veteran officer.[19]

As the main body of the brigade made its way along the old Iroquois trail that ran from Queenston to the Head of the Lake, Winder's officers were undoubtedly questioning settlers along the way to determine the size of Vincent's force. For a foreign army with limited knowledge of Upper Canada, a guide with local knowledge was essential. There is some evidence Winder's guide was the notori-

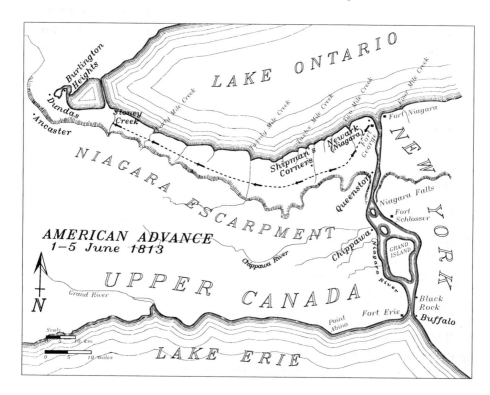

ous Canadian turncoat Joseph Willcocks. At least one Niagara resident identified Willcocks as the man who "led the American army in pursuit of ours."[20]

The Irish-born dissident, Niagara politician and journalist who fought with distinction on the British side at Queenston Heights had, in the wake of American victories at York and Fort George, become completely disaffected with British rule and was only weeks away from joining the American army.

Whoever his guides were, Winder had to have been alarmed by the intelligence he was receiving – Vincent, no longer in flight, was now strongly posted at Burlington Heights and gathering reinforcements.[21] That afternoon, as soon as he arrived at Forty Mile Creek, Winder despatched an express rider back to Fort George calling for reinforcements.

At the same time the American brigadier was making camp, Sir James Yeo was leading the Royal Navy squadron west from Kingston on its first foray into the lake, carrying 220 men of the King's Regiment, ammunition, clothing and food – all intended for Vincent at Burlington Heights.[22] Although he proceeded warily, the only adversary he would encounter was contrary winds, for his American counterpart, Isaac Chauncey, was in Sackets Harbor and going nowhere.

Jacob Cline, the 13-year-old son of Maryland Loyalists, was staying at his sister's house when Winder's brigade arrived at Forty Mile Creek and camped near the lakeshore on the property of William Crooks. "I remember well the arrival of the army, a lean, hungry-looking set about 2,000 strong.... I spent most of my waking hours

**"A lean, hungry-looking set"** is how 13-year-old Jacob Cline described the American infantry he saw at Forty Mile Creek when Winder's brigade first arrived. Cline said one of the American officers told him, "You'll soon be under the Yankey government, my boy" The soldier in this C.H. McBarron painting begins the loading process of his musket by tearing the end of a paper cartridge. (Parks Canada)

among the tents admiring the big guns and the cavalry and the gaudy uniforms of the general officers. The Americans were in high spirits and when I said I was a Canadian, one of the officers laughed and said 'You'll soon be under the Yankey government, my boy'. I was sassy like most boys of my age, and I said, 'I'm not so sure about that.'"[23]

They also asked Cline about the Indians they believed were shadowing them from the Mountain.

## 14 "Ensign No Coat."[1]

### CHANDLER'S BRAVE BOSOM, 3 JUNE 1813

Back at Fort George, the second part of Dearborn's bizarre two-stage strategy for defeating Vincent's army was unfolding with the dispatch of a yet another brigade commanded by yet another recently-minted general officer.

Up this time was a husky, grey-haired New Englander who had scrabbled his way from obscure poverty to become the most influential politician in his home territory of Maine. John Chandler – stiff in bearing, brusque in speech, prone to profanity and fond of parade and drill – at 51 was a remarkable success story. One of ten children of a French and Indian War veteran, Chandler joined the Revolution as a teenager. At 15 during a three-month enlistment he served at Saratoga, at 17 he crewed on the privateer *Arnold* until it was captured by the British; he subsequently escaped a prison hulk and enlisted for a second term in the army, this time for six months, during which he was befriended by a young field officer, Henry Dearborn.[2]

After the Revolution, "not only poverty-stricken but illiterate in the extreme," he settled in Monmouth, Maine, where Dearborn would become his mentor. At 21, Chandler learned to read and write, attending the settlement school with children a fraction of his age. He worked as a blacksmith – he was the fifth generation in his family to work the forge – cleared land, took census, kept a tavern and performed odd-job labour such as digging Dearborn's potatoes in return for every tenth bushel. The town historian, Harry Cochrane, said: "Wherever a dollar is to be found, there we find Chandler."

Commissioned ensign in the local militia, his lack of suitable wardrobe earned him the mocking epithet of "Ensign No Coat,"[3] but with Dearborn as patron, his rise was rapid and assured. "It was an easy matter for Dearborn to secure positions of honor and trust for his favorites," Cochrane said, "and whenever an office was vacated for a moment, he had Chandler in his hand ready to jam him into the crevice."[4]

The crevices Chandler filled included postmaster, town clerk, country sheriff, state senator, federal congressman and finally army officer. On 8 July 1812 he was appointed brigadier general in the U.S. Army. Four days earlier at an Independence Day banquet in Augusta, in a blush of patriotic fervour, he had confidently toasted the army: "Composed of free born sons of America, commanded by brave and experienced officers, again they will teach the haughty Briton and their savage allies to dance to the tune of Yankee Doodle." When he left his home in Monmouth on 31 July to join the army at Albany, the local militia colonel wished him "a pleasant and prosperous campaign … adorned with those laurels which time can never fade."[5]

In November of 1812 he had been with his mentor Dearborn at Plattsburgh for the farcical third invasion of Canada, which one contemporary historian, Charles Ingersoll, termed a "discreditable abortion … the feeblest of all attempts at invading Canada" and "the climax of our military degradation for that year." When General Joseph Bloomfield fell ill, Chandler had been briefly in command of the division. Chandler's action consisted of an overnight sortie into Lower Canada with 300 men including cavalry and artillery. A small breastwork at Odelltown was carried and one man captured. His losses were two wounded – "one had his ear bored and another his hand; but whether by the Indians or by their own cross fire, was not ascertained." Although hardly a shot was fired in anger, casualties on the late-fall campaign were enormous with nearly 500 of Chandler's brigade alone stricken with measles and attendant pleurisy, pneumonia and, not infrequently, death.[6]

**Brigadier General John Chandler (1762-1841)** was a blacksmith who rose from poverty and illiteracy to become one of New England's most influential politicians. He was one of several general officers appointed in the first years of the war who had never held a command of any rank in the regular army. Although fond of parade and drill, Chandler failed to impress many of his fellow officers. After the farcical thrust into Canada from Plattsburgh in November 1812, a subordinate said, "Chandler has neither sense nor discretion and is without any military knowledge at all." (Maine Historical Society)

At least one of the officers on that expedition assessed Chandler's military qualities and found them lacking. He "has neither sense nor discretion, and is without any military knowledge at all. This I assure you is a fact known to every officer who has had as good an opportunity of witnessing his folly as myself."[7]

Questions about his military competence combined with his blacksmith background gave the press a theme they could expand on: "Chandler, it is said, can form a *half moon* or a *horse shoe*, a *hollow square* or a *plough share* with equal skill and ability." Even the disgraced William Hull who had surrendered Detroit was "in every respect superior to Chandler," disparaged one newspaper in Chandler's home state.[8]

In the early spring of 1813 Chandler was ordered with his brigade to take command of the army gathering at Sackets Harbor for the invasion of York. En route, he was reported to have lost his temper with a lame sleigh driver and split the man's head with a hickory cane.[9] Assuming command of the outpost, he assured the troops in a General Order that only an application of discipline was needed "to render them the pride of their country and the terror of its foes."[10] Though pleased with the command at Sackets, he was less than impressed with the remote naval base. "Here I am on the banks of Lake Ontario," he wrote to a friend, "cooped up in a dirty little Village, every mouse hole & corner which can give shelter, crowded, which renders it very unpleasant."[11]

In early April the Thirteenth Infantry arrived from Utica and a young subaltern, Joseph Dwight, took measure of the brigadier and recorded it in his diary: "Gen. C. appears to be a man of very ordinary abilities and totally unfit for command of an army."[12] When Zebulon Pike[13] was given command of the York invasion force, Chandler was left behind to protect the new ship under construction that would become the *General Pike*.

While at Sackets Harbor, Chandler showed a keen interest in camp security, ordering that no officer "hazard his military reputation nor the safety of the army by quitting the guard to which he belongs until regularly relieved." At the same time he petitioned the secretary of war to clarify battlefield succession in the event the commanding officer was lost in action. Which of the two subordinate colonels with identical seniority would assume command, he asked. "Might not even a defeat be produced for want of rank being settled?" Both concerns would turn out to be eerily prescient.[14]

And he, who had been appointed brigadier general without having spent so much as one day as an officer in the regular army, complained to the secretary on the propriety of filling army vacancies with civilians. "The officers say that however great their services … they can have no hope of promotion."[15] Apparently county sheriffs appointed brigadier generals, as he had been, were excepted.

The Washington press corps, unimpressed with his elevation from blacksmith to brigadier, referred to him as "a hero who never feared the snapping of coal, the hissing of hot iron, nor the kick of a horse."[16] Clearly though, as a very successful politician he was not without admirers in the army. George Howard, a captain in the Twenty-Fifth Infantry, said Chandler "was like a father and friend to me" and one of his subordinates at Sackets Harbor described him as "a fine, firm zealous old gentleman."[17]

At the descent on Fort George, Chandler commanded the reserve brigade and saw no action. He later complained that he had been "improperly deprived of an opportunity to rendering essential service to his country and of gratifying that laudable desire of fame which always inhabits the bosoms of the brave." As a Dearborn partisan, he naturally made his mentor's enemies his own and in the wake of Fort George annoyed Morgan Lewis by second-guessing the decision to call off the pursuit and even questioning his courage.[18]

Which prompted Lewis's minions to retort: If Chandler was so anxious for action, why was he not commanding the advance instead of the reserve? "His rank entitled him to it as oldest Brigadier; his connection and standing with the Commander in chief assure it to him had he really wished it."[19]

In the hothouse of politics and ambition that was the U.S. Army in 1813, Chandler was well versed in the first and amply endowed with the second. That his combat command experience was virtually nil, however, apparently perturbed neither him nor his superiors.

So it was that on 3 June the former "Ensign No Coat," now rather impressive in dark blue coat with gold buttons and gold epaulets topped with a silver star, gilt spurs on high leather boots and fine felt cocked hat, led his brigade out from the Fort George encampment, doubtless expecting soon to gratify that laudable desire of fame that had so far eluded him. Morale was good, hopes were high. On their departure some American officers had "congratulated" the wives of British officers left at Fort George on the certainty of soon seeing their husbands again – as prisoners.[20]

The brigade that Chandler took up the Black Swamp road was composed of three infantry regiments – the Ninth, the Twenty-Third and the Twenty-Fifth, a company of riflemen, either Smyth's or Lyttle's, and Archer's company of the Second Artillery and Leonard's company of Light Artillery with five or possibly six field guns. The surviving record, including all of Chandler's various accounts, does not offer a total number but a reasonable estimate can be pieced together.

The Twenty-Fifth, unscathed in the attack on Fort George, was the largest regiment with well over 600 men, the Twenty-Third numbered about 350, while the Ninth, with perhaps 100 men, was really only a detachment with the bulk of the unit stationed at Sackets Harbor. Add in 200 for artillery and rifles, and Chandler's brigade weighed in around 1,300 men, although Auchinleck reckoned it closer to 1,700.[21]

As the burly brigadier departed, Winfield Scott, reflecting the optimism in the American camp, observed: "Chandler's & Winder's Brigades are again in pursuit.... Vincent will fall into our hands & and I think without much fighting."[22]

## 15   "The survivors were intensely excited."[1]

### NORTON CASTS A LONG SHADOW, 4 JUNE 1813.

On Burlington Heights, John Vincent was distressed to find he could not expect even token help from the Grand River warriors. He had directed the deputy superintendent of the Indian Department, William Claus, to seek a small party of warriors, "only thirty or forty," to join his troops. Despite repeated appeals by Claus, who had considerable influence with the Six Nations, the Iroquois remained adamant in their refusal. The dissidents on the Grand, more than 100 in number, were not only themselves refusing to fight but were also actively discouraging others from coming to the King's aid.[2]

Charles Askin, a captain in the 2nd Lincoln, in a letter to his father, summed up the view of many on the British side towards the Grand River warriors: "The Indians have behaved shamefully lately, and do us no service whatever. I hope they will do better. I would not give ten Hurons for two hundred of such as we have here."[3]

Norton remained the sole native presence, his force amounting to "my young Cherokee Cousin, a few Delawares, some Chippawas, one Mohawk, and a Cayugwa,"[4] no more than a dozen in total. Also missing were the militia. Save for Merritt's dragoons, Runchey's artificers, the artillery drivers and a handful of picked men, the militia had been sent home.

One of Prevost's aides de camp, Captain Robert McDouall, reflected the official pessimism in Kingston: "I set off in an hour to communicate if possible with Gen'l Vincent. I hope things are not so bad and that they are still retrievable."[5]

While Yeo's squadron, carrying crucial reinforcements and supplies, struggled against adverse winds, Harvey contemplated the prospects. June 4 was the King's birthday, normally cause for numerous salutes from artillery and small arms, yet on Burlington Heights the assembled troops honoured King George III with huzzahs – "the only mark of respect in our power to pay" – because there was no ammunition to be spared.[6]

By his calculation there were less than five rounds of ammunition for each of the 11 field guns and not enough musket cartridges to fill the 60-round boxes each redcoat carried. Moreover, not only did his troops know it, but the Americans as well. The emergency supplies recovered at Beaver Dams were exactly that – emergency. The victuals, three days worth, were gone. The troops needed clothing – "not one in 20 has an article more than what is on his person," according to one company commander. The chances of a successful retreat were slim, given the condition of the roads and the enemy's supposed control of the lake.[7]

No allies – militia or native – no food, no ammunition, no retreat and an opponent whose numbers increased daily.

Harvey, the seasoned combat veteran, knew the odds of success were lengthening. "The confidence which the knowledge of such a circumstance is calculated to give one party & the despair it must excite in the other, may be easily imagined," he wrote. "The Six Nations to a man held back & the few Militia who had hitherto remained with us, now retired to their homes considering our situation as desperate & and all as lost."[8] Should Vincent's army be defeated, he mused, the Americans could easily crush Procter in the south, take Kingston in the east and thereby gain control of all Upper Canada.

**United States Light Dragoon, 1813.** Under the command of Colonel James Burn, the Second Light Dragoons were part of Winfield Scott's pursuit column that came within a few miles of overtaking the British on 27 May 1813 before being called off. The dragoons were nicked up in a few subsequent skirmishes but took no part whatsoever in the Battle of Stoney Creek. This painting by H.C. McBarron depicts a trooper. (Parks Canada)

Yet for Harvey, who cut his teeth in combat at 16, fighting the French in Europe, and had seen action subsequently in South Africa, Egypt and India, the undeniably grim outlook was countered by the pride and resolve of a professional soldier facing a desperate situation.

"Our little band," he said, "stood resolutely in the 'Gap.'"[9]

At Forty Mile Creek, Winder's brigade made the best of the interim while they awaited Chandler's reinforcement. The previous two days had been an unending procession of quaggy ravines and defiles to be crossed, flooded creeks to be bridged and fallen timber to be cleared from the track. On top of that, the weather had suddenly turned oppressively hot. A break was welcome. On the morning of 4 June the officers took breakfast with "Mr. Cook," a wealthy settler, and Captain Mordecai Myers borrowed a clean shirt for the occasion from surgeon James Bronaugh with the proviso he not tell anyone where he got it.[10]

Although the Six Nations had so far refused to send any warriors to aid the British cause, Norton and his war party, their miniscule numbers notwithstanding, were actively intent on convincing the Americans otherwise. "I am determined to exert myself to the utmost to annoy the enemy,"[11] he assured Prevost, and went straight to the task at Forty Mile Creek

From the American camp the young farm boy Jacob Cline watched a scouting party of dragoons, impressive in snug hussar jackets and plumed leather helmets, canter off towards the settlement nestled near the base of the Mountain.[12]

Norton's warriors, skirting the road near the settlement, caught the glint of their arms and quietly slipped into the woods, "in order to gain their rear imperceptibly and intercept their return."[13] The group, their movements covered by

**John Smoke Johnson, Shakoyen'kwaráhton (1792-1886).** Smoke Johnson, a Mohawk of the Bear Clan and godson of Sir William Johnson, fought under Norton all through the war, including the battles of Queenston Heights and Lundy's Lane. At Stoney Creek he was one a handful of native warriors who took part in the action. The photograph was taken in Brantford in 1882 when Johnson was 89. (Library and Archives Canada, C-085127)

the forest, moved parallel to the road towards the dragoons. When they were abreast of the mounted men, a Mohawk, likely 21-year-old Smoke Johnson,[14] was spotted. Fearing the riders might escape, Norton led his men at a full run directly towards the dragoons, who responded by firing their muskets. As they closed within 70 yards the dragoons fired their pistols and Norton's natives answered with their muskets. One dragoon fell, a second was hit and nearly fell, before the scouting party wheeled and galloped back towards the lakeside encampment.

The skirmish was witnessed by 11-year-old Daniel Barber, the son of a New Jersey Loyalist, who was driving a flock of sheep to his father's house at the Fifty:[15] "I was overtaken by ten Yankee dragoons. Directly after they passed me, about a dozen Indians came out of the bush into the road behind me and in rear of the dragoons and fired at them. The dragoons, returning the fire, rode on.... I had gone some distance when I saw one of the dragoons sitting on the coupling of a lumber-waggon beside the road. He appeared to be in great distress, and had stuck to his horse for some distance, but soon fell off the waggon and died." The dead man was likely Ephraim Wilder, a 32-year-old bookbinder from Massachusetts.[16]

Back in camp, Jacob Cline saw the scouting party return in disarray: "They came galloping back in great flight. One horse was riderless, but kept its pace with the rest, and bloodstains on the saddle and mane showed that the rider had been shot. The survivors were intensely excited."[17]

Although the damage was minimal, the psychological effect of Norton's attack was profound. Already the myth of the large, unseen body of warriors stalking them from the shadows had taken root in the American psyche. Artillery captain Nathan Towson believed that Norton had 200 men with him at the Forty. From this point on the Americans were convinced, and would remain convinced, that the British had enlisted, in the words of one infantry officer, "all the Indians in Canada" to their cause.[18]

On Burlington Heights, militia officer Charles Askin, still recovering from malarial fever, joined the limited celebrations to mark the King's birthday, wondering if it might be for the last time, and reflected the anxiety shared by many Niagara settlers: "Our army, I think, must soon retreat from this. Whether they will go to Detroit or towards Kingston we do not know. I mean to follow it if possible. A great number of our gentlemen have taken protections from the enemy since they have come into the country. I shall keep out of their hands as long as I can. I wish we had Tecumseh here to help us out of our difficulties."[19]

John Vincent, while perhaps not pining for the great Shawnee chief, was certainly familiar with the misgivings expressed by Askin. The sightlines from Beasley's Georgian brick home, now his headquarters, perfectly framed his dilemma.

To the north stretched Little Lake and beyond it Lake Ontario, which he believed the American navy controlled. To the east lay the Queenston road upon which an overwhelming army was approaching. Retreat, without naval support? Or stand and confront superior numbers? A classic horned dilemma.

Just before completing the final few sentences of a report to Edward Baynes, the adjutant general in Kingston, Vincent was handed a message from his advanced post at Stoney Creek, warning him of the American advance. Perhaps at that moment, the beleaguered general began to realize he had a third option between retreat and full-fledged confrontation – that of some sort of pre-emptive strike. It was a faint hope to be sure, but maybe, just maybe with the right conditions, it might work. "An attack cannot be far distant," he wrote. "I am determined, if possible, to be beforehand with them."[20]

The 48-year-old career soldier was under intense pressure. He had already lost the most populous and prosperous part of Upper Canada and was contemplating abandoning the remainder. It mattered little that he was outnumbered on land and had no support on water; he was under the watchful eye of two of Prevost's aides[21] and if he was forced to surrender or retreat around the lake to Kingston, every detail of his conduct would end up before the governor general. In the wake of defeats at York, Sackets Harbor and Fort George, the future of the next hapless general officer to report bad news would not be bright.

At Fort George, an ailing Henry Dearborn updated the secretary of war on both the campaign and his health: "Chandler and Winder are in pursuit of the enemy who has halted about forty-five miles from here. I am still very feeble and gain strength but slowly."[22]

Once more, with American troops on the verge of major action, the commander-in-chief was nowhere to be found, having delegated the job to a subordinate, this time a crony whose combat experience in a command position was negligible.

At the same time a persistent rumour had taken hold in the American garrison that Vincent was about to be reinforced by Brigadier General Henry Procter with a strong detachment of regulars and Indians from Amherstburg.[23]

# 16 "Laden with the furniture of death and destruction."[1]

## CHANDLER'S DIVISION

By mid-morning on the 5 June, the vanguard of Chandler's brigade reached the American camp at the Forty, followed within an hour by the main body, including Chandler himself. As senior brigadier general the New Englander took command. It was here that the assistant adjutant general, Major John Johnson, calculated the combined brigades at 2,643 troops. This figure, which has been widely accepted as accurate, is unrealistically low given that approximately 6,000 troops landed at Newark a week earlier. Fort George was only lightly garrisoned by the Americans, as were Chippawa and Fort Erie. Unaccounted for are some 1,600 troops.[2]

Vincent's intelligence reported the combined U.S. force at the Forty to be 3,750; at least two other American observers put Chandler's division at 4,000 troops.[3] Chandler gave no figure, either for his brigade or for the division. The actual figure was almost certainly more than 3,000 and there is evidence of militia presence as well. Whatever the actual numbers were, it was undoubtedly an impressive force that formed up to march toward the Head of the Lake[4] laden, as one company commander said, "with the furniture of death and destruction"[5] – all or part of ten regiments of regular infantry plus three companies of artillery as light infantry, two companies of riflemen, a squadron of light horse and three companies of light artillery with nine field guns. From vanguard to rearguard, the American train would have stretched out at least three miles and the entire, squeaking, clanking, shuffling procession taken well over an hour to pass any given point.

Although American army uniforms were officially blue, it was by no means the only colour. Due to a shortage of blue woollen cloth, many infantry regiments were issued uniform coatees[6] made from whatever colour was in good supply. Hence in Chandler's army the Fourteenth Infantry was likely wearing brown coats, the Sixteenth black and the Twentieth and Twenty-Second greyish brown. The remainder of the infantry regiments, as well as the artillery detachments, were likely clothed in blue coatees with white cotton or dark, gaitered trousers. Infantry and artillery musicians, by regulation, wore red coatees but, again, chronic supply problems made green coatees a common alternative. The dragoons were all in blue, the riflemen, including Lyttle's U.S. Volunteers, all in green.[7]

At least seven of the ten infantry regiments would have been carrying a stand of colours, consisting of one national standard and one regimental colour. The national standard was not the familiar stars and stripes but rather a fully spread eagle on a dark blue silk field. Around the eagle on three sides were 17 stars and under it a scroll with the number of the regiment. The regimental colour was a simple scroll bearing the regiment's designation in blue on a field of buff silk. The national standard was slightly bigger – six by seven feet – and was carried on a staff slightly longer, ten feet versus nine feet, than the regimental colour.[8] On the march they were generally carried furled inside canvas tubes but at least one of the settlers that came to the Queenston road to see the blue army reported flags were flying.[9]

Colours served both as a practical point of reference amid the confusion and chaos of the battlefield and a revered symbol to the regiment that carried them, to be protected at all costs. A regiment that lost its colours was a regiment in disgrace, having essentially lost its soul. The colours were placed at the centre of a regiment's line, where the commanding officer took post, and were thus the object of considerable fire in battle. Usually entrusted to junior ensigns, the task of colour-bearer on the battlefield was extremely perilous.[10]

At the head of Chandler's division was the advance party under *de facto* command of Jacob Hindman, a captain in the Second Artillery. Winfield Scott, who led the advance at Fort George, had returned to his administrative duties as Dearborn's chief of staff. The cavalry colonel James Burn was senior officer in the advance but deferred to the young artillery officer. At 24, Hindman was an experienced and able officer. It was he who snuffed out the lighted fuses attached to the remaining two powder magazines at Fort George after the British evacuation. Expelled from Princeton at 17, he had studied law in Baltimore before entering the army in 1808 as a second lieutenant in the Fifth Infantry. At the age of 20 he was already adjutant of the Fifth. In 1810 he took a leave of absence to

**Colour bearer, Twenty-Fifth U.S. Infantry.** In this painting by Don Troiani, an ensign of the Twenty-Fifth carries the national standard, six by seven feet of dark blue silk emblazoned with a fully spread eagle over the regimental number, surrounded by 17 stars. The largest American regiment at Stoney Creek, the Twenty-Fifth was involved in some of the heaviest action and took the heaviest casualties, 45 killed and wounded, while fighting under this standard. (*Military & Historical Image Bank*)

resume his law studies before re-enlisting in the Second Artillery when war was declared.[11]

According to army regulations the officer commanding the advance "will take care to have a guide with him."[12] Perhaps it was the turncoat Joseph Willcocks who advised Hindman on potential ambush locations, which creek defiles to approach with caution and which plantations were extensive enough to encamp the army. Certainly as the Niagara member in the Upper Canada legislative assembly and a former newspaper editor in Newark, Willcocks would have known the country – and which settlers were sympathetic to the republican cause.

There is some evidence that known Loyalists in the area were persecuted by the American invaders. Daniel Barber, the young shepherd who lived with his grandfather at the Forty, was just reaching his father's house at the Fifty when he saw American troops approaching. "I ran to his house to tell him the Yankees were coming. He had just returned from the other side of the lines and did not wish to be captured, and at once jumped out a back window and ran away. I believe that as many as a hundred shots were fired at him."[13] Another farmer at the Fifty reported American troops stole his watch and were about to steal his prize mare when they were frightened off by native warriors.[14]

The advance was composed of the best troops the United States could field in the spring of 1813 – three companies of the Second Artillery as light infantry, two light companies of the Twenty-Second Infantry, a troop of the Second Light Dragoons, a company of riflemen and a fourth company of the Second Artillery, likely with a pair of 6-pdr. guns – in total about 400 men.[15]

At the very tip of the spear point, if army regulations were followed, would have been a patrol whose job it

**Private, Twenty-Second U.S. Infantry.** Two companies of the Twenty-Second were heavily involved in the early action at Stoney Creek, including McFarland's company to which Sergeant James Crawford belonged. Thanks to the chronic shortage of blue cloth in the first year of the war, the Twenty-Second were issued drab (light brown) coatees with green collars and cuffs and black binding. The overalls were a light blue weave. (Courtesy, James L. Kochan Collection and H. Charles McBarron Estate)

was to examine any creek valley or wood close to the road capable of concealing an ambush. In addition, flank guards fanned out a hundred paces on either side of the guard. Behind the advance was a detachment of pioneers, equipped with axes, billhooks, mattocks [16] and shovels to clear the fallen trees and repair broken bridges left in the wake of Vincent's retreat.

A mile or so behind came the main body of the army with Chandler and Winder at the head, trailing a knot of staff officers behind them, all mounted, followed by the core regiments. The two generals were exactly the same height – 5′8½″– but otherwise physical opposites. Chandler was 51 years old with a stout build, oval face, dark complexion and dark eyes. Winder, only 38 was slight, with a long, fair face and grey eyes. On horseback at the head of each regiment were its commanding officers – colonel, lieutenant colonel and major – if in fact they had accompanied their regiment. All other officers were on foot. As Niagara roads were rarely wider than 30 feet, a marching column would, by necessity, be narrow – probably six abreast. Officially, regiments were divided into ten companies of 90 men each. A full-strength company included five officers, 11 sergeants and corporals and two musicians. In reality, 1813 company strengths rarely exceeded 60 men with a commensurate number of officers. [17]

Following the main body came the artillery, as well as the baggage, which in this case was limited since most of it was being transported by bateaux along the lakeshore. Bringing up the rearguard [18] were the Thirteenth and Fourteenth Infantry, in total about 800 men.

The main weapon in Chandler's artillery was the iron 6-pdr. field gun. The black-barrelled smoothbore could effectively propel a 6-pound iron ball up to 800 yards, or case shot [19] up to 600 yards. Serviced by a crew of nine, a gun and carriage weighed 2,000 pounds and required four to six horses for transport.

The second piece of ordnance in his division was the shorter-range and lighter howitzer, which lobbed round and case shot on a much higher trajectory. Each artillery piece was accompanied by an ammunition wagon.

As the American army formed up and moved off from the Forty on the old Iroquois trail where it passed close under the Mountain, its progress was watched closely by three Stoney Creek men. Levi Green, his younger brother William and Samuel Lee – all members of the 5th Lincoln Militia – had come early in the morning to the Forty to see the invading American army. All three had Loyalist roots: Levi Green, 30, was born in New Jersey and Lee, 27, in Maryland. William, the youngest of the trio at 19, was believed to be the first European child born in Saltfleet township.

Descending to the edge of the bush that skirted the road, the three harassed the rearguard by whooping and hollering like Indians and occasionally emerging to harry stragglers. At one point the elder Green encountered a soldier wrapping a rag around his blistered foot. Before the man could reach his musket, Levi slipped in and cracked him with a stick. His cries alerted the rearguard and as the trio fled back into the bush they were followed by a few scattered rounds of musket fire.[20]

Ephraim Shaler, a junior officer in the Twenty-Fifth Infantry, reported Indians and militia "hanging around us all day, though generally at a respectful distance." Lieutenant Francis Cummins, adjutant of the Sixteenth Infantry, said that "along the brow of the mountain overlooking the route of the army, scouts could be seen through openings of the woods and passes of the hills, contemplating our progress and our strength."[21]

Rather than risk a frontal assault on Burlington Heights, Chandler's plan was to march from Stoney Creek to the lake, cross Burlington Beach and cut off Vincent's retreat route to York.[22] He believed the British were more inclined to retreat, thereby preserving their force – the classic give ground, not blood strategy – rather than hazard all in a decisive action.

The no-escape strategy was presumably on orders of Dearborn, who, in turn, had been told in no uncertain terms by the secretary of war that "battles are not gained when an inferior & broken enemy is not destroyed."[23]

**Burlington Beach.** This westerly view of the Beach Strip, with the King's Head Inn in the foreground, was sketched in 1796 by Elizabeth Simcoe. Brigadier General John Chandler, rather than making a frontal assault on Burlington Heights, intended to march along the beach road and cut off the British army's retreat route to York. (The Diary of Mrs. Simcoe)

# 17 "His Light Troops were already on the skirts of our Camp."[1]

### THE PRELIMINARY SKIRMISH, 5 JUNE 1813

The main British force was encamped on Beasley's hastily fortified farm on Burlington Heights with two advanced posts to the east. The first, with a small detachment of troops, was established at John Aikman's farm, about two and a half miles away. The former Butler's Ranger was in the process of building a frame house to replace his log cabin and would, on this day, have a wagon and harness set impressed by the army.[2]

The easternmost position, about seven miles away, was on the property of farmer and innkeeper William Davis, where the great road crossed Big Creek.[3] Here was posted the light company of the 49th under Queenston Heights veteran Major John Williams. In anticipation, Williams had advanced east on the Queenston road and halted just short of the hamlet of Stoney Creek. A vedette of provincial dragoons patrolled the area.

**Sixteenth U.S. Infantry.** Raised primarily in Pennsylvania and New Jersey, the Sixteenth took part in the attack on York and the capture of Fort George, taking 59 casualties in the process. The unit arrived in Stoney Creek under the command of Captain George Steele, all its field officers either on leave or sick. After Steele and the only other captain present were captured, command devolved onto a lieutenant. (Painting by H.C. McBarron. *Military Uniforms in America: Years of Growth, 1796–1851* © The Company of Military Historians, 1977)

The first contact was early in the afternoon when one of those dragoons, John Brady, brushed up against the American advance just east of Stoney Creek. According to Emerson Bristol Biggar,[4] who wrote an account of Stoney Creek 60 years after the battle, Brady was fired on but escaped by spurring his mount up a deer path to the top of the Mountain. By 3 o'clock the advanced guard was approaching the shallow brook that gave the settlement its name, one of the dozens of mill streams that drain the great limestone ridge running the length of the Niagara Peninsula.

In a township with less than 700 people and 100 dwellings,[5] Stoney Creek was the main settlement and could boast three taverns and a saw mill. Edward Brady's tavern, where the Queenston road crossed Stoney Creek, was the post for a small picket drawn from Williams's light company. Seeing a large body of infantry, riflemen, dragoons and artillery approaching, the picket prudently fired off warning shots and retired on the main body, which withdrew towards Davis's tavern.

Perhaps recalling the frustration of being called off the chase nine days earlier at Fort George and anxious to finish the job, or simply inspired by the brash example of Winfield Scott, the advance was clearly eager to have at the British and pushed forward aggressively.

The pursuit continued westward along the main road past Brady's farm and Stephen Jones's tavern, the land generally cleared and cultivated on both sides of the road. After half a mile, the road crossed an unnamed tributary of Stoney Creek that flowed through the farms of Mary Gage on the south side and her brother-in-law, William Gage, on the north. Both had log houses on high ground overlooking the road about 500 yards apart.[6] Some 200 yards west of the brook, the road rose slightly and ran through a thick wood. On the high ground south of the road stood a frame Methodist church, the only one in the township.

American reports put the size of Major Williams's company at 100 troops; in reality it was probably no more than 70, and certainly it was no match for the American advance, which numbered at least 400 men. Nevertheless, the 32-year-old Williams, a soldier since he was 16 and a seasoned combat veteran, was determined to make any advance as difficult as possible. First contact was likely in the last open ground before the church. Utilizing the standard light company tactics – two-man file partners, one musket always loaded and protecting the other – Williams' men gave ground in measured and deliberate steps, retreating into the woods.

British commanders were generally wary of bush fights with American troops, particularly riflemen. At Fort George, Harvey thought it "highly inexpedient & improper to commit the Troops to a contest in a thick wood with an enemy so thoroughly accustomed to that scene of fighting."[7] Yet Williams seems to have given at least as good as he got. Certainly, using the forest took the American dragoons out of the equation.

Lieutenant Jonathan Kearsley, adjutant of the advance, described a sharp, running action with occasional severe fighting. Another American officer, perhaps surprised at seeing redcoats take to the woods, decided he was facing British regulars *and* Indians.[8]

The riflemen, a detachment of U.S. Volunteers[9] under Captain John Lyttle, were eventually able to push the obstinate light company from the woods into the open ground to the west. From there, they fell back to Big Creek, crossed over and formed up on the far bank to give battle again, some of the troops taking cover in William Davis's barn.

As the advance approached, with Captain Jacob Hindman and Lyttle in the van, the light company opened up with their muskets. A gunner standing between Lyttle and Hindman was shot dead and at least two more wounded. Stood off on the far bank by a single under-strength company of redcoats, the Americans called up some extra firepower. At approximately 6 o'clock Chandler ordered the Twenty-Fifth Infantry, which had just arrived in Stoney Creek, forward to join the skirmish, nearly tripling the size of the advance. The American troops deployed in William Davis's wheat field, trampling his crop in the process. Williams, in the face of overwhelming numbers, retired yet again in good order.[10]

Casualty figures in this preliminary round are difficult to establish, with estimates ranging from hardly any to many. One British officer said there were eight

**Captain Jacob Hindman, Second Artillery (1789-1827).** A law student who retooled as an army officer, Hindman quickly gained a reputation as a tough disciplinarian and drillmaster. Under Winfield Scott and Hindman, the Second Artillery became the elite troops in the U.S. Army, equally adept as gunners or infantrymen. At Fort George he was in the first boat ashore and personally snatched a lighted fuse from one of the fort's powder magazines. Like Scott he was aggressive in the field. As an artillery officer he distinguished himself at Lundy's Lane and Fort Erie. (Portrait by John Wesley Jarvis. Maryland Historical Society)

American casualties, all dragoons, and one British soldier killed. One American officer said "many were killed and wounded," another that several were wounded on both sides and one dragoon horse killed and a third reported only a slight loss on both sides. Casualty rolls of the 49th show one man killed on June 5th – private Edward Little of the light company, a seven-year veteran. It seems likely that casualties were relatively low, probably less than 15 in total. In his 1873 account, Biggar says the American wounded were carried into Davis's tavern, the Red Hill House, to be attended by a nervous regimental surgeon, convinced they were all about to be scalped: "It seems he had heard the shouts of Williams's men and imagined them to be Indians." Clearly the spectre of Indian warfare – even when there were no Indians involved – had taken strong root in the American consciousness.[11]

Despite having bloodied and been blooded, Hindman was not ready to call it a day and "pursued briskly, his men generally running, until it was nearly dark," when the pursuit was halted on orders from Winder.[12] A question remains, however, just how far the advance actually tailed Williams's company.

The American historian Benjamin Lossing said the pursuit continued until the Americans were within sight of Burlington Heights.[13] Twilight in Stoney Creek would have occurred around 8:30 p.m. If the advance left at 6 p.m. and

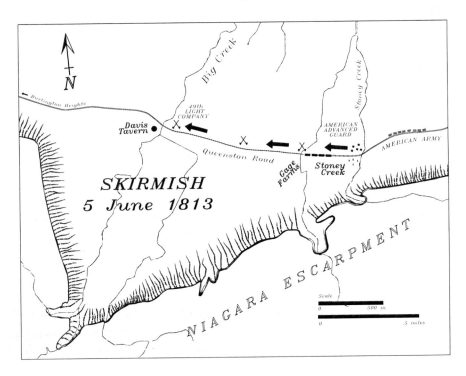

pursued rapidly it could have approached the sentry post at Aikman's farm and returned to Stoney Creek – total distance about six-and-a-half miles – before dark.

Chandler, according to his stated plans, did not intend a frontal assault on Burlington Heights, and so why would the advance be allowed to dash so recklessly close to the British camp? Was it a feint designed to fool the British into thinking a direct attack was imminent? Or a show of bravado by a young commander anxious to emulate his impetuous mentor, Winfield Scott?

We do not know. What we do know, however, is that Chandler thought the pursuit went too far and one of his senior officers even suggested the eagerness of the advance forced the American army to camp closer to Burlington Heights than Chandler and Winder intended, thereby alarming the British enough to consider a pre-emptive strike.[14]

Lossing said the audacity of the American vanguard in chasing the picket to the edge of Burlington Heights amazed and alarmed Vincent. Certainly there was consternation in the British camp from the moment the express rider came in with news of the skirmish at Stoney Creek. Late in the afternoon, the dragoon captain Hamilton Merritt was ordered to fall in with the main body of Vincent's troops at Barn's tavern about a mile in advance of the entrenched position on the heights. "The troops were formed in order of battle," Merritt said, "expecting the Enemy every moment."[15]

Harvey, astonished to hear that the American advance was "on the skirts of our Camp," rode forward to see for himself.[6]

**Canadian Light Dragoon, 1813.** A provincial corps raised in Lower Canada, the Canadian Light Dragoons wore essentially the same uniform as Hamilton Merritt's Niagara Provincial Light Dragoons – blue jackets with scarlet collar and cuffs, felt helmets with bearskin and grey overalls wrapped with leather. Merritt used his blue jacket to capture two soldiers at Stoney Creek after convincing them he was an American dragoon. (Painting by G.A. Embleton, Department of National Defence, Canada

# 18 "As sure as the morning dawn appears."[1]

## HARVEY'S DESPERATE GAMBLE

While waiting for the advance to return from its sortie, Chandler ordered the Thirteenth and Fourteenth regiments along with Archer's company of Second Artillery, with two guns, to take post on the lakeshore and protect the bateaux transporting his army's ammunition, baggage and provisions from Forty Mile Creek. Splitting his force and sending 800 troops and a company of artillery two miles away made sense, he reasoned, because they "would be on the route which I intended to pursue the next morning." Had Chandler consulted Armstrong's handbook, *Hints to Young Generals,* however, he would have found the first rule of offensive war, according to the old soldier, was: "Keep your forces in as undivided a state as possible."[2]

In the interim he surveyed the ground on which his main body had halted, "a grain and grazing farm" in the words of one company officer, judged it defensible and ordered all units to make camp. Somehow, in the midst of the Loyalist hotbed that was Saltfleet Township, Chandler had taken his position on property not belonging to Loyalists. Was it an accident? Probably not. Sixty-nine-year-old Mary Gage was the widow of an American militiaman killed fighting the British during the Revolution.[3] Through her brother, Augustus Jones, the Crown land surveyor in Upper Canada,[4] she secured a land grant in Saltfleet just below the escarpment. Living with her were her son, James Gage, his wife, Mary, and their five children ranging in age from three to 15 years. James Gage farmed the property and kept a general store. When the war started, he paid a substitute to take his place in James Durand's flank company of the 5th Lincoln, who subsequently deserted.[5]

**James Gage (1774-1854),** the son of an American militiaman killed during the Revolution, came to Upper Canada in 1790, establishing one of the farms Chandler chose for his Stoney Creek camp. The American army plundered his provisions, including flour and whisky, and slaughtered his livestock. (Portrait by unknown artist. Battlefield House Museum)

Across the road lived Mary Gage's brother-in-law, William Gage, who also fought the British during the Revolution. And, like his brother, he had also married one of Augustus Jones's sisters.[6] Whether Chandler was aware of their background is not known, although if Joseph Willcocks was the army guide he could have pointed out potential sympathizers.

Certainly from a military standpoint Chandler had chosen well; the two Gage farms offered a position that was unquestionably defensible. On the east side of the shallow creek that ran north toward the lake, a saucer-shaped meadow spread about 150 to 200 yards on either side of the Queenston road, the north side protected by a swamp, the south side by the foothills of the Mountain and heavy woods. One hundred and fifty yards east of the creek, a steep 20-foot bank carved by countless spring floods and thick with brush and fallen timber provided a natural earthwork on both sides of the road. Elevated and secure on both flanks, Chandler's position was one that could be approached only from the front.

**"A grain and grazing farm."** This view of the battlefield, looking south from William Gage's house, shows the ground Brigadier General John Chandler chose for his camp on 5 June. This pastoral scene was sketched by historian and artist Benjamin Lossing when he visited in 1860. The house visible in the background is the much-modified James Gage house. (Lossing, *Pictorial Field-Book of the War of 1812*)

**Two Gage farms.** This detail of a photograph from the early 20th century shows the relative positions of the two Gage farms looking north towards Lake Ontario. In the foreground is the house James Gage and his family lived in. The house in the background, just to the left above the chimney, marks the site of William Gage's home. Between them they mark the north-south extent of the battlefield. (Local History & Archives, Hamilton Public Library)

However, despite the natural advantages of the position, little care was taken in securing the encampment and posting the various units. Of course, Chandler and Winder had never been in a similar position before, their combat experience being limited and their knowledge of making camp in enemy territory confined to whatever they gleaned from books. Army regulations on the Order of Encampment, however, were straightforward – "infantry will on all occasions encamp by battalions as they are formed in order of battle"[7] – yet instead of enforcing the regulations, the two brigadiers allowed regiments to select their own ground.

"Most miserable generalship" is how Ephraim Shaler, a second lieutenant with the Twenty-Fifth Infantry, described the camp arrangement. "The whole brigade should have been camped in regular military order, having a rallying point designated by the commanding General, to be understood by every commandant of a regiment; but unhappily for us, no such point was designated. The several regiments of our brigade encamped wherever they found it most convenient."[8]

Virginian John Thornton, a captain in the Twentieth Infantry, said the units were "disposed in various and distant situations and too much scattered for a prompt cooperation in case of attack."[9] Indeed, the danger of a haphazard camp, well within striking distance of the enemy, appears to have concerned nearly everyone except the general officers. A captain in the Second Artillery observed: "Notwithstanding the opinion of all the officers that an attack would certainly be made that night, yet Generals Chandler and Winder permitted us to encamp without any order or regularity. One brigade of 800 men was three miles from the other. No order of battle, no watchword, not a rallying post assigned."[10]

Yet another angry officer sketched the scene. "Picture to yourself an army of between two and three thousand infantry, with artillery and cavalry halted on their arms, each commanding officer choosing such ground and place as he thought proper, some on a hill, others in a hollow, some one way, some another. No order of battle, no rallying point, no watchword."[11] For the Americans, confronting a desperate enemy, this carelessness would cost them dearly.

Lieutenant Francis Cummins, adjutant of the Sixteenth Infantry, surveyed the muddled camp arrangements with dismay. "Any one of the smallest military judgment can perceive the error of the commanding General. All was scattered, broken, disconnected – each part independent of the other; no point of rally, no pivot of operation, nor base line, nor combination. Effect is like cause. A battle in the night by forces under such arrangements, must necessarily be a chance medley, altogether *husteron proteron*."[12]

Back on the heights, Harvey and a small mounted escort collected the light company of the King's and headed for Stoney Creek, picking up Williams's light company of the 49th en route. To avoid any American patrols they travelled cautiously through the woods skirting the road. Just before Big Creek, Harvey halted the detachment and proceeded on with two of Merritt's provincial dragoons.[13]

With the bridge gone, they forded the muddy creek and were ascending the eastern bank when they encountered an American soldier with a British prisoner taken during the earlier skirmish. The soldier was quickly disarmed and questioned, and Harvey and his escort were able to advance close enough to reconnoitre the American camp just as the sun was setting behind them. Harvey was thrilled to discover the Americans had settled in for the night.[14]

Two crucial questions had been answered. Up to this point the British were uncertain what Chandler intended. The fact that the troops on Burlington Heights had been formed in order of battle indicated Vincent feared an imminent attack. Harvey, now certain that no further American offence was planned that night, could survey Chandler's defensive positions for any weaknesses.

How that was done is not clear. There are enduring stories that a spy, under cover of selling butter or potatoes, actually advanced right into the American camp for a first-hand inspection. Quite possibly it was a young Guards officer, Lieutenant Henry Milnes, who undertook the mission. Harvey himself said only that he got "sufficiently close to the enemy's Camp to ascertain its exact situation." However obtained, the intelligence gathered on troop and artillery dispositions was music to Harvey's ears – the camp was not secure, unit positions were haphazard and the guns poorly protected. In short the American camp was vulnerable.[15]

The idea of a night attack appears to have occurred to several people at the same time. One of the provincial dragoons who advanced with Harvey on the reconnaissance, Cornet Amos McKenny, may have the most credible claim. Others include Ensign James George of the 1st Lincoln Militia, native war chief John Norton, Prevost's ADC Captain Robert McDouall, and Lieutenant James Fitz-Gibbon of the 49th.[16]

Whoever first conceived the notion, Harvey was the one to set it in motion and dispatched Lieutenant Milnes, Prevost's other ADC, back to Burlington Heights proposing an immediate attack on Chandler's camp with the 8th and 49th regiments and one gun. About an hour after sunset, Milnes, distraught to the point of tears,[17] returned and delivered the response – the proposal had been submitted by Vincent to a council of all his field officers and had been unanimously rejected.

Harvey rushed back to the Heights, leaving the light companies at Aikman's along with Norton and a handful of warriors who had come forward. He found the troops lying on their arms and the council still sitting. Taking Vincent aside, Harvey made his desperate pitch. Failure to act now, he warned, would cost Vincent his reputation, his troops and quite likely the whole upper province. "I demonstrated to him that the Position which the Troops now occupied was not defensible with less than 4 or 5000 men. And as sure as the morning dawn appears, this handful of men under his command must either surrender or be cut to pieces in a fruitless & unequal contest."[18]

Aware the Americans possessed superior numbers, Harvey would also have known the British stood little hope in a conventional stand-up action; their best, perhaps only, chance lay in a surprise attack – to confuse the enemy and upset his battle plans. Vincent, to his credit, recognized the superior military talents of his subordinate. "His good sense & manly spirit," Harvey said, "had no difficulty in deciding upon the proper course. He gave a willing assent."[19] Regarding the field officers who, to a man, had rejected his bold plan, Harvey said nothing.

Realizing that the Americans would attack the following morning, Vincent acceded to Harvey's proposition "as offering the best chance of crippling the enemy and disconcerting all his plans."[20]

# 19 "The art of blundering."[1]

### CHANDLER'S DISPOSITIONS

In Stoney Creek it was dark before the last of the advance units returned to a camp which by then lay in a random sprawl over both Gage properties. Dozens of camp fires, fuelled by broken fence rails, burned on both sides of the road as soldiers cooked their first meal of the day. Just to the west of the shallow stream, a gated lane ran north to William Gage's log house. Second Lieutenant Ephraim Shaler marched into that lane with the Twenty-Fifth Infantry, "the men stacked their arms and lay down upon the grass: the regimental cooks built their fires along in the centre of the lane, and made preparations for cooking supper, a very large, fat ox was driven into the lane, butchered and divided among several cooks." The beast likely belonged to Isaac Corman, who had a yoke of oxen seized from his farm that day.[2]

On the south side of the road, James Gage's eight-year-old daughter Elizabeth witnessed the pillage of her home. "The cellar of my father's house was full of all sorts of provisions, enough to do the family during the year and the soldiers made free with everything. In the house were a number of bags of flour and there were twenty barrels of whisky in the cellar, all of which they took, the soldiers killed all the cows and sheep they lay their eyes on."[3] These were hungry and tired men. Elizabeth thought them "the most miserable, half-starved lot I ever saw."[4]

The two American brigadiers, Chandler and Winder, also made a strong impression on the young girl. "They were very proud and braggy and told us the old man (my father) would be shot in the morning if we didn't look out. They ordered the men to let down the fences for them, so they could ride into the meadow where the soldiers were."[5]

Some of the officers moved into the Gage home, bringing their cooks with them. They "were quite kind and friendly, and we got on first rate," she remembered, "but they used everything about the house and the soldiers carried away the quilts and forks and spoons to their camp."[6]

In a belated effort to secure the encampment, several inhabitants were rounded up, including the hapless oxen owner Isaac Corman and Jacob Springstead, both members of the 5th Lincoln Militia. Springstead, who was suspected of being a spy, was confined with two other men in a log cabin near the American artillery position. Corman, a member of Durand's flank company and veteran of Queenston Heights, was confined in his own home.[7]

Although army regulations governing order of encampment and camp duties were clearly defined in Alexander Smyth's 1812 manual, few appear to have been followed in the establishment of Chandler's camp. Despite rules restricting fires to kitchens in the very rear of the camp, dozens were set and maintained in the midst of the forward American line, essentially serving as beacons for an enemy approaching from the front.[8]

**Elizabeth Gage (1805-1889).** One of James Gage's five children, Elizabeth was eight years old when General Chandler's army camped on the family farm and his officers moved into the family home. His troops, she said, were "the most miserable, half-starved lot I ever saw." During the battle she took refuge in the wool loft. (Genealogical and historical records of the Mills and Gage families)

By regulation, slaughter of animals was restricted to an area at least 70 feet behind the kitchens, which were to be located well in the rear of the regimental lines. Entrails were to be buried immediately.[9] At Stoney Creek, oxen, sheep and cattle were killed, butchered and cooked in the forward line – along the lane leading to William Gage's house and on the meadow immediately south of the Queenston road. Regimental officers, including commanding officers, were expressly forbidden to lodge in civilian houses except in cases of sickness, yet officers and their servants moved into the Gage house.[10]

Perhaps the most telling infraction, however, concerned battle order. At Stoney Creek, with individual regiments selecting their own ground, it appears to have been the last thing on anyone's mind. Chandler's strongest regiment, the Twenty-Fifth, was camped on William Gage's lane with three elite companies of light artillery and an infantry light company on its right and two further companies of light on the extreme right as picket guard – in total probably close to 900 troops. One hundred and fifty yards in the rear of that lane, four pieces of artillery – three 6-pdr. guns and a howitzer – covered the road from the upland ridge that intersected it. Three more guns were parked on the south side of the road in the rear of the first position, rendering them useless in any action.

About 200 yards to the south of the artillery position and in the rear of the Gage homestead, three more regiments – the Twenty-Third, the Sixteenth and the Fifth – were encamped, facing the lake with their backs to the Mountain. Lyttle's rifle company of U.S. Volunteers was placed as the advance around James Gage's farmhouse. No infantry was posted to support the artillery. "We were encamped in detached parties," one American officer wrote, "so that when the firing commenced we knew not where to look for the line of battle."[11]

This is what Harvey and/or his spies saw when they reconnoitred the position – an erratic camp, too many troops forward in an exposed position with campfires to mark their location, the artillery orphaned without infantry support. A contemporary staff officer who examined Chandler's camp layout said the former blacksmith and tavern keeper, deficient in talent and experience, was in over his head: "Would not a commander of the most ordinary capacity have brigaded his artillery and made his order of encampment his order of battle? Had it been possible for the unfortunate gentleman to have learnt scientifically the art of blundering he could not have exhibited a more complete series of errors."[12]

An examination of how the outpost, picket and camp guards were selected raises further questions about Chandler's competence. Ironically the man who fussed over the responsibilities of sentries while in command of the U.S. naval base at Sackets Harbor,[13] gave little or no thought to security when camped in hostile territory with a desperate and dangerous enemy only seven miles away.

When the advance guard returned from the pursuit of the British picket, the adjutant, Lieutenant Jonathan Kearsley, was ordered by Chandler's brigade major, Captain Roger Jones,[14] to furnish a detachment from the advance to serve as sentries. Jones specified a company of riflemen, the light company from the Twenty-Second Infantry, and a company of the Second Artillery.

Kearsley resisted, both because his troops were tired and because he believed riflemen unsuitable for sentry duty. "They were excessively fatigued from the severe duties and fighting during the day, to which the other troops had not been exposed," Kearsley argued, and "the riflemen of Forsyth had never been disciplined to picket guard duty, and would therefore, probably, where ever they might be stationed, lie down and go to sleep."[15] When Jones refused to reconsider, Kearsley went directly to Chandler, pointing out the potential folly of entrusting the safety of the entire army to riflemen who "had never performed guard duty in their life." Unmoved, Chandler said picket arrangements had been made and would not be changed.[16]

And so, in spite of Kearsley's grave misgivings about rifles on sentry duty – "theirs was emphatically the discipline of fighting" – a company of rifles under a 21-year-old Virginian, Lieutenant Henry Van Swearingen, was detailed to guard duty at the Methodist church about 500 yards in advance of the main American line. And roughly midway between, on the lane leading to the William Gage house, the largest regiment in the brigade, the Twenty-Fifth Infantry, was posted as the bulwark of the advanced line. To the Twenty-Fifth's right, still on

**Lieutenant Jonathan Kearsley, Second Artillery (1786-1859)** came ashore at Fort George in the same boat as Winfield Scott and was adjutant in the advance of Chandler's army. At Stoney Creek he warned against assigning riflemen to guard duty and was proven correct when the entire picket at the Methodist church was captured after falling asleep. After the war he went on to become the mayor of Detroit and a regent of the University of Michigan. (Portrait by Alvah Bradish. Detroit Public Library, Burton Historical Collection)

the lane, four elite companies of light infantry – Peter Mills's Company of the Twenty-Third and Hindman's, Biddle's and Nicholas's Second Artillery. As the right flank guard, two companies of the Twenty-Second, under Captain Daniel McFarland and Captain David Milliken were posted on the northern edge of the meadow just below William Gage's house where the creek fed a swamp. Another guard was posted on the army's left flank approaching the Mountain.[17]

Burn's light dragoons took post 300 to 400 yards behind the artillery. A mile or two beyond the dragoons the Ninth Infantry, with two under-strength companies totalling 95 men, was posted as the rearguard.[18] In addition, Chandler said he ordered a chain of sentinels around the camp – as per camp guard regulations – with explicit instructions to put out constant patrolling parties toward Burlington Heights.[19]

As for the possibility of a surprise attack, it had crossed Chandler's mind but he did not believe the British would risk a major action: "I anticipated that the enemy would attempt to disturb us during the night, if he made any stand at all." Winder, his second in command, was even more convinced the British were retreating.[20]

Judging by the dispositions made to secure the camp, neither brigadier believed the enemy intended to fight. After all, as the secretary of war was fond of declaring, British commanders in Canada, chronically short of manpower, always "prefer the preservation of troops to that of his post."[21]

**Captain Thomas Biddle, Second Artillery (1790-1831).** Scion of a distinguished Pennsylvania family, Biddle left university to join Winfield Scott's Second Artillery. At Fort George he led his company ashore as part of Scott's advance and pursued the retreating British towards Queenston. At Stoney Creek he saw action in the skirmish of June 5 and in the main battle saw his company badly cut up when they were caught between British and American fire. He served with distinction through the Niagara campaign of 1813 and went on to become army paymaster. He was killed in a duel with Congressman Spencer D. Pettis in 1831. His portrait was painted by Thomas Sully in 1818. (Pennsylvania Academy of Fine Arts, bequest of Ann E. Biddle)

# 20 "Our little band."[1]

### JOHN BULL'S ARMY

On his way back to Burlington Heights, Harvey was met by John Norton with a small party of natives, no more than a dozen, at Aikman's farm. Distressed at not being able to field more warriors, Norton nevertheless offered "the few men I could collect" for a surprise attack on the American camp. To be sure, Norton's anxiety over the ominous reluctance of the Grand River warriors to join the fray was shared by the British high command as well. At Vincent's behest, William Claus had been sent to drum up support but none was forthcoming. A party of warriors had left the Grand River in the afternoon but stopped along the way, refusing to join the British on Burlington Heights. And Vincent worried that indifference was just the prelude to outright hostility.[2]

Harvey told Norton to remain with the light company of the 49th at Aikman's, promising to return as soon as possible.[3] Meanwhile at Barn's tavern, Hamilton Merritt, facing the prospect of imminent action, did what soldiers do in hurry-up-and-wait situations: he, along with several other officers, lay on the grass and napped.[4]

For the operation Harvey selected the 49th and the King's Regiment. Official returns indicate eight companies from the 49th and five companies from the King's, for a total of 704 muskets. There is, however, evidence that the 49th had men drawn from all ten companies in the regiment and the King's force included men from at least eight

**Private, King's (8th) Regiment.** One of the senior regiments in the British army, the 8th's Latin motto was *Nec Aspera Terrant* – which translates roughly as "Difficulties be damned." In 1813 alone, in actions at York, Fort George and Sackets Harbor, the unit had taken nearly 300 casualties. This painting by Peter Twist depicts a 1812 private in the grenadier company wearing a stovepipe shako and a trotter pack. (Peter Twist)

different companies. Possibly they were cannibalized to fill gaps in the light and grenadier companies but remained on the books of their original company.[5]

Founded in 1685, the King's or 8th Regiment of Foot was one of the senior regiments in the British army. Raised in Derbyshire and Hertfordshire, the unit's long and distinguished record included home service suppressing rebellion in Ireland and Scotland and active service all over Europe. During the American Revolution the King's men garrisoned Fort Niagara and other Great Lakes outposts. Against Napoleon they fought in Egypt, Germany, Denmark and Martinique. As a royal regiment, the 8th wore royal blue facings on its coats and used the Hanoverian motto *Nec Aspera Terrant* – which translates roughly into "Difficulties be damned." Certainly the regiment had no shortage of difficulties to face in Upper Canada; already in this war various companies of the 8th had been in combat at Ogdensburg, York, Fort George and Sackets Harbor, taking nearly 300 casualties in the last three actions.[6]

The 49th Regiment was formed in 1744 by the governor of Jamaica, Edward Trelawny, as his garrison regiment for "the service and defence of the King's plantations in America."[7] Which is exactly what the regiment did in New York during the Revolutionary War. The 49th, under General William Howe, was in successful campaigns to take New York City in 1776 and Philadelphia in 1777. In 1778 the 49th won its first battle honour, defeating a French force on St. Lucia. In 1788, the regiment successfully garrisoned Haiti for three years in the midst

of a revolution. In addition to the obvious martial dangers, the Caribbean was hard on garrison troops – malaria was rife, rum was cheap – and a posting there often amounted to a protracted death sentence.

Although recruited entirely from Britain and arbitrarily affiliated with

**Captain, Kings (8th) Regiment.** The 8th or King's Regiment had only 15 officers on the field at Stoney Creek, and almost half were wounded during the action, including two company commanders, Captain James Munday and Captain John Thomas Goldrisk. (Painting by J.C.H. Forster. Fort York Collection)

the county of Hertfordshire, the 49th did not set foot in England until the regiment was 52 years old, when fewer than 150 "fever-ridden scarecrows in red coats" landed in 1796. That same year, command of the regiment was taken over by an ambitious 28-year-old Channel Islander, Isaac Brock. Under Brock the 49th saw action against the French in Belgium and Holland and served with Nelson at Copenhagen before embarking for Canada in 1802. Ten years later Brock would report that while the 49th remained inordinately fond of rum "it is still respectable, and apparently ardent for an opportunity to acquire distinction." Distinction came with the decisive victory at Queenston Heights in 1812, albeit tempered by extreme sorrow at Brock's death while recklessly leading the 49th light company up the heights.[8]

Both regiments were stocked with lifers – career soldiers who would serve 20 years in the ranks or die in harness. They were professional warriors, well-trained and steady under fire. They were British redcoats, arguably the best infantry in the world.

The King's was an English regiment – barely. Slightly more than half its troops were English, the rest being Irish and Scots, mostly Irish. Nearly a quarter of the regiment had been in service for ten years or more, three-quarters had at least five years. Although there were a few teenagers in the ranks, 90 per cent were between 20 and 35 years. One quarter were short, 5'4", or less but the majority were between 5'5" and 5'8".[9] The King's was under command of 28-year-old Major James Ogilvie. In the army since 15, Ogilvie, the son of a general and the former colonial administrator of Cape Breton, had limited combat experience but was noticed at Fort George for his solid service.[10]

The 49th was an Irish regiment – overwhelmingly so. Nearly two-thirds of the troops, three-quarters of the NCOs and one-third of the officers were Irish. Two out of three enlisted men had ten years or more service with the regiment. A few were older than 50 but most were between 25 and 40 years old.[11] Major Charles Plenderleath, who commanded the 49th, was a 33-year-old Scot, scion of an old Border family who had also been in the army since he was 15. He was a young company commander aboard the fleet with Nelson at the Battle of Copenhagen, where the regiment won battle honours.

From the subalterns through the company commanders to the field officers, both regiments were led by experienced, professional officers. In 1811 the average length of service for officers in the 49th was 12 years.[12] On the other side of the line, few American officers had commissions that pre-dated 1812. Those who did had seen very little combat before the war.

At Burlington Heights it was close to 11 o'clock in the evening when Harvey led his party out onto the Queenston road. In addition to the 8th and the 49th, both carrying their colours, Harvey's force also contained a small detachment of Royal Artillery with one small field piece, likely a 6-pdr. There were 52 officers, including three from the 41st, two from the Royal Newfoundland Fencibles, one each from the Glengarry Light Infantry, Royal Artillery and the 1st Foot Guards, Harvey and Vincent himself.[13]

In addition to the regulars there may have been as many as 30 militia – officers and men – present as well, representing the five Lincoln regiments, the 1st and 2nd York, the Niagara Provincial Light Dragoons, the Incorporated Militia of Upper Canada, Cameron's Provincial Incorporated Artillery Company and the 1st Oxford. By the time they stopped at Aikman's to collect the 49th light company and Norton's natives, the total number was approaching 800 men.

An additional detachment of 200 men from the 41st Regiment was ordered to remain well in the rear of the main force on the Queenston road to protect against an American counterattack on Burlington Heights and as a reserve to cover the retreat.[14]

**49th Regiment of Foot.** Rigorous training and discipline were the keys to the superior performance of British infantry. The training manual of arms included 11 separate steps in the loading and firing of the .75 calibre Brown Bess musket. The private at left is tearing open a paper cartridge before priming the pan with gunpowder. The next step would see the remainder of the powder, a lead ball and the paper wadding rammed down the barrel. An experienced infantryman could deliver a sustained rate of fire of three to four rounds a minute.

In preparation for firing, the NCO at right has loaded his musket and is in the "make-ready" position, prior to the "present" command, at which point he will level his weapon and then fire on command. Like all infantry regiments in the British army, soldiers of the 49th would have spent countless hours perfecting battlefield drill. (© Craig Williams, used with permission)

In addition to the Canadian militia, there were at least another dozen Canadians in the ranks and officer corps of Harvey's regulars that night. Five lieutenants and two captains in the 49th Regiment were Canadian. Quebec-born Lieutenant Daniel Claus, son of William Claus, was 17 when he was commissioned in 1809 on the recommendation of Isaac Brock.[15] The Danford brothers, 20-year-old Edward and 23-year-old William, both lieutenants, were the sons of the Crown's ordnance storekeeper in Quebec and had been commissioned within months of each other in 1809.[16] Lieutenant Samuel Holland, grandson of Samuel Johannes Holland,[17] Wolfe's engineer at Louisbourg and Quebec, was also born in Quebec and commissioned in 1809.[18]

Lieutenant John Sewell, illegitimate son of Jonathan Sewell, chief justice of Lower Canada, had joined the Royal Navy when he was 13 as a midshipman but switched to the army at 17, gaining a commission in the 89th Foot[19] before transferring to the 49th.

Thomas Nairne, a 30-year-old captain in the 49th, was the son of John Nairne, a Scots army officer who helped Wolfe take Quebec in 1759, and Carleton defend it in 1775. Born on the family seigneury at La Malbaie, Thomas Nairne joined the army in 1801, attaining a captaincy in the 10th Foot by 1806. He had returned to Canada on half-pay when war was declared and was exchanged to the 49th.[20]

The senior Canadian-born officer was Captain Henry Smith Ormand, who was commissioned in the 49th in 1799. Born in Maugerville, New Brunswick, Ormand was the eldest son of Loyalist George Ormand, adjutant of Simcoe's Queen's Rangers during the Revolution. He served as a marine at Copenhagen on HMS *Glatten* and commanded the honour guard that welcomed Nelson on board.[21] And while the Royal Newfoundland Fencibles had no troops in the party, one of the unit's officers from Newfoundland, Lieutenant Alfred Andrew Armstrong, made the trek to Stoney Creek, probably as part of Vincent's staff.

**Lieutenant John Sewell, 49th Regiment (1794-1875).** The illegitimate son of the chief justice of Lower Canada, Sewell had spent four years in the Royal Navy before accepting a commission in the infantry at the age of 17. At Stoney Creek he was the youngest of the seven Canadian officers in the 49th. He is shown in this photograph wearing his General Service Medal with the Crysler's Farm clasp. (St. Lawrence Parks Commission)

Additionally, there were five Canadians in the ranks of the 49th and 8th as gentleman volunteers. In an era when almost one in five commissions was still purchased, this was one way for ambitious young men without means to make their way. They joined a regiment on active service as unpaid volunteers, uniformed as and marching with the enlisted men but messing with the officers. If their service was conspicuous or gallant enough to attract the attention of the commanding officer, they could, in the event of a vacancy, win an entry-level commission.[22]

A typical example in the 49th was Augustus Thompson. The son of New Jersey Loyalists who had settled 40 miles down the lake in Grantham Township, Thompson began the war in the 1st Lincoln Militia but was attached to the 49th as a gentleman volunteer just in time for the Battle of Queenston Heights, where he was noticed in dispatches.[23]

Remarked on in the same dispatches were two other volunteers, George Jarvis and Richard Shaw. Jarvis, the son of Connecticut Loyalists who had settled at York, was 15 when he joined the 49th. In the ranks at Queenston Heights he had witnessed the death of Brock. Richard Shaw, the son of the adjutant general of militia, Æneas Shaw, had joined the 49th in August 1812 and had already been in action three times.[24]

Also well-seasoned in the ranks was 19-year-old Donald MacDonell, son and grandson of distinguished Revolutionary War veterans. Although less than a year in the ranks with the 8th, he had seen hard action at York and Sackets Harbor. Fellow gentleman volunteer John Mathieson, nephew of the militia quartermaster general, Robert Nichol, had just undergone his baptism of fire at Fort George, joining the 8th's light company and winning favourable notice.[25]

**Lieutenant Daniel Claus, 49th Foot (1793-1813).** One of seven Canadian officers in the 49th Regiment who were at Stoney Creek, Claus was the son of Indian Department official and militia officer William Claus. He was 17 when he was commissioned in 1809 on the recommendation of Isaac Brock. Claus survived Stoney Creek but was fatally wounded at the Battle of Crysler's Farm in November 1813. (Library and Archives Canada, C-95817)

# 21 "We want experience in ... the Art of War."[1]

## UNCLE SAM'S ARMY

The two armies that clashed at Newark and eventually collided in the dark on the Gage farm were vastly different entities. One was a seasoned prize fighter and the other a young, green farmhand. The American administration had entered the war with hopelessly unrealistic expectations of its army, believing British control of Lower and Upper Canada needed only a solid kick to collapse like a house of cards. The shocks of 1812 – humiliating defeats at Detroit and Queenston – had been severe but implementation of lessons learned was still some ways off. "To be prepared for war is one of the most effectual means of preserving peace," George Washington had counselled. "A free people ought not only to be armed but disciplined."[2] In 1812 the United States was neither.

Just weeks after war was declared, one of the army's newly-appointed general officers, who would eventually become secretary of war, wrote: "Our standing army is but an ill-organized militia; and our militia not better than a mob."[3]

The regular army coming into the conflict was little more than "a frontier police force with no general staff or senior officers capable of strategic planning,"[4] and although Congress authorized a nearly six-fold increase in strength to 57,000 by 1813, actual recruitment was less than half that number. As a result, recruiting standards for age, height and health were all eased considerably and the quality of recruits fell.

The army surgeon James Mann said low pay – 20 cents a day for privates – attracted the dregs of society. "A large proportion of the army were not, when first enlisted, fit for soldiers ... many of these, habitually intemperate, with constitutions broken down by inebriation and its consequent disease.... It has been too much an object with officers on the recruiting service to fill up their rolls with numbers; without reflecting that the strength of an army consists in able-bodied men. These infirm men were always a dead weight, requiring a detachment of more efficient, as nurses or attendants. A body of five thousand composing our troops seldom have furnished more than three thousand capable of active duty in the field."[5]

An inspection report on the Fourteenth Regiment while camped near Buffalo in October 1812 damned just about every conceivable aspect of the unit and its equipment:

The regiment is composed entirely of recruits. They appear to be almost as ignorant of their duty as if they had never seen a camp and scarcely know on which shoulder to carry the musket.

The company officers are almost as ignorant of their duty as when they entered service....

The arms of this regiment are in infamously bad order. They appear to be old muskets that have probably been bought up at reduced prices by the contractors....

The knapsacks are very bad. Neither gun slings, picks nor brushes have been furnished ... some of the cartridges are said to have been made up in 1794. There is a scarcity of flints....

The tents never were any good and have been so abused on the march to this place that they afford little protection from the weather....

The surgeon states that he is without medicine, hospital stores and surgical instruments.

Though the month of October is partly gone, yet strange to tell, this regiment has not received a single article of woollen clothing. All the men are without coats and many without shoes or stockings....

The Lieut-Colonel states that the regiment is supplied with very bad provisions.[6]

The problems ran from the bottom to the very top, where the War Department, unable to determine accurate strength numbers for the army, was reduced to guessing, based on the number of uniforms shipped from the Philadelphia depot. Of the 18 infantry regiments raised in 1812, half were commanded by men with no previous military experience outside the militia. For general officers the situation was the same – the only experience anyone had came nearly 30 years before during the Revolution. When the war began, the majority of general officers were 60 or over, an age considered elderly. Politics and geography played a large role in every appointment. Many of the appointees, Winfield Scott wrote, were "swaggerers, dependants, decayed gentlemen and others – fit for nothing else, which always turned out utterly unfit for any military purpose whatever ... who on the return of peace, became the unscarred braggarts of war."[7]

The outspoken militia officer Peter Buell Porter, although a War Hawk, was equally scathing. "Our army is full of men fresh from the lawyers' shops and counting rooms, who know little of the physical force of man or the proper mode of its application. With them the whole of the *military* art consists in knowing how to manoeuvre a regiment, how to form and display a column, and the scientific shape in which the troops are to be presented ... with these acquirements they are sent out in quest of adventures, without object or design."[8]

Another army officer wryly derided the army from the brass hats to the rank and file. "Now-a-days a pair of epaulets and a splendid military coat are the only requisites to form able and great officers.... We have a horde of militia that are every thing except what they ought to be – soldiers! However they are very useful in their way, being inveterate enemies to all federalists, hen roosts, pig styes and sheep folds; and most renowned for their vigorous attack on corn fields and potatoe patches."[9]

Despite the obvious failings of the 1812 campaign, the same approach was still in play in 1813. A Pennsylvania infantry officer summed up the view of many of his colleagues: "We now had the experiment to repeat, of sending superannuated men of the Revolution to command. As the failure of the aged Poltroon, General Van Rensselaer, lost us everything in 1812, so was the age and infirmity of General Dearborn the cause of so many errors."[10] The influential *Niles' Weekly Register* reflected the widespread disaffection at the end of 1812 – "Never was a nation cursed with worse generals."[11]

By 1813 there had been some incremental improvements but the fundamental problems persisted. "Our troops are brave & our officers gallant men," artillery colonel Alexander Macomb observed, "but we want experience in the higher branches of the Art of War."[12]

In contrast to this amateur army of raw recruits, George III's redcoats were professionals – well trained, disciplined and experienced. Drawn primarily from the lower classes of Britain and Ireland and enlisted for life, the British infantryman had gained a worldwide reputation for steadiness under fire, tested and perfected over nearly two decades of fighting the French.

The Duke of Wellington held a low opinion of their moral character. "None but the worst description of men enter the regular service," he said, "some of our men enlist from having

**Gunner, U.S. Artillery.** Likely the best troops fielded by the American army in the first two years of the war, the artillery served the guns and served as infantry. The advance of Chandler's army included four companies of the Second Artillery – three as infantry and one as artillery. The gunner in this H.C. McBarron painting carries a sponge and rammer on his left shoulder. (Parks Canada)

got bastard children – some for minor offences – many more for drink." Yet his contempt was purely social, because militarily he "made his infantry into the best in the world by careful attention to organization, training and equipment. It gained also the priceless confidence which comes with continuous victories."[13]

After taking Fort George, one American infantry officer measured the value of the victory by the quality of the opposition – "the most choice troops in the British Army – (the 8th, 41st and 49th that have so frequently distinguished themselves in every quarter of the Globe)."[14]

In the spring of 1813 the overwhelming majority of American troops counted their experience in months while their British counterparts were "lifers." In 1811, when the 49th Foot was based in Lower Canada, two-thirds of the rank and file had been in service for ten years or better. The average length of service for officers was twelve years.[15] By comparison, on 23 January 1813, the senior officer in the Twenty-Fifth Infantry had been in service for ten months and eleven days, the junior officer, one day.[16]

Captain Peter Mills of the Twenty-Third Infantry had been in the army just over nine months. Samuel Hooker, a 32-year-old lieutenant in the King's Regiment, had been an officer for almost a decade. Sergeant James Crawford from western Pennsylvania and Private Samuel Lock, a 22-year-old farmer from Rhode Island, had both been in the Twenty-Second Infantry for a year.

On the British side, when Sergeant Charles Page and Private Michael Burke joined the 49th Foot in 1797, Crawford and Lock were still children.

## 22  "The victory they expected the next day."[1]

### DEALT IN THE DARK

Chandler's main position was well chosen. Overlooking a grassland meadow, it was on the brow of a 20-foot bank topped with a log and split-rail fence. His flanks were protected, on the left by the Mountain and on the right by swamp and bush. The Queenston road ran straight through the meadow. His line could only be approached from the front, lending his troops the advantage of high ground. Given reasonable care and competence, it should have been unassailable. However, on this uncommonly dark night in enemy territory,[2] with regiments camped willy-nilly, on hills and in hollows, and guarded by pickets drawn from exhausted, undisciplined units, the American camp was anything but.

Few of the troops in Chandler's division had eaten since breaking camp at the Forty. As a result, dozens of random bonfires, built of purloined fence rails, roasted slabs of mutton and beef taken from the Corman and Gage farms and baked bread made from James Gage's flour.[3] Had any British raiding parties been in the neighbourhood, locating the American camp would not have been difficult.

In the lane leading to William Gage's house, where many of the fires were kindled, the commanding officer of the Twenty-Fifth Infantry was anxious. Major Joseph Lee Smith, a rambunctious 35-year-old lawyer from New Britain, Connecticut, and the only field officer with the Twenty-Fifth, believed the American camp had been penetrated by spies[4]. A popular officer "much given to drinking, gambling and fighting,"[5] Smith did not like the low, exposed ground Chandler had chosen for his advanced line. Nor did he take to having the Twenty-Fifth's presence announced by cook fires. Considering his position "very dangerous & apprehending an attack from the Indians before morning,"[6] Smith rode the 150 yards back to the main American line and took his concerns to Chandler. Camped just to the right of Towson's artillery, the brigadier was in his tent playing cards with Winder. Smith conveyed his fears and requested permission to shift his regiment. His story contradicts Chandler's repeated insistence he was expecting a British attack: "Both generals told him the movement was unnecessary, as the British & their allies were too tired to make an attack that night."

Smith was dismissed, but an hour later, "much distressed by his fears," was back, and once again, asked to remove his unit from the forward position. The generals, apparently still playing cards, were irritated by his persistence but

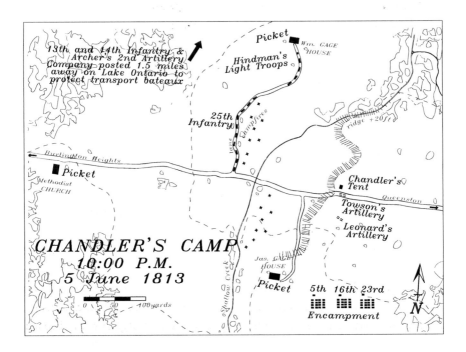

13th and 14th Infantry & Archer's 2nd Artillery Company posted 1.5 miles away on Lake Ontario to protect transport bateaux

Picket
Wm. GAGE HOUSE
Hindman's Light Troops
25th Infantry
Campfires
lane

Burlington Heights

Picket
Methodist CHURCH

Chandler's Tent

ridge +20ft

Queenston

Towson's Artillery

Leonard's Artillery

CHANDLER'S CAMP
10:00 P.M.
5 June 1813

Jas. GAGE HOUSE

Picket

0   50   100 yards

Shallow Creek

5th  16th  23rd

Encampment

N

acquiesced. "With consent of General Chandler," Smith said, "precisely at one o'clock I left that ground."[7]

Ephraim Shaler confirmed the sequence of events though not the timing: "Smith ... came to me about 11 o'clock and said we must get the men up and move them out of the lane for we shall be attacked before morning – there have been spies in the camp and they know the position of every regiment and if we remain where we are, we shall be cut to pieces."[8]

The troops, wearied by the march from the Forty, were asleep and difficult to rouse. Smith went from man to man, clapping them on the shoulder, "calling them his good fellows & urging them to rise instantly as he every moment expected an attack from the Indians."[9]

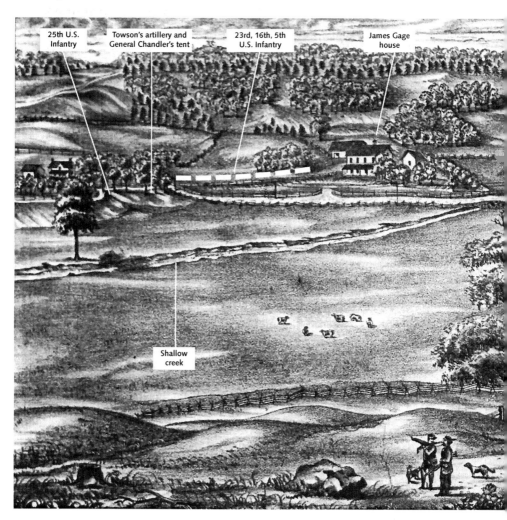

25th U.S. Infantry

Towson's artillery and General Chandler's tent

23rd, 16th, 5th U.S. Infantry

James Gage house

Shallow creek

Shaler assisted him in rousing the troops. On their feet, clutching arms and ammunition, "we then moved the regiment out of the lane into the road – marched up the road about sixteen rods [264 feet] and turned into an open field of elevated ground, and formed in line of battle directly opposite, and parallel with, the lane we had just left. The men were then ordered to load their muskets and lay down if they chose, but not a man to leave his place without permission."[10]

The Twenty-Fifth thus formed to the right of the artillery along the meandering 20-foot ridge that overlooked the creek's flood plain. Smith's apprehension and dogged insistence on shifting his regiment from the advance line would have a profound effect on subsequent events that night.

Left behind in the lane were the unit's cooks tending to the next day's provisions and, beside them, Hindman's command – three companies of the Second Artillery and Mills' company from the Twenty-Third – and beside them as pickets, Milliken's and McFarland's companies of the Twenty-Second. Hindman and his men were all asleep. Neither Smith nor Chandler thought to alert Hindman or the two companies on picket duty that the Twenty-Fifth, the largest regiment in the division, had been given permission to abandon the position because it was too exposed to enemy attack.

Chandler's version of how the Twenty-Fifth changed position is markedly different. According to

Methodist church.
Riflemen picket

Queenston road to
Burlington Heights

William Gage lane.
Hindman's advance
and picket

**Stoney Creek battlefield looking south, circa 1870.** This view of the battlefield, from the perspective of William Gage's house looking toward the Mountain, is adapted from *Wentworth County Illustrated.*

his accounts, it was all part of a defensive strategy designed to deceive and repel the expected attack. In his first full report on the battle, written 12 days after the action, he said fires were kindled on both sides of the road despite orders expressly forbidding them.[11] His second more-detailed account, polished with the aid of three years' hindsight and published in at least three major newspapers, offers a different story. In this version the Twenty-Fifth and the light troops were *ordered* to "kindle their fires at about 150 yards in advance of the high ground."[12] The idea was that the forward fires were really intended as a ruse to confuse the enemy as to the true location of the American line – "so that the enemy should not be able to calculate from reconnoitering in the evening what their position would be in the latter part of the night."[13] After they finished eating, in this version, the General "ordered that part of his forces which were in advance of the meadow to leave their fires burning, fall back to the upland and form on the right of the road." A third account, in Chandler's journal, further enhances the general's hindsight. After ordering the Twenty-Fifth back to the rear of the meadow at midnight "he ordered fuel to be added to their fires in large quantities … at the same time he ordered all the fires on the south side of the meadow to be extinguished, and in this state of things awaited the expected attack."[14] Nowhere however does he address why Hindman's command and the two picket companies were hung out to dry.

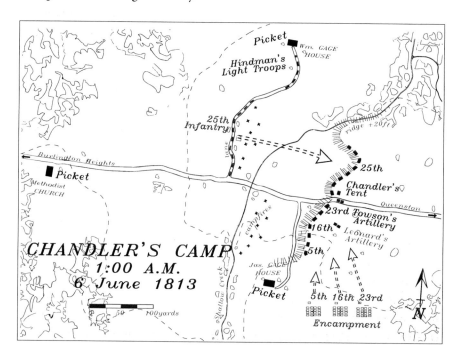

Chandler struggles to sound like a professional soldier explaining his dispositions but there is considerable evidence that the American camp was anything but prepared and, in fact, was in a shambles, before the attack. A plan of the encampment by Chandler's acting aide-de-camp, Lieutenant Donald Fraser, shows the earliest placement of infantry, artillery and dragoons (see page 125). Captain Nathan Towson's artillery – three 6-pdr. field guns and one brass howitzer – was posted on the Queenston road covering the western approach.[15]

If Chandler did indeed believe an attack was imminent, he neglected to inform his senior artillery officer. "My command," Towson said, "was assigned to the defence of the road by which the enemy would advance if he should venture to attack; but of that I had little expectation."[16]

On the right of the artillery was Chandler's tent. Another three pieces of artillery, under Captain Luther Leonard of the Light Artillery, were parked on the other side of the road and to the rear of the line – utterly useless in the event of an attack, unless it came from the rear. Major Joseph Smith's concern about the position of his regiment was entirely proper, as not only was it vulnerable to enemy attack but it was also in advance of the artillery. And on an extremely dark night. Some 200 yards away on the high ground to the southeast of James Gage's house, the Fifth, Sixteenth and Twenty-Third Infantry had encamped in a line facing the lake along with a detachment of riflemen from the First Rifle regiment, Lyttle's Company of U.S. Volunteers, and probably some militia.[17]

Chandler contended his line was secure because he posted the Twenty-Third beside the artillery on the south side of the road, flanked successively by the Sixteenth, the Fifth, the rifles and the light company. If, in fact, the movement of those units occurred on his orders just prior to the battle, as he asserts, why then, would it not have been effected hours earlier? If he was truly expecting a raid or some sort of reconnaissance in force on his camp, surely the time to make the dispositions necessary to secure the encampment against a nighttime raid was in the daylight? Considering his army was on unfamiliar ground, trying to change position on an uncommonly dark night would have been both difficult and dangerous.

It seems more likely that the decision to change troop dispositions was not part of an earlier-conceived defensive strategy, but a last-minute, late-night determination that originated somewhere other than the brain of Brigadier General John Chandler. His ADC, Fraser, claimed he put the bug in Chandler's ear: "Previous to the commencement of the action probably two hours, I suggested to General Chandler the propriety of our men removing from the fires, that in case we were attacked the Indians would be upon us unawares. He then gave me directions to order out some of the fires and the 25th to remove on the bank, which was immediately done."[18] Once more, the spectre of a surprise Indian attack was stalking Chandler's army.

Meanwhile, Hindman's elite light troops, who spearheaded the advance during a long day of marching and skirmishing, were somehow forgotten and left alone slumbering in what was left of Chandler's dangerously compromised advance line.

Whether the neophyte generals were playing cards is not mentioned by Chandler, but he does confirm they spent considerable time in his tent and that Winder, the brash, budding Bonaparte, did not believe the camp was in any danger.[19] The assistant adjutant general, Major John Johnson, who, along with the division's guide, was present at the meeting, maintained that, while an attack of some sort was anticipated, the two generals had spent the evening "making arrangements for the victory they expected the next day."[20]

Johnson remained with Chandler after midnight with their horses tethered close to the tent. Both lay down but did not sleep. Outside, "it was cloudy, misty and perfectly calm, and the fog which arose from the low land completed the obscurity."[21]

## 23 "Only the utmost daring."[1]

### NIGHT MOVES

Although only a handful of the current regiment were old enough to have been there, many of the officers and men of the 49th in 1813 would have known of an action during the American Revolution that bore a startling resemblance to Harvey's attack plan.[2]

In September 1777 the defeat of George Washington's army at Brandywine Creek in Pennsylvania had opened the road to Philadelphia. In an attempt to divert the British advance, Washington sent a force of 1,500 regulars and 1,000 militia under firebrand general Anthony Wayne to attack the rear of Sir William Howe's army.[3] The British, forewarned, opted for a pre-emptive strike. Twelve hundred select troops, spearheaded by the 2nd Light Infantry Battalion,[4] which included the light company of the 49th, all under Major General Charles Grey, were ordered to make a night attack on Wayne's camp near Paoli, Pennsylvania.

Grey's ADC, Captain John André,[5] recorded the specific instructions issued to the troops:

No firelock was to be loaded & express orders were given to rely solely on the Bayonet. No soldier … was suffered to load; those who could not draw [the charge from] their pieces took out the flints. We knew nearly the spot where the Rebel corps lay, but nothing of the disposition of their camp. It was represented to the men that firing discovered us to the enemy, hid them from us, killed our friends and produced a confusion favourable to the escape of the Rebels.... On the other hand, by not firing we knew the foe to be wherever fire appeared and a [bayonet] charge ensured his destruction; that amongst the Enemy those in the rear would direct their fire against whoever fired in front, and they would destroy each other.[6]

Shortly after midnight on 21 September, after a rapid, stealthy approach, Grey's troops slammed into Wayne's camp. One American brigade commander said the British came "with all the Noise and Yells of Hell ... the Impetuosity of the Enemy was so great – our men just raised from Sleep, moved disorderly – Confusion followed.... The Carnage was very great."[7]

Wayne's force was driven from camp, losing at least 150 killed, wounded and captured, plus eight wagons of baggage and provisions. British discipline held;

**Battle of Paoli, 1777.** During the American Revolution the light company of the 49th Regiment was part a daring nighttime raid on the camp of U.S. General Anthony Wayne near Valley Forge that was remarkably similar to Stoney Creek in intent. The British routed the Americans without firing a single shot. This detail of a painting by Xavier Della Gatta depicts the bayonet action. (Valley Forge Historical Society)

the only shots fired were by the American troops. All the wounds were inflicted by bayonet. British losses were negligible – three killed including one private from the 49th and perhaps a dozen wounded.[8]

Because of the gruesome nature of bayonet wounds, and perhaps the completeness of the rout,[9] the action became known in America as the Paoli Massacre, and the Continental Line regiments that had been so roughly used swore there would be no mercy in any return engagements. In response, the British light companies that were at Paoli dyed their green cap feathers red "so that their angry enemies should recognize them in future and not avenge themselves on other light troops who had not been engaged in the affair."[10]

There is no direct evidence that Harvey had Paoli in mind when he proposed a night raid on the American camp at Stoney Creek, but certainly the light company of the 49th would have known how their predecessors triumphed without firing a shot and perhaps suggested the all-bayonet tactic.

Sometime after midnight, Harvey's raiding party halted at or near the frame house of William Case, an American-trained physician who farmed on the south side of the Queenston road in Barton Township.[11] Here Harvey explained the plan of attack to his company commanders, including an Irish lieutenant, James FitzGibbon. A protégé of Brock's, FitzGibbon had come up through the ranks – no mean feat in itself – and it was a measure of his standing in the 49th that he was commanding the 6th company, Glegg's Company, in this action.[12]

"We were informed," FitzGibbon said, "that it was intended to surprise the Yankeys and that the work was to be done entirely by the bayonet – not a shot to be fired."[13] Compare that to Grey's instructions before Paoli: "No firelock was to be loaded & express orders were given to rely solely on the Bayonet."[14]

The standard infantry weapon of the British army was the .75 calibre India Pattern flintlock. This smoothbore musket, widely known as the Brown Bess, loaded via the muzzle from a paper cartridge that contained black powder and a lead ball. The spark necessary to detonate the powder was produced in the lock mechanism by flint slamming into a piece of steel. The killing kit of every British infantryman included a triangular, 17-inch steel bayonet that locked onto the end of the musket, thereby turning the firearm into a highly-effective stabbing weapon.

In accordance with his strategy, Harvey ordered every gun unloaded, every flint removed and every mouth shut. One member of the 49th light company said "not a whisper was permitted; even our footsteps were not allowed to be heard."[15]

Led by the light companies of the 49th and the King's, followed by the battalion companies of the 49th in the centre and then the remainder of the King's and the artillery detachment, the troops proceeded "with perfect order and profound silence." Bringing up the rear was a smaller column headed by Vincent and his staff that included dragoon captain Hamilton Merritt and a handful of militia. Small parties of the 5th Lincoln and the 2nd York were sent to the lakeshore and the Mountain, respectively, to warn of any surprise attack.[16]

Except for a short shower that fell at the beginning of the march, the night was calm and dark as pitch.[17]

The Prussian military theorist Carl von Clausewitz, in his seminal dissertation *On War*, devotes one short, four-and-a-half-page chapter to night operations. Difficult to execute and risky in the extreme, he wrote, "in practice they are very rare."[18] Applying Clausewitz's criteria to Harvey's Stoney Creek plan provides some insight into the situation facing the British commander on the night of 5 June 1813.

Although Harvey had personally scouted the American camp and almost certainly had further information from spies and deserters when he decided the encampment was vulnerable to a night attack, what he proposed was still high-risk because his intelligence was fallible. "It can never really be reliable," Clausewitz wrote, "for the simple reason that all such reports are always a little out of date and the enemy may in the meantime have changed his position."[19]

As well, the attacker has no way of knowing what dispositions the defender will make when the action begins – in other words, what Harvey saw at sunset from a distance might well have changed dramatically by the time he confronted it up close in the middle of the night.

In complete darkness, Clausewitz warned, even the best foreknowledge is rarely enough: "In a night operation ... the attacker seldom if ever knows enough about the defence to make up for his lack of visual observation ... the attacker needs his eyes in night operations just as much as does the defence."[20] To balance the risk, smaller detachments are preferable. Not only does that preserve the greater part of the army as a backup but it also gives the raiding party more

**Carl von Clausewitz (1780-1831).** "Night operations are not merely risky; they are also difficult to execute. This too limits their scale. Their essence being surprise, it must be a prime consideration to approach without being seen." (Combat Studies Institute)

chance of arriving undetected. "Night operations are not merely risky; they are also difficult to execute. This too limits their scale. Their essence being surprise, it must be a prime consideration to approach without being seen."[21]

Night raids, Clausewitz noted, are usually directed against detachments or outposts, hardly ever against whole armies. However, attacking an entire army at night can be justified when, one, the enemy has been exceptionally careless or provocative and, two, in "desperate situations in which one's troops are so heavily outnumbered that only the utmost daring offers any prospect of success."[22]

By those criteria the British raid was entirely justified: Chandler's army had been provocative – advance elements had ventured to the edge of Vincent's camp – his defensive position was carelessly laid out, and a night-time raid, risky as it was, represented the only real chance to avoid almost certain defeat and capture.

## 24 "A burglarious assault."[1]

### WHILE THE DEFENCE RESTS

It was close to 1:30 in the morning when the column headed by Harvey and the light company of the 49th reached Big Creek and Davis's tavern, where the two sides had skirmished the previous afternoon. Although the spring had been abnormally wet, the creek was still easily fordable by the British force. What was difficult, one redcoat said, was the constrained silence: "I shall never forget the agony caused to the senses by the stealthiness."[2]

The dragoon captain Merritt reported the distant crash of a musket from the direction of the American camp. The raiders paused and waited. Once more every musket was checked to ensure they were unloaded.[3] Perhaps a nervous or careless sentry had accidentally discharged his piece. After waiting long enough to ensure the alarm was not general, Harvey put the next phase of his plan in motion.

To get close enough to the American line for the British bayonets to do their work, his troops had to navigate through whatever net of sentries Chandler had placed in advance of his camp. To keep the pickets from raising the alarm, they needed to be disarmed with a password. The unofficial record is cluttered with password stories ranging from William Green's version to various American newspaper accounts blaming a spy or a deserter. The official record is silent – Harvey said only that the sentries were dealt with "in conformity with the directions I had given," but there is some intriguing evidence that may explain how the British got the American password.[4]

Frederick Snider, a neighbour of the Gage's, in a somewhat rambling account of the battle written after the war, claims it was Harvey himself who obtained the password by means of a simple ruse that took advantage of the complete darkness. In a section that shows more than passing familiarity with U.S. Army regulations on the service of guards, Snider wrote that Harvey, pretending to be the American officer of the day making Grand Rounds, approached the first sentry, "who challenged with the words, who goes there? Harvey answered, a 'Friend'. The sentry said 'advance friend and give the countersign'. Harvey advanced as he was ordered but not having the countersign to repeat, he did something else. He pushed the bayonet a little to one side and leant forward as if to whisper the word into the man's ear and as soon as he could reach, took hold of the man by the throat and threw him on the ground."[5]

On pain of death the sentinel surrendered the countersign.

Approaching the next picket, Harvey played the Grand Rounds ploy again, this time offered the countersign and found that it was correct. "They stood chatting for a minute or so in the darkness, when the British army came up … they quietly laid down their arms."[6]

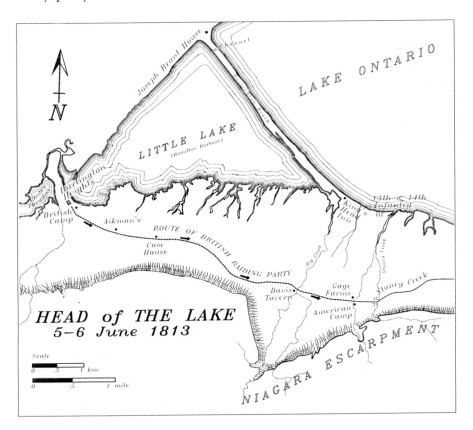

HEAD of THE LAKE
5–6 June 1813

As questionable as Snider's account may seem at first reading, it is lent some credence by witnesses from both sides in the action. One American officer said, "The British advanced silently with fixed bayonets, not a musket was allowed to be loaded for fear of blowing their design. Some officers and men advanced at some distance ahead of them, who hailed, amused and stabbed some of our centinels, pretending to give them the countersign."[7]

Another officer said, "By some means the enemy had obtained our countersign – it had been conjectured by the desertions of some of the inhabitants who had joined the American army in its advance. The American picket guard, who were within one fourth of a mile of the main body, were entirely cut off; the sentinels surprised and taken prisoners and no alarm given."[8]

Lieutenant Donald Fraser, Chandler's ADC, said, "Our picket guard suffered themselves to be taken without giving the alarm."[9]

Captain James Mundy, who commanded the 8th's light company was reported to have confirmed "the first centinel with whom he fell in near the church was totally ignorant of his duty, and was taken without noise. From him the Major [Mundy] unquestionably obtained the countersign, as he stated that no difficulty was experienced in capturing the other centinels."[10]

FitzGibbon, whose detailed account of the action is arguably the most balanced from either side, said the Americans had no advance post close to Davis's tavern and only three individual sentries on the Queenston road: "The 2 first were surprised and secured in succession by the Lt. company of the 49th which led, the third resisted and was bayoneted."[11]

At least one local history suggests that Harvey himself dispatched the sentries. E.B. Biggar cites a militia source that Harvey "spurred forward and clove him (the first sentinel) to the chin with his sabre," and an unnamed American orderly, who said Harvey approached the first sentry and "clove his skull with a broadsword, the second sentry being served in the same way."[12]

How many of those sentries were actually bayoneted is not certain. Harvey says four; Merritt says only that they were "made prisoners without giving the alarm." What is clear, though, is that the British were easily able to neutralize the sparse compliment of sentries posted on the only road by which the American camp could be approached.[13]

So where was the remainder of the 100-strong picket guard who, according to Chandler, had been ordered to send out constant patrolling parties toward Burlington Heights?[14] A good portion of them – a detachment of the First Rifle Regiment under Lieutenant Henry Van Swearingen – were sleeping in the Methodist church.

Just as the adjutant of the advance, Lieutenant Jonathan Kearsley, had feared when he so vigorously opposed detailing them to sentry duty, the weary and undisciplined riflemen "took up their quarters in a church and went comfortably to sleep, in the pews thereof."[15] The church stood on a small hill in the northwest corner of what is now Stoney Creek Cemetery in the midst of a wooded area that flanked both sides of the Queenston road for about 400 yards.[16] Armed with the countersign, the British troops quickly surrounded the church and bagged the sleeping riflemen, some of whom, according to one redcoat, "awoke in another world."[17]

Rudely awakened in this world, by bayonet thrusts to his left hip and right leg, was David Legg, who, along with his older brother Jeremiah, had joined the First Rifles six month earlier in Ogdensburg, New York.[18] Also captured was 19-year-old Pliny Story, a farmer from Bennington, Vermont, who was recruited from the Albany Volunteers to join the Rifles.[19] At this point, on the strength of boldness, discipline and good luck, Harvey's little force stood poised to successfully commit what one American staff officer described as a "burglarious assault"[20] on Chandler's camp.

So far the operation had been carried out in complete silence and the British force had crept to within 300 yards of the American line undetected. However, as the light companies of the 49th and the 8th emerged from the woods into the clearing that preceded the Gage farm, one sentry, alarmed

**Sleeping beauties.** Despite a well earned reputation for battlefield ferocity, the green coats of the First Rifle Regiment did not have their finest moment at Stoney Creek. Posted as a piquet well in advance of the American line, an entire detachment under Lieutenant Henry Van Swearingen was captured sleeping in the Methodist Church. (Painting by H.C. McBarron. Company of Military Historians)

apparently by the groan of a dying comrade, fired off his musket and fled toward the American line.[21]

The men in the column behind the light companies could make out what they believed was the American encampment by the fires still burning on both sides of the road.[22]

## 25 "That night a child might understand The De'il had business on his hand."[1]

### THE FIRST CONTACT, 2:20 A.M.

Although John Norton fielded no more than a handful of warriors at Stoney Creek and, by his own account, their part was limited, Indians nevertheless played a significant role – out of all proportion to their actual numbers – in how the action played out. The Americans believed at the time, and continued to believe for dozens of years afterwards, that they were attacked by a large contingent of native warriors.

There were plenty of survivors of Queenston Heights at Stoney Creek – particularly in the Second Artillery – who had first-hand knowledge of just how terrifying Norton's warriors could be in battle. Likely every soldier in Chandler's command had heard some version of the recent River Raisin massacre in Michigan Territory where, after the battle the American wounded were slaughtered by Indians.[2] All the way down the peninsula, the spectre of Indian ambushes had been a constant fear, even though Norton's numbers amounted to little more than a corporal's guard and had only made contact once.

These anxieties were probably not far from the mind of Second Lieutenant Ephraim Shaler of the Twenty-Fifth Infantry when he left his unit's new position to the right of the artillery and returned to its initial position on William Gage's lane. The young officer checked on the cooks left there to prepare the next day's meal and "just as I was about to leave the lane and go back to my regiment (it being at this time between one and two o'clock in the morning) I heard one of the most dreadful shrieks that ever fell on mortal ear and which seemed to come from one of the sentinels. I observed to an officer nearby that a sentinel had been shot with an arrow and the Indians were then tomahawking him, which I have no doubt was the fact, for not a gun had been fired."[3]

That silence, however, was only momentary before the first sentry discharged his musket, thereby raising the alarm. The assistant adjutant general, Major John Johnston, noted the time. It was 2:20 a.m.

On the edge of the woods the two British light companies moved rapidly to bag the remainder of the advance picket. They were now within a few hundred yards of the American line and still invisible. But as Clausewitz disciple Helmuth von Moltke so famously observed: no campaign plan survives first contact with the enemy.[4] For the British, neutralizing the pickets was the last thing that went according to plan that night.

Behind the light companies, some of Vincent's staff officers came forward to the head of the column to watch the action. Completely heedless of Harvey's "perfect order and profound silence" command, they began to cheer. Five companies back in the column, Lieutenant James FitzGibbon heard them and understood immediately what it meant: "The instant I heard their shout I considered our affair ruined."[5]

For the men in the ranks, constrained by the enforced silence, the outburst from the staff officers was both a welcome release from the tension and an invitation they could not resist. Section by section, company by company the troops began to cheer and yell "huzza!" And at least some of the men mimicked Indian war cries.[6]

"The moment I heard the shout spread amongst the men," FitzGibbon said, "I considered our situation very critical. For I was aware that it would be almost impossible to make the men silent again, and that consequently orders could not be heard or obeyed."[7] As Clausewitz warned, command and control of troops in a night action is crucial for success. FitzGibbon immediately told his company not to take up the shout and with the help of his three company sergeants, Joseph Buchanan, John Cole and Alexander Nicholl, "succeeded in keeping them silent and in good order," for the moment at least.[8]

The Irish subaltern was appalled at the behaviour of his fellow officers, considering them responsible for squandering a golden opportunity. "Never was surprise more complete – never was anything more brilliant than it would have been had we kept silence ... but our officers began that which they should have watched with all their care to prevent; for they ought to have known that in darkness and noise, confusion must be inevitable. I think I could have killed some of them had I been near them at the moment."[9] Certainly any chance of a Paoli-style rout had evaporated.

On the other side, the sudden tumult was also having an effect. Ephraim Shaler, the Twenty-Fifth Infantry lieutenant, was standing less than 50 yards away when the roar began. Though he could see nothing in the dark, he was convinced by the yelling that he was surrounded "by all the Indians in Canada. The war whoop was given and the air seemed rent with the yell of Indians, which was quickly followed by every sentinel discharging his piece and retreating to the main guard."[10]

Some of Shaler's countrymen claimed they distinctly heard Indians yelling *and* troops shouting, but Norton, who noted the troops were cheering loudly, made no mention of his small band of warriors taking any part. Of the dozens of accounts of the action from American officers, only one – that of Captain John Thornton of the Twentieth Infantry – appears to have got it right. "There were but few Indians with the British," Thornton wrote, "but the latter set up the savage yell before the attack was made. This artifice was unworthy of regular troops and it excited no other sentiment but contempt among our soldiers."[11]

Back on the American line, Chandler's acting ADC, Lieutenant Donald Fraser, was startled to discover the enemy – "British & Indians" – had penetrated American defences. "The first we knew was a horrid yell in Camp."[12]

Across the meadow behind the Gage homestead the adjutant of the Sixteenth Infantry was just passing a line of sleeping troops when "as in a serene and cloudless day, a peal of thunder would strike with awe and consternation, so in the midst of this profound repose that night, commenced an action embracing all the constituents of the awful and the sublime."[13]

In James Gage's house where several American officers had taken up quarters, the effect was bedlam. "What yelling and shouting there was," Gage's 8-year-old daughter Elizabeth recalled. "The officers rushed out of the house when the noise commenced and soon some of the soldiers came running in. I well remember how scared they were. They thought it was the Indians, from the yelling, and were afraid of being tomahawked."[14]

In his tent General Chandler heard "a tremendous savage yell" that instantly rousted him and Major Johnson from their cots and out onto their horses.[15] A few yards away, Captain Nathan Towson of the Second Artillery was standing by his battery of guns waiting for all the outlying pickets to come in and peering into the inky, dark night. His artillery – three 6-pdr. guns and a brass howitzer – was charged and the three iron guns, loaded with round shot and canister, levelled to rake the Queenston road.

As his gunners stood by, their slow matches close at hand, a horseman galloped out of the dark before them, reining in his mount at the muzzle of one of Towson's 6-pdrs. From his *chapeau de bras* it was clear he was an officer but in the gloom impossible to determine for which side. Lieutenant Patrick McDonough seized the bridle and putting his sword to the officer's breast demanded he identify himself. The answer was "a friend." McDonough dropped the bridle and the officer swung his mount around and galloped off. Towson immediately realized what had happened: "There was no longer a doubt this daring person must be a British officer, leading a force to attack us. He had thus unexpectedly gained the intelligence that our artillery was in position, ready to open up on his columns."[16]

Meanwhile, Chandler ordered the Twenty-Fifth, which was lying down in the field just north of the Queenston road close to the edge of the embankment, to form up for action. According to Chandler, "the line was formed with greatest facility on the right, as the men had only to stand up and they were formed." Major Johnson was sent with directions for Winder to bring the Twenty-Third, the Sixteenth and Fifth forward to the fence line on the south side of the road. All muskets were loaded, but the Twenty-Fifth at least was using a variation on the American favourite "buck and ball" ammunition. Instead of one .65 calibre lead ball and three buckshot, the muskets of the Twenty-Fifth were loaded with 12 buckshot balls only, effectively turning their Springfield muskets into 12-gauge shotguns.[17]

On the British side, the shouting in the ranks had become general, even Fitz-Gibbon's company joining in the uproar. The 49th, its blood up now, followed the light company in a rush toward the cook fires on the south side of the road.

Whether removing the Twenty-Fifth from William Gage's lane was a deliberate ploy or an accident is a moot point: whatever the reason, it effectively altered the course of the action. Had the regiment, the largest of the division, remained

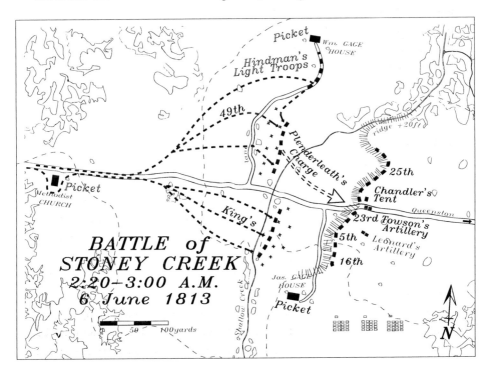

in the lane, the 49th's bayonets would have fallen on hundreds of sleeping men. Instead, as the regiment charged into the laneway, the only members of the Twenty-Fifth they encountered were about 20 cooks and one very startled Ephraim Shaler.

"I immediately started for my regiment," he wrote later, "when turning my head in the direction of the gate that led to the lane, discovered a column of British bayonets within twenty feet of me, I lost no time in making my way to the regiment. It was however, a narrow escape – a moment later I must have felt cold steel or been made a prisoner."[18]

A native New Englander in a unit raised in Connecticut, Shaler could not resist crowing over the Twenty-Fifth's good fortune: "The enemy charged furiously through the lane, upsetting in their way camp kettles and mess-pans and killing several of the poor cooks, and driving the rest out: and finally succeeded in taking quiet possession of – what? Not the 25th Regiment, for it contained too many Yankees to be caught in such a trap but they took possession of the bright fires the cooks had made and per force left."[19] Still in the lane, left to bear the brunt of the British bayonets, were four elite light companies from the advance and two companies from the picket guard. In total probably fewer than 300 men being charged by 424 men of the 49th in full battle cry.

Captain Jacob Hindman, like the rest of his men, had been sleeping along William Gage's fence line when the alarm went up. Upon forming his troops, Hindman withdrew a few paces behind the cook fires and sent his adjutant, Lieutenant Jonathan Kearsley, to find the Twenty-Fifth so that the advance could form on its left.[20]

**Lieutenant James FitzGibbon, 49th Regiment (1780-1863).** An independent thinker who came up through the ranks, FitzGibbon was an officer but not a gentleman. In his even-handed account of the action at Stoney Creek he was openly critical of fellow officers whose cheering aborted the British plan of attack. In this engraving by Alfred Sandham, he is wearing the uniform of a militia colonel. (McGill University Library)

Venturing into the murk, Kearsley encountered a mounted officer he took for Major Joseph Lee Smith, who habitually commanded the Twenty-Fifth on horseback. In reality he did find a regimental commander but this one was British, likely Major Charles Plenderleath of the 49th Foot. Addressing the figure, however he was cautious to give nothing away in the exchange.

"Don't fire, we are friends."

"What friends?" replied the figure.

"Friends," repeated Kearsley.[21]

Now close enough to see that the line of troops with charged bayonets were not American, Kearsley sprinted back to the advance.

An officer of the Second Artillery said, "The enemy, with Indians, surprised with horrid yelling and attacked our advance guard, which we composed. We were able to make but a feeble resistance as the enemy was not more than 15 yards from us ... and obliged us to retire in great confusion, as it was quite dark." Another officer confirmed the British attack was so sudden that the advance, unable to form, was completely dispersed.[22]

At the centre of the main American line Captain Nathan Towson was having troubles of his own – his guns would not fire. Three times the slow match was applied and three times the fuse failed to ignite. Fearing sabotage – "an indescribable feeling of horror came over me; I felt faint and sick at heart" – he leapt to the nearest piece to discover if a spike had indeed been driven into the gun's vent hole. None had.[23]

"The truth was," as Towson discovered, "the dews of the evening had damped the powder and our slow match was damaged."[24]

**Captain Nathan Towson, Second Artillery (1784-1854).** A native of Baltimore, Towson helped capture the British brig *Caledonia* from under the guns of Fort Erie in the fall of 1812 and over the next two years his artillery took part in every major action in Niagara, including Queenston Heights, Fort George, Stoney Creek, Chippawa, Lundy's Lane and Fort Erie. In 1848 he was brevetted major general for meritorious service in the Mexican war. (Portrait by Rembrandt Peale, 1815. Maryland Historical Society)

As the 49th swept into the American troops one of the first casualties was Captain Peter Mills of the Twenty-Third Infantry, who suffered precisely the sort of wound the bayonet was designed to inflict. The 17-inch blade ripped through the right side of his abdomen, perforated his intestines and continued on until lodged in his left hip.[25] Tearing the intestines would have spilled gut flora and septic bacteria into the abdominal cavity, setting up an almost-certainly fatal infection. It is not clear how many total casualties Mills's company took but six men at the minimum were taken prisoner.

To the right of Mills's company on the Gage Farm lane, Captain William Nicholas of the Second Artillery narrowly missed death when a bullet whistled through the crown of his hat. In his company, 33-year-old Samuel Palmer went down when a musket ball smashed through his left thigh.[26]

Impressed by the progress of the initial bayonet assault, Ensign James George of the 1st Lincoln Militia turned to Hamilton Merritt and declared the contest over, the British had won.[27]

While the 49th had followed the lane north and deployed on the adjoining creek flats, the King's advanced on the Queenston road and formed in the meadow to the south of it, fronting James Gage's farmhouse. The task they faced was daunting. The regiment, with fewer than 300 men, confronted at least three times that number in the Fifth, Sixteenth and Twenty-Third regiments, which also had the added advantage of high ground. However, the suddenness of the British attack that burst into the middle of the American camp, combined with a fear of Indians and amplified by the impenetrable darkness of the night, had sown considerable confusion in the defender ranks.

Unable to match the American firepower, the King's, still sticking to Harvey's plan, relied on the bayonet charge and the resulting melee further disrupted unit cohesion. The Americans, Harvey said, "poured a destructive fire of musketry upon us, which we answered on our part by repeated charges whenever a body of the enemy would be discerned or reached."[28]

The Sixteenth Infantry, according to one report, was so unnerved by the savage yelling that it broke, "and only a small part of them could again be formed and brought into action." Among the Sixteenth's casualties was James Huffee, described by the regimental surgeon as "brave, honest, faithful & dependable." Private Huffee, an Irish-born blacksmith, was shot in both legs, once just below the knee on the left leg, which splintered the calf bone, and the other through the thigh. James Simpkins, another private in the Sixteenth, was shot and bayoneted. The 19-year-old tanner from Philadelphia had a musket wound in his left thigh and bayonet wounds to his right thigh, left leg and left arm.[29]

Fraser identified dispositions and landmarks with a legend (his indications are circled for clarity):

"1. first position of the 25th in the afternoon" shows the regiment in William Gage's lane with light troops and a picket on its right.

"2. second position" shows the Twenty-Fifth perpendicular to the main line on the ridge.

"3. Position in action" shows the Twenty-Fifth deployed along the ridge on the north side of the road.

"4 & 5. That taken in the morning" shows the Fifth, Twenty-Third and Twenty-Fifth deployed in two separate positions after withdrawing to the east from the battlefield the following morning.

"6. Encampment of the 23, 16, 5th" indicates the camp of the three regiments prior to the battle.

"7. Position of the 5th in Action" shows the Fifth deployed on the south side of the road.

"8. Lieut McChesney of the 16th at the head of the companies of Steele and McEwen charged the enemy & recovered the field pieces except one and a Howitzer" erroneously shown on the road just east of the American line.

"IIII. Towson's Artillery on the main road" as the centrepiece of the American line.

"¦¦}. Archer's do" indicating what is actually Leonard's company of artillery behind the American line.

"9. Chandler's Quarters" shows his tent just to the right of Towson's artillery.

**Battlefield map.** This map, drawn by Chandler's ADC, Lieutenant Donald Fraser, shows the relative dispositions of American troops at different times before, and after, the battle. The perspective is westerly, Big Creek is mistakenly identified as Stoney Creek but otherwise it is relatively accurate. James Gage's house is on the left, William Gage's on the right at the end of the lane and the Methodist church is to the left of the road over the notation Piquet. (USNA RG 107, L110 (7))

The Fifth Infantry, under the hot-tempered Georgian, Lieutenant Colonel Homer Virgil Milton, the man Winfield Scott had called a coward, stood firm and commenced a fierce exchange, with the King's bayonets at times coming as close as 20 yards to the American line.[30]

In the darkness and confusion, some American units lost their bearings in combat and the British picked up on it. "In many instances," one American field officer wrote, "one of our regiments would fire upon another, when the cry was 'don't fire, you are firing on your own men.' The British caught the cry and made use of it to some advantage."[31]

However, for all the disorder and confusion the 49th was causing on William Gage's lane, troops on the main American line had been steadied enough to home in on the redcoats who were not only audible, but thanks to the numerous campfires in the meadow and lane, visible as well. "I must give the enemy's troops great credit," noted one 49th veteran, "for having recovered from their confusion and for having shown so bold a front so very soon after having been so suddenly and completely surprised."[32]

In sections and then in companies the Americans began to open up on the British troops. The range was extreme – nearly 200 yards on the north side of the road – but the psychological effect was telling. And at the same time Towson, taking matters into his own hands, finally got his artillery into the action: "Never was music so welcome to my ears as the report of the first gun."[33]

On the British side, there is no indication that an order to load and fix flints was ever issued and it appears unlikely one was. Command and control was becoming increasingly unsteady. Company commanders like FitzGibbon struggled to ensure that discipline kept panic at bay. "Before we formed line the enemy commenced firing," he said. "Our men never ceased shouting. No order could be heard. Everything was noise and confusion – which confusion was chiefly occasioned by the noise."[34]

In the ranks one redcoat from the 49th sketched the confusing medley of terror and grandeur. "Our troops deployed into line and halted in the midst of the camp fires and immediately began to replace their flints. This, though not a very lengthy operation, was one of intense anxiety for the enemy had now opened a most terrific fire.... We could only see the flash of the enemy's firelocks, while we were perfectly visible to them, standing as we did in the midst of the camp fires. It was a grand and beautiful sight … like the bursting forth of a volcano. Then again all was dark and still save the moans of the wounded, the confused click! click! noise made by our men in adjusting their flints and the ring of the enemy's ramrods in reloading. Again the flash and the roar of the musketry, the whistling of the bullets and the crash of the cannon. The anxious moments (hours in imagination) have passed; the trembling excited hands of our men have at last fastened their flints; the comparatively merry sound of the ramrods tells the charge is driven home; soon the fire is returned with animation; the sky is illuminated with continued flashes."[35]

No order was given to return fire but company commanders were helpless to prevent it as troops responded blindly to the artillery and musket fire from the American line. "Our men returned fire contrary to orders," FitzGibbon said, "and it soon became apparent that it was impossible to prevent shouting and firing. The scene at this instant was awfully grand. The darkness of the morning, 2 o'clock, made still more dark by the flashing of the musketry and cannon."[36]

In his house nearby, Frederick Snider had woken to "the sound of musket shots fired in rapid succession and soon [they] became as close together as rain on the roof accompanied every minute or so by the louder report of a cannon."[37]

In the Gage family home, Mary Gage acted quickly to protect her five children, including 8-year-old Elizabeth. "When the firing commenced," Elizabeth said, "my mother looked around for some place to put us children out of harm's way. It was a large log house, with a loft above the living rooms, and in the loft was stored all the wool that had been sheared that summer, so she took us up there and made us lay down among the wool. I remember it well. Every little while a bullet would hit the house but they did not go through the logs, and we were safe."[38]

Demoralizing as the American artillery fire was on the British, it was infinitely more so on Hindman's troops still on William Gage's lane. Their sharp fire fight with the British attracted the attention of Winder, who, unaware there were still American infantry in advance of the main line, directed Towson's artillery to fire on them.

It was with remarkable equanimity that Lieutenant Jonathan Kearsley described the harrowing hammer-and-anvil plight they faced:

> The advance of the American army was placed between two most galling and destructive fires – Vincent with his British column in front, and the grape and canister from Towson's pieces in the rear and upon the left flank.
>
> Such was the difficulty of extricating in any way the advance, that, after having many killed and wounded by the grape and canister of Towson's pieces, they were obliged to break and almost singly fall back on their own army.[39]

One of Hindman's lieutenants, his platoon completely dispersed by the British advance, took post in the rear of Twenty-Fifth and acted as a file closer.[40]

The advance would pay a heavy price for the negligence of its general officers, who left it isolated and alone to face the initial British assault. Among the wounded was company sergeant James Crawford, who took a musket ball just below the pit of his stomach.[41]

The chaotic spectacle of the battlefield, illuminated as Towson's artillery opened up, was captured by the descriptive pen of Lieutenant Francis Cummins, who witnessed it from the high ground on the south side of the Queenston road:

> The wild mountainous and lake scenery of the place, the impenetrable darkness of the night, the war whoops of the savage Indian, the shouts of battle, the rushing of horse and man in charge, the neighing of the war horse, the bellowing of the wounded cattle driven into the field the evening previous, the lightning of the arms in quick succession breaking upon and contrasting with the blackness of the night, the roar of artillery in the valley, rising, breaking and loudly re-echoing along the hills and mountains by repercussions which shook the earth, and rolling off like distant thunder along the waters of the lake, altogether formed a whole menacing, terrible and tremendous.[42]

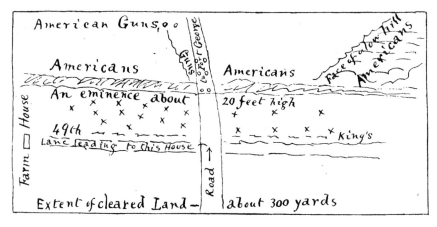

**FitzGibbon map.** Lieutenant James FitzGibbon of the 49th Regiment drew this battlefield map a day after the battle as part of a descriptive letter. The perspective is looking east toward the American line, the Xs represent campfires and the lane is William Gage's lane. Because there is no representation of James Gage's house, the map inspired some confusion over the years, including a 1913 map that placed the Queenston road to the south of the Gage house. (Cruikshank, *Documentary History* 6, 15)

## 26 "The Hill was a Continual sheet of fire."[1]

### HARVEY'S BOLD GAMBIT FALTERS.

Despite the initial shock of the attack and their belief it was supported by a considerable body of Indians, the Americans still held several trump cards. They occupied the high ground at the rear of the meadow, the slopes of which were thick with briars, limbs, brush and logs. To approach the position, the British had to run a gauntlet of massed musket fire and, if they got there alive, contend with a formidable natural abatis of brush and tree stumps. Anyone reckless enough to approach by the road, or even anywhere remotely close to it, would face the lethal effect of canister from the artillery. On top of it, this was all happening in the middle of the night on ground that was wholly unknown.[2]

With the exception of the advance, which had been seriously mauled, the entire American force was intact, safely behind the line, protected by artillery, and backed by cavalry and a rearguard. Any hopes the British harboured of a fast, decisive strike quickly vanished as their frontal attack on the American line bogged down under a terrifying onslaught of artillery and musket fire and began to disintegrate.

Hamilton Merritt witnessed the breakdown: "Colonel Harvey and the officers were using every exertion to get the men formed when the enemy opened a most tremendous fire on us from the Hill, likewise opened their guns.... I never heard so rapid a discharge of Musquetry, the Hill was a Continual sheet of fire. Our men were dispersed in every direction."[3]

The American officer of the day, Colonel James Burn, said that during the one-sided fire fight, "the enemy attempted by frequent charges to break our line, but without effect, being obliged to give way by the well directed fire of our brave troops."[4] On the right flank the Connecticut Yankee Major Joseph Lee Smith worked his way along the line encouraging his troops and "making remarks which made the soldiers laugh even in that moment of peril." Victory was assured, he insisted, if only they stood firm and fired low.[5]

Certainly the British were well within musket range. One of Smith's junior officers, Ephraim Shaler, could hear orders being issued. One British field officer directed his whole line to "charge the damned Yankees!" Three times they surged forward and three times "did his bleeding ranks fall back to their first position without affecting their object; for such was the effect of our buckshot at close quarters that no troops, however well disciplined, could long stand before such a shower."[6]

Harvey's bold gambit to turn on his pursuers when they least expected was beginning to take on the earmarks of rash failure. The noise, the confusion, the lack of visual references all combined to hammer away at unit cohesion. In daylight a unit's colours formed the centre of the line. In the Stygian darkness of Stoney Creek they were of no use whatsoever as a rallying point though both British regiments carried them. So ingrained was the ethos that colours represented the heart of a unit, that regiments would no sooner go into battle without them than they would without weapons.[7]

Traditionally the duty of carrying the embroidered silk colours fell to the two most junior officers in the regiment – for the 49th it was a pair of ensigns. Carrying the six-by-six King's colour – the union standard bearing the regimental number – was Ensign Francis Dury, scion of a distinguished military family.[8] The regimental colour, bearing the regiment's two battle honours, Egmont-op-Zee and Copenhagen, was probably carried by 17-year-old Ensign Sylvester Richmond. Given that the colours had no role on the field and were at considerable risk of capture in the chaos and confusion of a murky night action, it is likely they were with Vincent's staff, on the left of the British line and slightly in the rear of the action.

**Colour party, British infantry, 1813.** The King's colour and the regimental colour were the ethos of an infantry regiment, the source of immense pride and a practical marker on the battlefield marking the centre of the line. A unit's most junior officers were accorded the dangerous task of carrying the colours. At Stoney Creek, Ensign Francis Dury was carrying the King's colour when he was fatally wounded by a musket ball in the head. His last conscious act was to hand the colours to another officer. (Parks Canada)

Under the relentless artillery and musket fire in the opening stages of the battle, parts of the line on the left broke and retreated into the woods. Perhaps that was when Dury was struck in the back of the head by a musket ball. Although staggered by the wound he was able to hand off the King's colour to another officer before collapsing. Another casualty was Vincent's ADC, Lieutenant Thomas Barnard, who was injured when his horse was shot out from under him.[9]

On the south side of the road the King's was having problems as well, particularly Goldicutt's company, over which there was already a pall. Only ten days earlier its veteran commander, Captain Henry Francis Goldicutt, out of his mind with fever, had killed himself.[10] At Stoney Creek, under heavy fire and perhaps inexperienced leadership, the company was taking a severe beating. Privates Richard Hugill, a grinder from Nottingham, George Longly, a labourer from York, and Lawrence Mead, a shoemaker from County Carlow, all of them veterans of Copenhagen and Martinique, were killed. The 30-year-old Irish ser-

**"A continual sheet of fire"** is what the eight companies of the 49th Regiment faced when they deployed before the banks of this shallow stream that crossed both Gage farms, silhouetted by campfires behind them. Enemy fire was "most heavy," reported Lieutenant James FitzGibbon, "the men thought it terrible and fled." This photograph taken in 1915 looks south over King Street towards the Gage homestead and the monument. (Library and Archives Canada)

geant, George McCulloch from County Antrim, fell with a hip wound, Private William Phillips from Wiltshire, also 30, was shot in the thigh and Private David Best took a musket ball in the head. Quite possibly the company broke and fled into the woods.

Samuel Hooker, the 32-year-old senior lieutenant in the King's, was leading his company in a bayonet charge against elements of the Sixteenth and Fifth Infantry entrenched on the ridge when he was shot in the head and instantly killed. Ten years a lieutenant, he would die not knowing his promotion to captain had been approved.

Captain James Mundy, in command of the King's light company, was wounded three times; one of his sergeants, John Webb, a weaver from Somerset and a veteran of Copenhagen and Martinique, was killed. In Captain John Goldrisk's company, Sergeant Joseph Hunt, a Lancashire whitesmith, was mortally wounded, and in the ranks a 28-year-old Scot from Angus, John Mather, had a musket ball shatter his left arm.

The King's came into action with only 15 officers. Seven, including its commander, Major James Ogilvie, the regimental surgeon, William Hacket, and platoon commander Lieutenant John Thorne Weyland, were wounded by American gunfire. Ogilvie was shot twice and badly bruised when his horse was killed and collapsed on him, and Weyland took a musket ball in his left bicep.

In the meadow to the east of William Gage's lane, casualties in the 49th mounted. Private James Adams, a labourer from Herefordshire, was shot dead. Fourteen-year veteran Dennis Keough fell with a bullet in his head, Thomas Morgan, a private in Williams's company took a musket ball in the eye, and Private William Pronk took one in the neck. Major James Dennis was wounded and his horse shot under him. Fellow field officer Major Alexander Clerk was felled by gunfire.

**Lieutenant John Thorne Weyland, King's Regiment (1789-1873).** Shown here in his seventies, Weyland as a young subaltern was one of seven officers of the King's wounded during the Battle of Stoney Creek, taking a musket ball in the left bicep. After the war he served with the 1st Royal Veterans Battalion, 34th Foot, 65th Foot and finally the Royal Canadian Rifle Regiment. (Courtesy of Milton Loomis)

And so it went, officers and men, silhouetted against the laneway fires, tumbled and fell.

FitzGibbon watched as the British line began to crack and waver. Between the shouting of the men and the din of the weaponry, "officers could no longer control their men and they soon began to fall back. The fire of the enemy while it lasted was most heavy, and tho' not destructive, owing to the darkness, the men thought it terrible and fled."[11] The British advance, which had begun so confidently, was dangerously close to becoming a major reverse as troops broke and dashed to the cover of the forest on the western edge of the Gage farms.[12]

Unable to form "in extreme darkness upon unknown and rough ground covered with rail fences, fallen trees and stumps," FitzGibbon said the troops "on the left of and I believe every other portion of the line were in total confusion, shouting and firing, and ultimately breaking and flying into the woods in their rear.... General Vincent and the whole left of the line retreated, or may I say fled into the woods."[3]

## 27 "The enemy appeared to be completely broken."[1]

### CHANDLER MISSES A ROUT IN THE MAKING.

Every reverse of fortune, regardless of how stunning and apparently unforeseeable, can be traced back through a chain of otherwise obscure and seemingly unrelated incidents. Such was the case at Stoney Creek.

The initial British assault on the American line lasted between 20 and 30 minutes, and as the firing petered out and redcoats began withdrawing into the darkness beyond the bonfires, John Chandler watched and puzzled. He was relieved his casualties were low, but at a loss to determine what the enemy was doing. Likely still rattled by the audaciousness of the nighttime attack, Chandler could not read the withdrawal for what it was – a rout in the making that only required a little aggressive encouragement to become complete.[2]

Fearful the lull was just the prelude to a second assault on his position, Chandler heard what he thought were musket shots coming from the direction of the rearguard. "I ... expected that the enemy had gained our rear by some path unknown to me and were about to attack us. I instantly ordered Colonel Milton with the 5th to form in our rear near the woods."[3]

There is no evidence that order was ever received, and if it was, it certainly was not carried out for the Fifth remained a stalwart of the American forward line for the rest of the action.[4] Likely the reason the Fifth never got the order was because Winder, anticipating another frontal assault, had already ordered the

Fifth to secure its left flank by moving toward the Gage house, thereby opening a hole in the American line and leaving the artillery without infantry support on the south side of the road.[5]

*The first link in the chain of circumstance was in place.*

Chandler, noticing that Towson's battery was unprotected, then sent Winder directions to have the Twenty-Third Infantry support the guns. In subsequent accounts he tried to cast the Twenty-Third as scapegoats, claiming they had disobeyed his earlier orders to form on the artillery. In reality in his first account of the battle, written 13 June, Chandler said that at the beginning of the action the "5th, 23rd & 25 Regts of Infty were formed in the order and positions previously prescribed for them."[6]

It was standard practice to support artillery with infantry to guard against being overrun but in this case the gunners of Towson's battery were doubly vulnerable because, inexplicably, they had not been provided with small arms to defend themselves.[7]

Having tweaked his dispositions in the face of what seemed to be diminishing opposition, Chandler permitted himself the luxury of contemplating success. "By this time the enemy appeared to be completely broken, and the General had every reason to suppose he could keep him employed and at bay until daylight, when there could be no doubt of obtaining a decisive victory."[8]

At that moment however, while "anxiously expecting the first glimmer of dawn,"[9] he heard a new burst of fire on the far right of the American line held by the Twenty-Fifth Infantry. Suspecting the British were attempting to turn his right flank but without staff officers to investigate – all three had been despatched with orders – he resolved to reconnoitre the situation himself.

*The next link in the chain was forged.*

Through fog thick with gun smoke on "one of the darkest nights ever known," General Chandler spurred his horse at full speed.

It is uncertain whether the horse stumbled on the rough ground or was shot. Chandler, at different times, claimed both. Regardless, his mount went down, Chandler followed, his shoulder and head striking the ground heavily and knocking him out.[10]

Waking after a few minutes, he collected his thoughts and hobbled on foot to the right of the line, where he gave his directions to the Twenty-Fifth before turning back toward the centre of the line. On the way he found his ADC, Lieutenant Donald Fraser, and sent him running with orders for Winder to back-up the artillery with infantry.[11]

*All the links needed to effect a turnabout in fortune were now in place.*

# 28 "The moment must be seized."[1]

## ASSAULT ON THE BATTERY

On the other side of the line, close enough to Chandler to hear his shouted orders, FitzGibbon was having serious doubts about British prospects. Repeated assaults on the American position had been repulsed with attendant heavy losses, the artillery continued to pound the British line, and men, no longer able to bear the onslaught of noise and death from the dark, were breaking ranks and taking flight.

Historian John Keegan has observed that inside every army is a crowd struggling to get out.[2] Strung out across the Gage farm meadows at Stoney Creek, company grade officers struggled desperately to keep the crowd in. "The company I commanded," FitzGibbon said, "up to this moment, was kept in good order, neither shouting nor firing ... although I was almost convinced that their remaining under the enemy's fire could be of no use."[3] With no field officer present, FitzGibbon took matters into his own hands and ran along what was left of the line to the left trying to steady the troops.

Crossing the meadow at the same moment, the 49th's commanding officer, Major Charles Plenderleath, was tracking American defensive positions by their musket fire when two of Towson's field guns announced their position by discharging in succession. Surprised at how close the guns were, Plenderleath made a decision that would profoundly affect the outcome not only of this battle but of the entire Niagara campaign. Addressing FitzGibbon's and adjoining companies, "I told the men about me the moment must be seized to charge the guns before they were reloaded."[4]

First up was a 23-year-old Scottish sergeant, Alexander Fraser, who "very gallantly advanced, setting a noble example." The In-

**Major Charles Plenderleath (1780-1854), 49th Regiment.** The key figure in the Battle of Stoney Creek, without whom the British cause would assuredly have been lost, Plenderleath was awarded the Order of the Bath for his decisive charge. Five months after Stoney Creek he would distinguish himself again at Crysler's Farm against some of the same American troops. *(Canadian Geographical Journal)*

verness native had joined the army when he was 17 as a drummer, volunteered for the 49th in 1810 and for the past six months had been the regiment's assistant sergeant major. He was quickly joined by his 21-year-old brother Peter, a corporal in the company FitzGibbon commanded, along with 20 or 30 more volunteers.[5]

What Plenderleath had in mind was not fancy. With bayonets charged, the little party set off down the road at a run reverting to the most basic form of warfare when man-to-man combat with edged weapons was the standard and impromptu charges the norm. Certainly there was little in *Formations, Field Exercises and Movements of His Majesty's Forces* governing middle-of-the-night headlong dashes against enemy artillery. After the iron discipline of linear tactics, where command and control were everything, the bayonet charge was the ultimate release. No longer required to stand fast while the enemy smashed muskets balls and canister shot into your comrades, the soldier in a bayonet charge was licensed to run amok, avenge dead comrades but most of all, kill the enemy before he killed you. Close combat, where the assailants are near enough to smell each other's hot breath, is the essence of war. The fact that two Frasers from the Scottish Highlands were front and centre was likely not an accident as Highlanders had more than a passing familiarity with pell-mell charges. And, in place of the traditional Claymore was the ideal tool for wreaking the sort of havoc Plenderleath intended. The hefty Brown Bess musket, fitted with a 17-inch steel bayonet, became a six-foot pike capable of inflicting ghastly deep wounds.

While Plenderleath's forlorn hope gathered momentum on the Queenston road, a critical event was taking place on the knoll where Towson had placed his guns. The artillery captain received an order to cease fire. The origin of the order is uncertain but it probably came from Winder, who earlier in the action had been directing artillery fire.[6] Towson immediately complied and directed his gunners to take advantage of the lull to hitch horses to gun caissons so they could be rapidly moved, if necessary.[7]

That break in firing likely changed the nature of Plenderleath's mission from suicidal to homicidal for the only approach to the artillery position was directly into the mouths of the guns.[8] If Towson was still loading with round shot and canister, then a single discharge could have shattered the little party.

Thanks to the blackness of the night, the British were within a few yards of the battery before being discovered. The big Scottish sergeant, Fraser, said the men began shouting "Come on, Brant!" as they approached the guns, invoking the name of the fearsome Mohawk warrior Joseph Brant. Without warning or muskets to defend themselves, the American gunners were quickly overrun and the battery carried. One gunner was said to have been bayoneted in the very act of discharging a gun. Another, Fraser reported, touched off the priming but the gun did not discharge. Right through the artillery position Plenderleath's party charged – "stabbing every horse and man they met" – and slammed into the Twenty-Third Infantry, which had fired one damaging volley and then scattered on impact.[9]

That volley, had it been repeated, might have stopped the charge dead in its tracks and, as contemporary English historian William James noted, "changed the fate of the day." What fire there was, however, was concentrated on the mounted officer. Plenderleath's horse went down with six musket wounds, while Plenderleath himself had two balls pass through his thigh. Trying to get up, he laid hold of a soldier for support, and upon discovering the uniform was blue not red, ordered the man to surrender. Which he did.[10]

Meanwhile, Chandler, alerted to "some convulsion about the artillery"[11] on ground where he expected the Twenty-Third to be formed, limped in to investigate. "Knowing this regiment to be new and undisciplined, he naturally concluded it might have broken and, thereby occasioned the confusion he had discovered."[12]

Completely in the dark as to what had happened, the general, sword in hand, set about remedying the situation. "I hobbled in amongst them and began to rally them and directed them to form."

**Alexander Fraser (1790-1872), sergeant, 49th Regiment.** Fraser and his younger brother, Corporal Peter Fraser, were the sharp end of the stick that skewered the American line at Stoney Creek, overrunning the artillery and sowing confusion in the ranks. Alexander personally captured both the American generals, Winder actually surrendering his sword to the big sergeant. Promoted from the ranks to an ensigny for his gallantry, he settled in Upper Canada after the war and served during the Rebellion of 1837. When he died in 1872, the *Perth Courier* declared him "A soldier every inch." (Descendants of Simon Fraser of Laggan)

One officer said Chandler was running about crying, "Where's the line! Where's the line!" At the same time he called out for his adjutant-general, Major John Johnson, by name.[13]

The redcoats, realizing he was American, "immediately, with bayonets at his breast, demanded his surrender; and in his situation there was no alternative between a surrender and instant death."[14] Chandler was taken prisoner by Fraser, who had been binding Plenderleath's wounds when the American commander blundered into their midst.[15]

A few minutes later Winder fell into the same trap, reportedly exhorting the raiding party, "Come on my brave fellows, they are routed."[16] When he realized he was among British troops he pointed his pistol at Alexander Fraser. The sergeant, with his musket to Winder's breast, growled, "If you stir, sir; you die."[17] Dropping the pistol, Winder surrendered his sword to Fraser, who immediately presented it to Plenderleath. Moreover, Plenderleath took custody of Winder's horse, which, like his first mount, also attracted a deadly hail of musket fire – nine wounds were later counted on the beast.[18]

**Towson's artillery position,** the most critical piece of real estate on the entire battlefield. Pleaderleath's charge overran Towson's guns on this high ground and both American generals were captured here. This photo from 1910 shows King Street running west towards Burlington Heights. Plenderleath's party charged down the road visible through the trees. The guns, vintage naval ordnance of indeterminate provenance, are awaiting installation as part of the Lion Monument parkette. (Library and Archives Canada)

Despite two severe bullet wounds in his thigh, Plenderleath commandeered yet another mount, this time a nag without saddle or bridle, perhaps an artillery horse, and directed transport of the wounded to the rear.[19]

An alternative American version of the event has both American generals running into the British column asking excitedly "Where is the artillery? Where is the artillery?" In the dark an officer caught them by the arm saying he would show them the artillery and before they knew they were in the hands of the enemy and both had been whisked to the rear of the column. One source said they were bundled on artillery horses and packed off to Burlington Heights.[20]

An eyewitness from the 49th, almost certainly Fraser himself, denied that either officer was captured hiding under the guns. Chandler, he said, was taken "standing sword in hand by the last gun, encouraging his men to fight and stand by him. General Winder also a brave officer, was taken by the same party and upon the same spot, as well as several other American officers, and in justice to them I must say that I did not perceive the least appearance of cowardice on the part of any, and I am positive none were captured under a gun carriage, nor could such a thing happen without my knowledge."[21]

Nabbed with Chandler was his assistant quartermaster general, Major Christopher Van De Venter. His ADC, Lieutenant Fraser, had searched in vain for Winder and, returning to the guns, "found myself when I arrived there in company with guests I did not like, one of which claimed me as a prisoner, I however, declined the honor."[22]

Writing to a friend six days later, Fraser said, "I was very near being taken, having been ordered to surrender with a Bayonet to my breast but I knocked

**American field artillery, 1813.**
This painting by H.C. McBarron depicts a gun detachment from the Second Artillery similar to the gunners of Captain Nathan Towson's battery which was overrun by the 49th at Stoney Creek. These artillerymen all carry muskets, something Towson's men did not have. (Company of Military Historians)

it aside & escaped with two fingers cut a little." Chandler's brigade major, Captain Roger Jones, also eluded capture despite a serious bayonet wound.[23]

Bearing the savage brunt of the charge were the Second Artillery gunners and matrosses and the infantrymen of the Twenty-Third. FitzGibbon said the elder Fraser single-handedly bayoneted seven Americans while his brother was responsible for four more. Towson's company alone had a minimum of three killed, 19 taken prisoner and an unknown number wounded. And, of course, the battery, which consisted of three 6-pdr. guns and one brass howitzer, carriages, ammunition tumbrels and nine artillery horses, was taken as well. Among the American casualties was Peter Dempsey, a 44-year-old cooper from Philadelphia, who was shot in the thigh and lost an eye in the fray. William Peters, a 30-year-old shoemaker from Chester, Pennsylvania, had his arm smashed by a musket ball.[24]

Towson's own experience gives some idea of how completely the darkness cloaked, and isolated, individual occurrences. The artillery captain, refusing to credit reports his battery had been captured, went with Captain George Steele, the ranking officer of the Sixteenth Infantry to investigate. Both were taken prisoner by the 49th but Towson, "ever on the alert, watched for a favorable opportunity and by a bold exertion made his escape. Numerous shots were fired after him but by zigzag movements, and favored by darkness, he escaped unhurt."[25]

Also drawn into the dark melee around the guns was the Twenty-Fifth's commanding officer, Major Joseph Smith, who, like so many of his fellow officers, still believed Indians composed a significant portion of the British force. "It was so dark that he could neither distinguish their uniforms, nor tell whether they were friends or foe; he proceeded very slowly, peering forward until within a few

**Captain Roger Jones, Third Artillery (1789-1852).** As Chandler's brigade major, the officer responsible for distributing orders and directing troop movement, it was Jones who detailed riflemen for picket duty at Stoney Creek despite warnings they would fall asleep. He narrowly averted capture when Chandler was taken, sustaining a bayonet wound in the process. This portrait by unknown artist, circa 1833, shows Jones in the uniform of a brigadier general. (Virginia State Library and Archives)

yards of them, when an officer near him told him to surrender & he would give him good quarter. In his surprise, he said, he had the folly to refuse the officer in very uncourteous terms, and he instantly turned and fled ... and ran for life, the British and Indians in hot pursuit and yelling like so many evil spirits."[26]

Fraser, Jones, Towson and Smith all claim to have eluded capture but there is some evidence that they and others were actually captured and then escaped. Cruikshank says many bolted in the confusion and darkness, while 2nd Lincoln Militia captain Charles Askin said "several officers who were taken, after giving their word of honour they would not run away, made their escape."[27]

## 29 "None could conjecture what had happened to the Generals."[1]

### DECAPITATION

Although at least some staff officers knew their two brigadier generals had been captured,[2] the overwhelming portion of the American army was literally in the dark, unaware the command structure was missing two crucial bits.

James Burn, the cavalry colonel who was *de facto* commanding officer, would not know he had inherited the job for some hours. In a private letter, written a few weeks after the battle, Burn said when daylight came he still did not know the generals' whereabouts. Captain Jacob Hindman, who led the advance, said the fact both brigadiers had been taken was not generally known until the action was over.[3]

Major Johnson, Chandler's own adjutant general, was equally uninformed: "I lost sight of General Chandler and did not know he was taken until daylight." Captain John Thornton, one of the company commanders, said "the 5th Regiment remained at its new position until daylight impatiently waiting for new orders. None could conjecture what had happened to the Generals."[4]

Ephraim Shaler of the Twenty-Fifth said his first intimation of the capture was hearing Chandler's voice coming from the enemy side, ordering the Twenty-Fifth to cease fire. Perhaps it was Chandler who called out. Or maybe it was just the British taking advantage of the dark again to confuse American infantry.[5] Chandler himself claimed the British were unaware how big a prize they had bagged until they arrived at Burlington Heights,[6] but that seems unlikely, given that every foot soldier in the King's service would, at the very least, recognize the gold epaulet on each shoulder as belonging to a general officer.

The capture of the artillery and two brigadiers had a pronounced effect on the course of the battle, turning what had been an otherwise successful repulse of the British into a serious reverse. A significant portion of the British force having already quit the field in disarray for the security of the adjoining woods, what remained in action could easily have been crushed by the numerically superior American troops. If only they had known it.

When Plenderleath assaulted and overran the artillery, scattering the supporting infantry, he essentially smashed the centre of the American line. When he captured Chandler and Winder, he effectively reduced the American force from an army into a collection of individual regiments and detachments with no overall command structure. Already wobbly from the shock of the initial assault that came howling out of the night, the Americans were further staggered by Plenderleath's brazen thrust through the centre of their line.

"Finding our people so advanced in their centre," FitzGibbon said, "they broke and fled in every direction."[7] The assertion, that the Americans broke and ran, might be discounted as simply a partisan observation, except it is actually supported by several voices from the American side, including Chandler's and Winder's successor, Colonel James Burn, who admitted privately that "a good portion of the army … had skulked into the woods."[8]

Ephraim Shaler gave a graphic description of the American situation: "None knew where to go in the darkness of night, surrounded (as one might suppose from their yells) by all the Indians in Canada – there being, as I have before said, no rallying point designated, none could distinguish friend from foe; consequently all concept of action was lost, and confusion ensued – our men often firing upon each other by mistake. The brigade was composed of gallant men and officers who were ready and willing to engage the enemy, if they had known where to begin the work of death."[9]

According to the adjutant of the Sixteenth Infantry, Lieutenant Francis Cummins, at least three-quarters of the American army "had, in the confusion of the night, been broken and dispersed."[10] Ensign Joseph Dwight of the Thirteenth Infantry in his diary bluntly noted the chaotic breakdown of unit cohesion in American regiments – "most of them driven from the field in utter confusion."[11]

Another officer said the power vacuum at the top paralyzed unit commanders: "There was not a solitary instance of a single officer … endeavoring to retake either our officers, men or cannon, but stood, as the British retreated, waiting, as they said, for orders when both our Generals were taken prisoners.… No orders passing from or to any corps or any officer. May my eyes never witness such a scene again. Everything appeared to add to the confusion and disorder."[12]

And in the midst of the confusion and disorder, the British, with hardly a company left intact on the field themselves, were able to make off with the fruits of Plenderleath's audacity – two generals, one major, two captains, 75 men, two pieces of artillery plus accessories and nine horses.[13]

To FitzGibbon, Plenderleath's charge came at a point when the British, for all intents and purposes, were spent: "Our ruin would have been inevitable, but finding our people so far advanced in their centre they broke and fled in every direction and their fire consequently ceased at a time when our line was, as it were, entirely routed."[14] It was the equivalent of a Hail Mary pass in the dying moments of a football game. Or a boxer, down on the cards of all three judges, launching one last desperate haymaker in the twelfth round.

"I am convinced," FitzGibbon wrote, "that it was Major Plenderleath's party which drove the enemy off the field that saved us and gave us time to bring off our prisoners and guns."[15]

"For had it not been so made," he wrote, "the Americans would have maintained their ground till daylight, when they would have discovered that our force was dispersed in the woods and liable to be easily made prisoners."[16] So the Plenderleath/Fraser sortie cost the Americans their ground, their artillery and their general officers and it occurred at precisely the moment the British were ripe for the picking – dispersed in the dark, demoralized by the heavy gunfire and faced with their own particular leadership vacuum.

Sometime after the left part of the British line, including Brigadier General Vincent, "fled into the woods"[17] at the western end of the battlefield, the brigadier had disappeared. What actually occurred was never explained, or even acknowledged in any official document, but private letters, journals and memoirs – from both sides in the conflict – strongly suggest Stoney Creek was not John Vincent's finest moment. Fortunately for the British, Harvey was in command of the action from start to finish and Vincent's disappearance had little or no effect on the outcome.

However, with or without Vincent, the situation of the British was perilous. FitzGibbon, in a private letter written the day after the battle, and Hamilton Merritt in his journal do not hesitate to point out how close the British came to complete disaster. "The conduct of Major Plenderleath," FitzGibbon wrote, "and the pusillanimity of the enemy alone saved us from destruction."[18]

Merritt was equally frank: "Our men were dispersed in every direction, and had not Colonel Plenderleath charged and captured their Guns with 30 men, we should have been completely defeated."[19]

With the American line breached and a great portion of the troops driven into the surrounding woods, resistance along the upland ridge was likely sporadic, at best, in the immediate wake of Plenderleath's charge. One American officer said only two regiments held their position and kept up fire. Another, Ensign Joseph Dwight, said most had been driven from the field, only the Fifth and a portion of the Twenty-Third holding their ground.[20]

What remained in position of Chandler's division was a corps of between 450 and 500 troops composed of 250 of the Fifth Infantry bolstered by two companies of the Twentieth and the remainder from the Twenty-Fifth, the Twenty-Third and the Sixteenth. Lieutenant Francis Cummins, of the Sixteenth, did a count for Lieutenant Colonel Homer Virgil Milton at dawn and tallied 500 men. The rest, Cummins said, "had in the confusion of the night, been broken and dispersed." Captain John Thornton, who commanded one of the Twentieth Regiment's companies attached to Milton's Fifth, said the combined battalion had about 250 effectives. At daylight, he said, "there were the 5th Regiment and about 200 other troops in the field and well formed" for a total of 450.[21]

An officer of the Twenty-Fifth, almost certainly its commander, Major Joseph Lee Smith, said only a fraction – no more than 700 – of the total American force were ever in action and those that were, were almost all from the Twenty-Fifth. The British, he said, "attempted by a heavy fire and successive charges to break our line, but every man would have died before he would have given an inch – They wholly failed and never a man of them passed the line of the 25th – a very few in scattered parties passed the flanks of the Regt. at a distance, and were then speedily repulsed by other troops. Our Regiment being in advance was first and last engaged – indeed no other Regt. had an opportunity to share but little in the combat."[22]

Several other officers, though, reported a startlingly different version of events, one in which the Connecticut regiment broke and ran. "The 25th," they wrote in the *Albany Gazette,* "disgraced themselves and their country, by a precipitate retreat after the first fire. If they deserved any credit it is for their *rapid retreat,* not for their gallantry."[23]

Burn's cavalry, formed up perhaps 300 yards in the rear of the American line, never got into the action "on account of the darkness of the night and the thickness of the adjacent woods."[24]

Harvey, perhaps aware that a victory of sorts had been snatched from the jaws of utter defeat, wisely opted to withdraw. "Not choosing to expose the smallness of my force to the view of the enemy who though beaten & driven off the field, was still five times more numerous than us, I drew off the Troops just at Daylight."[25]

Although four pieces of artillery were captured, the British were only able to bring off two – a 6-pdr and a 5½ inch howitzer. According to FitzGibbon and the ranking Royal Artillery officer, Major William Holcroft, two were left behind because they had neither the horses nor the men necessary to draw them off. These two guns were spiked – that is a nail driven into their vent holes and broken off – and abandoned. Norton and the militia captain Charles Askin said two pieces were recovered by the Americans before the British could return with horses.[26]

The American version is somewhat different. Although Towson said he simply "regained possession of two his guns which had been spiked and left upon the field,"[27] at least three of his fellow officers insist they were retaken by force.

The lion's share of the credit was given to John Machesney, lieutenant in the Sixteenth Infantry, who, after the capture of the unit's two captains, became the senior officer in his regiment. Ephraim Shaler said Machesney "with a detachment of his regiment made a gallant charge and retook both pieces." Lieutenant Jonathan Kearsley said Machesney pursued the British and retook one gun. The third officer said "the 16th regiment, under the command of a subaltern (Lt. McChesney) discovering the enemy taking off our cannon, made a successful charge, and retook two pieces, with their caissons; this was done without any orders." A contemporary American historian said Machesney recovered one piece and Lieutenant Patrick McDonough of the Second Artillery another.

The brass howitzer the Americans failed to recover was an artifact from the American Revolution that had originally been captured from an invading British army at Saratoga in 1777 by a young infantry major, Henry Dearborn. Thirty-six years later it was the turn of an invading American army under the same Dearborn to give it back.[28]

With general officers, guns and prisoners to contend with as well as a considerable number of wounded, Harvey withdrew his force from the Gage farms just on the edge of dawn. The entire action, from the first alarm to the last parting shot, had lasted no more than an hour.[29]

# 30 "The awful dream of the night."[1]

## BY DAWN'S EARLY LIGHT

The first evidence of dawn in Stoney Creek appeared shortly before 3:30 a.m. Within half an hour – at the beginning of civil twilight – the grim effects of the battle would have been plainly visible. Bodies of men and horses from both sides along with cattle from James Gage's farm littered the battlefield, those of the dead beginning to stiffen and cool, those men still alive crying out for water and comfort.

Lieutenant Francis Cummins said the survivors looked out over "a field of desolation, anon looking at each other's countenances, blackened with smoke and powder, distorted by astonishment, as it were, the awful dream of the night." And all around them "broken swords, muskets, bayonets, caps and helmets strew the field. Friend and foe, savage and civilized, man and horse, lay commingled, stretched in their last repose."[2]

On the lane leading to William Gage's farm, where the advance guard was overrun by the 49th in the first contact, the urge that had prompted James Crawford of the Twenty-Second to write a will 13 days earlier was now seen to have been sadly prescient. The big sergeant from Mercer, Pennsylvania, lay still, the last of his life seeping out of a hole in his gut. "He died a brave man," one of his fellow soldiers reported, "with his face toward the enemy. He received a musket ball just below the pit of his stomach and breathed for several hours after, but was insensible." Also fatally wounded was Samuel Lock, a 22-year-old farmer from South Kingston, Rhode Island. His company commander in the Twenty-Fifth Infantry said it plain and simple: he "served with fidelity from June 13, 1812 to June 6, 1813." Among the wounded was Thomas Clark, the Scottish-born commander of the 2nd Lincoln, and Captain Thomas Manners of the 49th.[3]

Bodies and blankets were the first thing Elizabeth Gage saw when she ventured out of the family house and gazed on the strangely pastoral scene. "There was the body of a soldier lying between the house and creek and a lot of dead horses. I plainly remember seeing the blankets that the American soldiers had been sleeping on, lying in rows on the hillside just where they were sleeping when the surprise came. I thought at the time they looked like a flock of sheep on a green hill."[4]

Across the road, just below the William Gage house, Hamilton Merritt was looking at bodies as well, searching for any sign of the missing British general, John Vincent. Challenged by an American sentry while both his pistols were still holstered, the quick-thinking Merritt took advantage of his blue Provincial Light Dragoons' coat: "I was on the point of surrendering ... when I adopted the stratagem of enquiring, who placed him there? – and rode up to him – he, by my blue Military Coat, took me for one of his own party and answered, his Captain, who had just gone into the House with a party of Men. I then enquired if he had found the British General and pulled out my pistol, which made him drop his Gun. At the moment, a man without any Gun ran down the hill – I called him –

he came, when I had the good fortune to secure both and bring them off."[5]

Near the road, Nathan Towson, the artillery captain who had lost his guns in the battle, was relieved to recover two 6-pdrs. of his battery. Collecting some survivors of his company, he ordered the vent holes drilled and the guns made serviceable. "By firing a few rounds into the woods where red coats were still visible, the enemy were induced to retire altogether, and leave the Americans master of the field."[6]

The masters of the field, however, missing two generals, were in no mood to hold their ground. Overall command – strictly on the basis of seniority – had devolved on the 45-year-old cavalry colonel James Burn, who by his own admission did not even know which regiments composed his army. In a private letter, he gave a sense of how unprepared he was to assume command: "I was so much at a loss on that occasion as you would be if you were to be made President of the U.S. without any previous notice. When day appeared I found myself in command … not knowing what had become either of the generals or a good portion of the army."[7]

Fearful of another attack, Burn ordered an immediate withdrawal from the battlefield – at least one mile – to collect stragglers coming in from the woods and establish a new position on the east side of Stoney Creek. The initial position was in two sections with the Twenty-Fifth straddling the Queenston road, the Twenty-Third and the Fifth on the left and what was left of the artillery in the middle and then with the same three regiments in a continuous line across the road.[8]

**Colonel James Burn, Second Light Dragoons (1768-1831).** "Under the influence of an evil star" is how his friend Charles Jared Ingersoll described the North Carolina native. Although considered brave and competent, the commander of the newly-created Second U.S. Light Dragoons lacked two requisites of leadership – daring and resolve – that could have changed the outcome of the 1813 Niagara campaign. (Portrait by John Wesley Jarvis. Skinner, Boston and Bolton MA)

The new commander was anything but keen on shouldering the burden of command. The Charleston native, briefly a protégé of the lubricious James Wilkinson, had been appointed colonel of the newly-formed Second Light Dragoons in August 1812. Although a capable enough regimental officer, Burn lacked the essential elements of leadership – resolve and ruthlessness. His close friend and leading Republican Charles Ingersoll said Burn was "under the influence of an evil star," and lacking "what perhaps less courageous men would have shown in his exigency, fearlessness of responsibility: and fell back when a bold advance would probably have gained him a brigade with the applause of his country and his own confidence."[9] Lieutenant Jonathan Kearsley said that Burn actually tried to decline the command on the grounds he was a cavalry officer "and unacquainted with the duties appropriate to the corps."[10]

Despite having far superior numbers to the British, Burn could not decide what to do. "Being at a loss what steps to pursue in the unpleasant dilemma occasioned by the capture of our Generals,"[11] the cavalryman turned to the first choice of dithering commanders and summoned all the field grade officers to a council of war.

Down at the beach where Stoney Creek empties into the lake,[12] however, the other colonel in Chandler's army was experiencing none of the doubts that beset Burn. The sound of the battle had been clearly audible to the 800 troops of the Thirteenth and Fourteenth Regiments and their commander, Colonel John Chrystie of the Thirteenth Infantry, was particularly eager to get into the action. Chrystie, a native New Yorker and staunch Republican, had experienced the bitterness of defeat at Queenston Heights the previous fall.

Posted on the beach to protect the baggage vessels, his troops had slept on their arms and were formed up at the first alarm. As soon as it was light, Chrystie gave orders to advance west along the beach and then north along the road that tracked Big Creek to get behind the British and cut off their retreat. Just as they were about to depart an express arrived summoning all the field officers to join the main body of the army in its new position to the east of the original Gage farm encampment.[13]

Travelling from the beach, Chrystie's command arrived at the battlefield, now abandoned by both sides. On the way up they made prisoners of 40 British troops, all from the 49th, who had been lost in the woods.[14] Ensign Joseph Dwight was part of the detachment that briefly occupied the battlefield. In his diary he noted they arrived at 7 a.m., "collected our wounded, put them in waggons and at 8 o'clock took up our line of march to the rear."[15] There is no mention of burying bodies, and indeed in one hour it seems unlikely that any could have been.

Before the Twenty-Third had withdrawn earlier from the battlefield, its regimental surgeon, Silas Fuller, had examined the bayonet wound Captain Peter Mills sustained during the initial assault on the advanced line. The steel blade had punctured his intestines and penetrated his left hip. On the direction of the surgeon, "who entertained no hope of his living through the day," Mills was left on the battlefield.[16]

When the Thirteenth arrived, the 35-year-old officer was found by Major Richard Malcolm and Ensign Dwight and carried to a nearby house, where the seriously wounded militia officer Lieutenant Colonel Thomas Clark of the 2nd Lincoln – whom the Americans believed was commanding officer of the 49th – had also been taken. Both men were considered to be mortally wounded.[17]

In his account written from memory at least 20 years after the battle, Captain Mordecai Myers, also of the Thirteenth Infantry, said, "When we arrived at the ground we found it strewed with dead and wounded of both parties to the number of four or five hundred. The troops on both sides were scattered. We buried the dead and stacked and burned the arms and baggage for want of transportation. We brought off the wounded and prepared to follow our retiring forces."[18]

His account – other than the casualties, which are grossly overestimated, and his claim that they buried the dead – agrees closely with FitzGibbon, who said that at daylight the two American regiments from the lakeshore "pushed on to the scene of action, which was deserted. They occupied it, burned some waggons with flour, arms, accoutrements, blankets, in short everything which they found on the field and then retreated."[19]

The army, according to one American witness, "retired in great disorder, under command of Col. Burns [sic] of

**Colonel John Chrystie, Thirteenth Infantry.** A veteran of Queenston Heights, where he was wounded and captured, Chrystie was detailed by Chandler to guard the division's transport bateaux on the lakeshore with two regiments and a company of artillery. Eager to pursue the British the morning after the battle, he was overruled by a council of war. Artist unknown, print after a photo engraving. (*Uniforms and Equipment of the United States Forces in the War of 1812*)

the dragoons, leaving their dead on the field."[20] Robert Land, a lieutenant in the 5th Lincoln, told his grandson "they came to the camp, destroyed what they could not carry off, left their dead and some of the wounded on the field and retreated, a disorganized mob."[21]

Meanwhile, Burn, in his new position, had his hands full keeping his senior officers in line. Chrystie arrived believing overall command was rightfully his. "Chrystie thought that he ranked all the other officers," Myers said, "but on going to the council, he found, much to his chagrin and mortification that Col. Burns [sic] ranked by date of commission."[22]

Burn's own concerns about his fitness for command were apparently shared by some of his fellow officers. Small wonder. The officer the secretary of war referred to as "our modest cavalier" did not even know how many troops were in his command, reporting his main force at 1,000 and Chrystie's command at 300, which was somewhat less than half what he actually had in the field.[23]

Arguing that the troops who had been engaged were nearly out of ammunition and that the army was completely out of general officers, Burn suggested retiring to the camp at Forty Mile Creek, "where we could be supplied with ammunition and provisions and either advance or remain until further orders."[24] Burn said a majority concurred but the decision was neither harmonious nor unanimous. One officer said "a contention for rank took place between the respective Lieut Colonels present, of whom there were five or six, nothing could be decided on, as there was no one clearly in command of the others."[25]

Nathan Towson, the senior artillery officer, miffed at being excluded from the council of war, strongly protested the decision to retreat to Forty Mile Creek.

**Captain Mordecai Myers, Thirteenth Infantry (1786-1871).** With several years of militia service and training at a private military academy before the war, Myers was unusually well qualified for his regular army commission. At Fort George he took his company ashore just behind the advance and he was dispatched to pursue the retreating British army as part of Brigadier General William Henry Winder's brigade. He is portrayed here by John Wesley Jarvis in his New York Militia uniform. (Toledo Museum of Art)

Nor was it popular with the junior officers. Captain John Thornton of the Twentieth Infantry said the decision to withdraw "was disapproved by almost all the platoon officers, who wished for an immediate and vigorous pursuit ... the proceeding perhaps was prudent through not agreeable to my feelings nor glorious to our arms. Many stragglers, however would certainly have been taken." Another observer reported "every man and officer was in a rage for losing an opportunity to be revenged on the English and Indians."[26]

Chrystie appears to have made a last-ditch offer to pursue the British but was overruled by the council of war. "Had Chrystie taken command," Ensign Dwight confided to his diary, "not a doubt remains that the whole British force would have been in our possession."[27] An express rider was dispatched to Dearborn with news of the reverse and a request for instructions and more ammunition.

FitzGibbon characterized the confusing night action as a lose-lose situation: "Here then we find both parties leaving the scene of the action, each believing the others the conquerors."[28]

Certainly the British, with whole companies dispersed in the woods, heavy casualties on the field and a brigadier general missing, were in no position to claim victory. Back at Burlington Heights they were holding their own council of war and strongly leaning towards a further retreat around the lake. Merritt had found no sign of Vincent and a flag to the American line seeking to discover if he was a prisoner was equally fruitless. In the absence of Vincent, command fell to Lieutenant Colonel Cecil Bisshopp.

Returning from the battlefield, Prevost's aide de camp, Captain Robert McDouall, produced a letter from Prevost authorizing an immediate withdrawal to Kingston. According to the influential militia officer Robert Nichol, Bisshopp was on the verge of complying with the order until Nichol intervened. The letter, he argued, had been in McDouall's possession for some days and since he was only just revealing it then, it could only be considered as a discretionary order and thus, whether its instructions were followed or not was Bisshopp's call to make. Before abandoning the Niagara district, Nichol argued, he should consult his field and staff officers. Bisshopp agreed but before the council could assemble Vincent reappeared.

The official record is silent on what had happened to the brigadier and Vincent himself never acknowledged or explained his absence, but culling a variety of sources yields a picture of the general's fate that is neither gallant nor dignified. There are at least a dozen versions of the story that range from high misadventure to low comedy.

FitzGibbon said Vincent and the whole left of the British line fled into the woods and the general was missing until noon the following day. "A flag of truce was sent to enquire if he was taken but the Americans knew nothing of him. Indians were sent in search of him but without success. He at length found a road and joined us."[29]

Chandler, citing as his source Prevost's other aide de camp, Lieutenant Henry Milnes, claimed Vincent "lost his command in the dark, when his troops broke at the commencement of the battle and conceiving that the British were overwhelmed and cut up, he lay concealed in the woods until afternoon of the same day."[30]

The militia officer Charles Askin said Vincent was missing for six or eight hours after the action,[31] Mordecai Myers said the Americans looked for him but found only his blanket and pistol, and Lieutenant Jonathan Kearsley said his horse and hat were found but the general was lost for two or three days.[32]

One cheeky staff officer said the Thirteenth Infantry "early the next morning, captured the British commander's cocked hat in one place, and his horse, fully accoutred, in another; showing that the person who had rode under the one, and on the other, had wandered many degrees from the right point of his compass. The identity of these articles may not have been certain, though they bore the conquering motto of 'Vincent' stamped upon them."[33]

William Green said Vincent was found by two militiamen and the local historian E.B. Biggar said he was found by John Brant, son of Joseph Brant. York social doyenne Anne Powell reported that when found, Vincent was "greatly overpowered by fatigue and … a good deal bruised by the fall of his horse."[34]

Local amateur historian and phrenologist Peter Van Wagner claimed that an exhausted Vincent "had stimulated too freely that night and strayed into the bush at the Big Creek from his men and was found the next morning."[35]

Timothy Downs, a private in the 4th Lincoln, was 96 years old in 1875 when he applied for a war pension, claiming to have been at the battle where he "acted as an orderly … to Col. Vincent who ran away and left him."[36]

The flag party that approached the Americans seeking Vincent's whereabouts was accompanied by a woman and a small dog. The American officer who met the party was asked if a certain sergeant of the 49th, who was missing, was among the wounded or prisoners. A witness of the incident, the artillery officer Nathan Towson, said while the American officer was questioning the flag bearer, the woman's dog ran onto the battlefield.

The dog, Towson said, "seemed to comprehend the nature of her sad errand and ran round among the dead bodies, smelling each, until he discovered that of his master, when sitting down beside it, he commenced howling piteously.

'There' shrieked the poor woman, 'there is my husband' and rushing towards him, found it but too true."[37]

Towson never identified the man or his unfortunate wife but the only 49th sergeant killed in the action was Charles Page of Captain Augustine Fizgerald's company.[38]

## 31    "You will be surprised to find our loss so small."[1]

### COUNTING THE COST

By the time Vincent repaired to Burlington Heights, somewhat the worse for wear from his ordeal – "too much hurried and fatigued to write today," Harvey noted.[2] – the realization was beginning to dawn that the British has accomplished more than just an escape. They had bloodied the nose of the American army but more importantly they had shaken its resolve.

Although the losses were heavy and the action itself anything but decisive, Harvey's raid had effectively stemmed the American tide. Luck had played a huge part: Plenderleath's charge rescued what was almost certainly a failed mission, and the capture of artillery and general officers had decapitated the American colossus just at the point it was poised to overwhelm the British. Initial fears about the size of British losses were relieved somewhat as more and more of the stragglers who had fled into the woods found their way back to the heights. Very real concerns about an American counterattack faded on reports of panic in their lines. The American historian Benjamin Lossing said: "The Americans, fearing a renewal of the attack, retreated so precipitately that they left their dead unburied."[3]

Both Merritt and FitzGibbon returned to the battlefield after the Americans had retreated and saw first-hand the evidence of a hasty departure – unburied dead, abandoned wounded and the charred remains of provisions and arms. FitzGibbon initially counted only 19 American bodies and concluded "they must have carried off many of their dead. For in situations off the road where there was little done by us, I found many of them dead, and in the road where they have suffered most, I found but one dead man." After returning to Burlington Heights, however, FitzGibbon learned that another 12 bodies had been found on the line of retreat.[4] That would bring the total number of American dead on the battlefield alone to 31.

One soldier of the 49th who had been lost in the woods said he counted some 30 American wounded in the bush, all but one the work of the bayonet.[5] The Americans officially acknowledged 17 dead and 38 wounded, yet FitzGibbon counted 31 dead, one soldier alone found 30 wounded and the Fraser brothers between them accounted for 11 dead and wounded. Most certainly there were more fatalities following the battle.

Whether by design or by accident, reporting of American casualties from the battle was not accurate. A correct fix on the number of casualties remains elusive because no accurate unit-by-unit accounting has come to light. The assistant adjutant general, Major John Johnson, issued the report that has become the official record and the one that is cited in every account of the battle. Johnson's return lists a total of 155 killed, wounded and missing.[6] Like his earlier return for the number of troops in Chandler's division, his casualty figures for Stoney Creek are suspect, perhaps grievously so. How they have continued to be cited as reliable is a mystery, for there is ample evidence casualties were seriously under-reported.

Johnson says there were only 17 dead, although FitzGibbon, the most credible witness from either side, counted 31 American dead on the battlefield and believed than many others had already been removed. The figure of 31 killed is buttressed by one of Dearborn's staff at Fort George, Major Talbot Chambers, who on 6 June recorded "about thirty men killed" in the action at the Head of the Lake.[7]

Major Joseph Lee Smith, who commanded the Twenty-Fifth Infantry, reported his unit alone had 45 killed and wounded.[8] Henry Leavenworth, who commanded one of the nine companies of the Twenty-Fifth that took casualties in the action, said his company lost four killed and four wounded. If both Smith's and Johnson's number are correct, then the Twenty-Fifth – which was only one of the eight regiments in-

**Captain Henry Leavenworth, Twenty-Fifth Infantry (1783-1834).** A practising lawyer before he was commissioned captain in the Twenty-Fifth, Leavenworth commanded a company at Stoney Creek. While repelling repeated British bayonet charges, his regiment had at least 45 killed and wounded. A distinguished career soldier, he left his name on a military camp, a federal prison and the first incorporated city in Kansas. (Frontier Army Museum, Fort Leavenworth)

volved in the battle – accounted for better than three-quarters of all reported American dead and wounded.[9]

The Second Artillery, which served as light infantry in the advance guard at Stoney Creek and worked the guns, also took heavy casualties. A unit officer who fought in the action calculated the heavy price this elite unit paid: "You can imagine my astonishment and regret when at the approach of day we could not muster more than 60 of our brave companions, the rest were killed, wounded or made prisoners. Out of our fine battalion of artillery, which you saw leave Philadelphia, not more than 75 were left. Capt. Biddle's fine company musters only about 20 men."[10]

Again, if these casualty figures are correct and putting each of the four artillery companies conservatively at 50 men, for a total of 200, and "not more than 75 were left," then Towson's, Hindman's, Biddle's and Nicholas's companies alone took a total of 125 casualties – better than three-quarters of all reported American casualties. If Biddle's company could only muster 20 men, then at least 30 from that company alone were killed, wounded or missing. That makes two units – the Twenty-Fifth Infantry and the Second Artillery – that *each* took more than three-quarters of all acknowledged American casualties.

Separate letters from the front, reprinted in the Boston *Weekly Messenger* and *United States Gazette* in Philadelphia, put American losses at more than 350 and one company commander calculated the loss as "at least five hundred."[11]

The other oft-cited source for American casualties, Eaton's *Returns of the Killed and Wounded of American Troops*,[12] does a unit breakdown for eight regiments but the numbers cited are no more credible than Johnson's. The same Second Artillery companies cited above, according to Eaton, reported only three killed and seven wounded, a ludicrously low figure in light of the considerable anecdotal evidence. He reports the Sixteenth Infantry took no casualties whatsoever, yet a search of incomplete muster rolls and the enlistment registry turns up the names of six killed and four wounded at Stoney Creek. Doubtless there were more. Likewise the Twenty-Second Infantry, which is not even listed by Eaton as being at Stoney Creek. The same records produce the names of eight killed and four wounded from that regiment. The two companies of the Twentieth Regiment – Randolph's and Thornton's – which took five casualties are also nowhere to be found on Eaton's list.[13] The Twenty-Fifth Infantry, which according to its commanding officer lost 45 men killed and wounded, is credited with only 19 killed and wounded by Eaton.

And, as if the official record was not murky enough, the anecdotal record further complicates the picture with what can only be considered wilful suppression and deliberate misstatement of the facts. Sadly these attempts to save reputations and bolster careers, political and military, sully and obscure the sacrifice of dozens of troops maimed and killed.

Starting at the top: Dearborn, in a clumsy attempt to minimize the damage, reassured the secretary of war on 6 June "our loss was small (not exceeding thirty)."[14] No other casualty figures are included and there is no breakdown of killed, wounded or captured, but the implication is clear – the total loss was minimal, "not exceeding thirty." The report on the action he subsequently received from Colonel James Burn was in the same vein, leaving the impression casualties were almost too few to mention: "You will be surprised to find our loss so small; that of the enemy exceeds ours much."[15]

Chandler, even three years after the battle, was still insisting "the whole loss of those who were engaged on the American side did not exceed thirty in killed and wounded."[16] Ephraim Shaler's estimate – between 50 and 60 killed and wounded for the whole army[17] – ventures in the direction of reality but still seems improbably low, given Shaler's commanding officer reported nearly that many in his regiment alone.

For prisoners it is easier to get an accurate picture because there are always the enemy's figures on prisoners taken for comparison purposes. Johnson's official return lists 93 privates and non-commissioned officers and seven officers taken for a total of 100. The British returns of prisoners captured record 116 non-commissioned officers and privates and nine officers for a total of 125.[18] Somewhere along the line the British captured 25 prisoners the Americans did not know they lost.

On the other side of the ledger, there are two sets of entries for British losses in the action – the American estimates, both official and anecdotal, and the British

**Drummer, 49th Regiment.** Drummers were part of the British force at Stoney Creek and two from the 49th were among the wounded. In the absence of any visual reference in the dark, drums would have been a useful communication tool once the firing began. The drawing depicts the drummer in ceremonial bearskin, such as might have been worn to celebrate the King's birthday on 4 June. (© Craig Williams, used with permission)

records, mostly official. The gulf between them, which is wide and at times absurd, underlines the lack of professionalism in an infant army, whose leaders far too often reverted to the populist and blame-averting tactics of politics when it came to accountability for a reverse.

The worst offender was Chandler, who in the same breath as minimizing American killed and wounded, could put total British losses at nearly 500. In fact Chandler, years after the action, would claim that at Stoney Creek the British took the worst beating in any action up to that time in the war.[19] Other American accounts put British fatalities as high as 200 and total casualties at four times the number of the Americans.[20]

The official British figures, according to returns made right after the action, are 23 killed, 135 wounded and 52 missing for a total of 213.[21] Include the skirmish of 5 June and those that died of wounds after the battle and the final tally of British dead is probably 32.

Together with the militia – of which at least two were wounded and five made prisoner – the total number of British casualties must exceed 220. So, better than one-in-four of the nearly 800 officers and men who marched out from Burlington Heights were killed, wounded or taken prisoner. Given the risks involved in executing a night action, it could have been much worse.

## 32 "Never was a more compleat victory obtained."[1]

### DAMAGE CONTROL

Early in the evening of 6 June, an American dragoon officer, likely a cornet, reined in his exhausted mount inside the gates of Fort George. As he tethered the animal, every head turned toward him for some sign of the news. His face, however, swathed in French-style moustaches and large side whiskers, was "as inexpressive as a barber's block," with only the tip of his nose visible. "The shrewdest guesser among the spectators … found it difficult to determine whether the said tip bespoke victory or defeat."[2]

To Dearborn the express delivered the answer – sent not from his protégé Chandler, or even his second in command, the Baltimore lawyer Winder, but from his overmatched cavalry commander James Burn, who was "at a loss what steps to pursue."[3]

The complete contents of the express are not known – only an extract survives in the American State Papers – but the gist of it can be gleaned from two soldiers who were in Fort George at the time, one a high-ranking staff officer and the other a private in the Baltimore Volunteers.

Major Talbot Chambers, Dearborn's assistant adjutant general, wrote to a friend: "An express has this moment arrived from the head of the Lake with the news that our army under the command of gen, Chandler was surprised ... by a party of Indians and British and that a partial action took place which eventuated in making prisoners of Brigadier Generals Winder and Chandler and Major Van de Vente, with about thirty men killed."[4]

Significant of course are the admissions the camp was surprised and approximately 30 killed. In the garrison the news spread fast and the Baltimore Volunteer recorded the scuttlebutt, some of it remarkably accurate: "Our camp, they say, was badly and loosely laid out. The British advanced silently with fixed bayonets; not a musket was allowed to be loaded for fear of blowing their design. Some officers and men advanced at some distance ahead of them, who hailed, abused and stabbed some of our centinels; pretending to give the countersign. The advanced guard was first alarmed by hearing the dying groan of a sentry who had been run through. Five pieces of light artillery were seized and fired against our own troops; and they say, that gen. Winder was made prisoner in making a desperate attack on the British to retake them."[5]

The surviving extract of Burn's initial report to Dearborn describes what sounds like a different action, one that almost constitutes a victory. Assaults were gallantly repelled, fire was nobly returned and well directed, the army proved its firmness and bravery. Every enemy aim was completely frustrated, the battlefield was covered with his dead and only a small loss was suffered in return, which, however, happened to include two pieces of artillery and two brigadier generals. In somewhat tortured prose that hints at an agitated state of mind, Burn admitted the last event "prevented the future operations from being carried into effect with the promptitude which would have assuredly taken place had either of those officers been present to command."[6]

The following day Dearborn was further misinformed by the assistant adjutant general, John Johnson, who reported a decisive triumph of American arms in which commanders, fully anticipating the attack, were cool and brave and the troops valorous. "The fact is," Johnson wrote, "there never was a more compleat victory obtained." Johnson's missive, written 24 to 36 hours after the battle, is a model of damage control. Given that Dearborn already knew this information, Johnson's report sounds suspiciously like a press release, spin-doctored to put the best possible face on a bad situation.[7]

Later the same night, the sickly Dearborn, still suffering from the fever that had afflicted him from the start of the campaign, was forced to forward the news to his truculent secretary of war, who just three weeks previously had cautioned him that the British army "not be permitted to escape to-day that it may fight tomorrow."[8] Adopting the same tone as Burn, Dearborn struggled to ignore the elephant in the room, describing an action in which the enemy was "completely routed and driven from the field" and would have been pursued and destroyed but "by some strange fatality … both Brigadier-Generals Chandler and Winder were taken prisoner."

How he reacted to what could only be seen as a disaster is not known. Perhaps the old warrior still believed a decisive victory was within grasp. Certainly it did nothing to improve the state of his health.[9] Still too sickly to take to the field – "I never so severely felt the want of health as at present" – Dearborn ordered generals Morgan Lewis and John Parker Boyd to proceed immediately to Forty Mile Creek.[10]

An examination of the order he issued to Lewis that same night reveals no sense the action at Stoney Creek was anything other than what Burn had described – an American victory tarnished only marginally by the strange fatality of two lost generals. Clearly he needed only replace the leaders, and the remaining British force, already softened up, would rapidly collapse. His instructions were explicit: "You will attack the enemy as soon as practicable … every possible effort should be made for preventing the enemy's escape. May success and glory attend you." Brave words? Or hints of desperation from an old soldier who can see a once-distinguished career about to end badly? This was the fourth expedition dispatched by Dearborn to subdue an enemy that had been declared "beaten at all points," only 11 days earlier.[11]

In addition to Boyd, Lewis was told to take another brigadier general, Robert Swartout, and, presumably to add a little fire to the mix,

**American staff officers.** This drawing by H.C. McBarron shows two young "stafflings" such as the anonymous rookie staff officer who accompanied Major General Morgan Lewis to the Forty and chronicled the trip like a holiday outing in *The First Campaign of an ADC*, published in 1834. (Company of Military Historians)

hotspur Winfield Scott. Although instructed to act without delay, the comfort-conscious Lewis may have waited until the following morning. At least three sources say although Swartout and Boyd were ready to go immediately, Lewis delayed his departure because it was dark and rainy.[12]

Possibly Boyd or Swartout or even Scott marshalled the 400-strong Sixth Infantry under Lieutenant Colonel James Miller and left immediately, and Lewis followed in the morning, planning to make up the ground because his party was mounted.

A junior staff officer, relieved to be in the field, described Lewis's party as it left Fort George accompanied by an escort of Second Artillery equipped as cavalry: "The whole party was mounted, it being determined that no bipeds should be attached to it to retard its expedition. It was a small party but embraced a good deal of rank and would have been a fine haul for any way-laying fisherman of the enemy. But we relied much on our escort, that would have broken through any meshes of ordinary strength, and the Generals, staff and stafflings, were resolved on a good struggle rather than follow the captive brigadiers into bond."[3]

# 🎕 "An action … has quite altered the face of affairs."[1]

## ROLE REVERSAL

Safely back at Burlington Heights, Vincent quickly grasped that the British – more through good luck than good management – had gained the upper hand, and if he acted with resolve, the roles of hunter and hunted might be reversed.

Instead of the retreat around the lake to Kingston that his subordinates had been contemplating a few hours earlier – wagons had reportedly been loaded and knapsacks slung[2] – Vincent could now take the offensive. His first move was to forward a strong detachment, likely from the 41st Foot, to reclaim Stoney Creek as an advance outpost. Within a few hours of the American retreat, the Gage farms were back under British control.

News of the American reverse also had a positive effect on the Grand River warriors. On his return to Burlington Heights after the battle, Norton met a band of warriors "who had stopped the night on the Road and were now coming to look for us."[3] Undoubtedly they were the same party William Claus tried to coax into joining the British the night before. Perhaps heartened by the sight of so many American prisoners, they now were keen to join the fray. Charles Askin, a captain in the 2nd Lincoln, reflected the relief of the militia: "An action which took place on the sixth inst., which terminated much in our favour, has quite altered the face of affairs."[4]

In Stoney Creek, settlers from the outlying farms streamed in to see the battlefield. At James Gage's homestead, his daughter Elizabeth "remembered them coming to look at the bullet holes in our house. They carried home with them all they could carry of the blankets and things that the American soldiers had left. Among the stuff taken was a lot of quilts and things belonging to us"[5] Biggar said the ground was strewn with men, horses, guns, swords and baggage and the Methodist church was shattered and riddled with balls.[6]

On his way back to Burlington Heights, Harvey lodged many of his wounded, including Lieutenant Thomas Taylor of the 41st Foot, at the farm of Dr. William Case. Under the supervision of King's surgeon William Hackett, who was himself wounded in the battle, Case, his wife Ruth and some of his older children treated up to 30 of the seriously wounded of both sides. They were also assisted by Marie Archange Scott, the wife of Private John Scott of the 49th's light company. Among the wounded they cared for was Francis Dury, the 49th's colour bearer, who was dying from a musket wound to the head. According to one source, the American surgeon who initially attended Dury also relieved him of his watch and money.[7]

**Case homestead.** An early 20th-century photograph of physician William Case's house on the Queenston road, where many of the wounded from Stoney Creek were treated. The new frame residence would serve as a military hospital until the end of the war. Case, who was born and trained in the United States, was the first doctor to practise in what is now the city of Hamilton. His house was located on the northeast side of King Street at Lottridge Street in east Hamilton. (Local History & Archives, Hamilton Public Library)

Back in Stoney Creek the wounded of both sides had been parcelled out to several houses in the vicinity of the battlefield. James Gage's farmhouse became a makeshift hospital, both his wife and mother employed to gather lint for bandages.[8] The widow Letitia Gage, probably a sister-in-law of James Gage, who lived just west of the battlefield, found her house filled with wounded British soldiers and American prisoners. The day before, Chandler's troops had broken fences and trampled her wheat crop.[9]

At least three wounded officers were taken to William Gage's house at the north end of the battlefield, including Major Alexander Clerk of the 49th. The 34-year-old Scot, who had received his majority two days before, had been dangerously wounded and separated from the British army when it withdrew. The contemporary British historian William James, who spoke with many of the veterans of the battle, said Clerk was found by two stragglers – one British and one American – and carried to a bed in the Gage house. When Chrystie's two regiments arrived from the lakeshore, the wounded Clerk, bed and all, was trundled off in a wagon, the jolting of which nearly caused him to bleed to death. James's account is corroborated by William Gage's loss claim after the war in which

**Surgeon's tools.** Both civilian physician William Case and the surgeon of the 8th Foot, William Hacket, would have employed a similar amputation kit to deal with the shattered limbs of the wounded after the Battle of Stoney Creek. It contains saw, knife, scalpel, forceps and tourniquet and this one was the property of British army surgeon Henry Grasett. (Canadian Museum of Health and Medicine)

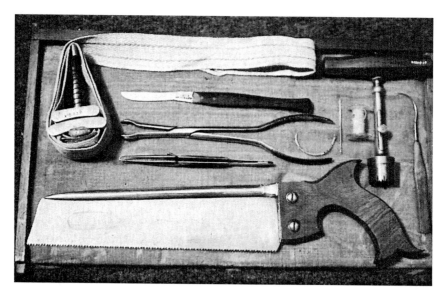

he sought £11 ($44) compensation for three beds, bedding and other furniture taken with the wounded officers after the battle.[10]

The wounded were also sheltered in William Davis's Red Hill tavern and Samuel Nash's house, where army surgeons used the family bedding to make bandages and the blood of the wounded left permanent stains on the floor.[11]

As for the dead, a group of young men that included William Green, Asiel Gage, Peter Gage, John Lee and John Yaeger used William Gage's ox sled to gather the bodies. Lee, a sergeant in the 5th Lincoln, said they collected 61 dead, who were buried in two mass graves, one beside the Methodist church and the other on the knoll where Towson's artillery stood.[12]

Meantime at Burlington Heights Chandler, hobbled by the effects of his tumble during the battle, was seen by a British army surgeon, who prescribed the default modality of 19th century medicine – bloodletting, likely with a six- or twelve-bladed device called a scarificator – after which he was carried to Beasley's wharf on the bay, and along with Winder and the other captured officers, bundled on board a bateau under the charge of Lieutenant Andrew Bulger of the Royal Newfoundland Fencibles. Bulger was anxious about escorting this high-profile cargo across the lake to Kingston lest they meet an American warship. Also on board was Prevost's young ADC, Lieutenant Henry Milnes, bearing Harvey's preliminary report on the action and his own first-hand observations including details of Vincent's embarrassing loss of command. In the short time Harvey was exposed to the captured American generals, Winder impressed him enough that he cautioned Prevost against any early exchange of the Baltimore lawyer: "He possesses more talent than all the rest of the Yankee Generals put together." Within a week the American officers were in Kingston, having eluded a search by the speedy American schooner *Lady of the Lake*, and three days after that in Montreal on their way to Quebec aboard a schooner in the charge of a militia colonel.[13]

Also loaded from Beasley's wharf were the dozens of seriously wounded from the battle. To ease their passage to York, sheaves of wheat where laid in the bottom of the bateaux.[14] While the small flotilla crossed the bay to the shallow inlet that connected with the lake, the Royal Navy squadron that had left Kingston on 3 June with reinforcements and supplies for Burlington Heights continued to struggle against adverse winds. Although still a day's sail from York and totally unaware of the events at Stoney Creek, Sir James Yeo's nine-vessel squadron would soon play a significant role in the final unravelling of Dearborn's 1813 Niagara campaign.

## 34 "The enemy's fleet have an intention on this place."[1]

### PUTTING THE WIND UP DEARBORN

On the morning of 7 June, sentries at Fort Niagara spotted the sails of Yeo's squadron on the lake and alerted Dearborn, bed-bound at Fort George. The ailing commander, who had complained the night before to have "never so severely felt the want of health,"[2] was clearly alarmed. And clearly losing his grip.

Knowing Chauncey would not leave Sackets Harbor until his new frigate was ready, Dearborn assumed the squadron was British and pondered its intent. Was it bound for the Head of the Lake to cover Vincent's retreat? Or was it carrying reinforcements with designs on the lightly garrisoned Fort George? A strong force, he worried, could easily carry Fort Niagara along with its newly erected batteries and then turn those guns on Fort George.[3]

With practically all his troops in the field and no realistic hope of relief from the navy, Dearborn succumbed to the latter scenario and dashed off another order to Morgan Lewis, the general he had so resolutely dispatched the night before with orders to seek and destroy the enemy. A British ship appeared this morning, he wrote, and "you will please to return with the troops to this place as soon as possible."[4] But then after a few hours deliberation he began to doubt his original assumption and wrote again, "It is possible the fleet in sight may be our own; a few hours will probably enable you to determine and act accordingly."[5]

Both orders reached Lewis en route and appear to have been ignored, for his party made excellent time, reaching the Forty late in the afternoon. The reinforcements were greeted with open arms by the veterans of Stoney Creek. Lieutenant Colonel James Miller, at the head of the 400-man Sixth Infantry,

would tell his wife, "I can scarce believe that you would have been more glad to see me than that army was."[6]

Dearborn however, was feeling isolated and increasingly fearful that something calamitous was

**Lieutenant Colonel James Miller, Sixth Infantry (1776-1851).** Despatched by Dearborn as part of the relief column sent to the Forty to reinforce the American army after Stoney Creek, Miller and his 400 troops were accorded a joyous welcome. He would write to his wife, "I can scarce believe that you would have been more glad to see me than that army was." (Essex Institute, Salem, Mass.)

about to occur. During the afternoon, two schooners from Yeo's squadron, probably the 12-gun *Beresford* and the similarly armed *Sir Sydney Smith*, spent at least three hours slowly cruising the shoreline at the mouth of the Niagara River. To the feverish general this was evidence they were seeking a suitable place to land troops. When they rejoined the squadron and sailed off, seemingly towards the Head of the Lake, he concluded an invasion force was being assembled to retake Fort George before the American army could return from the Forty.

Sometime during the evening Dearborn sent an express with his fourth set of directions to Morgan Lewis in 24 hours. There is a unmistakable whiff of panic in the tone:

> I am induced to suspect that the enemy's fleet have an intention on this place.... They may take on board additional troops near the head of the lake, and be here before you reach this place.
>
> You will please to send Milton's detachment and 500 of Chandler's brigade, and Colonel Burn's light dragoons, with all possible dispatch; they ought, if possible, to be here some time tomorrow forenoon. You will follow with the remainder of the troops as soon as practicable. It will be necessary to take care that your boats are not taken or lost.[7]

Endgame. The offensive that just days earlier had been poised to seize the heartland of Upper Canada had just collapsed. In less than 24 hours, the American strategy had lurched from pursuit and defeat of the enemy to flight and avoidance.

When Yeo's squadron moved off to the northwest, it was also seen by Lewis's army at the Forty. On the assumption it was British, he ordered his troops to sleep on their arms. Of course Yeo had no idea what had occurred at Gage's farm and had been merely scouting for any American vessels in the mouth of the Niagara when he sent schooners in to inspect the shoreline, but the timing of their appearance had a further unsettling effect on an American high command already unnerved by the reverse at Stoney Creek. So seriously was the invasion scenario taken that Fort George was kept under arms all night and, at 2 a.m., the alarm was beaten when pickets along the lakeshore opened fire on some approaching vessels. The intruders turned out to be American boats carrying wounded and prisoners from Stoney Creek.[8]

After thoroughly spooking all the American forces in the Niagara Peninsula, Yeo blithely sailed on to anchor off York in the late afternoon or early evening, sending Major Thomas Evans and a subaltern of the 8th Foot ashore, where they learned of the British success at Stoney Creek and the subsequent American withdrawal to Forty Mile Creek. Evans returned to the ship immediately to urge Yeo to harass the American encampment, while the junior officer, Lieutenant Edward Finch, was sent overland to apprise Vincent of the navy's co-operation.[9]

## 35 "We're going back to fetch a bigger army."[1]

### THE CAMPAIGN UNRAVELS, JUNE 7, 1813

Sick and tired. The American army that retreated to the Forty from Stoney Creek was in neither the best of spirits nor the best of health. Winder's brigade had been on the march for six of the previous seven days, Chandler's brigade for four straight days. Before that, most of the men had taken part in two extremely arduous waterborne invasions. The troops had gone days without food and nights without sleep. They had been in combat under the most terrifying circumstances – in darkness so complete that file partners could not find each other and units fired blindly at anything that moved, including their own comrades. Convinced they were under attack by British troops *and* hordes of Indians, many units had broken and fled into the woods.

In the midst of the confusion, the enemy had bagged two brigadier generals and a significant part of the artillery, which, short of regimental colours, constitute the ultimate battle trophies. There was shock and anger: British troops had reached the heart of the American camp before the alarm went up. And in the morning when they realized their losses were relatively small and the British were wide open to counter-attack, their leadership could think only of withdrawal. There was bickering and confusion at the top over who was entitled to command – Burn, the one that got it, did not want it; Chrystie, who coveted command, was denied

Physically, they were tired and many, because of poor food and sanitation, were sick. Typhus fever and diarrhea were particularly prevalent.[2]

Eleven-year-old Daniel Barber, who lived at the Forty with his grandfather, saw "the American army come straggling back along the road, and sorry looking men they were."[3] The young teenager Jacob Cline, who had seen the high-spirited invaders arrive at the Forty a few days earlier, noted the effect the night battle had had on the American troops. Early in the morning, he said, "the stragglers commenced to come in dusty and footsore. News of the defeat had preceded them and women and children laughed and jeered at them as they hurried by. Pretty soon the stream of fugitives got thicker and it was seen that the American army, or what was left of their 2,000 men, were in retreat. All the courage had oozed out of them and no-one wanted to stop till they were safely back in the

United States. I remember speaking to one soldier I knew and asking mischievously: 'I thought you were going to stay in Canada?'

"'We're going back to fetch a bigger army,' he replied."[4]

The Sixteenth's adjutant, Lieutenant Francis Cummins, said the army reached Forty Mile Creek at sunset "worn out with watching, fatigue and hunger."[5]

Joseph Dwight, the sharp-eyed ensign whose regiment had covered the retreat of the army from Stoney Creek, expressed the sentiments of many of his colleagues on political appointees when he confided somewhat bitterly to his diary: "Here we saw the blessed effects of having plough joggers for generals whose greatest merits consists in being warm partisans and supporting administration right or wrong."[6]

At least one regimental officer, however, still had enough brass to publicly beat his chest. The longtime lawyer Joseph Lee Smith addressed the Twenty-Fifth Infantry: "Among your brethren in arms you have acquired a name to which your future deeds will give additional lustre – Your enemies know and fear you – In the battle of this morning you alone withstood the united shock of the opposing army.... Thrice and finally you repulsed far superior numbers at their boasted charge – you stopped the incursion of the enemy and they retreated in confusion – For the brave soldiers of the 25th the savage war whoop and the English bayonet have no terrors."[7]

The position the Americans held at the Forty was the same ground that had impressed Harvey and Norton eight days earlier when Vincent's army occupied it. Between the Mountain, Forty Mile Creek and Lake Ontario, it was – particularly with the 3,500 to 4,000 men Lewis had in his command – virtually unassailable. Moreover, the British had less than half as many troops.

What caused Lewis to abandon such a strong position? It was a string of circumstances which, taken individually, could probably have been safely ignored, but bundled together were enough to derail a campaign that only a few days earlier was positioned to roll up the colony at least as far as Kingston.

## 36 "With all possible despatch."[1]

### FULL CIRCLE

Yeo's squadron set sail from York at first light on 8 June and, guided by the smoke from the American campfires, was by sunrise plainly visible offshore from the mouth of Forty Mile Creek.

Lewis's army was camped on the farm of William Crooks, brother and business partner of James Crooks, whose lakefront property in Newark had been the landing site for the American invasion 12 days earlier. On the east side of their position, two breastworks had been thrown up and along the beach, 19 boats – transport for provisions, camp equipment and baggage – were grounded.[2]

There are several widely diverging accounts of what occurred at the Forty, some of them, as to be expected, transparently partisan, others wildly fanciful. One that originated from a militia officer who almost certainly was not there claims Yeo used the ruse of approaching the shore under American colours and then, hoisting the King's colour, drove the American army off "with a few well directed shots."[3] That no other account from either side mentions the false colours tends to undermine this version's credibility.

Another, from a junior staff officer on the American side, had Yeo's entire fleet driven off by the American artillery fire. A Royal Navy officer claimed the exact opposite occurred, that fire from the squadron demolished earth works, dismounted the guns and drove the enemy into the woods.[4] Judging by the official reports from both sides, what did occur appears to have amounted to little more than a loud shouting match that ended indecisively.

The lake was dead calm, which made it virtually impossible for Yeo to bring the firepower of any of his big vessels to bear. At 6 a.m. he ordered two of his schooners, the 12-gun *Beresford* under veteran commander Francis Spilsbury and the 12-gun *Sir Sydney Smith*, as well as the gun boats, to be towed within range.[5]

In response, Lewis ordered two artillery captains, Nathan

**Royal Navy schooner *Sir Sydney Smith*.** Unable to bring the guns of his larger vessels to bear on the American camp at Forty Mile Creek, Commodore Yeo ordered his gunboats and two schooners, including the *Sir Sydney Smith* to bombard Lewis's army. The 12-gun schooner is shown in a detail of Peter Rindlisbacher's painting, *Engagement at the Genesee*. (Peter Rindlisbacher)

Towson and Samuel Archer, and four 6-pdr. guns to the lakeshore, where a furnace to heat shot was hastily thrown up. Yeo said his schooners and gun boats got in under the artillery and delivered "a sharp and well-directed fire." Lewis reported it was "returned with vivacity and effect," although there appears to have been no damage inflicted on either side, at least not materially.[6]

Thirty-five miles away an American officer stationed at Fort George wondered as the thunder of the artillery exchange rolled down the lake. "It must either proceed from the army or the enemy's squadron," he wrote, adding the vain hope "may the result retrieve what we lost on the 27th ult., when we ought to have slain or taken the very troops that have since given us so much trouble."[7]

The next act, in what was beginning to take on some elements of a comic opera, was set in motion by John Norton shortly after the action at Stoney Creek.

**Royal Navy schooner *Beresford*.** On the morning of 8 June, with the Royal Navy squadron becalmed off the American camp at Forty Mile Creek, the 12-gun *Beresford* under Commander Francis Spilsbury was one of the few vessels able to engage the American artillery in what was essentially a loud but indecisive shouting match. The *Beresford*, which began the war in the Provincial Marine as the *Prince Regent*, is shown here in a 1913 watercolour by Owen Staples. (Toronto Reference Library)

Meeting the Grand River warriors who had refused to commit to the British side before the battle, Norton proposed tracking the American retreat from the escarpment, from where the warriors could safely harass them with hit-and-run tactics. The plan was approved, but just before departure some of the Mohawks made their participation conditional on having British regulars accompany the party. Norton, perhaps sensing some treachery afoot, rejected the condition and appealed to their sense of honour, "that we should now attempt something alone, as in the last two Battles we had aided our father's Troops with very few Warriors indeed."[8]

While the council debate dragged on, Norton forwarded a small reconnaissance party of 12 Onondagas and Senecas to track the movements of the American army at the Forty.

With Yeo's squadron threatening the American encampment from the lake, a few miles east of the Forty Norton's warriors ambushed a small party of Second Dragoons under Captain Joseph Selden on the Queenston road, killing one and capturing another. The dead man was Trooper Charles J. Elliott, a 32-year-old former clerk from Northumberland County, Pennsylvania.

The main road blocked, the dragoons took to a second trail that cut across the side of the escarpment with the Indians in pursuit. The horsemen safely gained their camp and the warriors halted on a rock face that overlooked Robert Nelles's store. Venting their frustration at the escape of their quarry, they opened fire on a column of troops passing below them, wounding at least two.[9]

Captain Mordecai Myers of the Thirteenth Infantry was ordered to take a detachment and cut off the warriors' retreat but, before he could reach them, the regiment's adjutant, Lieutenant Joseph Eldridge, gathered a small group and took the direct route, "scrambling up the precipice with the agility of so many goats," and dispersing the warriors, who "scattered into the ravine along side like so many antelopes."[10] Although the timing of these two events was entirely coincidental, to American eyes it gave the illusion of a planned operation. Certainly Yeo was astute enough to take advantage of the situation and present Lewis with an impudent proposal – we've got you surrounded, give up.[11]

"An officer with a flag was sent to me from his ship," Lewis said, "advising me that as I was invested with savages in my rear, a fleet in my front and powerful army in my flank, he and the officers commanding His Britannic Majesty's land forces thought it their duty to demand a surrender of my army. I answered that the message was too ridiculous to merit a reply."[12]

After having withstood a naval bombardment, driven off an Indian war party and rejected Yeo's ultimatum, Lewis was then handed the express that had just arrived from Dearborn ordering him to abandon the offensive and rush the army back to Fort George.[13] It was an amazing turn of events. The commander who had been dispatched with orders to make every possible effort to prevent the enemy's escape less than 36 hours earlier was now tasked with managing his own escape.

Lewis's report to the secretary of war suggests a prompt and orderly departure from the Forty in compliance with orders – boats and wagons were loaded and 200 troops were detailed to protect the boats: "At 10 I put our army in motion on our return to this place."[14] The facts and the accounts of others, however, suggest something much closer to a state of panic.

While Lewis was getting his army in motion, Yeo and three ships of his squadron carrying five companies of the King's, about 220 men under Major Thomas Evans, sailed up to the Head of the Lake to deliver the reinforcements to Vincent. Before they had disembarked, a messenger arrived with news of the American retreat. Vincent, prodded by Harvey, immediately dispatched Yeo, Evans and the King's reinforcements back to the Forty just after 4:30 in the afternoon.[15]

Aided by a favourable breeze, the Royal Navy had Evans and his men landed on the beach at the mouth of Forty Mile Creek by 7:30 in the evening. What Evans found was a ghost camp – 500 tents, 200 camp kettles, 150 stands of arms and immense heaps of burned baggage.[16] "The enemy's flight and terror," he reported to Harvey, "is best evidenced by the precipitate manner in which he abandoned everything which was valuable or could be called to constitute his equipment for field operations."[17]

And, while Yeo had sailed west toward Burlington Heights with part of his squadron to deliver the companies of the King's, the *Beresford* and other light vessels had pursued and overtaken Lewis's train of boats, whereupon the crews ran them aground and fled. The supply vessels were easy picking for the navy because they had no infantry on board for protection. Twenty large bateaux containing hospital stores, provisions and baggage were captured by the British.[18]

Lewis, despite the specific caution from Dearborn about protecting the boats, was at a loss to explain what happened to the Sixth Infantry which he had detailed as an escort. His befuddled non-explanation rivals Dearborn's strange fatality defence: "By some irregularity, which I have not been able to discover, the boats put off without the detachments."[19]

Shortly after Evans's force landed at the Forty, a second British detachment, numbering about 230 men from the 41st and 49th, arrived overland under Major James Dennis, who was still serviceable despite two musket wounds from Stoney Creek.

Forty-eight hours after Vincent had been prepared to abandon Burlington Heights and retreat at least as far as Kingston, his army could not move fast enough to keep up with the Americans as they abandoned the Niagara Peninsula. Although the action at Stoney Creek was essentially a tactical standoff, the accumulated effects of the action itself, the loss of leadership and the timely arrival of the Royal Navy were rapidly turning it into a strategic victory for the British.

"The change operated in the minds of men, as well as on our real situation & the Character of the Campaign by this victory was astonishing," Harvey wrote. "Those who had desponded, all became elated – The Militia came forward not with congratulations only but real service. The Indians were no longer backward … but perhaps the most important result was that produced on the Morale of the enemy's Troops."[20] As word of their rapid withdrawal spread through the peninsula, the militia and the native warriors turned out in force.[21]

Native support of the British cause was no longer conditional. "All then moved on with great alacrity," Norton said, "no exhortations were wanting, no Council retarded their advance." Norton's warriors were quick to flush out the troops that had fled into the woods after abandoning the grounded transport boats. The revitalized militia likewise required little in the way of encouragement. Jonathan Petit and Henry Hixon, both officers in the 4th Lincoln, were active in rounding up stragglers after the American army left the Forty. The two militia officers sent 40 prisoners out to the Royal Navy schooners standing offshore. Even militia who had been paroled by the Americans took up arms again to harass the retreating army[22]

Among the prisoners taken was infantryman Samuel Boyd, a 52-year-old cordwainer from Virginia. Disabled by a shoulder wound at Frenchman's Creek in November 1812, Boyd had been on escort duty in the transport boats when they were run aground by Yeo's squadron.[23] Also captured was Ebenezer Knowlton, a 39-year-old private in the Ninth Infantry from Rhode Island, who was shot in the left knee on the retreat from Forty Mile Creek.[24]

Lewis may have had a well deserved reputation for the size of his baggage train and the slowness of his progress while on campaign, but there was nothing tardy about his departure from the Forty on 8 June. Unencumbered by baggage, the 59-year-old major general positively raced down the muddy peninsula, covering some 23 miles before stopping for the night at Twelve Mile Creek. One of his young staff officers attached to the rear guard compared Lewis's 4,000-strong column to a stream "that was sweeping everything back to Fort George."[25]

As the sun set behind him, he watched the head of the column descend into one of the deep ravines that can still be found on the old Queenston road, "at the bottom of which was one of those muddy streams, which, deprived of its bridge, had been so trampled and trenched of late, as to have become a seemingly bottomless pit of mire."[26]

The troops picked their way through the mud, but the guns, which were interspersed throughout the column, immediately bogged down. "Each one endeavored to avoid the rock on which its predecessor had split, by turning a little farther to the right or to the left; but it was all in vain, and they were soon most of them formed from column into line, sunk to the hubs of the wheels and about as immovable as the trees among which they were entangled."[27] After the infantry had all passed through the ravine, the artillery drivers consolidated their horsepower by hitching four and even five teams to a single gun.

It was well after midnight before the rearguard reached the tavern, quite likely Paul Shipman's, where headquarters had been set up, and slept a few hours on the floor before setting out again. "The enemy had thus far not presumed to tread on our heels," the officer wrote. "Had only a small part of his main body pounced on the rear guard and the artillery when the latter had been left in the lurch of the ravine, we should probably have abandoned the pieces to his care, and returned home much lighter than we came. But, luckily, neither Indians nor detachments from the main body took it into their heads to trouble us."[28] Likely the young staff officer never knew just how close to being realized his fears were.

Right behind Lewis's fleeing army was Norton's war party, now grown to a respectable force of at least 200 warriors. "About 10 o'clock in the morning, we came to a deep hollow, through which ran a small stream, – here we found that the heavy Artillery of the Enemy had remained the previous night," Norton said. "A mile & a half further on, the Main Body had encamped."[29]

Norton was told a 300-man detachment was returning to collect stragglers and boat crew – most of whom had already been bagged by Indians or militia. An ambush was set but the detachment never returned.

Lewis's single-minded obsession with reaching Fort George as soon as possible and his lack of concern for the wounded and stragglers angered at least one senior officer. Lieutenant Colonel George McFeely of the Twenty-Second Infantry wrote: "The consequence was that the Indians followed closely in the rear of our victorious but retreating division and killed and made prisoners of all the wounded and sick that fell in the rear of our division. The retreat was badly conducted and General Lewis ought to have been cashiered for it, for not protecting his wounded and sick; they ought to have been sent in front or a strong regiment to have protected and covered our rear."[30]

Captain John Thornton of the Twentieth Infantry said the troops were on the edge of exhaustion: "On this retreat the men were so much fatigued that whenever a halt was made they dropped down for rest in the ranks."[31] On reaching the security of Fort George, Thornton set a sheet of paper on his shako and catalogued the hard service of the campaign: "We have endured every hardship and privation, the officers in common with the soldiers. We have borne hunger, thirst and loss of sleep, we have endured the extremity of cold and heat and have frequently laid upon the wet ground in the open air and sometimes in rain, to seek the necessary repose."[32]

And it was not just the stragglers and the artillery that were at risk of capture. A case can be made that the entire division was vulnerable as it hastened back to Fort George. Charles Askin, a captain in the 2nd Lincoln, thought the British squandered a grand opportunity: "It's the opinion of those who saw them on their retreat that the whole of the army … would have surrendered but we lost this fine opportunity of getting rid of them."[33]

With the capture of their transport fleet by the British, the Americans lost not only baggage but food and ammunition. Arms, tents, cooking utensils and more provisions had been abandoned on the ground at the Forty. For Chandler's division, provision supply had been intermittent for several days and ammunition severely depleted at Stoney Creek. Amasiah Ford, a 17-year-old private in the Twenty-Third Infantry, said the troops that left Forty Mile Creek "were out of provisions & had but very little ammunition to defend ourselves with."[34]

Lieutenant Jonathan Kearsley, the adjutant of the advance, which formed the rearguard on the retreat, summed up their predicament: "The American army, then in the enemy's country and without provisions or military munitions, must necessarily fall without a struggle into the hands of the British. A precipitate retreat was therefore made to Fort George."[35]

Precipitate yes, and circumspect as well. So wary was Lewis of the Royal Navy springing any more surprises on him that, instead of the direct route from Twelve Mile Creek to Newark via the Swamp road, which edged toward the lakeshore, he chose instead the longer but safer inland route through Queenston.[36]

Casualty returns, as Clausewitz observed, "are never exact, seldom truthful, and in most cases, full of intentional misrepresentations."[37] Certainly the American returns for the action at Stoney Creek met that standard. Although precise figures will likely never be known, the record shows American losses were considerably higher than anyone in command was willing to acknowledge. Chandler, the division commander, insisted less than 30 men were killed and wounded even though one of his unit commanders would report his regiment alone counted 45 killed and wounded. As for the retreat from the Forty, where the casualties were almost exclusively prisoners taken, there has never been any official accounting. The American Baptist preacher and writer Michael Smith said the retreating army "lost a considerable number, being taken prisoners by the Indians and militia, who hung on the skirts of the army, nearly throughout the march." Lewis himself would acknowledge only the loss of "a few stragglers." Contemporary newspaper accounts of the aggregate loss for the whole offensive – usually from American officers – range from trifling to catastrophic. The *Albany Gazette* said, "The residue of the American army effected a retreat to Fort George – having lost in the different engagement 1000 men in killed, wounded and prisoners."[38]

*Niles' Weekly Register*, one of the most authoritative American newspapers of its time and a detailed chronicler of the war, reflected the conflicting nature of reports on the Niagara offensive: "We have a strange confusion of accounts from Fort George; and are completely foiled in all attempts to extract truth from the chaos of rumors. We therefore, prefer to let them rest pretty much as they are till better informed of events that have a singular aspect."[39]

Other papers, such as the Georgetown *Federal Republican*, saw a deceitful method in the government's selective release of war information. Its fiery editor, Alexander Contee Hanson, wrote: "Petty successes were borne on eagle's wings, while snails were constituted the heralds of our evil tidings…. No success too small to be embalmed; no disgrace too great to be buried alive and kicking…. Every man who dies for his country has a just claim to be remembered. Instead of concealing, as is too much the case, the time, place and manner of the death of every soldier, it ought to be the enjoined duty of every commanding officer to state as far as he can discover, the particulars of every soldier's death, and such statements should be transmitted to the war department, there to be registered in justice to the memory of the man who has died for his country, in testimony of her love, for the consolation of his friends."[40]

Echoes of that chaos endure. There are still no absolute casualty figures for the Winder/Chandler/Lewis sortie into the Niagara Peninsula. Cruikshank put the American losses in the battle and the retreat at "nearly 500," which may be somewhat high. Captain Mordecai Myers of the Thirteenth Infantry put the loss at 300.[41]

According to British prisoner returns from Stoney Creek and the retreat, a total of 205 Americans were taken prisoner.[42] American casualty returns admit to 55 killed and wounded at Stoney Creek, which makes an aggregate loss of 260. Based on considerable evidence that official casualty returns for the battle are inaccurate and incomplete, and that none exist for the retreat, the true figure must be at least 350.

In the late afternoon of the 9 June, less than two weeks after the Niagara campaign had opened in a burst of glory and high hope with the routing of Vincent's army, and one week after two brigades were dispatched to finish him off, the remnants of the American army, demoralized, sick, hungry and bordering on panic, scuttled back inside Fort George and barred the gate.

The previous night, Fort Erie had been evacuated and burned, positions at Chippawa and Queenston abandoned, and an evacuation flotilla of boats stood ready to cross the Niagara River. Clearly, the ripple of alarm that had dogged Lewis's division had reached the highest level of command. "Preparations were making for a retreat from Newark," the *Albany Gazette* reported, "boats being stationed along the east bank of the river. Great consternation prevailed at that place. Colonel Proctor and forces had joined gen. Vincent and ... it is said, [are] within 20 miles of Fort George."[43]

The young staff officer who accompanied Lewis to and from the Forty, and chronicled it like a holiday outing, reflected on the army's good fortune in regaining the security of Fort George relatively intact: "On the whole, reasoning like the man who having broken his leg, consoled himself with the belief that it would have been worse if his neck had suffered ... we had lost only two generals when we might have lost two brigades into the bargain."[44]

Mordecai Myers, who had been with Winder in the original brigade sent out to corral Vincent, summed up the failed promise of the Niagara offensive: "We arrived at Fort George having gained no laurels and having lost nearly three hundred. We were now on the defensive."[45]

The anonymous junior staffling took it a step further: "Had a map of the United States been published on or about the first of June, it would have exhibited quite a respectable addendum to our territory. But the expansion proved to be only a bubble on the frontiers of New York, which burst after a few weeks inflation."[4]

# **37** "More contradictory statements we have never seen."[1]

### THE FIRST CASUALTY

The first public notice of Stoney Creek was probably the terse summary of events compiled by the postmaster at Niagara on 9 June and forwarded to his counterparts to the south in Buffalo and to the east in Sackets Harbor, Canandaigua, Geneva and Albany.

Cue the spin.

Information just received states that our army at the head of the lake have been surprised in their camp – Generals Winder and Chandler, Capt. Jones, quarter-master Vandeventer and 150 men were taken prisoner and 4 pieces of artillery lost. The enemy were however repulsed, Gen. Vincent (their commander) killed in our camp, one gun retaken, 60 prisoners and a great many killed.[2]

In the absence of any information from the army, that report, relatively accurate as it is, sparked a media firestorm over the following weeks. Fuelled by rumour, false reports and misinterpretation, the press presented a chaotic mosaic of claim and counter-claim that veered from total defeat to outright victory.

The *Plattsburgh Republican* declared that in addition to regulars and militia, the British raiders also had "a powerful body of Indians under chief Norton." The *New York Evening Post* upped the ante, reporting that Vincent had been reinforced by Brigadier General Henry Procter, all the way from Amherstburg with his force *and* 1,000 Indians.[3]

---

## BY THE MAIL.

### Particulars of the Defeat of the Grand Army.

BLOOMFIELD, JUNE 15.

*Messrs. Websters & Skinners,*

THE following detail of the events of the war on our Western frontier, is collected from numerous and authentic sources, and will be found in the main to be correct.

It will be remembered that the American forces, supposed to consist of 6 or 7000 men, under Gen Dearborn, made a landing at Newark, on Tuesday morning, the 27th of May; the British, after a short contest, retreating to 40 mile creek, about 35 miles distant from Fort George, and that the next day, Col. Preston, with a small body of men, entered Fort Erie, without resistance. The British had destroyed or removed all the publick property at that post, and on their whole line on the river—except a small quantity of flour, which fell into our hands

---

## BY MAIL.

### BAD NEWS FROM THE ARMY.
ALBANY, June 19.
BY THE STEAM BOAT.

On Tuesday morning at an early hour the British fleet made their appearance off the 20 mile creek, where the American army then lay, and demanded by a flag its immediate surrender. Gen. Lewis received and treated this demand with great indignation. An attack was then made upon the American boats, all of which escaped excepting nine, containing baggage of the officers, &c., the rescue of which was prevented by the British landing a force to protect them.

After the rencontre the residue of the American army effected a retreat to Fort George—having lost in the different engagements 1000 men, in killed, wounded and prisoners. They reached Fort George on Thursday last. We are further informed that on Saturday evening preparations were making for a retreat from Newark, boats being stationed along the east bank of the river. Great consternation pervaded that place. Col. Proctor and forces had joined Gen. Vincent, and were on Friday, it is said within 20 miles of Fort George.

[Merc. Adv.

**The press was not good.** As details of the action at Stoney Creek began to leak out, American newspapers were quick to pass on the bad news, as the headlines from the *Boston Daily Advertiser* and the *Gleaner* in Wilkes-Barre indicate. (American Antiquarian Society)

The *Geneva Gazette* reported Chandler and Winder were captured sleeping in James Gage's farmhouse. The *Boston Patriot* improved the story by putting Procter "at the head of the British forces; and that the enemy rushed into the Generals' house and carried them off, before they could be protected."[4]

Then the *Albany Argus*, citing a "respectable gentleman," retracted earlier reports and announced "the news of Gens. Winder and Chandler being prisoners to the enemy was no longer credited."[5]

In reporting on the action itself some unlikely recipients were credited with gallantry. The *Geneva Gazette* said one of the captured guns was recovered by "the bravery of capt. L. Leonard of the light artillery who made a charge into the thickest of the enemy, sword in hand, his men on foot." When the British retreated, "our dragoons gave them hot chase, and took 60 prisoners."[6]

Several newspapers reported that Vincent had been killed during the battle but credit must go to two New York papers for creatively elevating the story to an entirely new level. The *New York Evening Post*, citing Dearborn's assistant deputy quarter master general, Captain Thomas P. Baldwin, reported that orders found on Vincent's body directed his troops to embark at a certain place and make their way to Kingston. An express was immediately sent to Major General Morgan Lewis, who intercepted their embarkation, rescued Chandler and Winder and captured 1,500 British regulars. Earlier the New York *War* had reported Lewis was transported across the lake to York to get ahead of the retreating British while Chandler's division pursued them from behind "and being thus placed between two fires, it was confidently expected he would be compelled to surrender."[7]

By the third week in June there was virtually no coherence whatsoever left in the story line. In Boston the *Weekly Messenger* surveyed the dissonance and offered readers a gentle caveat: "In these accounts there are slight contradictions and possibly there may be little truth in them."[8]

In Albany the editors of the *Argus* lamented the dearth of factual information: "The Western Mail of last evening has furnished nothing to relieve the public mind from the anxious solicitude which has been excited by the thousand rumors which have been afloat during the current week."[9]

And in New York, the *Columbian* was contrite: "We are sorry to be obliged to leave our readers at a loss to form possible conclusions on the relation of events. More contradictory statements we have never seen … one says the Americans were *attacked in open day on their march*; another says they were *surprised at night in camp*. And the further we proceed in the narrative the more difficulty we meet with."[10]

## 38 "That approval which valor and discipline must ever receive."[1]

### ROYAL APPROBATION

The collapse of the American offensive left a vacuum in the Niagara Peninsula which the British quickly recognized and moved to fill. By the time the rearguard of Lewis's army reached Fort George on 9 June, forward elements of the British army were only a few miles behind. Vincent himself was sufficiently emboldened to move his headquarters to the Forty along with the main part of his army. The DeCew house at Beaver Dams was reoccupied and restocked as a supply depot, a strong advance post was established at the Twenty and the militia reoccupied Queenston. With a promised reinforcement of regular troops on its way from Kingston as well as more Indian warriors from the west and Lower Canada, Vincent felt comfortable enough to finally heed Procter's call for aid and sent a 100-strong detachment of the 41st to Amherstburg.

The strategy was driven by Harvey – maximize the presence of the Royal Navy, exploit the skidding morale of American troops, deny the enemy access to any provisions from the land and "leave him only the ground on which he stood." It represented an extraordinary change in fortune for an army that, only two weeks before, was on the run after narrowly avoiding the sort of crushing defeat that could have heralded the end of British rule in Upper Canada. As the realization dawned that Harvey's brash sortie, while attended by considerable losses, had landed a telling blow on the American army, a sense of euphoria took hold that stretched from the local command all the way to the Prince Regent in London. The one notable exception was the 49th subaltern James FitzGibbon, whose account of the battle in a private letter is likely the most accurate and evenhanded account written from either side.[2]

> This business was, I think, very ill executed by us, and the great error was shouting before the line was formed for the attack. Had we maintained silence and not fired I believe we should have taken and destroyed four-fifths of the Americans and with them all their guns – 7 in number. The instant I heard their shout I considered our affair ruined, and after circumstances confirmed this opinion.[3]

Regardless, ill-executed or not, the end result was an immense morale boost in the ranks. Norton wrote of "the Soldiers exulting with patriotic Joy at having retaliated on the Enemy the affair of Fort George." The militia, which only days before had been dismissed in what was considered a prelude to the abandonment of the whole upper province, was elated. Captain Charles Askin of the 2nd Lincoln said Stoney Creek "put us all in high spirits again." On the other side, the Americans complained that the militia "have lost confidence in us, and are joining the enemy in great numbers." Vincent's brigade major, Captain John Glegg, wrote in a private letter that "a wonderful change has taken place in our prospects since the nocturnal visit to the enemy's encampment at Stoney Creek … we are all well and in the highest spirits."

Still hardheaded but notably less censorious than FitzGibbon is Harvey's report on the action, which reflected the experience of a veteran officer adept at massaging facts to maximum benefit. Harvey acknowledged serious losses and the initial breach of discipline but noted the artillery was gallantly carried, the troops firm under fire and, most importantly, the end result a "complete and brilliant success."[4]

Vincent, who missed most of the action, nevertheless pronounced a totally *veni vidi vici* operation in which the "enemy was completely surprised and driven from his camp." Declaring himself "at a loss for language" in his District General Orders, the brigadier still managed to find nearly 400 words "to do justice to the distinguished bravery and good conduct of the troops."[5]

Betraying the relief of a man who just dodged a rather large round shot, Vincent sounds almost giddy promising Prevost he will hold Burlington Heights even "if their whole force of twelve thousand is brought against me." And a week later, with the news of a large Indian reinforcement on its way, he was positively cocky: "I make bold to say, one thousand men more added to this army will drive every part of the enemy out of this country."[6]

And if Vincent's relief was manifest, it was no less so than Prevost's, whose adjutant general could not resist punching up the results – an American army of more than 4,000 "completely defeated and dispersed … the British loss has been very slight."[7]

The governor-general ordered a 21-gun salute be fired from the bastions at Kingston "in celebration of the splendid achievement," and three days later, after detailing "the rout and complete dispersion … the capture of their artillery and of their ablest generals … their subsequent flight with the loss of the whole of their baggage, provisions and tent equipage," urged residents of Niagara to remain loyal to their King. In apparent response, a group of prominent York citizens publicly thanked Vincent for "an achievement history must select as one worthy of her page."[8]

On the same day Prevost would dispatch his ADC, and Stoney Creek eyewitness, Captain Robert McDouall with "the particulars of a feat of distinguished valour and enterprise achieved near Burlington Bay" for delivery to the secretary of war, Lord Bathurst, in London.[9]

Although the Duke of Wellington's Spanish campaign dominated the English press, Prevost's and Vincent's reports on the action at Stoney Creek both appeared in *The Times* in late July along with a fulsome tribute to "the zeal, enterprise and intrepidity of His Majesty's forces on this station." Two weeks later, Lord Bathurst instructed Prevost to convey "His Royal Highness's approbation of the enterprising spirit and professional ability displayed by Lt.-Col Harvey in suggesting and Br. Gen'l Vincent in making the attack on the advance of the American army."[10]

At the same time the Duke of York himself wrote to Prevost, bestowing the royal gratitude on Vincent and his troops: "The judgment and talent evinced by the conception of that gallant enterprise, and the glorious conduct of the troops in carrying it into execution against a greatly superior force, are too conspicuous to fail of meeting with that approval which valor and discipline must ever receive."[11] The royal pat on the head.

Lost in the congratulatory swirl was a grand opportunity to take advantage of the American reverses. A week after Stoney Creek, Vincent, arguing that the Americans were sick and demoralized, urged Prevost to authorize an immediate assault on Fort George: "I am determined, if Sir James Yeo thinks he can cooperate with us, to push on and retake Fort George."[12]

Prevost, having reverted to the defensive form that characterized his war strategy, quickly vetoed the plan: "Although I approve the energy and applaud the valour which has been so conspicuous … I cannot allow you to dissipate your force uselessly."[13] Vincent, whose proposal for a pre-emptive assault on Fort Niagara in April had been rejected,[14] could be forgiven if he privately cursed Prevost's safety-first approach to war for once again stifling his initiative.

Stoney Creek, a significant triumph in its own right, could have been much more had only John Harvey's tactical daring been applied at the strategic level.

**The grand old Duke of York, Frederick Augustus Hanover (1763-1827).** News of the army's good showing at Stoney Creek prompted the Commander in Chief of His Majesty's Forces to laud "that gallant enterprise and the glorious conduct of the troops in carrying it into execution against a greatly superior force."

# 39 "Poor victims to fear."[1]

### DESERTERS AND PRISONERS

Among the more than 200 American prisoners taken at Stoney Creek and on the subsequent retreat to Fort George none were more hapless than James Gready and Thomas Hunt. For most of the prisoners, capture meant a year or so in confinement until they were exchanged or the war ended. For Gready and Hunt, capture meant death. Within a month of the battle, both had been executed by firing squad, for they had committed the most serious crime possible under the military code – they had deserted their units and then taken up arms with the enemy.

Hunt, who was a gunner in Luther Leonard's Company of the Light Artillery, was taken at the Gage farm along with at least ten other members of the same company. At Burlington Heights, a sergeant of the 41st recognized Hunt among the prisoners and told the brigade major he was prepared to swear the man was a deserter. Little is known about Hunt beyond his enlistment in the army sometime before 1799 and his desertion in July 1803, while his unit, the 6th Foot, was garrisoning St. Jean in Lower Canada. Presumably he fled to the United States, where he lived until war was declared and then enlisted in the American artillery.[2]

The second deserter, James Gready, a private in the 8th, had deserted while his regiment was stationed at Prescott on 23 March 1813. Likely he crossed the St. Lawrence to New York, where he joined the American army. Gready was arraigned before a General Court Martial on 22 June at Forty Mile Creek, convicted and sentenced to death. In the General Order announcing the sentence, troops were cautioned to heed "the awful consequences which, under the present circumstances of the country, must inevitably await the crime of desertion, more particularly desertion to the enemy."[3]

Although the verdict was clear and the sentence appropriate to the crime, Vincent nevertheless lobbied vigorously to have Gready spared "in consequence of the high character of the King's Regiment to which the unfortunate man belongs, and in which corps instances of desertion have so seldom happened since their arrival in this province."[4] Aware of the heavy losses the King's had sustained at Stoney Creek, Sackets Harbor, Fort George and York, Vincent was clearly concerned about the effect an execution would have on unit morale.

His entreaty was in vain for Major General Francis de Rottenburg, newly appointed military and civil commander of Upper Canada, was determined to make an example. On 9 July, James Gready was executed by firing squad in the British camp on Twelve Mile Creek. While in custody he was placed back on the army payroll and earned 11 shillings ($2.20), which was applied to his accumulated debt. He died owing the Crown £1 12s 7½d ($6.52).[5]

There appears to have been no appeal made on Hunt's behalf. In the general order announcing his conviction and sentence the troops were reminded there was no statute of limitations on desertion. Hunt had deserted ten years before his capture, which was doubtless the reason for the admonition: "No length of residence or service in a foreign country can absolve them from their allegiance to the King or secure them from the just punishment which sooner or later must attend their desertion of his cause."[6]

Prevost decreed Hunt's execution in Kingston "be conducted in the presence of the garrison under arms with all that awful solemnity which the occasion calls for."[7] At dawn on 1 July the Kingston garrison – 89th Foot, Canadian Voltigeurs, Glengarry Light Infantry, de Watteville's Regiment and Royal Artillery – formed in front of the number 3 blockhouse in open column of sections to witness six privates from de Watteville's carry out the sentence.

Ten months later, Captain Daniel McFarland of the Twenty-Second, a veteran of Stoney Creek, would witness a similar scene at Sackets Harbor: "This day saw two soldiers executed by shooting, the sight was truly affecting and horrible. They kneeled down without hesitation and rec'd the fatal volley with apparent resignation. Poor victims to fear, to [prefer] security in Desertion to War. How unfortunate your end, how distressing to friends, how dishonourable to your country."[8]

For the rest of the rank and file captured at Stoney Creek, life, albeit diminished, would go on for most, while others would perish in prison ships at Quebec, on Melville Island at Halifax or in the dark confines of Dartmoor Prison in England. The soldiers captured ranged in age from 16 to 52, and the civilians included at least two black servants and a boy of 10. From Burlington Heights, escorted by a detachment from the 41st, they were sent by bateaux to York and then on to Kingston by foot. At Gananoque the 41st was relieved by a detachment from the 89th Foot and the prisoners were transported on the St. Lawrence River to Lachine and on to Montreal by foot, where they boarded John Molson's steamboat for the final leg to Quebec.[9]

One prisoner who covered the same route a few weeks later said that, apart from the wormy bread and bad pork diet, he was "treated as well by the enemy as we could expect." Ned Myers, however, the celebrated American sailor, spent three weeks in a York jail and was not impressed. "Our treatment was every way bad," he reported, "as to food … the bread was bad and the pork little better." Pliny Story, the young rifleman captured at the Methodist church, complained that he was stripped of his clothing by Indians.[10]

On reaching Quebec, Myers, like most of the enlisted men, was lodged in a prison ship anchored off shore: "Our provisions were very bad, and the mortality among us was great." While the officers were lodged ashore in relative freedom and comfort in the nearby village of Beauport, the other ranks lived and died in squalid hulks, old merchant ships and naval vessels that were converted into floating prisons. Most of the Stoney Creek prisoners were confined in the troop ship *Hydra* and the aged store ship *Malabar*, which were likely an improvement on most prison hulks as they were still active vessels.

Because of overcrowding, disease was always a concern on prison ships and *Hydra* and *Malabar* were no exception. John Chandler, after one of his weekly visits to the ships, wrote the ranking military officer in Quebec, "so alarming is the sickness getting on board that I cannot avoid saying to you how desirable it is that the prisoners should be got on shore ... should they be kept on board I fear but few will survive by November. With respect to clothing many of the prisoners are quite destitute." Little survives in the way of prison narratives but British prisoner of war records illustrate the harsh realities of prison hulk confinement.[11]

John DeFriend, a 30-year-old from Pennsylvania who signed up in Milliken's Company of the Twenty-Second Infantry, died less than three weeks after arriving in Quebec. Forty-five-year-old Rhode Islander Caleb Wells, probably one of Lyttle's volunteer riflemen, lasted four weeks. Thomas Girton, 28, from Salem, New Jersey, and likely also one of Lyttle's company, lasted seven weeks. Samuel Luckey, a private in the Twenty-Third Infantry, died in September, eight months after enlisting in the army. German-born Charles Stocker, captured when the British swept over Hindman's artillery company on William Gage's lane, lasted until October. He was 36. The sick returns for one week in August 1813 report 89 men in hospital, dying at the rate of nearly one a day. One third had fevers, mostly from typhus, another third had dysentery or diarrhea, and the rest influenza, pneumonia, consumption, sore throat and lesser ailments.[12]

In October many of the remaining Stoney Creek prisoners were loaded on the *Malabar* and shipped to Halifax, where the majority were confined at the British military prison on Melville Island while some, usually the Irish-born, who were considered British subjects, were sent on to England.[13]

Infantryman Bernard Hoy, a native of Sligo who emigrated to New York, was captured when Mills's company of the Twenty-Third Regiment was overrun in the opening phase of the battle. The 27-year-old was transported to England, where he was confined in three different prisons – Spithead, Gravesend and Chatham – and "suffered great hardships"[14] before returning to the United States at the end of 1814.

Thomas Sturtevant, a sergeant in the Twenty-Fifth who was captured at Stoney

Creek, said his Melville Island captivity was "a thralldom worse than Egypt for bondage." On his release he described the appearance of the exchanged prisoners who arrived with him in Salem, Massachusetts, in February 1814: "Had you seen us, you would have said, surely bedlam had broken loose. Nothing but dirty rags covered us, excepting immeasurable multitudes of the plagues of Egypt who formed and display'd columns about our ranks and marched over our backs in eschelon like an army with banners!"[15]

For the 60 British prisoners brought to Fort Niagara two days after Stoney Creek, conditions in American prison camps would be equally grim. John Stewart, a private in Glegg's company of the 49th, said rations were short on the 300-mile trek to the prisoner depot at Greenbush, near Albany: "In consequence of the want of their usual allowance of Food, many of the Prisoners became so weak as to be unable to perform the journey of each day, from 25 to 30 Miles, and in their falling behind were Bayonetted by the Escort."[16] As they passed through Albany, a witness reported, "their situation was deplorable, many of them being without shoes, and barely sufficient clothes to cover them."[17]

At Greenbush, Stewart said prisoners were kept in barracks that were locked each night before dark, "and were not permitted to go out to relieve the Calls of Nature, and if any attempted to make water at a window they were immediately fired at by the Sentinels; on one of these occasions Patterson of the Glengarry Regiment was shot through both knees after he had shut the window. On the same night that Patterson was wounded, several other Shots were fired into the rooms and two Men of the Light Company of the 8th Regiment, who were lying on a Table, narrowly escaped being killed … very frequently the Sentinels were in the habit of indulging themselves in that amusement."[18]

Thomas Delaney, also of the 49th, witnessed an American officer, Lieutenant Colonel Guilford Dudley Young, strike a prisoner in the head with his sword causing a 4½-inch wound that had to be dressed by a surgeon. Delaney further said another prisoner, an epileptic who missed Roll Call because of a fit, was also abused: "An officer went to the room in search of him, dragged him from the Bed and cut him on the head with his sword in a most shocking manner, he was afterward sent to the Provost, another Prison where he remained three days.[19]

## 40  "Canada will not be conquered this year."[1]

### AFTERMATH

Although American battle casualties were relatively low during the 1813 Niagara campaign, losses due to sickness and disease were not. Ill health took many more men out of action than British arms. A cold, wet spring, poor food, bad sanitation and lack of shelter combined to produce an epidemic of typhus fever and diarrhea. The army that returned from Stoney Creek contained hundreds of sick men. The army surgeon James Mann reckoned that during the 1813 campaign, the proportion of those unfit for duty by reason of illness was seldom less than 40 per cent. And among the sufferers, none was more prominent than the former physician and current major general, Henry Dearborn, whose health was in apparent lockstep with American fortunes in the field. On 6 June with Chandler's division rattled and leaderless after Harvey's daring night raid, Dearborn delivered the bad news to Washington, then added that because of his poor health little in the way of redress could be expected from him.[2]

By 8 June with the Royal Navy squadron apparently stalking his headquarters at Fort George while all his troops were at Forty Mile Creek, Dearborn was threatening to "retire some place where my mind may be more at ease."[3]

On 10 June the day after the army returned to Fort George from Stoney Creek, Dearborn's adjutant general, Winfield Scott, posted the order giving Morgan Lewis temporary command of the whole military district.[4] Two days later Dearborn's ADC would report to Armstrong that "in addition to the debility and fever he has been afflicted with, he had, within the last twenty-four hours, experienced a violent spasmodic attack on his breast, which had obliged him to relinquish business altogether."[5]

The Maine historian Harry H. Cochrane said, "Dearborn's condition now became so critical that he was compelled to relinquish the immediate sight of the troops. Disaster after disaster followed. It seemed as though the officers in command were inspired by cowardice or some kindred principle to effect the overthrow of the American army."[6]

Within two days of his appointment Lewis, the temporary commander, was acting as though his assignment had been made permanent, announcing that Dearborn had resigned his command: "I have doubts whether he will ever again be fit for service," Lewis wrote to the secretary of war, "he has repeatedly been in state of convalescence but relapses on the least agitation of mind."[7]

By 16 June the first word of Stoney Creek reached Washington and influential congressman and Revolutionary war hero Benjamin Tallmadge observed: "We have this morning read unpleasant intelligence from our Northern Army. It is said Genl Chandler & Winder with about 170 Men, were surprised & captured. We seem to be doomed to suffer disgrace from that quarter."[8]

On 19 June, Armstrong, with reports on Stoney Creek and the subsequent retreat before him, dripped venom as he hectored and lectured an old soldier whose combat experience far exceeded his own. "There is indeed some strange fatality attending our efforts," he wrote Dearborn from Washington. "I cannot disguise from you the surprise occasioned by the two escapes of a beaten enemy; first on the 27th ultimo, and again on the 6th instant. Battles are not gained when an inferior and broken enemy is not destroyed."[9]

In nearby Georgetown, the anti-government *Federal Republican* took aim at army leadership: "The war has been conducted by the most curiously selected Generals that have ever borne the title. Dearborn, Hull, Smyth, Lewis, Chandler, &c. &c. have all debased the reputation of the country, and with the co-operation they have received at Washington, have held up the heart-rending spectacle of all the disposable military forces drawn from every part of the country, being successively captured or routed by a handful of men in a comparatively defenceless foreign colony which was calculated to be ours with scarcely any exertion."[10]

On 20 June Dearborn told Armstrong his troop strength was seriously depleted by casualties, sickness and resignations from the officer corps. At the same time the number of enemy troops was increasing because their fleet controlled the lake. As to his own health, "I have been reduced in strength as to be incapable of any command."[11] If Dearborn was indeed relapsing on the least agitation of mind, the events four days hence were guaranteed to completely sabotage any recovery.

Emboldened by Stoney Creek, Vincent had established forward crossroad positions at Twenty Mile Creek, Ten Mile Creek and the DeCew House from which to observe and harass Americans movements from Fort George. Foraging patrols sent out from the fort were at constant risk of attack. The chief irritant was a special command under Lieutenant James FitzGibbon consisting of some 50 Irishmen from the ranks of the 49th – the regimental troublemakers according to one source – who called themselves the Bloody Boys or the Irish Greens.[12]

FitzGibbon conducted a successful guerilla campaign in the Niagara, skirmishing with cavalry patrols and attacking pickets but principally clashing with the mounted freebooters under Cyrenius Chapin who were terrorizing the peninsula. Chapin, whose mounted company was known by both sides as the Forty Thieves, convinced Brigadier General John Parker Boyd to move against Fitz-Gibbon's headquarters at the DeCew House. Boyd got approval from Dearborn and on 23 June ordered Lieutenant Colonel Charles Boerstler to lead a force of 575 troops comprising his own regiment, the Fourteenth Infantry, companies from the Sixth and the Twenty-Third Infantry, two pieces of artillery, a squadron of dragoons and Chapin's partisans. Significantly absent was a company of riflemen which had been ordered to join the force but had been placed on sentry duty by Lieutenant Colonel Homer Milton.[13]

Boerstler, who had been at Stoney Creek as part of Chrystie's command guarding the bateaux on the lake, was about to experience for real what Lieutenant Ephraim Shaler supposed was happening in the dark at Gage's farm – "surrounded by all the Indians in Canada."

Word of the expedition's target was overheard by Laura Secord, the wife of a Queenston Loyalist, who walked a roundabout route of 20 miles to warn FitzGibbon. By a stroke of luck, a newly-arrived force of 465 Iroquois warriors from the Grand River and Lac-des-Deux-Montagnes and Saint Regis in Lower Canada, along with about 70 Ojibway and Mississauga warriors, was between Boerstler and the DeCew House. On the morning of 24 June near an area known as Beaver Dams, Boerstler's force was ambushed from a beechwood forest. Without riflemen, Boerstler was unable to drive the Indians from the forest and gradually his force became surrounded. After three hours of fierce fighting, FitzGibbon arrived with 46 men and told the American commander he was outnumbered and more troops were on their way. He also raised the spectre of a possible massacre. This audacious bluff, reminiscent of Brock at Detroit and Yeo at the Forty, worked and the entire force, demoralized and nearly out of ammunition, surrendered.[14]

The Americans losses included about 30 killed and 50 wounded, 492 prisoners, two pieces of artillery and the one prize that had eluded the British at Stoney Creek, a stand of colours belonging to the Fourteenth Infantry. It was one of the most decisive defeats ever suffered by the U.S. Army at the hands of native warriors. The Indians, FitzGibbon said, "beat the American detachment into a state of terror." From captivity Boerstler wrote to his father, "On the score of humanity I determined to capitulate, as it was extremely doubtful whether a man of us would reach Fort George."[15]

Dearborn, echoing the strange fatalism of his earlier bad-news missives, began his report on the battle to Armstrong: "I have the mortification of informing you of an unfortunate and unaccountable event...."[16]

On 30 June a visitor to Fort George reported on the condition of the army: "Every night our piquets have a skirmish with the marauders. They are very troublesome. They keep our troops under arms through the night, which exhausts and wears them fast away. Our force has decreased very much by many causes.... Our men are in a wretched condition for clothing, many barefooted and half naked.... The enemy's fleet plague our forces very much. It has been making demonstrations for near two weeks off Fort Niagara.... It is powerful in size of vessels, number of guns and weight of metal."[17]

By 1 July Dearborn had recovered sufficiently to resume command and by 6 July to inform Armstrong that his "health and strength have hourly improved, and I hope shortly to regain them in their wonted vigor – notwithstanding the gloomy opinions which have been formed and disseminated on my case."[18]

It was too late: the gloomy opinions had been heeded. In Washington, several influential congressmen, fed up with continual tidings of mismanagement and misfortune, demanded Dearborn's head. Armstrong needed no encouragement and on the same 6 July, with the approval of the president, his cabinet and congress, sent his doddering, dithering senior general a one-sentence dismissal.[19]

Dearborn, according to James Burn, was surprised and "much mortified at the manner in which it was communicated to him – I really felt for the old buck." On 15 July after word of his removal became known, 26 field officers and the one general officer still in camp, John Parker Boyd, assembled to pay respect and offer *pro forma* regrets. According to Winfield Scott, this "short, emphatic valedictory did much to sooth a wounded heart."[20]

Fearing perhaps that the army had worse major generals in reserve – indeed, the venal and self-serving James Wilkinson was next in line – some of the officers apparently believed Dearborn should stay. Burn, his cavalry colonel, said in a private letter the field officers were much surprised at the recall and "we all regret it as he is a persevering good officer and had recovered his health sufficiently to do his duty."[21]

Scott said Dearborn "possessed more energy, zeal & comprehension than any General with whom I have served since the war. His courage, patriotism & devotedness to his country have never been impeached & are unimpeachable."[22]

A junior staff officer observed that the government had done the very "thing which it ought not to have done – namely – it ordered home our Big Bug in chief," largely on the strength of a health report penned by the antipathetic Morgan Lewis. "This taking away the head at the very moment when such part of the body was most wanted, struck the whole army as being both unwise and ungracious, and looked very much like a blundering. The commander in chief had been sick – too much so for effective service – but he was now convalescent and ready to think of another York or Fort George."[23]

A band played and an artillery salute was fired from Brock's bastion as Dearborn made his way to the boat that would take him across the Niagara. With most of the army watching, he waved his tricorn, acknowledging the salute which the staffling said bespoke "the regret of the camp at the unmerited disgrace of an old officer, who had done the state much service."[24] Some of the Washington papers however were not so deferential, the *Federal Republican*, among others, disparaging "the old stupid, doting, creeping driveller Dearborn."[25]

A few months later William Duane, the army's adjutant-general, assessed

Dearborn's performance in a private letter: "It was a great mistake to place him in these times at the head of a new army – and it was still worse to give him co-adjutors incompetent from various causes to supply any of his deficiencies."[26]

With Dearborn dismissed and Lewis posted to Sackets Harbor, Armstrong's lame-duck replacement for command at Niagara was the former mercenary John Parker Boyd. His first order from the secretary of war could hardly be mistaken as a vote of confidence: "You will pay the utmost attention to the instruction and disciplining of the troops and engage in no affair with the enemy that can be avoided."[27]

Despite the short leash imposed by Armstrong, Boyd was cut a little slack when Commodore Chauncey finally got his new 26-gun frigate *General Pike* into service and brought the American fleet back onto the lake for the first time in nearly two months. Although the British had been defeated at Sackets Harbor, crucial fittings, sailcloth and stores had been destroyed during the battle, delaying completion of the biggest and most powerful warship on the lakes. Until the *Pike* was in service at the end of July, Chauncey refused to leave port, thereby ceding control of Lake Ontario to the Royal Navy and effectively dooming Dearborn's Niagara offensive.

**USS *General Pike*.** This 26-gun corvette, imperilled while still on the stocks when the British attacked Sackets Harbor on 29 May 1813, kept Commodore Isaac Chauncey off the lake until it was finally finished at the end of July. The most powerful ship on the Great Lakes, it tipped the balance on Lake Ontario in favour of the Americans. (Plan by C. Ware, U.S. Naval Historical Center, NH57006)

Chauncey's belated appearance off Niagara on 27 July afforded the Americans yet another run at Burlington Heights. Reports from the partisan leader Cyrenius Chapin and deserters indicated the British had a large depot of ammunition and stores at the Head of the Lake, including the guns taken at Stoney Creek, and Boyd organized a smash-and-grab expedition to "surprise, take, destroy, or bring it off."[28]

Before 6 a.m. on 28 July, the fleet, with 250 infantry under Winfield Scott on board, left Niagara, but light winds and calms delayed arrival off Burlington until the night of the following day. The 13-vessel fleet anchored three miles from the shallow outlet that drained Little Lake into the big lake.[29] Two landing parties discovered that the British had been sent reinforcements – the light companies from different outposts in the Niagara Peninsula – totalling 200 men.

On the morning of 30 July, Scott's 250 infantry along with 250 marines and seamen from the fleet landed on the beach strip to observe the British position on Burlington Heights seven miles across Little Lake. Scott, who had a life-long reputation for never avoiding a fight, nevertheless found plenty of reasons to reconsider after peering across at Vincent's position. The outlet that drained Little Lake was far too shallow to admit even the smallest of Chauncey's fleet but the Royal Navy, three days before, had managed to get a vessel inside. The small schooner *Vincent*, stripped of guns, stores and masts, had been dragged across the inlet and into Little Lake.[30] To approach the heights, Scott and Chauncey would have to row their force across in small boats without any artillery support whatsoever. The British, however, had the approach covered with seven guns on the high ground, and the *Vincent*, reunited with its 18-pdr. carronade, positioned to harass the small craft.

At the same time, Scott and Chauncey learned the British had also been further reinforced by the Glengarry Light Infantry from York. And once more, the Indian factor came into play, even though there is no record of any natives among the British force. A navy midshipman was convinced – with the help of a canny local citizen – that the Americans faced a massacre if they persisted: "I was informed by an inhabitant that our men who fell or were taken at the battle of Forty Mile Creek were most shockingly butchered. Their heads skinned, their hearts taken out and put in their mouth, their privates cut off and put in the places of their hearts – We owing to someone's imprudence, narrowly escaped a similar fate."[31]

Scott was undoubtedly the best and most active field officer in the American command yet even he knew there were limits on what he might accomplish. "Perceiving the strength of the enemy's position," he wrote, "and learning from the inhabitants that the force on the heights, independent of the reinforcements above mentioned, was nearly equal our own, the Commodore determined not to risk an attack … in the above opinion I fully concurred."[32]

Discretion having overruled extreme valour, the force re-embarked. Perhaps reluctant to return home empty-handed, Scott and Chauncey elected to take another swipe at York, stopping just long enough to burn the barracks and public stores, seize a 24-pdr. gun, 11 bateaux and 400 barrels of flour, and release a handful of prisoners from the Crown lockup.

Harvey, who watched the fleet back off, was scornful of Plan B. "The prudent commander thought it expeditious to carry the armament to a place where they were sure to meet no resistance & they accordingly paid a second visit to York (where there was not so much as a Corporal's guard) and having carried off a few barrels of Flour, returned in Triumph."[33]

Boyd, however, remained convinced Burlington Heights was indeed pregnable and just a week later attempted one more expedition that sounds strangely similar to Dearborn's original plan. The newly-minted brigadier general, David R. Williams, a congressman and lawyer from South Carolina, and 1,500 troops were to be transported by the navy to the other side of Burlington Heights to cut off any retreat. After carrying the heights, Williams was to march back toward Fort George. Meanwhile Boyd with the main part of the army would advance in two columns from Fort George. The British, outnumbered and denied any means of retreat, Chauncey reckoned, "must have surrendered in the course of a few days."[34]

However, just as the troops were about to embark, Yeo made yet another inadvertent, just-in-time appearance with his fleet off Niagara at dawn on 7 August, enticing Chauncey to join him on the lake for a dance that would continue, on and off, for the next two months and effectively stymie any combined operations in Niagara.[35]

The allure of Burlington Heights was strong though, and in November yet another expedition was in the works. The bulk of the American garrison at the mouth of the Niagara, 4,500 regulars, had been shipped down-lake as the backbone of Wilkinson's planned descent on Montreal. But the future president Major General William Henry Harrison, flush from his crushing defeat of Procter's army at Moraviantown, arrived at Fort George in late October with 1,300 regulars. Together with 1,000 short-term militia and volunteers and 400 Iroquois from New York, Harrison proposed to assault Burlington Heights, but on 14 November Chauncey's fleet arrived with orders directing Harrison to Sackets Harbor immediately. Nevertheless the militia commander, Brigadier

General George McClure, was determined to make a demonstration at least, and on 25 November he led 1,000 militia up the peninsula as far as Twenty Mile Creek, where he called a council of war. "The undisguised opinion and advice of every field officer," he wrote, "imperatively bound the General to acquiesce in the necessity of retiring." Some 400 barrels of flour were seized and the force returned to Fort George.[36]

The artillery colonel, Alexander Macomb, had been eerily prescient when he predicted in late June, "the campaign will terminate rather to our disgrace than advantage on the Niagara frontier.... Canada will not be conquered this year."[37] Indeed as the year wound down and the last and most ambitious invasion attempt fizzled out, disaffected war hawks like Charles Ingersoll could only watch in despair as "the bubble of Canadian conquest burst and evaporated, if not forever, at any rate for that year."[38]

Stoney Creek was indeed the turning point in the 1813 campaign. Easy victories at York and Fort George had heartened the American command to the point they believed the conquest of Upper Canada was at hand. The pursuit and defeat of Vincent's little army was really only part of the mopping-up operation.

Stoney Creek changed all that. The course of events was marked by an unpredictable ebb and flow of fortunes. This chaotic, night action hardly an hour in duration – really a desperate, last-ditch effort by the British to avert almost-certain defeat the following day – actually began as though it might succeed brilliantly.

Then they began cheering and firing back, and the British lost the one critical advantage they held – that of being invisible to the enemy. The American cook fires that had marked the edge of their advance had turned against them: rendered visible by the fires, the attackers suddenly became easy targets. Unable to withstand the withering volleys, they disobeyed orders and returned fire, which made them even easier to pinpoint. Under even more intense fire, companies and sections began to break and melt into the surrounding woods.

But just at the moment when it seemed the Americans, having weathered the initial shock and steadied their lines, were poised to rout the jostled raiders, Plenderleath intervened with his impromptu charge that in one fell swoop fractured their position, overran the artillery, bagged Chandler and Winder and neatly decapitated the whole division.

In the ensuing confusion the British were able to make their escape.

The battle cost the Americans two generals, two guns and all their momentum. Above all, it probably cost them Upper Canada. This minor battle would portend major implications. In the Middle Ages it fell to the heralds to declare a victor and name a battle site, usually according to the nearest castle. Stoney Creek had neither heralds nor castles and the battle itself was probably too close to call but the naming rights went to the mill stream that tumbled over the escarpment on its way to the lake.

As the sun came up over the Gage farm on the morning of 6 June, the Niagara campaign of 1813 was effectively over. And the ripple effect of the Battle of Stoney Creek would unseat the senior military commander in the American army.

Six months later, the surgeon for the Twenty-Fifth Infantry looked back at everything that transpired after Stoney Creek and declared: "The British have taken possession of the whole frontier from Fort Erie to Fort George ... our whole summer's work seems to be at an end, the campaign in this section of the country is all for naught and ended in disgrace."[39]

In Connecticut, home of the Twenty-Fifth Infantry, which took more casualties than any other American unit at Stoney Creek, the *Connecticut Mirror* indicted Madison and his cabinet: "They are answerable for all the lives that have been sacrificed, the towns that have been plundered, the disasters that have happened and the disgrace that has been incurred ... we have proved ourselves incompetent to combat, even with the feeble province of Upper Canada.... Where then, is the glory which was so certainly to be won in Canada the present summer?"[40]

## 41 A Time for Peace

### FATE DECREED

#### John Chandler

John Chandler never escaped the stigma of Stoney Creek and bore it like a curse until he died. The physical injuries sustained when his horse was shot lessened but never completely left him – he needed help getting dressed for the rest of his life. Likewise, he never overcame the damage his reputation sustained. An outsider in Washington from the beginning, forever marked as a blacksmith who should never have left the forge, Chandler came to symbolize the folly of political appointees to the army.

Surveying the shambles of the Niagara campaign a month after Chandler's capture, the *Connecticut Mirror* noted:

Our Administration appear to have supposed that they could, in all cases, make a good general out of a hairbrained partisan; and that forty-eight hours was a sufficient time for him to learn the trade.

Why, it probably took Gen. Chandler at least half a dozen years to learn the art and mystery of a blacksmith. Does it require less skill to do the duties of an accomplished officer, than it does to make a hoe?[1]

On the occasion of American Independence Day 1813, the *Herald of Liberty*, a paper from Chandler's own county of Kennebec, printed this item:

> At the celebration of Independence in Augusta on the 4th of July, 1812, General Chandler gave the following toast: 'The fourth of July 1813 – May we on that day drink wine within the walls of Quebec!'
>
> This was certainly prophetic, and Gen Chandler will have his wishes granted; not however by his own military prowess, but by the politeness of the enemy.[2]

This story, widely reprinted as an example of retribution for a foolhardy comment was, however, completely spurious.[3] Nevertheless it continued to have currency and was repeated in at least two books.[4]

In North Yarmouth, only 50 miles from Chandler's home town of Monmouth, citizens marked Independence Day in 1813 by derisively toasting "The capture of General Chandler – American loss, *a Brigadier General*, British gain, *a good blacksmith*."[5]

In Windsor, Vermont, the *Washingtonian* snidely reviewed the military career of "a certain *Blacksmith* in the Province of Maine ... enrolled on the list of Fame as one of the Conquerors of Canada! His exploits in the field of *Mars*, have been known and celebrated. In the *rapidity* of his movements he has copied *Caesar*. In much less than six weeks he has *run over* both provinces."[6]

And in the national capital, the editor of the *Federal Republican* directed a shrill rant at the disastrous army appointments of the Madison administration such as Dearborn, Smyth, Hull and "the low-bred, ignorant Chandler."[7]

While the troops captured at Stoney Creek were kept on makeshift prison hulks anchored off Quebec, Chandler and the other officers were on parole in the nearby village of Beauport. As a prisoner during the Revolution, he had experienced the squalor of prison hulks; in Quebec when disease broke out on board he actively petitioned the British to alleviate crowding on board the two prison ships.[8]

In December the relative freedom Chandler enjoyed on parole was curtailed by a long-standing dispute between Washington and London over the Crown's right to treat British subjects found in arms with the enemy as traitors.[9] Chandler, along with Winder and three other officers, ended up in close confinement until they were exchanged on 19 April 1814 and returned to the United States.

The brigadier spent the remainder of the war as military commander of the

District of Maine,[10] relinquishing his commission in the spring of 1815 when the army was reduced to a peace establishment. He returned to politics a strong supporter of Maine statehood and was elected to the U.S. Senate as the first representative of the new state. Still, he was never able to escape the taint of Stoney Creek and the ignominy of having been snatched from the head of his army by a raiding party. His request for a court of inquiry into his conduct was denied, perhaps because Washington believed there was nothing to be gained from drawing attention to an action that reflected badly on army leadership and the administration that appointed it.

In 1816, a long, anonymous account of the battle appeared in most of the major newspapers, supposedly penned by a subordinate officer. But it was widely believed at the time that Chandler was the author and indeed large passages of it, some identical and some nearly identical, appear in his autobiography. When the *Eastern Argus* in Portland ran the piece it was accompanied by a fawning editorial contending Chandler, "having committed the unpardonable crime of being unfortunate," was the victim of a smear campaign and "has been suffered to retire from the public with unmerited censure resting upon his name." Its publication did little, however, to retrieve his military standing.[11]

In 1817, his mentor and patron, Henry Dearborn, struggling to maintain his own reputation, offered his protégé a limited absolution: "I am fully satisfied that any misfortunes which occurred at Stony Creek, where Chandler was captured, were the effects of unavoidable accident and in no degree chargeable to his want of judgment in the disposition of the troops, or to any neglect of duty on his part."[12]

Chandler ended his public life at the age of 75 as the collector of customs for Portland and Falmouth, retiring to Augusta, Maine, where he died in 1841 in relative obscurity with little more than perfunctory notice in the New England Press. The *Eastern Argus* noted his command and capture, without comment, and the *Kennebec Journal* added that "as a citizen and a neighbor he was always highly esteemed."[13]

Seven years later, army historian Fayette Robinson assessed his military career in the light of Stoney Creek: "Winder and Chandler bore the commission of generals, but no one who looks attentively at their military history will call them soldiers. The consequence was, Vincent grown up in the correct school, dashed into the centre of their line of battle on the morning of the 6th and managed to capture both generals, neither of whom had taken care to see that the outposts were attentive to their duty or commanded by officers familiar even with the routine of what was required of them."[14]

A measure of the obscurity that has overtaken John Chandler is his official biography from the United States Congress, which limits his war service to three years in the state militia.[15]

## William Henry Winder

Through a combination of good connections and good luck, Winder managed to avoid almost all of the Stoney Creek fallout. Although the circumstances of his capture were hardly more glorious than Chandler's – taken while trying to rally enemy troops that had just broken through the centre of the American line – Winder was never cast as anything worse than unfortunate.

Maryland judge Joseph Nicholson said Winder had been "untimely snatched by one of those accidents which no human foresight can prevent," a view widely shared by the eastern press. Even his British captor, Lieutenant Colonel John Harvey, after only the briefest exposure declared Winder had "more talent than all the rest of the Yankee Generals put together," and warned against exchanging him.[16]

The reality of his situation was brought home to Winder in Montreal when he realized the exchange process had ground to a halt and he would not be going home anytime soon. Writing to the secretary of war, he referred to the calamity of his capture and the impenetrable darkness of his fate. "The prospect of a protracted confinement as a prisoner of war," he wrote, "bears with the most oppressive weight upon my hopes & feelings."[17]

Within three weeks of arriving in Quebec, Winder had petitioned Prevost for a temporary parole to visit his family and was summarily denied. Nevertheless he continued the correspondence with Prevost, positioning himself as the facilitator who could break the hostage logjam and six months later was granted a highly unusual 60-day parole to do just that.[18]

Winder travelled to Washington to convince the Madison administration to drop the retaliatory system and although initially unsuccessful, an order granting him authority to negotiate an exchange convention was issued while he was on his way back to Quebec. Within three weeks a deal was struck for the mutual exchange of prisoners and Winder was headed for home and his next military adventure, which turned out to be an even bigger disaster than his last.

Still confident of his brigadier's martial capabilities, Madison put him in charge of a new military district comprising Washington, Baltimore and Annapolis. In August 1814, when the British advanced on the American capital, Winder was in command of a largely militia force drawn up in the Maryland village of Bladensburg to oppose them. Although numerically superior, the Americans withered before the disciplined British regulars and soon broke and ran, leaving

Washington defenceless. A young British lieutenant, George Gleig, would note: "Never did men with arms in their hands make better use of their legs"[19]

In the wake of the subsequent sacking and burning of Washington, Winder was widely censured, most notably by Henry Adams, who said he was without equal among his contemporary general officers in his inability to organize, fortify, fight or escape. "When he might have prepared defences, he acted as scout; when he might have fought, he still scouted; when he retreated, he retreated in the wrong direction; when he fought, he thought only of retreat."[20]

Winder survived a court martial and was discharged from the army in June 1815. Winfield Scott, one of his judges, would later say Winder had the elements of a good soldier but no luck: "It is a misfortune to begin a new career with too much rank, or rather too late in life."[21]

Winder resumed his extensive Baltimore law practice, and when he died nine years later of tuberculosis at 49, was widely mourned in his home town. Newspaper accounts said it was the largest funeral procession ever seen in Baltimore with 15,000 people accompanying the body to the grave site.[22]

### Henry Dearborn

Humiliated by his summary dismissal from command, Dearborn sought a court martial but was denied. As a face-saving sinecure he was given command of New York City. Curiously, he presided over General William Hull's court martial which convicted the hapless general of cowardice and neglect of duty for surrendering Detroit. Considering Dearborn was Hull's commanding officer and his negligence a contributing factor in Hull's surrender, his participation in the court martial was highly improper, to say the least.

In March 1815 Madison nominated him as secretary of war but was forced to withdraw the nomination in the face of adamant opposition. Seven years later he was named ambassador to Portugal, a post he held only two years before retiring to Roxbury, Massachusetts, where he died in 1829 on the 16th anniversary of the Battle of Stoney Creek. His obituaries were generally complimentary, playing up his Revolutionary War service and singularly ignoring his failings during the War of 1812.[23]

### Jonathan Kearsley

The artillery lieutenant who had warned Chandler of the perils of assigning undisciplined riflemen to guard duty survived another disastrous battle in 1813, Crysler's Farm, and then in the spring of the following year became a rifleman himself, transferring to the Fourth Rifle Regiment.

Kearsley saw hard service at Fort Erie in 1814, winning promotion to brevet captain and major but losing a leg in the bargain. After the war he was appointed Receiver of the U.S. Land Office in Detroit, twice served as mayor of that city and was appointed trustee and regent of the University of Michigan.

In the latter role he was in the habit of personally examining each graduating student in Latin, which earned the old soldier the epithet Major Tormentum.[24]

### John Harvey

A career soldier, certainly one of the most capable British field officers to serve in Canada during the war, Harvey also distinguished himself at Crysler's Farm, Lundy's Lane and Fort Erie, where he was wounded. While stationed in Niagara he formed an enduring friendship with the American officer Winfield Scott, who spared his life once and nearly captured him twice. That friendship would go a long way to avoiding another conflict between Britain and the United States, in the 1839 Maine–New Brunswick boundary dispute.[25]

Although he once complained "no credit was to be gained in Canada,"[26] Harvey would spend almost all of the rest of his life as a colonial administrator in pre-Confederation Canada as lieutenant governor of Prince Edward Island, New Brunswick, Newfoundland and finally Nova Scotia. Knighted for his army service in 1824, he reached the rank of lieutenant general in 1846.

When he died in Halifax in 1852, two Toronto newspapers carried the same long, admiring obituary lauding his gallant bearing and enlightened civil service – reprinted from the *New York Herald*.[27]

### James FitzGibbon

Perhaps the most reliable witness of the Battle of Stoney Creek, FitzGibbon, in his letter to a Montreal clergyman, James Somerville, was unsparing in his criticism of fellow officers who began cheering after the light company overran the American pickets – "I think I could have killed some of them."[28] That independent turn of mind, not unusual for an outsider who came up through the ranks and therefore had little in common with the gentleman officer class, would serve the Irishman well.

In the wake of Stoney Creek, FitzGibbon was given a separate command based at the DeCew House from which he disrupted enemy communications and conducted a small guerilla war throughout the peninsula. During his watch a combined force of Iroquois, Ojibway and Mississauga warriors won a spectacular victory at Beaver Dams. FitzGibbon cleverly negotiated the American surrender. Although the credit was due the native warriors, FitzGibbon reaped the rewards, including a gold medal from his fellow officers and a company command in the Glengarry Light Infantry.[29]

On the strength of an outstanding war record he secured a number of significant militia and minor civil service posts in Upper Canada, and during the Rebellion of 1837 overcame considerable difficulties to organize and lead the militia force that broke and scattered Mackenzie's rebels.

Despite his capable and loyal service, FitzGibbon was treated shabbily by authorities in Canada and in England and he spent the last 16 years of his life as a military knight at Windsor Castle availing himself of a modest Crown indulgence for indigent army officers.

### Alexander Fraser and Peter Fraser

If any individuals can be considered crucial to the outcome of the Battle of Stoney Creek, they would most certainly be the ferocious 49th sergeant and his younger brother. Plenderleath's last-ditch charge of the artillery would have been a decidedly forlorn hope without the Fraser brothers at the tip of the spear. A two-man wrecking crew, the Frasers between them killed or wounded 11 men, which if the highly suspect American casualty figures are to be believed, amounts to one fifth of all American casualties. The charge, which broke the centre of the American line and netted two guns, five officers and 75 men prisoners, marked, for the British, the difference between almost certain defeat and qualified success.

"In consideration of his gallantry and good conduct,"[30] Alexander was promoted from the ranks to an ensigncy in the New Brunswick Fencible Infantry, where he served capably as adjutant, rising to lieutenant by 1815.

Placed on half pay in 1816, he was part of the large military settlement of 1812 and Peninsular War veterans who founded the town of Perth in eastern Upper Canada. He built a fine stone house called *Annsfield* and sired 13 children, 11 of whom survived infancy, one of whom was named Charles Plenderleath after his old 49th commanding officer.[31]

Fraser saw active service again in the 1837 Rebellion in Toronto and Gananoque, as an officer in the Lanark Militia, eventually rising to colonel. He was also a justice of the peace with a reputation for occasionally unruly behaviour. Charged with libelling the district surveyor, Fraser's behaviour in court when he was arrested after threatening the plaintiff with a bludgeon and attempting to occupy the bench, was reported fully in the *Bathurst Courier*: "This was done in Court of Justice – in our Court – by a Magistrate and a Colonel of Militia! What a fearful example to evildoers!"[32]

**Annsfield.** Alexander Fraser settled in Perth, Ontario, after the war, where he built this stone home to house the 13 children he would sire. Named for his wife, Ann, the 1824 building had double stone walls and eight fireplaces, three of which are still in use by the current owner. (Irene Spence)

Although he fathered 13 children, Fraser petitioned district council to be excused the increased assessment for a new school, arguing that he would derive no advantage.[33] Nevertheless when he died in 1872, at 82, he was fondly remembered in his adopted home town. "The beau ideal of a Highland gentleman," wrote the *Perth Courier*, "he came of a race famed for its fighting qualities of two clans who left their mark on the history of the Highlands, the Frasers and the Macdonalds ... the Colonel in his day must have been a powerful active and robust young man. A soldier every inch."[34]

Alexander Fraser is buried in plot #125 of the Old Pioneer Cemetery on Craig Street in Perth, Ontario.

Peter Fraser was also rewarded for his part in the Battle of Stoney Creek with promotion to sergeant, but after returning to England with the 49th at the end of the war, was broken back to private. In the summer of 1816 he re-enlisted for unlimited service and was posted to Ireland, where he once more made sergeant. In 1821 Fraser was posted to the Cape Colony in Africa, where he rose as high as colour sergeant before returning to private. In 1828 he was sent with the regiment to Berhampore in West Bengal, where he died four years later at the age of 40 leaving a wife, Mary, with the regiment.[35]

## Charles Plenderleath

Plenderleath's split-second decision to charge the artillery recalls the opening lines of Kipling's *If* – "If you can keep your head when all about you are losing theirs...."

With the entire British initiative collapsing around him, whole companies breaking and running for the woods under massive American musket and artillery fire, the veteran 49th major had the presence of mind to sum up the situation and conclude the only hope lay in a headlong dash right into the artillery. Initiative, speed and surprise led to psychological victory. He lost his horse and was wounded twice but his decisive action retrieved British fortunes from the edge of disaster.

For his courage and initiative on the battlefield he was promoted lieutenant colonel, and despite his wounds he was back on active duty in Niagara within three weeks. In November he commanded the 49th at Crysler's Farm, again exhibiting uncommon initiative and skill in manoeuvring the regiment out of a deadly field of artillery fire. He was one of seven field officers awarded a gold medal for the action.[36]

John Vincent had campaigned unsuccessfully for a similar medal for Stoney Creek and Plenderleath was one of his nominations.[37]

His wounds having proved more serious than originally thought, Plenderleath was relieved of his command in late 1813 and returned to England. There he retired on half-pay but not before a grateful government made him a Companion of the Order of the Bath for his service at Stoney Creek.[38]

Plenderleath became involved with the Italian Waldenses, a pre-Reformation Christian community, visiting their settlements in the Italian Alps and developing an information program. The man FitzGibbon said saved Vincent's army and "most probably the whole of Upper Canada" died in 1854 at the age of 73 in Florence, where he was buried in the city's Protestant Cemetery.[39]

## John Vincent

Although Vincent garnered the official accolades for Stoney Creek, including promotion to major general, the nasty little secret that he was nearly the third general officer captured during the action did not advance his career. Prevost had two ADCs keeping an eye on Vincent and they most certainly furnished the governor general with detailed accounts of the brigadier's ignominious disappearance in the heat of the battle. In the wake of Stoney Creek Vincent moved aggressively to reoccupy the Niagara Peninsula and the complete victory of Beaver Dams reflected positively on him. However, after Procter's defeat at

Moraviantown in October, he once more abandoned the peninsula in the face of Harrison's planned assault on Burlington Heights. For that hasty, albeit entirely understandable withdrawal, he drew the ire of Prevost, who declared Vincent "incapable of performing an arduous task." Although defended by de Rottenburg, he was replaced in December by Major General Phineas Riall and returned to his earlier command at Kingston. By the summer of 1814 he was on his way back to England on sick leave, and although he would reach lieutenant general in 1825 and general in 1841 via the seniority list, it was his last active command. He died in London in 1848 at the age of 83. There were no eulogies from his former subordinate, James FitzGibbon: "He was at all times a feeble man, both in mind and body."[40]

### Thomas Taylor

One of Vincent's staff officers who accompanied the brigadier to Stoney Creek, Taylor, a lieutenant in the 41st, was critically wounded during the battle, perhaps during the action that drove Vincent and his party into the woods.

He was treated in the farmhouse surgery of Dr. William Case for chest and arm wounds and spent the summer recovering at Fort York.[41] Trained in law, Taylor held an administrative post at the fort (fort major) until he was ordered in 1816 to rejoin his regiment in England. Reduced to half-pay with five children to feed, he qualified to practise law and returned to Canada in 1819, settling near Burlington Heights. Within a year of his return he was called to the Bar of Upper Canada and named a judge. Within five years he was colonel of the 3rd Battalion, Gore Militia.

By 1833 when the nascent settlement of Hamilton qualified as a Police Town, Taylor was appointed president of the town's board of governance, making him, in essence, Hamilton's first mayor. He was 59 when he died in December 1837.[42]

Seventy-three years later, his grandson, Hamilton Plantagenet MacCarthy, an English-trained sculptor, would design the Imperial Lion sculpture that presides over the American artillery position on the Stoney Creek battlefield.[43]

### James Yeo

Yeo's early career was storied – the term swashbuckler comes to mind. His appointment as Great Lakes commodore, under the cautious thumb of Prevost, was probably not the best use of a bold and original talent but without him the Niagara Campaign of 1813 would have had a completely different ending.

The attack on Sackets Harbor, through no fault of Yeo's, was a costly failure but kept the American fleet in harbour for seven weeks and denied Dearborn water transport. With free rein on the lake, Yeo's opportune appearances off Niagara and the Forty confused and intimidated the American command into retreat.

For the remainder of the war Yeo and his American counterpart, Commodore Isaac Chauncey, circled each other like a pair of wary prizefighters and conducted a shipbuilding war that culminated in the 112-gun behemoth *St. Lawrence* as Yeo's flagship.

Yeo's already rocky relationship with Prevost worsened over the loss of his Lake Erie and Lake Champlain squadrons (both pressured into premature action by army commanders) and his health deteriorated. In spring 1815 he returned to England and was given responsibility for the anti-slavery patrol off West Africa. He died at sea on 21 August 1818 of "general debility." He was 35 years old.[44]

### George Prevost

The governor-general, whose intervention at Sackets Harbor was crucial in buying Vincent's army enough time to regroup and turn on the Americans, did not come out of the war well.

A deft administrator who endeared himself to the Canadiens in Lower Canada for his conciliatory measures, Prevost struggled to prosecute the war in the face of chronic shortages of manpower and supplies. Given the hand he was dealt, he succeeded reasonably well, adopting a cautious defensive stance designed to avoid major losses.

Unfortunately on the two occasions where he actually led an army into action, Sackets Harbor and Plattsburgh, he was found wanting. Summoned to London to answer for the failure of the Plattsburgh campaign, he requested a court martial but died of edema, probably due to congestive heart failure, before it could be held in January 1816. He was 48.[45]

**"The lightning of the arms in quick succession."** Hundreds of re-enactors representing many of the units that fought at the Battle of Stoney Creek gather at Battlefield Park every year to mark the anniversary. This photo, taken in 2005, demonstrates the dramatic effect of nighttime gunfire, described by one veteran of the 1813 battle as "a grand and beautiful sight, like the bursting forth of a volcano." (Barry Gray)

# Appendix A

## Billy Green: The Scout and the Rout

No history of the Battle of Stoney Creek can be considered complete without an examination of the role of Billy Green. For well over a century the tale of the plucky scout has been part of the popular consciousness surrounding the battle and, in some ways, has achieved the status of a minor legend.

Broadly speaking the saga goes like this. When the American army arrived in Stoney Creek, a local settler, Isaac Corman, was detained by the advance guard. His wife[1] asked her younger brother, Billy Green, to find out what had happened to him.

Corman, on his way home after having been released, met Green and relayed the password necessary to cross American lines. Green took his brother's plough horse, rode to the British camp at Burlington Heights and told them all he knew.

Pressed into service as a guide, Green led the British force back to Stoney Creek, where he killed at least one sentry in the prelude to a battle he subsequently witnessed. For his deeds, Scout Green has been hailed as a Canadian Paul

**William Green (1794-1877).** A member of the 5th Lincoln Militia who may have been on active duty the night of the battle, Green during his lifetime claimed a role no larger than his presence. However, in 1889, at the founding of the Wentworth Historical Society, he was presented as having played a significant part in the battle. The subsequent appearance of a "diary" detailing his exploits created a folk hero. Largely unknown though is his brother Freeman's land grant petition of 1836, in which he claims the laurels. (Battlefield House Museum)

Revere, first for raising the alarm and second for guiding the redcoats through the darkness to surprise the American camp.

Since then, Billy Green has been the subject of three books, at least three recorded songs and numerous articles, celebrated by Stan Rogers, cited by historians ranging from George F. Stanley to Pierre Berton and even recognized on the floor of Parliament.[2]

The record shows that William Green, youngest child of New Jersey Loyalist Adam Green, was born 1794 in Stoney Creek and died there in 1877. In 1813, he was a private in Samuel Hatt's Company of the 5th Lincoln Militia. After the fall of Fort George on 27 May 1813 the name William Green appears on the list of militia paroled on condition of not bearing arms against the United States. Nevertheless Green continued to collect his militia pay and, according to one source, at least part of his company was indeed on active duty the night of 5 June 1813. Under the command of Queenston veteran Lieutenant Robert Land, a detachment of Hatt's company travelled with Harvey as far as Big Creek and was detailed to the beach to keep on eye on the two American regiments posted there to guard the transport boats. There is no indication the detachment was involved in any action nor are there any known corroborating sources.[3]

In 1908 the Wentworth Historical Society published "An Old Diary: Entries from D. Slater's Diary, Stoney Creek,"[4] which included a long account of Billy Green's part in the Battle of Stoney Creek. Society vice president Rose Holden was credited with transcribing the diary, but no source was given.

In 1938 the museum at Dundurn Castle was given an 18th-century geography textbook that had come via the Corman family of Stoney Creek and the Hamilton Scientific Association.[5] On the back of three maps, opposite pages 117, 149 and 571, were hand-written entries identified as copied from the diary of a school teacher, S.D. Slater, covering his departure from Ireland on 3 September 1818 and concluding 5 June 1819. There are only 13 entries, which up until the last are brief in the extreme – "Dec 8. Landed in Quebec," "Feb. 1 Arrived in York," "Feb 16 Arrived in Hamilton," "March 17 Boarding at Samuel Nash." But then on 5 June 1819 he apparently recorded Billy Green's 937-word account of his role in the Battle of Stoney Creek.

Some time before he died in 1877, Green is said to have dictated a second expanded version to his grandson.[6] Between them, these two accounts have become the basis of an authentic early Canadian fable.

No other primary source confirms whether the 19-year-old paroled militiaman played a pivotal role in the battle, or indeed whether he was even there. Examination of his two statements does however suggest a possible peripheral involvement. His timing of the American advance from the Forty – late morning to noon – coincides with primary accounts. Green and his brother Levi, along with fellow 5th Lincoln Samuel Lee, whooping and yelling like Indians, is mirrored in the account of an American officer who reported "militia and Indians who had been hanging around us all day." However, his claim American troops fired on civilians in Stoney Creek and narrowly missed hitting his sister-in-law and her infant daughter sounds unlikely, although having two officers question her about the whereabouts of the Indians seems eminently reasonable, given American fears.[7]

The story of Corman being released because he could trace his roots to Kentucky and was a first cousin to American Major General William Henry Harrison[8] is well entrenched in the oral histories of both the Green and Corman families. However, genealogists have yet to prove the link. And the story itself, including the password derived from Harrison's name, seems hardly credible. It is difficult to imagine what sort of officer would reveal the countersign to a civilian who had just been detained because of security concerns.

Green said the British thought he was a spy – "I had to tell them all I knew before they would believe me" – yet as an active member of the 5th Lincoln his identity and character would have been easy enough to determine. Did the British really need a guide to find Stoney Creek? The answer is no. The Queenston road ran directly from Burlington Heights to Stoney Creek, the British had already travelled it back and forth as recently as a few hours earlier, when Harvey made his reconnaissance. Perhaps in the darkness, a local guide might be useful but hardly essential.

**Billy Green's monument.** Three years after the Toronto *Mail and Empire* declared Billy Green "God's instrument in saving Upper Canada," public subscription funded this memorial in Stoney Creek Cemetery, which was dedicated in September 1938. (Hawthorn Ink)

On the approach to the American camp, Green has four different sentries discharging their muskets – three at Big Creek[9] directly at the British and one at the Methodist church as an alarm. If this had actually occurred, the entire American camp would have been roused long before the British were able to get close enough to engage. In fact his whole battle account sounds suspiciously like it was confected from second-hand information after the fact. It is simply inconceivable that a seasoned professional like John Harvey would allow a militia man to guide the light troops and actually count on him to know how to quickly and silently kill a sentry in a crucial situation.

From the battlefield Green presents a confused picture of the "middle rank" rushing, the "south flank" charging, the "centre flank" capturing and concluding with the Americans "running in all directions." In the expanded version he describes the charge on the artillery position: "Major Plenderleath, with thirty men of the 49th, and Major Ogilvie with the 8th or King's Regiment, charged and captured four field pieces in very gallant style."[10]

Harvey, in his initial report of the battle wrote: "The 8th or King's Regiment and part of the 49th charged and carried the four field pieces in very gallant style.[11]"

In 1820, Green applied for a land grant based on his service in the 5th Lincoln during the war. His petition, an ideal place to toot his own horn, notes nothing more distinguished than "the said William Green did his duty."[12]

In 1836, William's older brother, Freeman Green, filed his own land grant petition in which he relates an experience that is remarkably similar to the one credited to his brother. Freeman, nine years older than William and a 5th Lincoln veteran who saw action at Queenston Heights,[13] claimed a central role in the battle and, whether his claim was valid or not, he paid a huge personal price.

In his statement, prepared by his attorney, Samuel Smith of Ancaster, on 7 May 1836, he said he assisted in the capture of the American generals, Chandler and Winder, and "as a private volunteer he discharged his duty and distinguished himself on Secret Services as well as a brave soldier and a good loyal Subject during the late war."

"I must further state," the attorney's statement went on, "that he lived with his family at Stony Creek where the American army encamped no more than three hundred yards from his house & he left his wife sick in bed and went to the British army and gave information where the American Generals had pitched their camp and then joined the 49th Regiment in the engagement. The Battle so frightened his wife (as she expected he was in the battle) that she left her bed undressed and ran out of the house & took Cold and a violent fever set in & carried her off."[14] After the war Freeman Green resettled on Lake Erie near what is now Ridgetown, Ontario.

In 1851 or 1852, amateur Hamilton historian Robert Nisbet was given a guided tour of the battlefield by James Gage, then 77 or 78 years old. Gage told Nisbet the attack began when "the British scout, a large Scotch sergeant" pinned an American sentry to a tree with his bayonet. If Gage mentioned the role of William Green, Nisbet never reported it.[15]

Eight years later American historian Benjamin Lossing visited Stoney Creek as part of the research for his massive *Pictorial Field-Book of the War of 1812*. Lossing wrote mysteriously about "Harvey's Scout" who guided Vincent's army to Stoney Creek: "By one of the inhabitants of the neighbourhood who had treacherously joined the Americans and deserted, Vincent had obtained the countersign for that night and through it he was able to secure the sentinels without giving alarm."[16]

In 1873 on the 60th anniversary of the battle, Emerson Bristol Biggar, a young journalist from Winona, published a careful reconstruction of events.[17] It was the first serious – and relatively even-handed – attempt to organize and make sense of an otherwise confusing action and stood for nearly 40 years as the standard reference work. Biggar, who had five great uncles who served in the 5th Lincoln during the war, three of them in the same company with Green,[18] made no mention of William Green, although several local settlers are referred to by name. He did, however, relate the adventures of one of Merritt's dragoons who encountered the American advance guard just as it arrived in Stoney Creek on 5 June. The account of how trooper John Brady escaped by riding up the Mountain on a deer path and then made his way to Burlington Heights to report what he had seen, sounds not unlike William Green's account of leading his brother's horse up the Mountain, riding along the brow and then descending to Vincent's camp on the heights.

In 1875 when the federal government issued a one-time $20 payment to the surviving local veterans of the War of 1812 at Hamilton City Hall, William Green, age 82, was second in line. Although some of his contemporaries gave detailed statements of their war service, Green said only that "he fought at Stoney Creek and was not wounded."[19]

In 1887, ten years after Green's death, Sarah Anne Curzon published the blank verse drama that made Laura Secord a household name in Canada and fed a growing hunger for Canadian heroes and heroines in the new dominion. Two years later in 1889 the fledgling Wentworth Pioneer and Historical Society attracted 500 people to its inaugural Pioneer Picnic in Stoney Creek, where one of the featured guests, phrenologist and amateur historian Peter Van Wagner, credited William Green with conveying the countersign to the British. The subsequent report in the *Hamilton Evening Times* may be the first published account of Green's deed.[20]

In the same year, John H. Land, grandson of William Green's company commander, Robert Land, first read his paper on the battle before the Wentworth Historical Society. According to Land, on the afternoon of 5 June 1813 when the only British presence in Stoney Creek was an advanced picket, "a scout brought word that the Yankees were just on the other side of the 'Big Creek.'"[21] Assuming for a moment that the scout could be Green, perhaps this modest accomplishment of warning the picket that "the Americans are coming" could be the genesis of the grander version of warning the entire British army of the approaching peril.

In 1893 Emerson Bristol Biggar, who had interviewed Green for his 1873 account of Stoney Creek, wrote an updated 16-page account of the battle for the *Canadian Magazine* in which he scoffed at Van Wagner's claim. "In the account which this Wm. Green gave the writer years ago," Biggar wrote, "he made no mention of this incident, which one would think he would not have forgotten."[22]

In 1909, the first real War of 1812 historian, Ernest Cruikshank, weighed in with a compact, 4,600-word history of the battle. Typically document-driven, Cruikshank's version makes no mention of William Green. In his only reference to intelligence, he writes that Harvey, on his evening reconnaissance of the American camp, "picked up two prisoners and was joined by a deserter, from whom he obtained some important information."[23]

By 1913, when the battlefield monument was officially unveiled on the 100th anniversary of the action, Green's profile in Stoney Creek was such that "Scout Green" was chiselled in the limestone façade along with the rest of the cast –Vincent, Plenderleath, FitzGibbon, James Gage, Merritt, Ogilvie and Harvey.

In 1916, Hazel Corman, grandniece of Isaac Corman, published her account of the battle, which became, after Slater's diary, the standard reference for the role of Green and Corman. In it, Corman, after being released, is apprehended a second time by five American soldiers, who hold him captive in his own home overnight. According to Corman, the noise of the battle was dismissed by the sergeant in charge as merely the sound of reveille in the camp. William Green, she writes, "better known as Billy Green the Scout," was a great, unsung hero.[24]

By 1926 when Stoney Creek became a police village, the formal William Green the Scout had been fully replaced by the more familiar Billy Green the

Scout.[25] Five years later, *Hamilton Spectator* columnist and local historian Charles McCullough cast a skeptical eye over the Slater diary and suggested "Billy the Scout was pulling the leg of the too credulous newcomer ... and that too much telling of the story of the night fight at Stoney Creek had made the resourceful Bill believe in each stage of the tale from the original fact to the finished fiction."[26]

By the middle of the Depression however, Green's exploits were recognized in Toronto, where on the anniversary of the battle in 1935 the *Mail and Empire* proclaimed him a national hero: "And so Canada remained British ... due to the cool-headed, yet audacious courage of Billy Green, the farm lad who was God's instrument in saving Upper Canada."[27]

The fact the story did not emerge until a decade after Green's death and that it appeared in neither his land petition nor his War of 1812 pension application, nor in the interview he gave E.B. Biggar on the battle but did appear in his *brother's* land petition, strongly suggests that it was fabricated, or appropriated, long – perhaps 75 years – after the fact, as part of the great patriotic awakening of the 1880s.

Other than the Slater diary and the revised version produced by his grandson, John W. Green, there is no evidence whatsoever that William Green ever claimed to be a major player in the Battle of Stoney Creek. The diary itself is suspect. Why would a schoolteacher emigrating from Ireland to the New World in 1818 find nothing worthy of recording in his diary for ten months other than the Billy Green narrative? Apart from his name on the diary – two initials only – S. D. Slater left no trace of his time in Upper Canada. What seems more likely to have occurred is that sometime between Biggar's 1873 account of the battle and Van Wagner's "revelation" of 1889, the persona of Billy Green the Scout was cut from whole, or nearly whole, cloth to create a Stoney Creek hero who could stand beside Laura Secord.

There is, of course, no smoking gun to identify the tailor or tailors, but a circumstantial case can be built against Van Wagner. Perhaps he was familiar with the Freeman Green petition. Or at least Freeman's story. Possibly the names got confused. Freeman had left town in 1816 and was likely forgotten. Billy had lived his entire life in Stoney Creek and was well known.

The following is the Statement of Freeman Green accompanying the land grant petition written by his attorney Samuel Smith:

NAC RG 1, C-2035, L3, vol 212, G Bundle 20, petition 14.

Ancaster, May 7, 1836

I do herby certify that Freeman Green is a son of Adam Green of Saltfleet a U.E. loyalist and said Freeman Green was a Volunteer in a Flank Company commanded by Captain Duran in the late war between Great Britain and the United States of America and that he was in the battles of Queenston and Stony Creek and assisted in the taking of two of the American generals at Stony Creek. As a private volunteer he discharged his duty and distinguished himself on Secret Services as well as a brave _____ soldier and a good loyal Subject during the late war .

I must further state that he lived with his family at Stony Creek where the American army encamped not more than three hundred yards from his house & he left his wife sick in bed and went to the British army and gave information Where the American Generals had pitched their camp and then joined the 49th Regiments in the engagement. The Battle so frightened his wife (as she expected he was in the battle) that she left her bed undressed and ran out of the house & took Cold and a violent fever set in & carried her off.

Samuel Smith

Local History & Archives at the Hamilton Public library holds a 1794 leather-bound atlas, donated by the Corman family, in which the following is written on the back of three maps. The whereabouts of the original diary is unknown.

Copied from S. D. Slater's Diary.
Sept. 3, 1818 – Left Ireland for America.
Dec. 8 – Landed in Quebec.
Feb 1, 1819 – Arrived in York.
Feb 16 – Arrived in Hamilton.
Feb. 17 – Am chopping wood for Robert Land.
March 3 – Am at Stony Creek teaching school. Am boarding at Mr. Samuel Green's for this week.
March 10 – Boarding at Isaac Corman's.
March 17 – Boarding at Samuel Nash.
March 24 – Boarding at Henry Van Wagner's.
April 14 – Boarding at Thomas Davis'.
April 28 – Boarding at Brady's Hotel.
June 5 – Took walk up the mountain met Billy Green, he told me his experience as the battle of Stony Creek

I was 16 or 17 years old then. We heard the Americans were camped down below the Forty, so my brother Levi, Sam Lee, and me went down the top of the mountain about six o'clock in the morning. We got to the Forty and stayed out on the peak til noon. When the troops came marching up the road we stayed till all the enemy but a few were past. Then we yelled like Indians I tell you them simples did run, then we ran along the mountain and took down to the road. Levi ran across a fellow with his boot off, putting a rag on his foot. The soldier grabbed for his gun but Levi hit him with a stick. He yelled and some of the scouts fired. We made our way to the top of the mountain again. I whooped and Levi answered. Lee went home and the rest of us went to Levi's place on the side of the hill. When we heard them going the Creek we all went out on the hill to see them. Some of them spied us and fired, one ball struck the bars where Teenie[28] was sitting holding Hannah on her arm. We all went back in the mountain to one of Jim Stoney's trapping huts. Teenie went to the house, after a while two officers came up and asked her if she had seen some Indians around there. She said there was around back on the mountain. They left and Teenie came out where we were hed and whistled, I answered, I told them I would go down to Issac's. When I got down there I whistled and out came Dezi. I asked where Isaac was and she said "they have taken him prisoner and taken the trail to the Beach". I wanted to know how she knew. She said Alph had followed them to the Swamp. Where is Alph? "I am in the cellar with Becky and Dezi."[29] I went down and he told me where to go. I started and ran, every[30] now and then I would whistle until I got across the Creek when I heard Isaac hoot like an owl. I thought they had him there but he was coming back. I was going to raise an Indian War whoop and scare them when I saw Isaac coming. I asked how he got away. He said the major and he got a-talking and said he was a second cousin to Harrison, I said I was a first cousin. After talking a little longer a message came for him. He said I must go. You may go home "but I can't get through the line" "I will give you the countersign" and he did.

I got it and away I went. When I got up to the road I forgot it and didn't know what to do, so I pulled my coat over my head, I went up on the hill and got Levi's Tip and led him along the mountain till I could get to the top. Then I rode away round by the gully where I tied old Tip to a fence around a stack bottom. I made my way to the camp on the Heights when I got there they took me for a spy and then I had to tell them all I knew before they would believe me. It was about twelve o'clock and they commenced to hustle. We got started about one o'clock, the officer asked me if I knew the way and I said "Yes; every inch of it." He gave me a corporal's sword and told me to take the lead. Sometimes I would get away ahead and go back to hurry them up. I told them it would be morning before we got there. Someone said that would be soon enough to be killed. We got down this side of the big creek when three sentries fired and ran over the South Creek. Then we came on more careful after that. I spied a fellow crouched against a tree, I told the man behind me to shoot but the officer said "No, Run him through." The next was at the church, he demanded a pass, I commenced to give him the countersign and walked up, I grabbed his gun and put my sword to him. The old gun had no load in it, he had shot the ramrod away. Then we could see the camp fires. We cut across and got in the lane when the order was given to "fix flints – fire" and we fired three rounds and advanced about one hundred yards. Then we banged away again. There was a rush in the middle rank. Their south flank charged. Then came orders for our flank to charge. There's where we lost most of our men. We got bunched right down under them. The centre flank captured their two guns. Then the general order was to charge and we drove them back. We could hear them scampering. We were ordered to fire and we shot all our powder away. When it commenced to get light they were running in all directions. We lost about eighty killed and one hundred and fifty wounded. Their loss was two hundred killed and two hundred and fifty wounded. The settlers helped to scare them by giving war whoops on the top of the hill.

Appendix B

# Bones of Contention

The dead of Stoney Creek confound researchers still. Not only are their actual numbers unknown – although most certainly they are higher than the official tally – and the extent of their burial uncertain but there are also disturbing hints on how some of them may have died and distressing questions about how their remains have been treated.

Despite some American claims that they buried their own dead on the battle-field, it is clear from the number of first-hand accounts that all the dead were buried after the American army retreated to the Forty early in the morning of 6 June. James FitzGibbon, who commanded a company of the 49th, reported 31 American bodies left behind on the morning after the battle. John Lee, a private in the 5th Lincoln, said he personally counted 61 bodies from both sides that were buried on 6 June.[1]

Lee does not indicate where the bodies were buried but fellow militiaman William Green identified the knoll where Towson placed his artillery just to the north of the Queenston road (now King Street). E.B. Biggar, writing in 1873, said there were two burial sites – the knoll and the graveyard beside the church where the American pickets had fallen asleep. At the latter, he said, the dead were buried "without distinction of country," which suggests a mass grave. An anonymous, undated document in the Thompson Papers at Hamilton Public Library, listed as an eyewitness account of the battle, described burials beside the Methodist church of as many as 22 bodies.[2] "At this spot four little mounds could be seen for a long time after, with a soldier in each – likewise a sunken pit, in which sixteen or eighteen were said to be buried." The Methodist church, which served as a barracks for the British garrison in the latter part of 1813, was torn down in 1871.[3]

In 1888, 75 years after the battle, a Hamilton mortician, Charles Blachford, unearthed bones of what he believed to be those soldiers in the old church graveyard. Unfortunately this is all that is known about battle dead buried in the old cemetery.

The knoll presents a somewhat more detailed history and therefore looms larger in any investigations. On the southeast corner of the original Crown grant made to William Gage in 1802, the knoll was part of a 12-acre fruit farm owned by Gage's great granddaughter, Louisa Smith, and her husband, Hiram Smith. According to family history, it was their son Allen who first uncovered human remains while ploughing, probably around the same time Blachford made his discovery in the cemetery.[4]

Perhaps it was at this time as well that millwright and local historian Peter Van Wagner began digging up bodies at Smith's Knoll. Van Wagner, who was born in 1818, grew up near the battlefield at a time "when single graves and mounds were quite fresh and bullets, bayonets and buckles, and brass ornaments and decaying straps turned up by the plow were gathered and battle tales ad infinitum were in order."[5]

A one-time teacher and eventually a justice of the peace, Van Wagner also lectured in phrenology, a 19th-century pseudoscience which held that the shape and protuberances of the skull revealed character and mental

**Owners of Smith's Knoll.** Hiram (1843-1924) and Louisa Smith (1849-1927), shown here in 1912 with their grandson, Harold Coleman, owned the 12-acre fruit and flower farm that included the elevated piece of ground where Towson's artillery was located during the battle and many of the dead were buried afterwards. Their son, Alan Smith, was reputed to have first ploughed up human remains on the site in the late 1880s. (Louise Wilson)

capacity. In 1889, at the first Stoney Creek outing for the newly-formed Wentworth Pioneer and Historical Society, Van Wagner referred to "a long trench in which forty friends and foe lie sleeping and waiting the last bugle call." Ten years later Van Wagner told George Mills, president of the same society, that 40 bodies had been dug from the knoll and he had personally exhumed 22 because he wanted the skulls for phrenological examination.[6]

The knoll, of course, was the epicentre of the battle and the most strategic piece of real estate on the field. The embankment that snakes north from the knoll, overlooking the floodplain of Battlefield Creek, was where the Twenty-Fifth Infantry formed up and where some of the fiercest and most sustained fighting took place. According to Smith family lore, ploughing on the knoll was restricted after Allen Smith found the first bones. However, spring furrowing on the rest of the property regularly yielded up more bones and artifacts, the latter, which included flattened bullets, buttons, cloth fragments and edged weapons, collected in several bushel baskets.[7]

In 1894 Hiram and Louisa Smith agreed to cede Smith's Knoll to the Wentworth Historical Society for a monument site on condition that $50 was paid

**Knoll consecrated.** A crowd of 1,000, including 600 members of the militia, gathered in the spring of 1908 to witness the consecration of Smith's Knoll as a cemetery by the Anglican Bishop of Niagara, John Philip DuMoulin. Pictured here are members of the County of Wentworth Veterans' Association. (Battlefield House Museum)

to remove an old building on the site and an iron fence constructed around the plot. However, despite the Smiths' apparent civic-mindedness, it would be another 14 years before the deed of transfer was registered and the plot officially consecrated as a cemetery by the Anglican Bishop of Niagara. The Smiths were paid $400 for the site.[8]

In the interim between the Smiths' initial commitment and the legal transfer of the deed, an electric railroad was built along King Street that could well have uncovered human remains when the rail bed was dug directly in front of the knoll.[9] In 1907 the president of the County of Wentworth Veteran's Association complained that the site "has been entirely neglected & left to the mercy of relic hunters, who take away anything they can dig up belonging to the deceased soldiers."[10]

By 1910 a $1,500 stone cairn topped by a stone lion was constructed –another opportunity to disturb burials – and the site stood for the next 88 years largely as a monument to the "memory of 23 good and true King's men, who fighting in defence of their country, died and were buried on this knoll." Stewardship was entrusted to the County of Wentworth Veterans' Association,[11] which held it

**Smith's Knoll.** In the spring of 1910 this stone cairn was erected on Smith's Knoll marking the spot where Plenderleath's charge overran the American artillery position. The funds to buy the site and erect the monument, still awaiting a stone lion, were raised by public subscription. Two hulking 32-pdr. guns can be just be seen behind the cairn on the two western corners of the knoll. (Library and Archives Canada)

until 1995 when ownership passed to the municipality of Stoney Creek.

In 1998 as part of a $200,000 rehabilitation of the site, a Hamilton archaeologist was hired to locate and catalogue the burials. Rita Griffin-Short, working in the summers of 1998 and 1999, uncovered the remains of at least 24 bodies in a shallow, irregular trench. Although aware that Peter Van Wagner and others had already disturbed the graves, she said what she found was more garbage pit than burial site. There were no in-situ burials, only disarticulated human bones mixed in with animal bones and domestic rubbish.

"It really is a terrible thing to have to be digging this kind of site," Griffin-Short said in the spring of 1999, "because the bones have been so mashed up, obviously some of it has just been left outside … to be chewed on by animals. None of my colleagues have ever seen or heard of anything like this. If we didn't know we were digging in a cemetery we would be hard pressed to figure out what was going on. All sort of indignities have occurred to these bones. Most of the heads have been broken off because it looks like when they took these out they probably just weren't fussy about how they were taken out. And all this stuff

**Lion monument.** In 1910 the site the Wentworth Historical Society had championed finally got its monument with the dedication of a stone cairn topped by the Imperial Lion on Smith's Knoll. The lion was sculpted by Hamilton Plantagenet MacCarthy, the grandson of Stoney Creek veteran Lieutenant Thomas Taylor. In this picture, taken in 1913, a pair of naval carronades are visible at the base of the cairn. (Local History & Archives, Hamilton Public Library)

is reburied with demolition debris, animal bones. You find cow bones in with human legs. It's just really depressing."[12]

Griffin-Short's licence restricted her excavation to the monument site even though the trench, showing evidence of further bones, clearly continued on under the property immediately east of the knoll, a women's spa.[13] In other words there are more bodies, or body parts, under the lawn next door.

Griffin-Short also reported finding several dozen military buttons. Those she was able to identify were mostly American, predominately the Second Artillery Regiment, which manned the guns on the knoll during the battle. Four buttons from the 49th regiment were identified plus one Royal Artillery. Perhaps the most puzzling find was a single regimental button from the 66th Foot, a British line unit that never served in Canada during the war. Two musket balls and one gun flint were also recovered. The relative scarcity of military artifacts she attributed to looters.[14]

In her 2000 report to city council, Griffin-Short chastised the descendants of the Smith family for not surrendering artifacts they had inherited. "Their apparent lack of remorse and willingness to come forward to do their civic duty, I find shocking … whatever the family has should be returned to the people of Stoney Creek."[15]

The farm adjoining the knoll was inherited from Hiram and Louisa Smith by their daughter, Nellie Victoria, and her husband, Dilly Coleman, and continued to produce tender fruit and cut flowers for the Hamilton Market until it was sold to developers in 1963, who covered the entire area with apartment buildings.[16]

At least two descendants have artifacts that were originally collected by Allen Smith. One of his granddaughters, Bernice Ott, who was born in

**In situ.** This is one of the scenes that confronted archaeologist Rita Griffin-Short when she excavated Smith's Knoll in the summer of 1999 – a pile of disarticulated bones and bone fragments. Finding the reburied remains mixed with animal bones and demolition debris, she said, was one of the most distressing experiences of her professional career. (Rita Griffin-Short)

1925, has several dozen buttons, predominately 20 mm copper buttons from the Second Regiment of Artillery, a pair of 20 mm gilt-on-copper officer's buttons from the 49th and a couple of Royal Artillery – one 14 mm, one 20 mm – copper buttons, which raise more questions because no more than a half dozen Royal Artillery took part in the action and none were reported as casualties. Ott also has an American oval brass belt plate, some gun flints, several American .63 calibre lead shot and some buttons with fabric and leather attached. Her older sister, Helen Crichton of Winona, has a similar, smaller collection of buttons – pewter and copper – as well as some small-calibre round shot.

Ott said that when her grandmother, Norma Mae Smith, died in 1954, the family's extensive collection of artifacts was divided among several descendants, including her mother, Viola Rose. "Mother didn't have a big interest in this stuff, she didn't ask for anything, it was just what was given to her."[17]

Along with the buttons, arrowheads, flints and bullets in the collection was a human skull that was kept in the back of a storage cupboard. "It had been in my mother's relics and they were hidden away, they weren't something that was out on display by any means, it was just something that we had." During a move in 1960 the skull was destroyed. "I

**Battlefield buttons.** Through the late 19th century literally bushels of artifacts were ploughed up on Smith's Knoll and the adjoining farm, including hundreds of buttons. Most have been lost but some are still held by descendants of Hiram and Louisa Smith. From top, Second Regiment of U.S. Artillery, 19 mm; U.S. Infantry, 19 mm; Royal Artillery, 19 mm; Royal Artillery, 19 mm; 49th Regiment, officer's, 19 mm; 49th Regiment, other ranks, 24 mm. (Hawthorn Ink)

hated having it. We were moving into a new home and I just could not see taking that with me. We had a big bonfire going out in the field and I was burning a lot of stuff and I had this skull. I said 'mother, it is such a crime that this poor man hasn't been allowed to be buried' and she said 'Bernice, you do whatever you want to do.' I can remember my friend and I stood there and we put it on the fire. There's a few people that would like to murder me when they found out what we had done ... [but] I didn't have the [fore]sight to see that it could be very important to a lot of people."[18]

Ott said she offered to let Griffin-Short examine the artifacts but was rebuffed: "She didn't want to talk to us.... She said we were grave robbers. We knew we had the relics that our grandfather had found and we just assumed they came from the farm, it never entered our heads 'til this, that he could have got them from the grave"[19]

Louise Wilson, great granddaughter of Hiram Smith, grew up on the original Smith farm and lived there until it was sold to a developer in 1963. From her paternal grandfather, Dilly Coleman, who lived on the farm for more than 50 years, she learned that the knoll became a no-plough zone after the bodies were discovered but bones and artifacts continued to turn up all over the property for some years after. "This was a farm. Ask any farmer about spring ploughing ... all kinds of things emerge from the ground over years of thawing and freezing." The recovered bones, she was told, were collected under a large white cherry tree that stood about 100 yards northeast of the knoll. If these bones were re-interred prior to the consecration of the knoll in 1908, it may account for the weathered, exposed condition of the remains Griffin-Short reported.[20]

Wilson insists there was no willful desecration: "My great-grandparents, grand parents and my parents were respectful of any bones they found in the fields."[21] Wilson said that when she was a child, artifacts were still turning up on the farm, which her grandfather collected in his home. "He had a dining room off to the side, it was full – maybe a dozen bushel baskets full of stuff, heaped right up – arrowheads, tons of buttons, bits of cloth, swords and flattened bullets." After his death in 1956 everything disappeared. "Stolen in the night."[22]

The hundreds of bones and bone fragments the archaeologist Griffin-Short recovered from the knoll were shipped to the University of Waterloo, where Maria Liston, a physical anthropologist, used them as a component of an osteology course. Liston, who had previous experience studying military remains from the 18th-century Fort William Henry site in New York, was able to draw some general conclusions about age, size and health of the soldiers. Of the 15 she was able to age, 11 were between 25 and 40 and four between 40 and 50.

The average height, based on the literally fragmentary evidence, was estimated at 172.7 cm or almost 5′8″. Their health, compared to their 1757 Fort William Henry counterparts, was good – some minor arthritis but otherwise "a pretty healthy, able group."[23]

Liston's background also included forensic work for police on murder victims, experience that served her well when dealing with the Smith's Knoll remains. Only four skulls were found, all had to be reconstructed from fragments and all showed evidence of gunshot wounds – three at the base of the skull and one through the temple.

"I'm still troubled by the position of these cranial wounds," Liston said in 2004. "They're just such classic execution wounds. They're either here, right square in the temple – that classic blow-your-brains-out position – or they're here at the back of your head. If you're going to kill somebody at close range kneeling on the ground in front of you, you shoot them in the back of the head. Or right through the middle. Those are the only two locations we've got – clear musket ball entry wounds – there's just no doubt what they are."[24]

One of the reconstructed skulls – the different parts were found at separate ends of the dig– had two holes, one the size of a quarter, the other the size of a loonie coin. The smaller hole bevelled on the inside, the larger hole on the outside. Assuming the weapon to be a .75 calibre Brown Bess musket, Liston theorized that a musket ball fired at close range would travel through the brain,

flattening along the way, and exit larger than it came in. Because there was little forensic literature on what a musket ball wound looks like, Liston conducted her own controlled

**Every shard tells a story.** Maria Liston, a physical anthropologist at the University of Waterloo, made the Stoney Creek bones the centre of her osteology class in 2000. Her first direction to the students was, "No jokes about the bones, they were human beings, somebody loved them and they died awfully, a long way from home." (Barry Gray, *Hamilton Specator*)

experiment. Four pig heads from a slaughterhouse were shot with a reproduction Brown Bess musket at four distances from point blank to 100 feet. Liston then boiled the heads to remove the flesh and observed: "The wounds produced using a standard black powder charge produced entry and exit wounds similar to those found on the Stoney Creek (skulls). In particular, the appearance of the five-metre distance and contact (point-blank) experimental wounds most resembled those found on the Stoney Creek cranial bones."[25]

The incidence of head wounds in the only recovered skulls adds emphasis to Peter Van Wagner's 1899 statement to the president of the Wentworth Historical Society, George Mills, that of the 22 bodies he had exhumed from the Knoll, "several were shot in the top of the head."[26]

What happened? Prominent War of 1812 historian Donald E. Graves suggests a combination of panic and fear. "The fact they have head wounds is really unusual, it could have been a volley but it's more likely they were shot at close range. I suspect it was done in the heat of the battle or immediately afterwards. Night attacks are the worst because all your fears and worries are magnified. In close-quarters combat at night – it's dark, it's confused – guys get very frightened and frightened soldiers do bad things. I think it likely that the British having taken the gun position just shot at anything that moved. The probability is, they're the remains of the gunners who were in that position when it was captured. You've got guys crawling around, crawling away and they just simply shoot. When you use the bayonet you have to be very careful … if you get the blade stuck in the rib cage, which is quite easy to do, it's hard to get out, it gets stuck in there. It makes more sense to simply put the muzzle of the musket near their head and *boom!*"[27]

Bayonets in rib cages are exactly what happened to several of the soldiers bur-

**Musket ball wound.** This reconstructed skull – the different parts were found at different ends of the dig – shows the spalling of an exit wound the size of a loonie coin on the right frontal. The entrance wound on the left side of the temple is the size of a nickel and spalled on the inside. Such a wound would break down the sutures that bind the cranium and in the ground the skull would literally fall apart. (Barry Gray, *Hamilton Spectator*)

ied on Smith's Knoll. Liston found 30 rib fragments with evidence of trauma, identifying dozens of tiny triangular nicks and several bones that were actually split. The damage was completely unlike the wound made by a knife blade, leaving the obvious suspect the 17-inch triangular steel bayonet used during the War of 1812. Again, modern forensic literature having no reference to early 19th-century bayonet trauma, Liston turned once more to pigs. This time the experiment took place at the reconstructed Fort George in Niagara-on-the-Lake, where two Parks Canada interpreters took turns thrusting reproduction Brown Bess muskets fitted with bayonets into a crown rack of pork ribs.

In the Napoleonic era the bayonet transformed a standard Short Land Pattern musket into a six-foot pike that in the hands of a trained infantryman was capable of inflicting severe wounds in close quarter fighting.

While directing the stabbing of the pork roast, Liston came to appreciate the essentially grisly nature of the bayonet charge and that it was not for the squeamish or the inexperienced. Her volunteers found that retrieving a vigorously thrust bayonet from the pork ribs literally required the strength of two men with their feet braced against the roast. "We made sure we stabbed every single rib. It

took a lot of force to penetrate that tissue and then get it back out. It's a nasty wound, that was very clear in the experiment ... difficult to sew up or get to heal."[28]

Again the ribs were boiled

**Charge bayonets!** Confronted with dozens of triangular nicks in rib bones excavated at Stoney Creek, anthropologist Maria Liston conducted an experiment to determine if they were bayonet-inflicted. Peter Mitchell, an interpreter at Fort George National Historic Site, repeatedly stabbed a rack of pork ribs. After the flesh was boiled off the ribs, the resulting bone cuts were identical to those on the Stoney Creek ribs. (Maria Liston)

to remove the flesh. The resulting bone cuts were found identical to those on the Stoney Creek ribs, right down to the piece of bone fragment left in the centre of each nick. The bones that broke from contact were likewise sheared in a manner similar to the Stoney Creek bone fragments.

On 4 June 2000 the remains of the 24 soldiers were re-interred at the refurbished parkette in a single grey wooden box. When the site opened in 1910 it had been furnished with an array of vintage naval artillery of indeterminate provenance – two hulking 32 pdrs. on garrison mounts and three small carronades – that bore little relation to the light field guns that defended the knoll in 1813. Ninety years later the same wobbly concept of historical accuracy was evident in the re-interment ceremony. Neither the pallbearers, members of the American Old Guard dressed in uniforms of the American Revolution circa 1784, nor the circa-1860s horse-drawn hearse that conveyed the casket, had anything to do with 1813. Only the re-enactors dressed in War of 1812 uniforms watching from the sidelines conveyed an authentically appropriate background. The bones of four-and-twenty were sealed in a new crypt on the site which the mayor of Stoney Creek declared redress for nearly two centuries of neglect. However, there are perhaps as many as 16 more bodies on the adjoining properties that seem to have been officially ignored. The archaeologist, Rita Griffin-Short, said her proposal to investigate further and follow the bone trench into the property adjoining the knoll was approved by Stoney Creek but died when the municipality was amalgamated as part of greater Hamilton in 2000.[29]

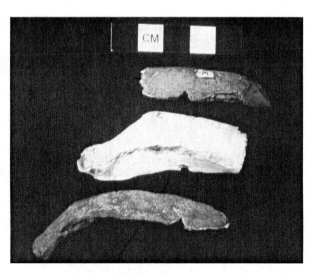

**Bayonet wounds.** The darker rib fragments on the top and the bottom were excavated from Smith's Knoll at Stoney Creek. Both exhibit uniform triangular nicks. The white bone fragment in the centre, one of the pork ribs stabbed with a bayonet, displays a similar nick. Bones that broke from contact were likewise sheared in a corresponding manner to the Stoney Creek bone fragments. (Maria Liston)

Appendix C

# The Second Battle of Stoney Creek

The 1887 publication of Sarah Anne Curzon's blank-verse drama *Laura Secord: The Heroine of 1812* heralded a burgeoning public hunger for Canadian history, particularly from the War of 1812. Within a year of publication, the Pioneer and Historical Association of Ontario was founded in Toronto, followed shortly after by the Wentworth Pioneer and Historical Society in Hamilton. Established on 8 January 1889 by six of Hamilton's most prominent citizens, the new society's coming-out party was a picnic held five months later on property adjoining the original Stoney Creek battlefield. Despite cold, blustery weather and the threat of rain, an estimated 500 people turned out on the 76th anniversary of the battle for a program that included a guided tour of the ground. In the speeches that followed there was an almost evangelical tone that reflected the patriotic groundswell Curzon had initiated. To hearty applause, society president and former Hamilton mayor George Mills said the society's mandate was to collect and preserve "a truthful record of the historical events of this part of the country, and thus aid in welding together a patriotic and distinctively Canadian national spirit, which will enable us to hand down this grand inheritance as we have received it from our forefathers."[1]

The future lieutenant governor of Ontario and co-founder of the society, John Gibson, lauded Curzon's plucky heroine, declaring "Laura Secord's patriotic and heroic endeavours should never be forgotten by loyal Canadians."[2]

Expanding on that theme, wealthy Hamilton meat packer Frederick Fearman invoked "memories of the brave men who laid down their lives on this never-to-be-forgotten soil ... we must acknowledge the neglect of years past, and regret that suitable care and attention have not been given."[3]

And finally to *Hamilton Spectator* editor, Augustus Toplady Freed for the closer: "We in Canada have a history. We can look around us and say, on these fields our fathers fought. Let us prove that we are worthy sons of worthy sires."[4] And with that Freed moved a formal resolution that would resonate for the next quarter century and provoke a second battle on the old Gage farm, this one with the lines drawn not between nationalities but between sexes.

It was resolved: "That the Dominion Government be respectfully requested to grant a reasonable sum of money in aid of the erection of suitable monuments on the battle ground of Stony [sic] Creek and on Burlington Heights"[5]

The *Hamilton Evening Times*, before listing the names of 166 men who attended the picnic, noted "a goodly proportion" of females in the crowd, although none were identified. It was a prescient – though likely unintentional – observation that foreshadowed a forthcoming conflict that would go from merely impolite to downright nasty.

Unacknowledged but undoubtedly present at the picnic was a middle-aged socialite and amateur painter who had something none of worthies on the dais could claim – a blood line that ran directly back to the heart of the battlefield. Sara Galbraith Calder, wife of prominent Hamilton clothier John Calder, was the granddaughter of James and Mary Gage, on whose farm part of the battle had occurred. An acute sense of her hereditary connection and zealous nationalism combined to make a formidable package. Society president George Mills could well have been describing Calder when he singled out "the women of this district, their daughters and granddaughters ... signifying and testifying their interest in what is now going on."[6]

The resolution seeking federal funding for monuments was heartily endorsed, doubtless by male and female picnickers alike, but few present that day could have imagined how it would ultimately play out, how Wentworth's nameless "daughters and granddaughters" – driven by the indomitable will of Sara Calder – would show they were not to be trifled with or taken for granted. Obsessed with the idea of honouring history, the 43-year-old Calder

**Sara Calder (1846-1914).** "It can be done, it must be done, and it will be done" was the watchword of the Victorian dynamo as she fought a 20-year battle with the Wentworth Historical Society to have an imposing monument built on the hill behind the Gage homestead. In 1913, on the 100th anniversary of the battle, she fulfilled her dream. (Battlefield House Museum)

became a local version of Joan of Arc, striding into battle under the old flag and smiting her enemies with the sword of self-righteousness. Described by one historian as a "hard-driven Victorian dynamo," Calder was energetic, creative and, most of all, single-minded. Her compulsive watchword was: "It can be done, it must be done, and it will be done."[7]

Following the picnic, the WHS officially petitioned parliament for monument funding and was unofficially ignored. Despite counting captains of industry, wealthy merchants, lawyers and politicians of all three levels of government among its membership, the society made little headway dealing with the Department of Militia and Defence in Ottawa. "I scarcely need draw your attention to the importance of the Stony Creek battle," Mills wrote the minister in 1890, "but for the reverses resulting from that engagement the loss of this southern peninsula would certainly have followed." The official response to the grant requests was tepid and non-committal. Calder's patriotic ardor, however, was not in the least diminished and she moved to infuse some vigour into the staid hierarchy of the historical society. In 1893, she commissioned and paid for an embroidered silk banner commemorating the Battle of Stoney Creek, which she donated to the society at a gala reception in the handsome old Hamilton Court House.[8]

The banner was an extravagant gift. Weighted cream silk and blue velvet embroidered with gold and silver bullion, it depicts an armorial design featuring a beaver and a wreath of maple leaves surrounding a crown inlaid with 36 faceted, cut-glass jewels. It cost $200 in 1893 – when labour could be had for 20 cents an hour.[9]

In her presentation address to the 700 invited quests, Calder gave a glimpse of the motives that would drive her over the next 20 years – patriotism and loyalty to the British connection. "Perish the people," she declared, "who have no spirit of patriotism to warm and stir the pulse of national life.... I am proud to be able to claim descent from United Empire Loyalists as my great grandfather, Captain James Gage, was killed while fighting under the old flag.... God grant that Canadians may never dishonour the memory of that noble band of exiles."[10]

Ironically Calder's claim to Loyalist descent through the Gages – the bedrock of her faith – was in reality anything but solid, although she undoubtedly believed what she had been told. The flag her great-grandfather died fighting for was not the King's colour but the Stars and Stripes.[11] Calder, however, never suffered a moment's doubt about her Loyalist pedigree and the banner was a mark of her faith.

In accepting the gift, society president George Mills recognized and applauded Calder's personal connection to the battlefield as "a direct descendent of patriotic United Empire Loyalists, upon whose farm the brilliant engagement took place.... It is well that memories of such events be perpetuated and you madam, have contributed not a little to that end."[12] It was probably the last time Mills and Calder agreed on anything pertaining to the Stoney Creek battlefield.

At the behest of the province, the banner was immediately dispatched to the World's Columbian Exposition in Chicago – already in progress – to become part of the Ontario exhibit. Calder too was destined for bigger things.

A year later at the society's annual meeting, the membership approved a resolution authorizing "the lady members of this Society" to form to an auxiliary "to aid the Society in carrying out its objects."[13] Few in the hierarchy of the society could have foreseen how that tiny sliver of autonomy would grow into a giant wedge that would split the society along gender lines.

In the fall of the same year when two potential monument sites in Stoney Creek became available – the former James Gage homestead with four acres of land and Smith's Knoll, the American artillery position during the battle – the choice to Calder was immediately obvious. The Gage parcel included an option on a commanding hilltop lot behind the house and Calder, with the eye of an accomplished amateur painter, had visions of Brock's soaring monument on Queenston Heights in mind. The owner of the Gage property, George Fisher, was asking $1,600 for the main parcel plus an additional $300 for the hilltop and road access to it.

**Calder vision.** The view from this hill behind the Gage house, looking north across the battlefield towards Lake Ontario, inspired Sara Calder's castle-in-the-air concept for a Stoney Creek monument. She envisaged something along the lines of Brock's Monument on Queenston Heights and would struggle for two decades to bring it to fruition. (Library and Archives Canada)

Smith's Knoll, a 240-square foot plot on the north side of King Street, was owned by Hiram Smith and his wife Louisa, a descendant of the original owner, William Gage. The Smiths agreed to sell the knoll for $50 and a promise to enclose it within an iron fence.

According to society minutes, Calder actively promoted the Fisher parcel but the WHS committee of five men had a different view and recommended Smith's Knoll, which was accepted. Although rebuffed, Calder had no intention of abandoning her quest. A consummate networker and savvy fundraiser, she was the organizational genius behind a ten-day art show in 1888 that attracted 20,000 people – nearly half the city's population – and raised $2,000 for the Hamilton Art School. She had a touch of the impresario, handled the press easily and built her fundraisers around big, spectacular paintings or curios like Marie Antoinette's watch or a lock of Napoleon's hair.[14]

In the spring of 1895, the Ladies' Committee of the Wentworth Historical Society was formed with Calder as vice president and the remainder of the executive drawn from prominent Hamilton families. Of note is the press coverage of the inaugural meeting, which reflects prevailing attitudes about the role of women in society: "About 40 ladies gathered in the Board of Trade rooms this morning to organize a feminine auxiliary to the Wentworth Historical Society," the *Hamilton Spectator* reported. "The meeting was enthusiastic and entered into the scheme of dabbling into archaeology and historical research with apparent zeal."[15]

Within three months Calder had taken over as committee president and within six months the "dabblers" had mounted a lively eight-day exhibition in the Hamilton Drill Hall to raise funds. "Mrs. Calder is the busiest woman in town," the *Spectator* marvelled. "Under her direction a large corps of workman are 'making the waste places bloom like a rose' with buntings, flags, flowers and streamers."[16]

Loosely based on a pioneer theme, the Military Encampment of 1895 featured theatrical performances, a minstrel show, Highland dancing and an 1812 tent and cabin. Relics on display included a saddle used at Waterloo, Sir Walter Scott's ink stand, flintlock pistols and muskets, swords, the key to the Bastille and the form of a stuffed dog that was purported to have accompanied Laura Secord (and perhaps her cow) on her famous night-time trek.[17]

Some insight into the Calder character can be gleaned from an incident that occurred during the event. When the Highland dancers continued their performance after being told by Calder to curtail it, she summoned a policeman to enforce the order, eliciting considerable resentment in the process. The wife of a prominent politician observed: "Mrs. Calder was again the cause of offence ... [she] is a very hard worker, and overdoes herself and thus she loses self-control."[18]

Calder pique notwithstanding, the encampment was an unqualified success – the provincial lieutenant governor, George Kirkpatrick, was only one of 3,000 people who attended opening night festivities – and the Ladies' Committee realized more than $1,000. The funds had originally been earmarked to build a log museum on Burlington Heights, for which the committee had undertaken earlier in the year to raise the money, but after the Military Encampment the ladies had a change of heart. Citing their right to "absolute control and disposal of all funds that may be raised by the said committee,"[19] they refused to hand the money over to the society.

The issue, of course, was where the Stoney Creek monument would be sited. Calder argued the prominence of the hill site outweighed any objections that it was not part of the actual battlefield. The men charged her with wilfully ignoring history and acting out of self interest. The cash stayed in the Ladies' Committee account. Even in the dryly polite minutes of the WHS it is possible to get a sense of the turmoil Calder's committee caused. "Shortly after the money had been raised for the building in Harvey Park," the WHS secretary recorded, "some of the leading members of the Ladies Committee came to the conclusion that the Society was wrong in its choice of sites for monuments and museum and took such action as prevented the erection of the proposed building. In consequence considerable friction arose in the Society."[20] Indeed, the ladies' show of independence torpedoed the museum plans and cracked open a giant schism within the society.

By 1898, after nine years of unsuccessfully pestering Ottawa for money and dealing with a revolving door at the Ministry of Militia and Defence that saw seven different ministers hold the portfolio, the WHS had little to show for its efforts. The society president complained "that three of the memorable battle grounds of the War of 1812-14, Lundy's Lane, Chateauguay and Cryslers Farm have already been decorated with national monuments while the most memorable of them all, *still* remains unrecognized though every minister of militia from Sir Adolphe Caron to the present minister has given the society fair reason to believe than an appropriation would certainly be made for Stony Creek."[21]

The pattern continued with the latest minister, Frederick Borden. In March he informed the society that $2,000 was to be put in the estimates for a Stoney Creek monument but by June the offer was withdrawn when it failed to gain cabinet approval. The society however, did have one staunch ally in Ottawa, an accomplished English sculptor, Hamilton Thomas Carleton Plantagenet MacCarthy. Already well known for his sculptures of Sir John A. Macdonald and Egerton Ryerson in Toronto, MacCarthy approached the WHS about sculpting a monument for Stoney Creek. His reasons were more than simply professional.

MacCarthy's maternal grandfather, Thomas Taylor, a lieutenant in the 41st Regiment and one of John Vincent's staff officers, had survived a severe wound at Stoney Creek and gone on become the first judge in Hamilton and president of the municipality's first governing body. MacCarthy created at least two models of the work he proposed – an officer leading a charge of men à la Plenderleath – and actively lobbied to get the commission, telling the society, "the carrying out of the statue of the monument I should make the crowning work of my life."[22]

But, while the society mounted yet another futile letter-writing campaign to prod the federal government into action, politicians with short attention spans were not the only adversary the WHS faced.

In June of 1899, on the anniversary of the battle, the Ladies' Committee of the Wentworth Historical Society held its last meeting. With Calder in the chair, the committee voted to secede from the WHS and form its own distinct society, the Women's Wentworth Historical Society, finally annulling a marriage that had been on the rocks for five years. And just to underscore their newly won independence, the new society announced that the first order of business would be the purchase of the Gage homestead. Calder, wisely realizing the value of grass roots support, said the money would not come from the society treasury but from public subscription.[23]

The $900 down payment was quickly raised and, to seal the deal, Calder personally assumed a mortgage for the remainder until it too could be raised by subscription. Three well-connected Hamiltonians, including steel pioneer and MP Andrew Trew Wood, were appointed trustees of the site. Calder then made her pitch to the Department of Militia and Defence, offering to donate the elevated land immediately south of the Gage House for a monument. The hilltop site, Calder wrote, "is the most appropriate one that can be, owing to its commanding position and being the center of the Battlefield." On 26 June the deputy minister, Lieutenant Colonel Louis-Felix Pinault, informed Calder that the offer

**Battlefield House.** The Gage house in 1897, two years before the Women's Wentworth Historical Society bought it. A visitor said it had "a decided let-me-lean-against-you style" and had not seen paint for at least 40 years. Shortly after Julian Seavey made this sketch, the portion to the left of the middle chimney was demolished. (Wentworth Bygones)

had been accepted. Three weeks after declaring independence, the former ladies' auxiliary now sat in the catbird seat. Calder had apparently scored a stunning victory, deftly scooping the prize that had evaded the WHS for ten years.[24]

The executive of the Wentworth Historical Society was caught completely flat-footed. While Calder was executing her coup, they were innocently contemplating the happy prospect of a $3,000 monument grant finally winning Parliamentary approval. To consolidate their case for Smith's Knoll, they had marshalled official support of several branches of the Canadian Club and had a petition in hand signed by 63 prominent Stoney Creek citizens. Right up until the last moment neither George Mills nor anyone else on the executive appears to have had any inkling of what was happening, which raises the question of whether the Ministry of Militia and Defence fully understood that the Women's Wentworth Historical Society and the Wentworth Historical Society had become separate entities. Three days before his deputy minister accepted Calder's offer, the minister of militia had his secretary write Mills confirming the society would be notified as soon as the monument estimates were approved by Parliament.[25]

Certainly Mills had ample evidence to believe the WHS had the inside track. "I think from correspondence with the Minister of Militia," he wrote on 29 June "that he is inclined to place in the hands of Wentworth Historical Society the selection of the site for the Stoney Creek monument." And on the following day, "the Minister of Militia has already, if my memory serves me rightly, stated in some of his letters to me, that it would be highly probable that the site chosen by the Wentworth Historical Society would be adopted by the Govt." Even when news of the Calder's coup appeared in the *Hamilton Spectator,* Mills could not bring himself to believe it. "I paid very little attention to the paragraph," he wrote to Wentworth MP Thomas Bain, "because from the correspondence with the Minister of Militia I feel assured that the question of Site will not be settled without consulting the Wentworth Historical Society."[26]

**Rundown relic.** When the Women's Wentworth Historical Society bought the altered and expanded Gage house in 1899 for $1,900, the property had been on the market for five years and was suffering from long-term neglect. (Library and Archives Canada)

Bain too heard the rumblings: "I observe by the *Globe* & *Times* of yesterday that the Women's Historic Society were also active and if the report is correct, claim that an Order In Council had been passed accepting the site offered by them … evidently some one is working hard to create an impression in favour of the site advocated by Mrs. Calder." And then he added, "These are days of Womens Rights."[27]

Finally, on July 15, nearly three weeks after handing the prize to Calder, the minister's office got around to telling the WHS – and only then in response to the citizen's petition endorsing Smith's Knoll. "The spot for the monument is naturally the one where the battle on the 6th of June 1813 was fought," Borden's secretary wrote, "and I must let you know that the piece of ground in question has already been offered to the Crown by the Women's Wentworth Historical Society and accepted."[28]

It took two days for the secretary's bombshell to reach Hamilton. Shocked at the turn of events, Mills wrote directly to the minister. "I fear some great mistake has been made.… I fear that your department has recognized the Women's Wentworth Historical Society, incorporated only a few weeks since, as being the Wentworth Historical Society. This Women's Society has had nothing whatever to do with any negotiations with your department for the proposed monument at Stoney Creek. The Site they propose is far away from the main travelled road on a high hill and not on the battle field at all. A monument there, such as the Government would recommend, would look like a tomb stone from the main road. I cannot believe that your Department, after the correspondence between us, will allow a mistake to be carried out, therefore rely upon the right thing being done."[29]

Later the same day Mills took up pen again to launch a second salvo at the minister, suggesting that Calder was motivated by a desire to enshrine her grandparents and should be disregarded: "I do sincerely trust that you will give this important matter your grave consideration … historical exactness should be preserved and prevail over personal regards."[30]

In private, the 72-year-old Mills, his health beginning to fail, was disgusted with the department of militia and complained bitterly that "the Wentworth Historical Society has been ignored altogether, after all the years of effort to secure the Monument, and people acknowledged who didn't even know anything about the matter."[31]

On the 19 July, Borden, clearly under siege, sputtered a confusing reply that sounded something like "the Gage site if necessary, but not necessarily the Gage site." The precedent, Borden said, had been set at Lundy's Lane, Crysler's Farm and Châteauguay that monuments were sited at the heart of the battlefield. "Under these circumstances there can be no negotiations in regard to the place for the monument, as history itself decides the matter. The Women's Historical Society are on no account to determine this point, except that if they own the real grounds, the Department must obtain it from them."[32]

Mills, likely sensing some leverage, redoubled his efforts, entreating the aged skull collector Peter Van Wagner to write in favour of Smith's Knoll, forwarded the Canadian Club resolution and wrote again to the minister restating the society's case, disparaging Calder's and suggesting a solution:

> Smith's Knoll was the very heart of the battle ... from this knoll the American cannon were captured and the fact can be established, while the hill to the south of the Gage house was not occupied by the enemy at any time during the battle, or by the British soldiers; In fact it did not form part of the battle ground. Mrs. Calder of the "Womens Society" whose grandfather occupied the "Gage house" during the war, is naturally anxious that the monument should be built on some part of her Grandfather's farm. If the spot offered by the women be accepted by the Government and a monument erected thereon, a great historical mistake will be made. All that this Society wants is to receive fair treatment and see that no perversion of historic facts be permitted.... Might I venture to suggest that some competent person be sent by your department to report the facts connected with this matter."[33]

Clearly the message had hit home, for Borden responded the very next morning promising immediate attention, adding the text of a brusque note he had just sent to Calder. "On the assertion contained in your communication ... that the Gage Farm was 'the centre of the battlefield' I naturally answered that the spot in question was accepted. But it would appear now that this assertion is contested, and the Department will investigate the matter by sending an officer there."[34]

Now it was the turn of the other side to be outraged. Trustee Andrew Trew Wood let loose a salvo at the militia department declaring he would not "in any way countenance the change desired by a few, old hide-bound Tories of placing the monument on the north side of the road, simply because one or two old fogies have given Mrs. Calder a great deal of opposition all through." Wood never names the fogies but the main one is undoubtedly Mills, "a certain gentleman in this city who has not anything like the knowledge of the whole matter possessed by Mrs. Calder or myself."[35]

The government, understandably reluctant to get caught in the crossfire between the two factions, appears to have quietly absented itself at this point, at least until hostilities died down. There is no record extant of any officer being sent to make an evaluation.

Calder's nervy pre-emptive strike had come very close to succeeding, and only a desperate counter-attack by the WHS old guard denied her band of dab-blers complete victory. The male hierarchy of the society had been challenged and severely shaken. "Mrs. Calder is rushing things in her usual crooked way," Mills grumbled. "I should not be surprised if she meant this Society be ignored altogether."[36]

Calder was indeed pushing the issue, serving the Department of Militia and Defence with an impassioned defence of her high-ground vision. "The battle ranged all round the spot the Women's Wentworth Historical Society have cho-sen as a site for the monument," Calder wrote, "all authorities of established reputation hold the same view. The various members of my own ancestral fam-ily who lived in the house ... have assured me that the fighting took place all around the house and at the foot of the elevation for the monument."[37]

Promising a site as imposing as Brock's at Queenston, Calder said local citi-zens were enthusiastic in their support. "A prominent member of the Stoney Creek Historical Society, Mr. Corman, [is] promising to supply enough stone to erect a Monument a thousand feet high." As to her detractors, Calder was dismissive. Mills, she wrote, "can scarcely be considered an authority on this subject. He is not associated in any way with the township in which the Battle of Stoney Creek was fought. His evidence is secondhand."[38]

With the battle lines now distinctly drawn, both sides would settle in for a drawn-out campaign. The senior society would continue to write letters; the dis-taff upstarts turned their attention to the historic property they had just bought. The house that Calder so strove to preserve was, by the summer of 1899, scarcely recognizable as the modest farmhouse her grandparents had occupied in 1813. Considerably altered and neglected, the two-storey frame house was badly in need of repair, which Calder's committee undertook immediately. A visitor in 1897 described a ramshackle structure, seriously in need of paint with "a de-cided let-me-lean-against-you style from one end to the other." The foundation was rebuilt, floors replaced and the grounds cleaned up with the help of local citizens. In all, nearly $1,000 was spent. The house was redecorated and stocked with antique furniture and relics of the 1812 period.[39]

The visitor's register in the Gage house bore a motto composed by society historian Mary Emily Holden. It read, "Victory Swift on Heels of Action," and true to it, Calder wasted no time. On 21 October only four months after buying the rundown homestead, she scored yet another public relations coup. Before an admiring crowd of 2,000 with Lady Aberdeen, founder of the Victorian Order of Nurses, as guest of honour, the five-acre property was officially declared a public park. Calder's doughty band became the first historical society in Canada to purchase and donate to the public a historically significant property. Reflecting the confidence of the society president, the *Hamilton Herald* declared "ultimately there will be a monument erected to the British and Canadian soldiers who fell ... and the monument will be in the park."[40]

In the meantime the monument proposed by the other side continued to tantalize the sculptor Hamilton MacCarthy. Based in Ottawa, MacCarthy became a de facto lobbyist for the Stoney Creek monument, staying abreast of any federal funding plans and bringing the Minister of Militia and various MPs to his studio to view the model he had made. On 21 November MacCarthy wrote to the WHS suggesting a financial commitment would favourably affect the government decision on a monument grant. "I have [been] given reason to believe it would be adopted if a sum of not less than $1,000 could be raised by your Society."[41]

The very next day, the Minister of Militia and Defence would pose exactly the same question to the society. "I am told," Frederick Borden wrote, "that the

**Calder delivers.** Just four months after forming the Women's Wentworth Historical Society and buying the run-down Gage homestead in June 1899, Calder declared the renovated house and property a public park. With Lady Aberdeen, an early and active campaigner for women's rights, as guest of honour, more than 2,000 people attended the opening ceremonies. Calder, on the verandah to the left of the hanging plant, listens while Lady Aberdeen speaks. (Battlefield House Museum)

amount voted by Parliament is not sufficient to cover the expense of a construction such as the people of Hamilton and vicinity desire. I would like to ascertain from you whether your society is prepared to contribute any sum to supplement the grant in question."[42]

However, despite being offered the same frank advice from two separate sources, to put their money where their mouths were, the WHS either missed or ignored the point and essentially passed on the issue. Instead the executive council airily declared that the "amount that can be raised and contributed by the Society to supplement the grant of Government will be governed to a large extent by location of site, owing to difference of opinion."[43] Any legitimate chance the WHS had of coming out ahead in the monument site dispute effectively disappeared at that point.

Less then two weeks later the same point would be underscored by Calder in a letter to the militia department that promised everything the WHS would not: "The Women's Wentworth Historical Society are an active body of workers and if they had the assurance that the Monument would be erected on the Site which they have chosen, they would cheerfully assume the responsibility of doing good and effective work in securing such a sum of money, which added to the Government grant, would ensure the erection of a Monument."[44]

As to the opposition, Mills and Fearman, she said they "have never contributed financially in support of their views … they have never made an effort as we have done to raise funds to add to the Government grant … our society is the only one that has rendered effective service in securing funds."[45]

Calder, in contrast to her counterparts in the parent society, understood how Ottawa worked, how proactivity and a willingness to roll up your sleeves and get to it, would trump an essentially passive academic interest, no matter how well rooted in history. While Mills talked a good game, the society never really did anything other than write letters looking for handouts from Ottawa. Even when it came down to buying the site they were convinced constituted the true heart of the battlefield – Smith's Knoll – they shied away from buying, even when it could have been had for $50, preferring instead to lay the whole issue at Ottawa's feet and act only as advisors. Compare that to Calder's bold decision to buy the Gage property and present the government with the easy political option of accepting a site that had been bought by public subscription, not public funds. Calder had even opened negotiations with the prominent Hamilton architectural firm F.J. Rastrick & Sons to design a monument.[46]

However, for all her canny strategies, Calder was still at the whim of Ottawa, where the distraction of sending Canadian troops to a new war in South Africa,[47] put monument funding for an old war on the back burner again.

In 1901 Calder's chief adversary, George Mills, died after a period of illness at the age of 74. Four months later, her husband, John Calder, after suffering several business reverses, would follow from the effects of a massive stroke. Calder, who had more than her share of personal tragedy in her life – seven of her nine children died in childhood – soldiered on. Duty beckoned, and Calder was instrumental in raising $10,000 to honour the 64-year reign of Queen Victoria with an imposing bronze statue in downtown Hamilton.[48]

In 1905, the indefatigable Hamilton MacCarthy once more queried the WHS about the monument, suggesting the time was ripe to approach the government afresh. "If the project were brought again," the sculptor wrote, "I think the Militia Department would cause the vote to be re-made & perhaps increased. I understood at the time from the late Mr. Mills that the Society had some funds at their disposal."[49] There is no record of any response from the society, which is not surprising, since after Mill's death, responsibility for championing Smith's Knoll appears to have fallen to the County of Wentworth Veteran's (sic) Association.

The county veterans held the first official commemoration ceremony at Smith's Knoll in 1907, in the midst of a $400 fund-raising campaign to buy the property. When asked for support, the WHS responded with a $50 donation, matching pledges already made by the King's Regiment and the local MP. Since 1894 the society had been trumpeting the knoll as the historic heart of the battlefield and the only appropriate site for a monument but, when it came down to backing it up with hard cash, they could only find $50. Indeed, by early 1908 the society had apparently all but given up hope of Smith's Knoll winning government approval, and was instead supporting the quick placement of a monument "somewhere on that battle-field."[50]

Meanwhile, the women's society, through several years of fundraising of its own, had completely paid off the mortgage on the Gage property by October 1907 and, with characteristic flair, had the provincial lieutenant governor, Mortimer Clark, burn the mortgage and symbolically convey title to the park's trustees before a crowd of 500 people. Suitably impressed, the minister of militia promised to promote "a handsome grant toward a monument,"[51]

The path to Calder's dream of an imposing monument on an imposing site[52] finally seemed straight and clear – the opposition was in retreat, the government was poised to restore the monument grant and Battlefield Park was debt-free. But as had been demonstrated several times over the previous two decades, progress was seldom straightforward and unforeseen bumps and twists were the rule rather than the exception when dealing with government bureaucrats.

In July 1908 the women's society was told that their monument proposal was in line for a $5,000 government grant but, once again, the militia department, somehow having forgotten the sectarian rivalry the monument site engendered, managed to mishandle the file. The county veterans, to their astonishment, also received a letter from the department informing them, the monument grant had been awarded because "of the representations received from your association and other sources." The letter was reprinted in the *Hamilton Spectator* under the heading: "Grant of $5000 – Government Contributes Towards Cost of Soldier's Monument."[53] The militia department sent the letter mistakenly believing the opposing factions had reconciled and agreed on a monument site.

The veterans' association, which had been resigned to building their Smith's Knoll monument without government money, could scarcely believe their luck and moved quickly to exploit the advantage. "I see by the estimates that $5,000 has been granted toward the erection of a monument," the president, John Gardner, wrote. "Our association together with Wentworth Historical Society petitioned … for a grant for that purpose & we guaranteed $1,000 towards the erection & we would also hand over a portion of the ground lately purchased by us. Not having received any word or official notification, are we to understand that our petition has been granted?"[54]

The women, who believed they had already sewn up the grant, were stunned. "To our great surprise and dismay the enclosed paragraph appeared in last Saturday's local paper," Calder wrote Borden. "We confess ourselves unable to understand it. It can not surely be that the benefit from all our hard work during these years, is to be reaped by the Veteran's Society, which has only recently appeared on the scene."[55]

Once more, Borden found himself in a confusing crossfire of claim and counter-claim, and the women's society, who had so bedevilled the Wentworth Historical Society a decade earlier, found itself the object of exactly the same tactics by the county veterans.

The militia department, thoroughly confused, was reduced to pleading with Hamilton MP Adam Zimmerman for direction. "Surely there is not more than one Monument being erected, and therefore, there can be no doubt as to whom the money should be, in due time, paid … who are the responsible parties in the matter of the erection of this Monument?"[56]

The vets, sensing a breach in the Calder line, moved quickly to exploit it, corralling official support of the Saltfleet Township Council and donations from the prime minister, Wilfrid Laurier, and the Earl of Minto, Gilbert Elliot.[57]

By the end of August, Oscar Seeley, the government MP for Stoney Creek, in considerable lather, was calling for a ceasefire. "The men are proceeding with their Foundation as well as the Women," he informed the Militia Department, "and in order to avoid serious difficulty for all concerned it seems important that your Dep't take some action … calling a halt to both associations immediately seems necessary."[58] On the same day Calder posted a copy of the women's monument plan to the minister, Frederick Borden, promising to have all the work completed within seven months.[59]

The militia department, beset from both sides, finally grasped the essential difference between the two groups and the possibility of two monuments being built. "There will be no dividing the Parliamentary grant," the militia council secretary warned, "it will be applied, if applied at all, towards the erection of one Monument only."[60]

Meanwhile, as the vets sought to get the Wentworth Historical Society, as the originators of the monument quest, back into the game as full partners and allies,[61] Calder simply refused to acknowledge any competition for the grant. "I found Mrs. Calder very unreasonable," the veterans' association president John Gardner reported after approaching the WWHS. "They say they are sure they will get the grant, therefore there is no sense in having a meeting. Mrs. Calder positively refused to allow her Society to send representatives."[62]

Hamilton lawyer and WHS member Kirwan Martin then tried to bring the three parties together but met the same intransigence. "There is no difficulty with the Wentworth Historical Society or the Veterans' Association, they are ready to meet but the Women's Wentworth Historical Society absolutely refuses …the position here is now a deadlock. As the Women's Wentworth will not meet, we cannot make any progress. I have exhausted every effort and it seems the time is come for the Department to take the matter into their own hands and deal with it."[63]

Finally in late November, the deputy minister, Eugene Fiset, issued Calder an ultimatum – settle or kiss the grant goodbye:

> It is understood that Wentworth Veterans' Association and the Wentworth Historical Society are prepared to meet your society with a view to deciding on a site and that your Society refuses to meet them.
>
> The course that the Women's Historical Society is pursuing is much regretted as, if persisted in much longer, it cannot but result in the parliamentary grant lapsing. That has already occurred once and if it occurs a second time, it is most improbable that the Minister will ask Parliament to again revote it. The responsibility … would then rest with your Society.[64]

With resolutions in hand from both the county veterans and the WHS proclaiming their willingness to settle the issue, Fiset waited for some response from

Calder. Finally after nearly three weeks of considering her options, Calder agreed to meet the other two groups.

Appropriately enough, the meeting took place on 6 January, Epiphany. Calder brought three members of the society executive as well as former Hamilton mayor and future lieutenant governor John Hendrie.[65] The Wentworth County Veteran's Association had three representatives, as did the Wentworth Historical Society. The three local MPs represented the government, with Hamilton West MP Adam Zimmerman in the chair.

After 15 years of often acrimonious contention, the meeting, according to the surviving minutes, played out like a model of decorum. Hamilton East MP Samuel Barker set the tone early when he suggested two monuments be built – a stone marker on Smith's Knoll and "a higher shaft on a greater height to commemorate the battle." Perhaps the years of wrangling had taken their toll. Certainly without George Mills the WHS mission had lost much of its steam and there was likely some serious arm-twisting in private – and in addition to which, Calder's site was still the government's first choice. In any case, both the WHS and the county veterans complied with scarcely a whimper.[66]

In a terse 96-word resolution Calder dictated her terms. All three groups would co-operate in raising $1,500 for a monument on Smith's Knoll – which would be built first – and $10,000 for a monument on the Gage homestead. The Women's Wentworth Historical Society would receive the entire government grant of $5,000. The motion was unanimously carried.

The Calder vision – imposing monument, imposing site – had prevailed over the more prosaic objective of the men's society. Peace had been achieved and Smith's Knoll would get its marker but there was no doubt who won the big prize. Cessation of hostilities, however, was only the end of the beginning

**Viceregal support.** Sara Calder was a skilled networker. When Governor General Earl Grey visited Hamilton in the spring of 1909, Calder arranged a visit to the Stoney Creek battlefield, where the Countess of Grey turned the first sod for the monument. From left, Sara Calder, Lord Grey and Lady Grey. (Battlefield House Museum)

and, predictably, the route to the final realization of Calder's dream was neither straight nor smooth.

It would be October before a contract was signed with the Hamilton architectural firm F.J. Rastrick & Sons and a month after that before Hamilton contractor F.W. Dickenson agreed to build it for $11,798. The deadline for the 1909 grant, however, was seven months past and work on the monument did not begin until the spring of 1910, when the cornerstone was laid by the prominent British general, Sir John French, in a ceremony carried off with typical Calder panache before a large contingent of uniforms – militia and boy scout – singing school children and local dignitaries.[67]

The Rastrick design, the work of Edward Rastrick with input from the executive of the WWHS, described an octagonal, castellated tower, 100 feet high, rising from a square base. The Gothic Revival structure, with corner turrets, battlements and wall buttresses, may have been loosely based on the 1807 Nelson monument in Edinburgh.[68]

Among contemporary War of 1812 monuments, the Stoney Creek design was by far the most ambitious, eschewing airy classicism for the solidity of a medieval keep. Where the battlefields of Châteauguay, Lundy's Lane and Crysler's Farm

**Monument cornerstone.** With an architect and a contractor on board, work on the monument finally began in the spring of 1910 with the official laying of the cornerstone. With characteristic flair Sara Calder orchestrated an impressive public event featuring the prominent British general Sir John French, then Inspector General of the British army. French is at the centre of the photograph holding his sword with Calder on his immediate right in the flowered hat. (Battlefield House Museum)

were marked with modest granite shafts, the hill behind the Gage farmhouse was to be topped with a grand landmark more on the scale of Brock's monument. And, to provide a bigger stage for such a structure the women's society had just bought a 13.5-acre adjoining parcel for $2,700, taking a $2,000 mortgage. For all the energy and enthusiasm of Calder and the executive, the society was nevertheless limited in its ability to raise money: causeries and entertainments could generate a few hundred dollars each year, but the $10,000 Calder promised to raise for the monument was well beyond their grasp. By June of 1911 the $5,000 government grant was spent. A foundation had been laid and the base built to the height of 25 feet built when the contractor halted work. The WWHS, despite earlier assurances, had nothing to add. The only alternative was to ask the government for more. Calder wrote directly to the new militia minister, Sam Hughes, for another $5,000.[69]

"It would seem now, from Mrs. Calder's letter, as if little more, if any, has been expended on the monument than the Government grant," Hughes' deputy minister dryly commented. "This does little credit to those who have had the matter in hand, as there was never a word of further government aid being expected."[70]

The nationalistic Hughes, however, was sympathetic and no doubt delighted Calder with his response, which must have left the society president pinching herself to ensure she was not dreaming. "Your suggestion that the government un-

**Construction stalls.** Construction began in spring 1910 but within a year the entire government grant of $5,000 had been spent and work stopped. It would take another six months for Calder to convince the Minister of Militia to finance completion of the $14,158 project. This photograph, taken in the winter of 1911-12, shows the 25-foot base and piles of building stone at the foot of the hill. (Battlefield House Museum)

dertake the completion of the work is most gratefully received," Calder purred in reply. "The society will be glad to be relieved of further worry on that account."[71]

With government funding now secure, the contractor announced he could not complete the work at the old price because building materials were up 15 per cent, stone cutters and layers wanted five cents more an hour and the teamsters were seeking a 50-cent-a-day increase for each team.[72]

In support of his contractor, the architect outlined some of the difficulties the project presented: "Mr. Dickenson had to haul all his materials to the Site from a distance, he also had to dig out for, and make a road up the side of the hill so the materials could be taken up, the Concrete was wheeled up in Barrow by Labourers, the Steam Mixer and Materials being at the base of the hill. The stone for walls was cut into shape at the base of the hill and hauled up by Horse stone Boat and when at top, a derrick was used to place the Materials on Scaffold for use. All this work cost money."[73] Dickenson won a 20 per cent increase and the cost of the job went from $11,798 to $14,158.[74]

Specifications ran to seven pages and included 43 subsections covering everything from the use of hot manure to cover cold-weather concrete to the type of wood in the window frames – hard pine. The contract stipulated that all materials be Canadian and "the whole of the Work to be left perfect at completion."[75]

The contractor complained about the dearth of competent stone cutters and masons, the Union of Masons and Bricklayers complained about the use of non-union masons and the architect complained about his subcontractors not being paid, but by 21 May 1913, the stone work was complete and only pointing, plastering, painting and glazing remained The final cost to the government was somewhere between $15,000 and $16,000.[76]

Although it had taken 20 years for Calder to realize her dream, the final timing of its de-

**Transitory view.** This coloured postcard, from photographs taken in 1911, shows the monument in a state of suspended construction, which would not have pleased Sara Calder. Her soaring tower is but a stubby base and the centrepiece of the card is the Smith's Knoll monument which she vehemently opposed for 20 years. (Battlefield House Museum)

but – exactly 100 years after the battle – could not have been more appropriate. Estimates of the crowd that jammed Battlefield Park on 6 June 1913 ranged up to 15,000, including 1,800 schoolchildren and several hundred boy scouts and girl guides, detachments from four battalions of militia, four regimental bands, a large contingent of Six Nation Indians, dozens of politicians and army brass and the granddaughter of the celebrated Stony Creek veteran James FitzGibbon. None of them however, could have been more gratified than Calder.[77]

The reporter from the *Hamilton Evening Times* declared her "probably the happiest lady on the grounds." Fittingly enough, she was presented with a large basket of American Beauty roses by the organizing committee. The monument architect, Edward Rastrick, added a bouquet of red and white roses. The program began in the morning with a parade to the battlefield, followed by a picnic under cloudy June skies. Standing with her schoolmates from SS #2 Fruitland, each one tagged with a blue and white ribbon, nine-year-old Ethel Lounsbury tried to keep track of her younger brother while the minutes ticked down.[78]

At exactly 1:25 in the afternoon the crowd, prompted by a fanfare from the mounted heralds, fell silent and the men removed their hats awaiting the pleasure of a famously shy monarch 3,500 miles away.[79] Thanks to an arrangement with Canadian Pacific Railway, a cable connection had been made between the draped monument and Buckingham Palace in London.

**"All roads seemed to lead to Stoney Creek,"** declared the *Hamilton Herald* reporter who watched as thousands of citizens from Ancaster, Dundas, Hamilton, Stoney Creek and Grimsby poured into Battlefield Park in street cars, rail cars, motorcars and buggies for the unveiling ceremony. By 4 p.m., radial cars alone had delivered 8,000 people to the battlefield. (Local History & Archives, Hamilton Public Library)

**Five hundred Boy Scouts** camped out on the battlefield on 5 June as a guard of honour. Some are shown here flanking the dais to the east of monument. The dignitaries in the background include the executive of the Women's Wentworth Historical Society on the left, with Sara Calder on the extreme left. (Battlefield House Museum)

**Girl Guides** in their distinctive middy blouses and wide-brimmed campaign hats were also well represented in the ceremonies. Their numbers were impressive given than guiding was only introduced to Canada in 1910. (Battlefield House Museum)

**Colours on the battlefield, 1913.** A century after Ensign Francis Dury was fatally wounded carrying the King's colour of the 49th regiment into battle at Stoney Creek, two fresh-faced ensigns parade the colours of the 77th (Wentworth) Regiment on the same ground. The regiment, under Lieutenant Colonel William Edward Knowles, awaits the order to march past in review. (Local History & Archives, Hamilton Public Library)

As the multitude waited in hushed expectation, Queen Mary, Consort of George V, pressed an ivory telegraph key, launching a trans-Atlantic signal that arrived at Battlefield Park, burning a tiny fuse to begin the process. A bell rang, the white fabric veil fell away from the stone tower, the Union flag rose on its staff, the crowd issued three hearty cheers and the massed bands played *God Save the King* followed by the schoolchildren, who sang *Rule Britannia* and *The Maple Leaf Forever*.

Ethel Lounsbury would remember the unveiling for the rest of her long life – as the fabric fell the children saluted the King's colours while the bands played – "it was really a marvellous thing."[80]

For Sara Calder, the dedication ceremony provided a storybook culmination of the extraordinary personal vision that had driven her since 1894 when her grandfather's homestead first came on the market. Her personal watchword – the imperious "it can be done, it must be done, and it will be done" – had been vindicated.

Three years earlier Calder had spoken of the uphill fight her society had faced in securing the monument. "We started with no money – only great hopes and enthusiasm and, ladies, we have accomplished much." The *Hamilton Evening*

**School children.** Tagged with a blue and white ribbon, nine-year-old Ethel Lounsbury from School Section #2 Fruitland was one of more than 1,800 schoolchildren who took part in the opening ceremonies, singing *Rule Britannia* and English Canada's unofficial national anthem, *The Maple Leaf Forever*. (Battlefield House Museum)

*Times* reflected approvingly on Calder's accomplishment: "In the hearts of the people, especially the children of the district, were sown seeds which in time will produce nobler thoughts and aspirations … the whole future life and thought of many a boy and girl who stood on the historic ground yesterday may be influenced by what they saw and heard."[81]

Seven months after the dedication, Calder was once more petitioning the militia minister for funds, this time for landscaping the park – "the ground, of great natural beauty and eminently suited for a public park, is however, in a very neglected condition and requires attention and treatment from competent hands."[82]

It was the last time the militia department would hear from Sara Calder – the Victorian Dynamo, now 67, was not well. A very private 14-year struggle with diabetes was coming to an end. On 16 March 1914, she died of diabetic acidosis in her Aberdeen Avenue home after a three-week illness. "She served her generation well," noted the *Hamilton Spectator*, "and her best memorials are her works that remain."[83] Certainly it can be said without any exaggeration that little or any of the Stoney Creek battlefield would remain today were it not for the efforts of Sara Calder.

SCHOOL CHILDREN AT STONY CREEK
CELEBRATION, JUNE 6TH 1913

**"In days of yore, from Britain's shore."** Ethel Lounsbury would long remember the moment when the monument was unveiled: "It was really a marvellous thing – as it fell we saluted the flag and the band struck up." (Local History & Archives, Hamilton Public Library)

**Soldiers on the battlefield.** Four militia battalions were strongly represented at the unveiling, including the 13th Royal Regiment and the 91st Regiment Canadian Highlanders from Hamilton, the 77th (Wentworth) Regiment from Dundas and 37th Regiment, Haldimand Rifles, from the Six Nations Reserve. All four brought their regimental bands. The following year many of these men would be on their way to active battlefields in Europe. (Battlefield House Museum)

**Unveiling the monument, 1:24 pm, 6 June 1913.** This photograph from the *Hamilton Times* was taken moments before Queen Mary pressed a button in Buckingham Palace, symbolically unveiling the monument before a crowd the *Toronto Star* estimated at 15,000.(Local History & Archives, Hamilton Public Library)

The former lieutenant governor, Sir John Gibson, a trustee for Battlefield Park, attested to her unwavering determination: "No one was more deeply interested and no one individual did more to have that work carried out … she never knew what failure meant … never in all her experiences acknowledged defeat. When she made up her mind that something was desirable and ought to be done, she worked in season and out of season. A strong-minded woman … she was capable of arguing out any proposal … and also capable of downing any unreasonable opposition."[84]

The feisty, never-take-no-for-an-answer Calder style would endure in the society. In the spring of 1925, Calder's successor, Adelaide Lynch-Staunton, petitioned the government for money to complete repairs and build a staircase inside the monument. When defence minister Edward Mortimer Macdonald tried to brush her off with the excuse the government did not own the property and never agreed to maintain it, her response was pure Calder.

"I think you have misunderstood," she wrote, "the case in short is this. The Government undertook to build this monument and did not complete it, and has left it in such a state that we cannot maintain it."[85] After clearing its throat and shuffling its feet for another two months, the Department of National Defence coughed up a $500 grant.

Landscaping, including tree-lined paths and flower beds, was completed but Calder's dream of a tourist attraction to rival Queenston Heights never came to be, and the women's society had to constantly rely on the federal government for maintenance funding. In 1949, the original pledge of 1899, to deed the monument site to the federal government, was finally fulfilled. By the early 1960s[86] with the site attracting only a few thousand visitors a year, the federal government opted for local stewardship and transferred ownership to the Niagara Parks Commission, which held title until 1989 when Stoney Creek became the landlord. The following year, inspections revealed serious structural problems – rebars had rusted, causing shifts and cracks in the limestone. A public save-the-monument fund was established, all three levels of government stepped up and a $400,000 restoration saw the top of the tower rebuilt, interior landings and stairway rebuilt and all glass and frames replaced. Eighty years after it had been built, the cost of window repairs alone exceeded the original construction cost of the entire project, yet few complained.

Sara Calder's gift to Stoney Creek, a permanent testimonial to its early colonial history, endures, as much a tribute to her perseverance as it is to the battle that inspired it.

**Battlefield vista.** This view from the parapet of the Stoney Creek monument was taken by a *Hamilton Spectator* photographer in 1963 to mark the 150th anniversary of the battle. Looking north toward Lake Ontario, the considerably-altered Gage house sits in the centre. To the left a shallow stream, now called Battlefield Creek, passes under a small bridge on King Street – the old Queenston road – into the wooded strip that

runs parallel to the street. The first contact with the advance took place to the north of the two square, flat-roofed buildings on the left of the wooded strip and the general action on a ridge that runs north across King Street to Smith's Knoll, where the two American generals were captured, and beyond. (Local History & Archives, Hamilton Public Library (labels added))

Appendix D

# Weapons and Capability at Stoney Creek

## *Infantry Weapons*

### British Short Land Musket, India Pattern, "Brown Bess"
| | |
|---|---|
| Furniture: | Brass |
| Calibre: | .75 |
| Calibre of projectile: | .71 |
| Projectile: | lead ball slightly over one ounce |
| Propellant: | 190 grains black powder |
| Range – theoretical maximum: | 250 yards |
| Range – effective maximum: | |
|    Volley: | 150-200 yards |
|    Single round: | 100-150 yards |
|    Favoured range: | less than 100 yards |
| Weight: | 9.5 pounds |
| Rate of fire | |
|    Optimum: | 4-5 rounds per minute |
|    Actual: | 2-3 rounds per minute |
|    Misfire: | at least one in five |

### American 1795 Springfield
| | |
|---|---|
| Furniture: | Steel |
| Calibre: | .69 |
| Calibre of projectile: | .65 |
| Projectile: | lead ball slightly under one ounce, or a "buck 'n ball" combination of one musket ball and three buckshot or 12 buckshot only. |
| Propellant: | 160 grains black powder |
| Range – theoretical max. (ball): | less than 250 yards |
| Range – effective maximum | |
|    Volley: | 150-200 yards |
|    Single round: | 100-150 yards |
|    Favoured range: | less than 100 yards |
| Weight: | 9 pounds |
| Rate of fire and misfire: | Similar to British musket |

## *Artillery Weapons*

### American light iron 6-pdr. gun
| | |
|---|---|
| Calibre: | |
|    Bore | 3.66 inches |
|    Projectile (roundshot) | 3.49 inches, 6 pounds |
| Range – roundshot | |
|    Theoretical maximum: | 1,000 yards |
|    Effective maximum: | 800 yards |
|    Favoured range: | 600-800 yards |
| Range – cannister (case shot): | 200-600 yards |
| Rate of fire: | 1 to 2 rounds per minute |
| Propellant (round shot) | 1.5 pounds black powder |

**"An outspoken, flinty-lipped, brazen-faced jade** with a habit of looking men straight in the eyes," is how Rudyard Kipling described the Brown Bess musket, which was the standard weapon of British infantry for more than a century. The .75 calibre smoothbore fired a lead ball that was capable of penetrating five inches of oak at 30 yards. Although stopping power was impressive, the maximum effective range was only about 200 yards. (Cherry's Fine Guns)

**Land Pattern socket bayonet.** For close combat situations, such as occurred at Stoney Creek, the Brown Bess could be fitted with a three-sided, 17-inch bayonet which effectively turned the gun into a six-foot pike. Excavations at the site where the British overran the American artillery have turned up several rib fragments bearing the triangular nick of a bayonet thrust. (Hawthorn Ink)

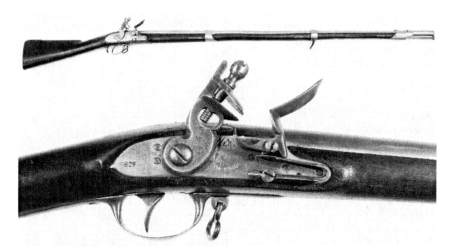

**1795 Springfield.** Inspired by the 1763 French Charleville musket, the .69 calibre Springfield was the first military gun produced at the Springfield arsenal in Massachusetts and was standard issue for U.S. troops. Although a slightly smaller calibre, the Springfield performed comparably to the British Brown Bess. The detail shows the lock without a flint. (Parks Canada)

| | |
|---|---|
| Weight of gun and carriage: | 2000 pounds |
| Gun detachment: | |
|     Trained gunners: | 3 |
|     Assistants: | 6 |
| Number of horses in gun team: | 4-6 |
| Ammunition scales: | 18 roundshot carried in chest in carriage chest and 30 cannister rounds in caisson |

### Sources

Donald E. Graves, *Field of Glory*, "American Ordnance in the War of 1812." *Arms Collecting*, Vol 31, 4 ; René Chartrand, *Uniforms and Equipment of the United States Forces in the War of 1812;* Mike Willegal, *The Accuracy of Black Powder Muskets.*

## Appendix E

# British Order of Battle and Strength

### *Brigadier General John Vincent's Command*
### *British Army, 6 June 1813*

| | |
|---|---|
| **Commanding General:** | Brigadier General John Vincent |
| **Second in Command:** | Lieutenant Colonel John Harvey |

**Staff**

| | |
|---|---|
| Aides to General Vincent: | Lieutenant Thomas Barnard |
| | Paymaster James Brock |
| | Captain Hamilton Merritt |
| Brigade major: | Major John Glegg |
| Quarter Master General's Department: | Captain Peter Chambers |
| Fort major: | Lieutenant Thomas Taylor |

**Infantry**

49th Regiment of Foot (8 companies, 424)

| | |
|---|---|
| Commanding officer: | Major Charles Plenderleath |

King's (8th) Regiment of Foot (5 companies, 280)

| | |
|---|---|
| Commanding officer: | Major James Ogilvie |

**Artillery**

Royal Artillery (est. 20)

| | |
|---|---|
| Commanding officer: | Lieutenant Richard Armstrong, RA |

1 × 6-pdr. gun

**Militia**

1st, 2nd, 3rd, 4th, 5th Lincoln, 1st, 2nd York, 1st Oxford, Niagara Provincial Light Dragoons, Incorporated Militia of Upper Canada, Cameron's Provincial Incorporated Artillery Company (30 est. officers and men)

**Native Allies**

Cherokee, Delaware, Chippawa, Mohawk, Cayuga (est.12)

| | |
|---|---|
| Commanding officer: | Captain John Norton |

**Capitulation**

| | |
|---|---|
| Infantry: | 704 |
| Artillery: | 20 |
| Militia: | 30 |
| Natives: | 12 |
| **Total:** | **766** |

**Sources**

NA WO12/6044 muster book and pay lists of 49th Foot March-June 1813 NA WO 12/2575 Muster Book & Pay List 8th Foot, March-June 1813. LAC, RG9, IB7, Vol. 24, 5th Lincoln 1812-1814, AO MS-MU 2095 item 26, Irving, *Officers of the British Forces in Canada*. Sutherland, Stuart, *His Majesty's Gentlemen*

## Appendix F

# American Order of Battle and Strength

*Brigadier General John Chandler's Division*
*United States Army, 6 June 1813*

| | |
|---|---|
| **Commanding General:** | Brigadier General John Chandler |
| **Second in Command:** | Brigadier General William Winder |
| Staff | |
|     Aide to General Chandler: | Lieutenant Donald Fraser |
|     Assistant adjutant general: | Major John Johnson |
|     Brigade majors: | Captain Roger Jones |
| | Captain Richard Whartenby |
| Deputy quarter master general: | Lieutenant Christopher Van De Venter |

**Infantry**

| | |
|---|---|
| Fifth/Twentieth U.S. Infantry (est. 250) | Lieutenant Colonel H. V. Milton |
| Ninth U.S. Infantry (est. 100) | Captain George Bender |
| Thirteenth U.S. Infantry* (est. 400) | Colonel John Chrystie |
| Fourteenth U.S. Infantry* (est. 350) | Lieutenant Colonel Charles Boerstler |
| Sixteenth U.S. Infantry (est. 270) | Captain George Steele |
| Twenty-Second U.S. Infantry (est.100) | Captain Daniel McFarland |
| | Captain David Milliken |
| Twenty-Third U.S. Infantry (est. 350) | Major Henry Armstrong |
| Twenty-Fifth U.S. Infantry  (est. 650) | Major Joseph Lee Smith |

**Artillery**

| | |
|---|---|
| Second Artillery  (est. 250) | Captain Jacob Hindman† |
| | Captain Nathan Towson |
| | Captain William Nicholas† |
| | Captain Thomas Biddle† |
| | Captain Samuel Archer* |
| Light Artillery (est. 60) | Captain Luther Leonard |
| 8 × 6-pdr. guns, 1 × 5.5 inch howitzer | |

**Cavalry**

| | |
|---|---|
| Second U.S. Light Dragoons (est. 150) | Colonel James Burn |

**Rifles**

First Regiment U.S. Rifles (est. 50)    Lieutenant Henry Van Swearingen
U.S. Volunteers, Riflemen (est. 50)    Captain John Lyttle

**Capitulation**

| | |
|---|---|
| Infantry: | 2,470 |
| Artillery: | 310 |
| Cavalry: | 150 |
| Rifles: | 100 |
| **Total:** | **3,030** |

Note: British POW records indicate the presence of at least some American militia at Stoney Creek even though official U.S. Army records and reports acknowledge none.

*posted to the lakeshore to protect transport bateaux.
†fought as infantry

**Sources.**

U.S.NA, Registry of Enlistments. RG94 Army Muster Rolls 1812-1814; Heitman, *Historical Register and Dictionary,* (2 vols.) Dwight, *Diary,* 13 May 1813 Gaves/Chartrand, *Army Hand Book,* 240, 244 ; *Enquirer,* 2 July 1813, Extract of a Letter from an Intelligent Captain, 10 June 1813; Myers, *Reminiscences,* 19 ; *NWR,* 4th January, 1817, General Chandler and the Affair of Stoney Creek Chandler, *Autobiography,* 187; Walworth, *Letters.* Walworth to Simonds, 13 May 1813

## Appendix G

# British Regulars and Canadian Militia Casualties at Stoney Creek

| | Age | Place of origin or enlistment |
|---|---|---|
| **49th Regiment of Foot** | | |
| Ensign Francis Dury, | – killed | England |
| Major Charles Plenderleath | 33 wounded | Peebles, Scotland |
| Major Alexander Clerk | 34 wounded | Scotland |
| Major James Dennis | 36 wounded | Ireland |
| Captain Thomas Manners | – wounded | England |
| Lieutenant Joseph Stean | – wounded | – |
| **Dennis's Company** | | |
| Pte. Michael Gillispie | – killed* | – |
| **Glegg's Company** | | |
| Pte. Henry Carroll | – killed | – |
| Pte. John Hostler | – killed | – |
| Pte. John Marvell | – killed | Hilsea Depot |
| Pte. Timothy Bresland | 27 pow | Monaghan |
| Pte. Soloman Donally | 29 pow | Armagh |
| Pte. John Stewart | 29 pow | Monaghan |
| Pte. James Ryan | 27 pow | Clare |
| **Williams's Company** | | |
| Pte. Edward Little | – killed | – |
| Sgt. Mathew Reily | – pow | – |

| | Age | Place of origin or enlistment |
|---|---|---|
| Cpl. Peter Owens | 28 pow | Sligo |
| Pte. Andrew Armstrong | 29 pow | Monaghan |
| Pte. Joseph Burns | 31 pow | Ireland |
| Pte. Michael Eagen | 26 pow | – |
| Pte. William Macrow | 27 pow | Armagh |
| Pte. Thomas Morgan | 30 pow, w. | Glamorganshire |
| Pte. James Nauton | 31 pow | Bedfordshire |
| Pte. William Farmer | 30 pow | Kerry |
| Pte. Josiah Hardingham | 31 pow | Cork |
| **Lewis's Company** | | |
| Pte. Peter Henley | – killed | – |
| Sgt. Patrick Jordan | 27 pow | – |
| Pte. Patrick Looney | 39 pow | Limerick |
| Pte. William Pronk | 34 pow, w. | Scotland |
| **Fitzgerald's Company** | | |
| Sgt. Charles Page | – killed | – |
| Pte. Thomas Brannon | – pow, w. | – |
| Pte. Samuel Crooks | – pow | – |
| Pte. John Neal | 32 pow | Dublin |
| Pte. Christopher Davis | 29 pow | Kildare |
| Pte. Alexander Wales | 27 pow | Monaghan |

**Clerk's Company**

| | | | |
|---|---|---|---|
| Pte. Nathaniel Catlin | – | killed | – |
| Pte. Alexander Brown | 28 | killed | Berwickshire |
| Sgt. Alexander Milrose | – | pow | – |
| Pte. Thomas Burke | 28 | pow | Mayo |
| Pte. Titus Elliott | 27 | pow | Berwickshire |
| Pte. Michael Jennings | 29 | pow | Sligo |
| Pte. John McKenna | 31 | pow | Armagh |

**Ormand's Company**

| | | | |
|---|---|---|---|
| Pte. Patrick Martin | – | killed | – |
| Pte. John Hondell | – | killed | – |
| Pte. John Callahan | 30 | pow | Ireland |

**Manner's Company**

| | | | |
|---|---|---|---|
| Pte. James Adams | – | killed | Herfordshire |
| Pte. Michael Burke | – | killed | – |
| Pte. Thomas Armstrong | – | pow, w. | – |
| Pte. Richard Conlon | 31 | pow | Roscommon |
| Pte. William Binnoy | 30 | pow | Hampshire |

**Johnston's Company**

| | | | |
|---|---|---|---|
| Pte. Thomas Adams | 29 | killed | Armagh |
| Pte. John Brown | 34 | pow | Staffordshire |
| Pte. Richard Collins | – | pow, w. | |
| Pte. Henry Granger | 28 | pow | Edinburgh |
| Pte. Dennis Keough/Hough | – | pow, w. | |
| Pte. John Whiteside | 29 | pow | Armagh |

**Heriot's Company**

| | | | |
|---|---|---|---|
| Pte. Martin Donally | – | killed | – |
| Pte. Martin Curley | – | killed | – |
| Pte. Edward Killorne | – | killed | – |
| Pte. Joseph White | – | MIA | – |
| Pte. James Hay | 30 | pow | Middlesex |
| Pte. James O'Neil | 31 | pow | Dublin |
| Pte. Benjamin Sapwell | – | pow, w. | – |
| Pte. James Sweetman | 29 | pow | Tipperary |
| Pte Adam Burnside | 48 | pow | Ireland |
| Pte. Robert Carr | 35 | pow | Monaghan |

**King's (8th) Regiment of Foot**

| | | | |
|---|---|---|---|
| Lieutenant Samuel Hooker | 32 | killed | Herfordshire |
| Major James Ogilvie | 28 | wounded | Banff |
| Captain James Mundy | 33 | wounded | English |
| Captain John Goldrisk | – | wounded | – |
| Surgeon William Hacket | 33 | wounded | – |
| Lieutenant Edward Boyd | – | wounded | – |
| Lieutenant John Weyland | 24 | wounded | Devonshire |

**Goldicutt's Company**

| | | | |
|---|---|---|---|
| Pte. Richard Hugill | – | killed | Nottingham |
| Pte. George Longley | – | killed | York |
| Pte. Lawrence Meade | – | killed | Carlow |
| Sgt. George Mccolloch | 30 | pow, w. | Antrim |
| Pte. John Burns | 30 | pow, w. | Cork |

| | | | |
|---|---|---|---|
| Pte. John Mcdonnell | – | pow, w. | Down |
| Pte. John Blunt | 30 | pow | Richmond, Cork |
| Pte. David Best | – | pow, w. | – |
| Pte. William Phillips | 30 | pow, w. | Wiltshire |
| Pte. Michael Guinan | 28 | pow | Dublin |
| Pte. Edward Parker | – | pow | – |
| Pte. James Sparroway | – | pow | – |
| Pte. John Hodgson | 30 | pow | Durham |
| Pte. William Stringer | 28 | pow | Worcester |
| Pte. William Jackson | 45 | pow | Durham |

**Robinson's Company**

| | | | |
|---|---|---|---|
| Pte. John Boys | 24 | pow | Mullaglass, Newry, Armagh |

**Goldrisk's Company**

| | | | |
|---|---|---|---|
| Sgt. Joseph Hunt | – | killed | – |
| Pte. James Morrison | – | killed* | Armagh |
| Pte. John Mather | 28 | wounded | Brechin, Angus |

**Bradridge's Company**

| | | | |
|---|---|---|---|
| Pte. John Wale | – | killed | Somerset |

**Mundy's Company**

| | | | |
|---|---|---|---|
| Sgt. John Webb | – | killed* | Somerset |

**Blackmore's Company**

| | | | |
|---|---|---|---|
| Pte. Phillip Donaghoe | – | killed* | Cavan |

**McDouall's Company**

| | | | |
|---|---|---|---|
| Pte. James Daig | – | killed | Forfar |
| Pte. John Walker | – | killed | Lincoln |

**Cotter's Company**

| | | | |
|---|---|---|---|
| Pte. Thomas Fearnsides | – | killed | Blackburn |
| Pte. John Piglar | – | killed | Gloucester |
| Pte. John Smith | – | killed | Youghall, Cork |
| Pte. John Cuff | – | pow, w. | – |

**41st Regiment of Foot**

| | | | |
|---|---|---|---|
| Lieutenant Thomas Taylor | 25 | wounded | London |

**Lincoln Militia, 1st Regiment**

| | | | |
|---|---|---|---|
| Ensign James George | – | wounded | Niagara |

**Lincoln Militia, 2nd Regiment**

| | | | |
|---|---|---|---|
| Lieutenant Colonel Thomas Clark | 43 | pow, w. | Dumfries |

**Lincoln Militia, 4th Regiment**

| | | | |
|---|---|---|---|
| Pte. Lewis Campbell | – | pow | – |
| Pte. William Martin | 37 | pow | – |
| Pte. George Pettit | – | pow | – |

**York Militia, 2nd Regiment**

| | | | |
|---|---|---|---|
| Pte. Samuel Loree | – | pow | – |

**Niagara Provincial Light Dragoons**

| | | | |
|---|---|---|---|
| Pte. Godfrey Huffman | 17 | pow | Burford |

**Sources**

This list was compiled from NA WO12/6044 muster book and pay lists of 49th Foot March-June 1813, WO25/1829 Casualty returns 49th Foot, WO25/1549 Casualty returns 1st Batt 8th Foot from 25/12/13 to 24/06/13 and 25/06/13 to 24/09/13, WO12/2575 Muster book and Pay List of 8th Foot 1813 Mar-June; NYS Library, Gardner Papers, SC12914 List of prisoners brought to Fort Niagara, June 8 1813 and USNA RG-94 Entry 127c – List of Br POW Ft Niagara 8 June 1813, Descriptive list of British POW at Greenbush 6 Sept. 1813.

Appendix H

# American Casualties at Stoney Creek and Retreat to Fort George

| | Age | | Origin or place of enlistment |
|---|---|---|---|
| Brigadier General John Chandler | 51 | pow | Mass. |
| Brigadier General William Winder | 38 | pow | Md. |
| Major Christopher Van De Venter | 24 | pow | N.Y. |
| Captain Roger Jones | 24 | wounded | Va. |

### First U.S. Infantry

| | | | |
|---|---|---|---|
| Pte. James Lowery | 35 | pow | Ireland |

### Fifth U.S. Infantry

**Bell's Coy**

| | | | |
|---|---|---|---|
| Pte. Joseph Boyce | 20 | killed | Duchess, N.Y. |
| Pte. George Williboughy | 26 | pow | Baltimore |

**Dorman's Coy**

| | | | |
|---|---|---|---|
| Pte. Henry S. Rose | 29 | pow, w. + | Va. |
| Pte. Samuel Parsons | 33 | pow | Va. |

**Opie's Company**

| | | | |
|---|---|---|---|
| Pte. John Barlow | 32 | pow | Yorkshire |
| Pte. Elisha Clay | 25 | pow | Va. |
| Pte. James Dugan | 26 | pow | Md. |
| Pte. Tunis Ostrander | 28 | pow | Ballston, Mass. |
| Pte. Solomon Scott | 20 | pow | Va. |
| Pte. Alfred Wilson | 26 | pow | N.Y. |

**Wallace's Company**

| | | | |
|---|---|---|---|
| Sgt. Jesse Joy | – | killed | – |
| Pte. Gray Barber | – | wounded | – |

**Whartenby's Company**

| | | | |
|---|---|---|---|
| Pte. William Lyndsay | 17 | pow | Delaware |
| Pte. David Horney | 29 | pow | Md. |
| Pte. William Kelly | 50 | pow, w. | Va. |

### Ninth U.S. Infantry

**Bender's Company**

| | | | |
|---|---|---|---|
| Pte. Ebenezer Knowlton | 39 | pow, w. | Cumberland, R.I. |

### Thirteenth U.S. Infantry

**Kearney's Company**

| | | | |
|---|---|---|---|
| Pte. Elnathan Davis | 33 | pow | Stonington, Conn. |

**Sproull's Company**

| | | | |
|---|---|---|---|
| Pte. Christian Evener | 24 | pow | N.Y. |
| Pte. Nathan Robinson | 20 | pow | Wales, Vt. |

**Wool's Company**

| | | | |
|---|---|---|---|
| Henry Foote | 25 | pow | Albany, N.Y. |

**Barnard's Company**

| | | | |
|---|---|---|---|
| Pte. Zebediah Woodland | 25 | pow | Baltimore |

**Morris's Company**

| | | | |
|---|---|---|---|
| Pte. William Tuffs | 19 | pow | Charlotte, N.Y. |

**Uknown company**

| | | | |
|---|---|---|---|
| Pte. Elijah Smith | 36 | pow | Fredricksburg, N.Y. |

### Fourteenth U.S. Infantry

**Fleming's Company**

| | | | |
|---|---|---|---|
| Pte. Edward Walton | 22 | pow | Steuben Cty., N.Y. |

**McIlwain's Company**

| | | | |
|---|---|---|---|
| Pte. Peter Stout | 41 | pow | Northumberland, Penn. |

**Mckenzie's Company**

| | | | |
|---|---|---|---|
| Pte. Patrick English | 36 | pow | – |

**Sullivan's Company**

| | | | |
|---|---|---|---|
| Pte. Samuel Boyd | 52 | pow | Va. |

**Grindage's Company**

| | | | |
|---|---|---|---|
| Pte. Alexander Wilson | 26 | pow | Hardyston, N.J. |

**Unknown company**

| | | | |
|---|---|---|---|
| Pte. Thomas Soran | 38 | pow | Dublin |

### Sixteenth U.S. Infantry

| | | | |
|---|---|---|---|
| Captain George Steele | 28 | pow, w. | Va. |
| Captain Alexander McEwan | 33 | pow | Penn. |

**Davenport's Company**

| | | | |
|---|---|---|---|
| Pte. George Hertzell | 31 | killed | Penn. |
| Pte. Peter Eaton | 42 | wounded | N.Y. |
| Pte. James Simpkins | 19 | wounded | Philadelphia |
| Pte. John Adams | 28 | pow | – |
| Pte. Jacob Bays | 21 | pow | Lancaster, Penn. |
| Pte. Henry Bear | 24 | pow | Berks, Penn. |
| Pte. John Croninger | 38 | pow | Penn. |
| Pte. Owen Mullin | 23 | pow | N.J. |
| Pte. John Raudolph | 31 | pow | – |
| Pte. William Taylor | 21 | pow | Berks, Penn. |

**Gray's Company**

| | | | |
|---|---|---|---|
| Pte. Morris Shay | 28 | MIA | N.Y. |
| Pte. Jacob Rheam | 23 | wounded | Penn. |
| Pte. John Barron | 44 | pow | Springfield, Penn. |
| Pte. Joseph Flemming | 28 | pow | R.I. |

**Greenwood's Company**

| | | | |
|---|---|---|---|
| Pte. Michael Viner | 27 | pow | Penn. |

**Machesney's Company**

| | | | |
|---|---|---|---|
| Pte. John Updike | – | wounded | – |
| Pte. James Huffee | 24 | wounded | Ireland |
| Sgt. James Doyle | – | MIA | – |
| Pte. George Bowyer | 27 | pow | Egg Harbor, N.J. |
| Pte John Lynch | 50 | pow+ | Ireland |

**McElroy's Company**

| | | | |
|---|---|---|---|
| Pte. Enoch Marsteller | – | killed* | – |

**Uknown company**

| | | | |
|---|---|---|---|
| Pte. Thomas Dore | – | MIA | – |
| Pte. Morris Morris | 45 | pow | Montgomery, Penn. |

## Twentieth U.S. Infantry

**Thornton's Company**

| | | | |
|---|---|---|---|
| Pte. Thomas Pettus | – | wounded | – |

## Twenty-First U.S. Infantry

**Tobey's Company**

| | | | |
|---|---|---|---|
| Pte. David Fowler | 29 | wounded | Northfield, N.H. |

## Twenty-Second U.S. Infantry

**Foulk's Company**

| | | | |
|---|---|---|---|
| Pte. David Shupes | 37 | pow | Uniontown, Penn. |

**McFarland's Company†**

| | | | |
|---|---|---|---|
| Sgt. James Crawford | 23 | killed | Westmorland, Penn. |
| Abraham Vallaly | 22 | killed | Washington, Penn. |
| Pte. James Reed | 52 | pow | N.Y. City |
| Pte. Robert McCann | 21 | pow | Penn. |
| Pte. Zadock McIntire | 22 | pow | Va. |
| Pte. Benjamin Davis | 23 | pow | Vt. |
| Pte. Samuel Robb | 38 | pow | Chester, Penn. |

† Company muster rolls cited in The Western Penn. Historical Magazine, "The Papers of Major Daniel McFarland" by John Newell Crombie, April 1968, indicate McFarland's company lost 11 men.

**Milliken's Company**

| | | | |
|---|---|---|---|
| Pte. Solomon Brininger | – | killed | – |
| Pte John Brandford | – | killed | – |
| Pte. Mathew Campbell | – | killed | – |
| Pte. Michael Stover | – | killed | – |
| Pte. James Jordon | – | killed* | – |
| Sgt. Robert Brown | 36 | wounded | England |
| Pte. William Beaty | – | pow | – |
| Pte. John Defriend | 30 | pow+ | Penn. |
| Pte. Josias Moore | 35 | pow+ | Morris Cty., N.J. |
| Pte. John Nappertandy | 50 | pow | Dublin |
| Pte. John Winton | 25 | pow | Pittsburgh |

## Twenty-Third U.S. Infantry

| | | | |
|---|---|---|---|
| Captain Derck Van Veghten | 37 | pow | N.Y. |

| | | | |
|---|---|---|---|
| Captain Peter Mills | 35 | pow, w. | Mass. |

**Armstrong's Company**

| | | | |
|---|---|---|---|
| Pte. Jonathon Race | 24 | pow | Hudson, N.Y. |

**Finney's Company**

| | | | |
|---|---|---|---|
| Pte. Daniel Baker | 20 | pow | Williamstown, Mass. |

**Mills Company**

| | | | |
|---|---|---|---|
| Pte. John Cox | 34 | pow | Kent, Conn. |
| Pte. James Evans | 48 | pow | Laois |
| Pte. Bernard Hoy | 27 | pow | Sligo |
| Pte. Solomon Little | 23 | pow | Lebanon, Conn. |
| Pte. Stephen Scudder | 19 | pow | Hillsdale, N.Y. |

**Unknown company**

| | | | |
|---|---|---|---|
| Pte John Haney | – | killed | – |
| Pte. Samuel Delong | – | MIA | – |
| Pte. Samuel Luckey | – | pow+ | – |
| Pte. John Burger | 32 | pow | N.Y. |
| Pte. Elias Countryman | 21 | pow | Kingston, N.Y. |
| Pte. Richard Goodwin | 27 | pow | Newport, N.H. |
| Pte. Henry Newman | 54 | pow | Germany |
| Pte. Robert Price | 19 | pow | Pequannock, N.J. |
| Pte. Jeremiah Rathburn | 26 | pow | Petersburg, N.Y. |
| Pte. Stephen Emery | 26 | pow | Jeffrey, N.H. |

## Twenty-Fifth U.S. Infantry

**Cone's Company**

| | | | |
|---|---|---|---|
| Cpl. Joseph Decker | 23 | pow, w. | Orange Cty., N.Y. |
| Pte. John Littlefield | 28 | pow, w. | Essex Cty., Conn. |
| Pte. Elijah Wells | 17 | pow, w. | Glastonbury, Conn. |

**Howard's Company**

| | | | |
|---|---|---|---|
| Sgt. Thomas Sturtevant | 35 | pow, w. | Middleborough, Mass. |
| Pte. John Lynes | 22 | pow, w. | Reading, Conn. |
| Pte. Anthony Spinks | 28 | pow | East Greenwich, R.I. |

**Ketchum's Company**

| | | | |
|---|---|---|---|
| Pte. William Walter | – | killed | – |
| Cpl. John Smith | 40 | pow, w. | Hamburg, Conn. |
| Pte. John Godfrey | – | wounded | – |
| Pte. Daniel Mathews | 18 | pow, w. | Windsor, Vt. |
| Pte. Joseph Corkins | 21 | pow | Derby, Conn. |

**Kinney's Company**

| | | | |
|---|---|---|---|
| Pte. Benjamin Eddy | – | killed | – |
| Pte. James Ward | 24 | pow, w. | Freehold, N.J. |
| Pte. Clark Tinker | 19 | pow | Waterford, Conn. |

**Leavenworth's Company†**

| | | | |
|---|---|---|---|
| Pte. Issac Odle | 19 | killed | Westchester Cty., N.Y. |
| Cpl. Daniel Loomis | 22 | pow, w. | Granville, N.Y. |
| Pte. Hontice Couse | 27 | wounded | Nine Partners, N.Y. |
| Pte. Thomas Jones | 24 | pow, w. | – |

† Captain Henry Leavenworth said he had four killed and four wounded at Stoney Creek. George Howard Letterbook, CHS micro 80005, Leavenworth to Howard, 26 June 1813.

**Read's Company**

| | | | |
|---|---|---|---|
| Pte. William Curtis | – | killed | – |
| Pte. Samuel Lock | 22 | killed | South Kingston, R.I. |
| Pte. James Brown | 46 | pow | Windham, N.H. |
| Musician Andrew Peck | 20 | pow | Conn. |
| Cpl. John Reynolds | 26 | pow | Newcastle, Mass. |
| Pte. Michael Rous | – | pow | – |
| Pte. Elisha Wel | – | pow | – |
| Pte. J. MacPherson | – | pow. w. | – |
| Pte. Edward Morse | – | pow, w. | – |

**Unknown company**

| | | | |
|---|---|---|---|
| Sgt. Elisha Warren | 25 | pow | Upton, Mass. |
| Pte. Samuel Hawkins | – | wounded | – |
| Musician Nathan Spicer | 40 | pow | Duchess Cty., N.Y. |

## Second U.S. Light Dragoons

**Burd's Troop**

| | | | |
|---|---|---|---|
| Trooper Thomas Dodson | 25 | pow | Franklin Cty., Penn. |
| Trooper John Tomlinson | 21 | pow | Orange Cty., Va. |

**Selden's Troop**

| | | | |
|---|---|---|---|
| Trooper Charles J. Elliot | 32 | killed | Mount Carmel, Penn. |
| Trooper Benjamin Phillips | 27 | wounded | Richmond, Va. |

**Smith's Troop**

| | | | |
|---|---|---|---|
| Sgt. Ephraim Wilder | 32 | killed | Mass. |

## Second Regiment Artillery

**Biddle's Company**

| | | | |
|---|---|---|---|
| Pte. Elias Doughty | 36 | pow | Philadelphia |

**Hindman's Company**

| | | | |
|---|---|---|---|
| Pte. William Melvin | 30 | pow | Sligo |
| Pte. Peter Morris | 39 | pow | Stransburg, Germany |
| Pte. Charles Stocker | 34 | pow | Frankurt, Germany |
| Pte. William Stiles | 37 | pow | Morris Cty., N.J. |

**Nicholas's Company**

| | | | |
|---|---|---|---|
| Pte. William Hunter | – | killed | – |
| Pte. Samuel Palmer | 33 | wounded | – |

**Towson's Company**

| | | | |
|---|---|---|---|
| Pte. Michael Kelley | – | killed | – |
| Pte. Richard Williams | – | killed | – |
| Pte. William Peters | 30 | killed* | Chester, Penn. |
| Pte. Henry Bowermaster | 18 | pow | Brunswick, Germany |
| Pte. Thomas Bowen | 24 | pow | Willistown, Penn. |
| Artificer Stephen Gorsuch | 31 | pow | Md. |
| Pte. George Foster | 39 | pow | Philadelphia |
| Pte. Anthony Fisher | 23 | pow | Baltimore |
| Pte. George Hedrick | 18 | pow | Baltimore |
| Pte. Truman Johnson | 29 | pow | Cape Ann, Mass. |
| Pte. Enoch Jones | 32 | pow | Baltimore |

| | | | |
|---|---|---|---|
| Pte. William McElroy | 30 | pow | Newry, Ireland |
| Pte. Edward T. Plante | 19 | pow | Ovid, N.Y. |
| Pte. Thomas Renark | – | pow | – |
| Pte. Michael Roe | 30 | pow | Baltimore |
| Pte. Cornelius Rosepaugh | 38 | pow | N.Y. |
| Pte. Samuel Stansbury | 25 | pow | Baltimore |
| Pte. James Trainor | 19 | pow | Baltimore |
| Pte. Hugh S. West | 33 | pow | Va. |
| Artificer William Wheeler | 25 | pow | Baltimore |
| Pte. David R. Whiteley | 26 | pow | Baltimore |

**Unknown company**

| | | | |
|---|---|---|---|
| Pte. John Pitzpatrick | 34 | pow | Ireland |
| Pte. James Hamilton | 23 | pow | – |
| Pte John Allen | 29 | pow | N.Y. |
| Pte. Abraham Lazier | 26 | pow | Hackensack, N.J. |

## Regiment of Light Artillery

**Leonard's Company**

| | | | |
|---|---|---|---|
| Pte. Paul Cilley | 35 | pow | Hillsborough, N.H. |
| Artificer James Colburn | 31 | pow | Wilton, N.H. |
| Pte. Thomas Clayton | 42 | pow | Cork |
| Pte. William Crayton | 22 | pow, w. | Boston |
| Pte. John Ervine | 33 | pow | Hanover, Md. |
| Pte. Terence | – | executed for desertion | – |
| Pte George McKendrick | – | pow | – |
| Pte. Thomas Nowlan | 49 | pow | Dublin |
| Pte. John Sanderson | 28 | pow | Woodstock, Vt. |
| Pte. Curtis L. Stanhope | 28 | pow | Greenfield, Mass. |
| Pte. William Sumner, | 22 | pow | Schoharie, N.Y. |
| Pte. Samuel Vaughn | 30 | pow | Waterbury, Vt. |

## U.S. Regiment of Riflemen

| | | | |
|---|---|---|---|
| Lieutenant Henry Van Swearingen | 21 | pow | Va. |

**Smyth's Company**

| | | | |
|---|---|---|---|
| Cpl. William McCune | 26 | pow | N.Y. |
| Cpl. Francis Ledman | 28 | pow | Va. |
| Pte. David Legg | 22 | pow, w. | Hartford, N.Y. |
| Pte. Joseph Myers | 36 | pow | N.Y. |
| Pte. Benjamin Pearl | – | pow | – |
| Pte. Nicholas Roberson | – | pow | Penn. |
| Pte. Pliny Storey | 19 | pow | Bennington, Vt. |
| Pte. Joseph Sampeteau | – | pow | – |
| Pte. Benjamin Smith | 25 | pow | Gosham, N.Y. |
| Cpl. Francis Ledman | 28 | pow | Va. |

## Miscellaneous

The following names are identified in *General Entry Book of American Prisoners of War* LAC C Series, 694A, as Stoney Creek prisoners. At least three of them, Amasa Lackey, Thomas Girton and Caleb Wells, were state militia, Daniel Lee was a N.Y. Volunteer and Jacob Quick a U.S. Volunteer. Joshua Chase was a black servant probably attached to one of the officers. The affiliation of the remainder is not known but they are probably militia.

| | | | | | | | | |
|---|---|---|---|---|---|---|---|---|
| Nathan Campbell | 35 | pow | Ireland | | Jacob Quick | 29 | pow | Germany |
| Joshua Chase | 21 | pow | Baltimore | | Thomas Richards | 24 | pow | Va. |
| Edward Evans | 35 | pow | Ireland | | Russell Welsh | 21 | pow+ | Penn. |
| Thomas Girton | 28 | pow+ | Salem, N.J. | | Caleb Wells | 45 | pow+ | R.I. |
| Elisha Hardy | 17 | pow | Canada | | Oliver Wilkinson | 22 | pow | N.Y. |
| George Hemmick | 21 | pow | Va. | | | | | |
| William Jones | 20 | pow | Baltimore | | | | | |
| Amasa Lackey | 26 | pow | Mass. | | | | | |
| Daniel Lee | 32 | pow | N.Y. | | | | | |
| John Muncreef | 33 | pow+ | – | | | | | |

*denotes died of wounds, *pow+* denotes died in captivity, *pow, w.* denotes prisoner and wounded

## Sources

This is an incomplete list of killed, wounded and captured compiled from *Registry of Enlistments in the United States Army, 1798-1914, Vol. 1-2*, USNA, *Muster Rolls United States Army1812-1814* RG 94 and the *General Entry Book of American Prisoners of War at Quebec*, LAC C-3233.

# Endnotes

## Abbreviations

AO      Archives of Ontario
ASPMA    American State Papers, Military Affairs
BHM     Battlefield House Museum
CHS     Connecticut Historical Society
DAB     *Dictionary of American Biography*
DCB     *Dictionary of Canadian Biography*
DHB     *Dictionary of Hamilton Biography*
DocHis   E. A. Cruikshank, ed. *Documentary History of the Campaigns on the Niagara Frontier in 1812-1814.* Volume and page number citied first, followed by document.
HPL     Hamilton Public Library
LAC     Library and Archives Canada
LOC     Library of Congress
MCHS   Mercer County Historical Society
MHS    Massachusetts Historical Society
NA      National Archives, United Kingdom
NYSL    New York State Library
NWR    *Niles' Weekly Register*
RG      Record Group
USNA   National Archives of the United States
WO     War Office

## Preface

1. A.R.M. Lower, *Colony to Nation,* 171.

## 1: "Perhaps the last time I will write."

1. MCHS, Mercer County Estate # 126 OS. James Crawford's will.

2. On 6 July 1759, Brigadier General John Prideaux landed 2,500 troops and 1,000 Iroquois allies at Four Mile Creek. Within three weeks Fort Niagara had fallen; within two months, Quebec had fallen. Four Mile Creek is now the site of a state park. *First Campaign of An A.D.C.* 3: 10, hereafter ADC. The anonymous aide de camp, a junior staff officer who came ashore with Boyd's brigade at Newark, left a witty, impressionistic account of the 1813 Niagara campaign.

3. MCHS, Mercer County Estate # 126 OS. James Crawford's will, written 23rd May 1813, was probated in the town of Mercer on 4 February 1814. USNA, Registry of Enlistments. RG94 Army Muster Rolls 1812-1814.

4. *New York Evening Post,* 3 December 1816, The Descent on the British Shore at Fort George, hereafter Descent. This detailed, subjective account of the 1813 Niagara campaign signed "one of the staff" is widely believed to have been authored by Major General Morgan Lewis; The time, more than a century before the introduction of Daylight Sav-

ing, is a rough approximation of Eastern Standard Time. In 1813 there was no time standard; watches were set at noon when the sun was at its highest point which of course occurred at different times as one moved east or west. Nautical dawn, when the sun is 12 degrees below the horizon, general ground objects can be discerned and limited military operations are possible, occurs on the Niagara at 3:24 a.m. EST on 27 May; Stagg, *Mr. Madison's War,* 165. The British minister in Washington, Augustus Foster described Henry Dearborn as "heavy, unwieldy-looking."; Graves/Chartrand, *The United States Army and the War of 1812: A Handbook,* 257, henceforth *Army Handbook*; ADC 3:12.

5. Shaler, *Memoirs,* 413. McFeely. *Journal,* 260 ; Boyd, *Documents and Facts,* 13-14;. ADC 3, 11-12 ; *LOL,* 125. *ADC* 3, 11.

6. Boyd, *Documents and Facts,* 14. ADC 3: 12. LOL, 125.

7. Myers, *Reminiscences,* 28. ADC 3: 16

## 2: Modern Times

1. *Boston Patriot,* 9 January 1811, From the Anthology. Zerah Colburn.

2. Scripture, "Arithmetical Prodigies", 11-17; Dodge, *Encyclopedia Vermont Biography,* 151-152. Believed backward until he suddenly began solving complex math problems at the age of six. Zerah Colburn was victimized by a father intent on exploiting his gift. Dragged around America and then to Europe, where his father died in 1824, Zerah attended pubic school at Westminster in England and College Royal in Paris, but gradually lost his powers. He was briefly an actor and studied under the physicist and physician Thomas Young before returning to America in 1823 where he became a Methodist preacher and a teacher of languages. He died of tuberculosis at the age of 35.

3. Named after the likely mythical Ned Ludd, who reputedly destroyed some stocking frames in the late 18th Century.

4. *So We'll Go No More a Roving,* Lord Byron.

5. *The Times,* 16 July 1816, We remarked with pain.

6. The Bohemian-American composer, Anthony Philip Heinrich is credited with conducting the first Beethoven symphony in America in Lexington Kentucky in 1817.

7. This was in fact the Democratic Republican Party, ancestor of the present Democratic Party. In opposition was the Federalist Party which would disappear by 1820. The current-day Republican Party dates from 1854.

8. *Federal Republican*, 31 August 1812, Invasion of Canada.

9. Steiner, *The Life and Correspondence of James McHenry*, 589, Tallmadge to McHenry, 29 November 1813. *The Repertory & General Advertiser*, 8 January 1813, From the Connecticut Mirror.

10. Fulton's steam warship, renamed *Fulton the First* and launched 29 October 1814, was a defence vessel for New York harbour. This visionary craft proved perfectly viable and predates the infinitely more famous USS *Monitor*, by nearly half a century. Fulton's submarine gun, which he called *Columbiad*, proved successful in trials – provided the range was no greater than twenty feet.

11. *Northern Whig*, 5 January, 1813. Perpetual Motion. *New York Mercantile Advertiser*, 16 November 1812, Valuable Discovery. Ord-Hulme, *Perpetual Motion: The History of an Obsession*, 123-133 NWR, 14 November 1812, 2 January 1813. *Commercial Advertiser*, 11 January 1813, Perpetual Motion. *Mercantile Advertiser*, 9 January, 1813, Perpetual Motion.

12. Unfortunately after contaminated vaccine was accidentally distributed in 1821, Congress repealed the act and left the issue in the hands of individual states, an abdication that resulted in thousands of unnecessary infections. Not until 1902 would Congress redress the error and make smallpox vaccination a federal responsibility again. See *Missed Opportunities: The Vaccine Act of 1813* by Rohit K. Singla.

13. U.S. Bureau of Census, Urban Place Population, 1810-1820. *American Statesman's Kalendar and Register for 1813*, 22.

14. The 1810 census was 7,239,881, over the next ten years it would increase an average of 240,000 a year. U.S. Bureau of Census, Urban Place Population, 1810-1820. *American Statesman's Kalendar and Register for 1813*, 22. Matthews, "Uncle Sam". *Proceedings of the American Antiquarian Society*, Vol 19, 33. The first use of Uncle Sam, inspired by the letters U.S. on government wagons, is credited to the *Troy Post*, 7 September 1813.

15. *Albany Argus*, 5 February, 1813, Upper Canada ; *Columbian*, 30 December 1812, Seat of War.

16. The first public library in Canada was established in Montreal in 1796. See the Quebec History Encyclopedia, Libraries in Canada. *.La Gazette du commerce et littéraire* was founded in 1778 and would become *The Montreal Gazette* in 1785, the same year *The Times* began publishing. Molson's steamboats were the *Accommodation*, 1809 and the *Swiftsure* 1812. See DCB 7.

17. The Constitutional Act of 1791 which divided the province of Quebec into Upper and Lower Canada recognized the English-speaking, largely Loyalist society that had settled along the Upper St. Lawrence and Lower Lakes following the American Revolution. NA, WO1/537. 75-106, "Memorandum [on the defence of Canada]", cited in Latimer,

*1812*, 42. Stanley, *Land Operations*, 49; Sheppard, *Plunder, Profit and Parole*, 13; Merritt, *Desire of Serving*, 68; Gray, *Soldiers of the King*, 18: Statistics Canada, Estimated Population of Canada, 1605 to Present. Dunlop, *Recollections*, 89.

18. English traveller John Maude, quoted in Cruikshank, *The Battle of Fort George*, 14. Smith, *A Geographical View of the British Possessions in North America*, iii.

19. The act – (1813) 53 Geo. III, C. 3 (U.C.) – produced great consternation in the British army over the loss of whisky supplies and was suspended long enough for distillers to build up adequate reserves. The initial proclamation expired 1 March 1814 and was not renewed. See William R. Riddell, "The First Canadian Prohibition Measure," *Canadian Historical Review*, 1, (1920) 187-190

20. LAC, CO 42, Vol 146, Prevost to Liverpool, 18 May 1812 ; Sheppard, *Plunder, Profits and Paroles*, 42. In 1813, £1 was worth $4. Twelve pence made one shilling, twenty schillings made one pound.

21. Niagara was Newark officially only from 1792 to 1798 when it served as capital of Upper Canada but the name stubbornly endured into the 19th Century. Contemporary American documents refer to it exclusively as Newark, British military maps continued to refer to as Newark throughout the war. The present name, Niagara-on-the-Lake was officially adopted in 1970.

22. Burghardt, "Origin and Development of the Road Network of the Niagara Peninsula", 431 ; Smith, *Topographical Description of Upper Canada, 27;* Cruikshank, *The Battle of Fort George*, 13 ; Melish, *Travels in the United States of America*, Vol II 337; *Albany Argus*, 5 February 1813, Upper Canada. The Niagara Escarpment is a 1,000-mile limestone cliff that begins in western New York and terminates northwest of Chicago near the Wisconsin border. It is the defining feature of the Niagara Peninsula, towering up to 30-storeys above the flatlands south of Lake Ontario.

23. Smith, *Topographical Description of Upper Canada*, 27. In the 1808 election Barton Township had only 62 eligible voters. See Hobbs, *Thomas Taylor's War*, n 6.

24. Gourlay, *Statistical Account of Upper Canada*, 389, 394-395, 398, 399, 423, 426, 427.

25. The battalions were numbered according to the electoral districts of Lincoln County, representing from three to five townships. 1st Lincoln – Niagara, Grantham and Louth, 2nd Lincoln – Stamford, Thorold and Pelham, 3rd Lincoln – Bertie, Crowland, Willoughby, Humbertson and Wainfleet, 4th Lincoln – Clinton, Grimsby, Caister and Gainsborough and 5th Lincoln – Ancaster, Barton, Glanford, Saltfleet and Binbrook. See Paul Couture,. *The Non-Regular Military Forces on the Niagara Frontier: 1812-1814.* Cruikshank, *The Battle of Fort George*, 14 ; Smith, *A Geographical View of the Province of Upper Canada*, 65.

26. Melish, *Travels in the United States of America*, 338.

27. *American Statesman's Kalendar and Register for 1813*, 35.

**3: "So unequal a contest"**[1]

1. *DocHis 6*, 70. Vincent to Prevost, 28 May 1813.

2. *DocHis 5*, 250, Vincent to Prevost, 28 May 1813 ; *DocHis 4*, 257, Fowler to Baynes 29 May 1813 ; *ADC*. 3: 11. Numerous witnesses on both sides remarked on the thickness of the fog

3. Fifty yards equals forty-six metres. The lighthouse, built at Point Mississauga in 1804 as one of the earliest on the Great Lakes, was demolished in 1814 and the stone used to build Fort Mississauga, which survives as part of the Niagara-on-the-Lake Golf Course, itself an historical artifact dating from 1875. Norton, *Journal*, 323. According to Merritt, Vincent believed the Americans would split their force in two and attack Fort George from two different directions.

4. *DocHis 5*,221, Glegg memo 8 May 1813. Estimates of the American invasion force vary widely. Winfield Scott said 4,700, John Armstrong, the secretary of war in 1813, said 6,000, the British Deputy Assistant Quarter Master General , Captain George Fowler put the number landed at 8,000. Starting with Scott's figure of 4,700 and adding in 500 camp guards and 300 artillery and dragoons at Five Mile Meadow, the figure of 6,000 becomes approachable. Less than three weeks before the invasion, Captain Isaac Roach of the Twenty-Third Infantry, noted "We had now assembled about 6,000 men." Two days after the invasion, Captain John Walworth of the Sixth Infantry reported: "Our Army at this Station consists of upwards of Six Thousand effective men" ; Cruikshank, *Records of Niagara*, 44, 28. Sheaffe to Prevost, April 1813. Vincent, encouraged by intelligence that only 200 men defended the old fort, proposed an assault by 400 troops. The plan was rejected by Major General Sir Roger Sheaffe as contrary to Prevost's strictly defensive policy.

5. *DocHis 5*, 257, Fowler to Baynes, 29 May 1813.

6. Cruikshank, *Battle of Fort George*, 42.

7. *DocHis 6*, 179 Hamilton to Henderson, 4 July 1813. *ADC 3*, 12.

8. AO MS 842, Harvey, *Journal* ; *DocHis 5*, 237-238, Myers to Baynes, 26 May 1813 (the date is incorrectly stated as 20 May)

9. *New York Evening Post*, 3 December 1816, Descent ; Anonymous ; *Taylor and his Generals*, 276.

10. *ADC 3*, 12-13. The intentional explosion of the Fort York magazine on 27 April 1813 wounded 222 and killed 38 American soldiers including the commanding officer, Brigadier General Zebulon Pike. See Malcomson, *Capital in Flames*.

11. Cruikshank. *Battle of Fort George* 38, 44.

12. *DHB* 8. A brewer, distiller and provisioner, the Scottish-born Crooks, commanded a flank company of the 1st Lincoln at Queenston Heights and

was mentioned in dispatches ; Cain, *Ghost Ships*, 90. The *Scourge*, one of a pair of 1812 warships discovered in 300 feet of water offshore from Port Dalhousie, Ontario in 1973, was seized on Lake Ontario thirteen days before war was declared, supposedly on suspicion of violating Embargo Laws. The ship was promptly sold to the US Navy for $2,999.25, renamed and fitted for war. It would take the Crooks family another 115 years to wring a $15,546.63 compensation/settlement from the US government.

13. *ADC 3*, 14. Long toms were long-range cannon, typically ranging from 12 – 32 pdrs, mounted admidships on a swivel.

14. *Buffalo Gazette*, 8 June 1813, Battle at Newark. *ADC 3*, 16

15. *DocHis 6*, 257, Fowler to Baynes, 29 May, 1813.

16. Harvey, *Journal* ; *National Advocate*, 23 June 1813, Extract of a Letter.

17. *DCB 6*. Teyoninhokarawen ; Norton. *Journal*. *323*. Norton's men, disheartened by the overwhelming odds, continued melting away. Within an hour he was down to fifteen warriors.

18. *DocHis 5*, 258. Fowler to Baynes. 29 May 1813. Captain George Fowler, the deputy assistant quartermaster general, said ninety Glengarries, forty Royal Newfoundlanders, twenty-seven Black Corps and 100 militia.

19. *Republican Star*, 22 June, 1813, Buffalo, June 8 ; Anonymous, *Taylor and his Generals*, 276.

20. Boyd, *Documents and Facts*, 5 ; *ADC 3*, 16 ; *Baltimore Patriot*, 17 June 1813, Extract of a Letter from an Officer ; *Baltimore Patriot*, 12 June 1813. Extract of a Letter from an Officer of the 16th Infantry.

21. *ADC 3*, 17, 18.

22. *ADC 5*, 201.

23. Although trained as artillery, the gunners of 2nd Artillery were also excellent light infantry, "The 2nd Regiment of Artillery was the best unit in the army during the war." – *Army Handbook*. 203. Scott was 6'5" and weighed 230 pounds in an army where the average height was 5'7" ; NYSHS, Dearborn Letterbook. Dearborn to Armstrong, 23 June 1813. "There is no officer in the Northern Army who…possesses the necessary requisite for forming a great officer, in so imminent a degree as Col. Scott."

24. *ADC 3*, 19 ; Anonymous, *Taylor and his Generals*, 277.

25. Boyd, *Documents and Facts*, 5.

26. Cruikshank, *Battle of Fort George*, 54. Mann, *Medical Sketches*, 62. Mann provides a casualty figure of 391, Cruikshank furnishes the size of battlefield – 200 yards by 15 yards – less than half the playing area of a Canadian Football League field – 110 yards by 65 yards.

The official British returns did not include any militia or Indians killed. Cruikshank, *The Battle of Fort George*, says eighty-five militia were killed or wounded and at least two Indians killed. Boyd,

*Documents and Facts,* said 107 British troops were buried on the initial battle ground. A captain in the Sixteenth Infantry, *Baltimore Patriot,* 12 June 1813, said the British "loss amounted to 140 killed (at least we buried that number of them this day) 130 wounded, 130 prisoners."; *ADC* 4, 73 ; *DAB,* John Parker Boyd 1764-1830. Boyd spent nearly twenty years as a mercenary in India, selling his services to various native princes. He returned to the U.S. in 1808 as regimental commander of the 4th Infantry. He fought under William Henry Harrison at Tippecanoe in 1811 and was named brigadier general in 1812.

27. *DocHis* 6, 247 Loss Returns ; *Boston Patriot,* 30 June 1813, Extract of a Letter from an Officer.

28. *ASPMA, 1* 445, Lewis to Dearborn, 27 May 1813. Second in command, Morgan Lewis reported at 1 p.m. "Fort George and its dependencies are ours. The enemy, beaten at all points"

29. So thorough was the destruction of Fort George that even the garrison fire engine was destroyed. See "The Journal of Major Isaac Roach", *Pennsylvania Magazine of History and Biography,* July, 1893 ; *DocHis* 6, 70. Vincent to Prevost, 28 May 1813.

30. Niagara Provincial Light Dragoons – a locally-raised cavalry unit primarily used for communication and observation. The unit was commanded by a 19-year-old Niagara Peninsula native, William Hamilton Merritt, who after the war would go on to build the first Welland Canal. See DCB, 9 ; Lossing, *Pictorial Field-Book,* 600. Lossing quotes from Merritt's narrative, a different passage from surviving versions. "We formed again at the Council House when I was sent up to order down the light company of the King's, who we understood, were at the Eight-mile Creek. I rode through the woods, around the American regiments, followed the lake to the Twenty-Mile Creek (was two hours on the road) where I met Commodore Barclay with his sailors and the King's."

Commander Robert Barclay's party, on its way to Lake Erie, included three lieutenants, a surgeon, a purser, a mate and nineteen sailors, twelve of whom were discards from Sir James Yeo's Lake Ontario squadron, and the rest "the most worthless characters that came from England with him." Wood, *Select British Documents,* 2, 298.

31. *ADC* 3, 79 "The distant spectators, who had cheered the descent of one flag, were not less loud in their acclamations on the ascent of the other." ; *Columbian Phenix,* 19 June 1813, Extract of a Letter from an Officer.

32. *Baltimore Patriot,* 22 July 1813, The Fall of Fort George, the Bulwark of Upper Canada.

33. *National Advocate,* 23 June 1813, Extract of a Letter.

### 4: "We ought to have pursued the enemy night and day."[1]

1. McFeely, *Journal,* 265.

2. *DocHis* 5, 246, Dearborn to Armstrong, 27 May 1813.

3. For an account of the abortive 1775 expedition under Richard Montgomery and Benedict Arnold to capture Quebec, see *Canada Invaded* by George F. G. Stanley, Canadian War Museum, 1977.

4. The official figures of the *Historical Register of the United States,* Vol 2, 229 are thirty-nine killed and 111 wounded, the actual figures are undoubtedly higher with at least forty-three killed. See *Poulson's American Daily Advertiser,* 12 August 1813, Extract of a Letter from an Officer.

5. Mann, *Medical Sketches,* 60. Mann said Dearborn has "a fever of the synochal type." See M. C. Gillette, *The Army Medical Department: 1775-1818.* "The type of dysentery seen by physicians in the North at this time 'was attended in most cases with a fever of the synochal type, accelerated action of the arteries, and heat increased considerably above the healthy standard.' Mann favored treating it by depletion, preferably a single bleeding of 16 ounces followed by a 'full cathartic of calomel and jalap.' 'Anodynes,' or painkillers, might be administered after the 'intestines were well evacuated.' Mann also discovered that 'There were cases when calomel and opium, in small doses, at intervals of 4 or 6 hours, were found beneficial.' Emetics were generally used only when all else failed, but dysentery could take on 'a typhoid form' which made the administration of wine or diluted brandy, up to two pints of the former, as well as purgatives, advisable." *Sketch of the Life of Major Gen Henry Dearborn,* campaign literature 1817, 10-11. Cruikshank, *Battle of Fort George,* 49.

6. Ingersoll, *Historical Sketch of the Second War,* 99-101.

7. *Carolina Federal Republican,* 12 June 1813, Copy of Letter from an Officer.

8. William Duane. *Proceedings of the Massachusetts Historical Society,* 262. Appointing Lewis quartermaster, Duane said, was the equivalent of "sending a vessel to sea without raising her anchors."

9. Armstrong, *Notices 134.* The truculent, pugnacious and politically ambitious Armstrong – no friend of Dearborn's – was furious Vincent had been allowed to escape : "A contingency of this kind, was never provided for in the original plan of attack nor by any subsequent order given on the field; and would, perhaps, have entirely escaped notice, had not Scott, from his advanced position, made the discovery and deemed it his duty to institute and continue a pursuit of five miles; not merely without orders, but in evasion of such as was given, until at last, a mandate reached him, of a character so decided and peremptory as, by leaving nothing to discretion, could not fail to recall him to Fort George." Ironically, Armstrong laid none of the blame at the feet of his brother-in-law, Morgan Lewis.

10. McFeely. *Journal,* 265. Scott vowed to sleep

wrapped in the British flag that night. *Buffalo Gazette*, 22 June 1813, To the Editor of the Buffalo Gazette. No horses were landed with the troops, therefore all artillery had to be transported by manpower.

11. NYSL, Gardner Papers, Scott to Gardner, 4 June 1813.

12. Five Mile Meadow was two miles below Lewiston, NY ; *Buffalo Gazette*, 22 June 1812, To the Editor of the Buffalo Gazette. Joseph-Geneviève Le Comte de Puisaye, *DCB* 6. A French royalist resettled in Upper Canada after the French Revolution, de Puisaye built an estate on the Niagara River three miles south of Newark, now Niagara-on-the-Lake. His house, moved from the original site, survives near the present-day Iniskillin Winery. The original site is marked by a plaque on the Niagara River Parkway.

13. Ingersoll, *Historical Sketch of the Second War*, 286-287

14. NYSL, Gardner Papers, Scott to Gardner, 4 June 1813. Brackenridge, *History of the Late War*, 114. One eager company of the Fifteenth Infantry, commanded by Lieutenant Thomas Riddle, is said to have pursued Vincent almost to Queenston, collecting stragglers along the way.

15. *Buffalo Gazette*, 22 June 1813, To the Editor of the Buffalo Gazette.

16. *New York Evening Post*, 3-4 December 1816, Descent.

17. *Independent Chronicle*, 3 April 1817, Capture of York and Fort George. Dearborn regarded the combined operation against Fort George as "the handsomest military display on the northern frontier during the war."

18. *DocHis* 6, 4. Armstrong to Dearborn ,15 May 1813.

19. Tucker, *Poltroons and Patriots*, n 356. Tucker says the nickname is supposed to have originated with Andrew Jackson while Dearborn was secretary of war from 1801 to 1809.

20. DocHis 5, 269.

21. McFeely, *Journal*, 265.

22. Boyd, *Documents*, 47.

23. The Baltimore Blues or Baltimore Volunteers was one of the 12-month, U.S. Volunteers' units that were trained similarly to, and served alongside, regular troops. *Albany Register*, 22 June 1813, From the Baltimore Whig – June 17.

24. Myers, *Reminiscences*, 9.

25. *New York Evening Post*, 3-4 December 1816, Descent. Historians have not been kind to the American leadership for recalling Scott. Robert Quimby suggests a conspiracy. "The old generals, Dearborn and Lewis, were fearful that he might run into an Indian ambush laid by the British and suffer disaster. The brigadier generals concurred, possibly because they had no desire to see a junior harvest all the laurels." To which the Scott biographer, A. D. Smith adds: "Caution, always caution. That was the watchword with most of them. My God, Colo-

nel, there might be Indians in those woods!"

26. Cruikshank, *Battle of Fort George*, 53. The British losses were severe – more than a quarter of their fighting force – the 8th alone sustained 202 casualties out of 310, the Glengarries, with 108 men took eighty-one casualties, one forty-man company of the Royal Newfoundland Regiment lost seventeen men, and two companies of the 1st Lincoln Militia lost five officers and eighty men ; *DocHis* 5, 257, Fowler to Baynes, 29 May 1813.

27. Harvey, *Journal*. Newark was indeed deserted and damaged, a captain in the 16th Infantry reported "There is scarce a house in town that is not perforated with bullets, which have done great damage. The inhabitants had generally left it before we took possession.". See *Baltimore Patriot*, 12 June 1813, Extract of a Letter.

28. *DocHis* 6, 4. Armstrong to Dearborn 15 May 1813.

29. *Ibid.*

30. *War*, 15 June, 1813, Latest from the Army.

31. On the northeast coast of Lake Ontario, thirty-five miles southeast of Kingston, Sackett's Harbour was the principal American naval base during the War of 1812. Malcomson, *Lords of the Lake*, 129

32. Wilder, *The Battle of Sackett's Harbour*, 68.

33. *DCB* 4. An active soldier with a distinguished service record and an able administrator, Prevost was saddled with managing the war with limited resources and no mandate other than avoiding defeat.

34. *DocHis* 5, 134. Prevost to Sheaffe, 27 March, 1813.

35. *Sir Isaac Brock.*

36. *DCB* 5. ADC 5, 269.

37. Wood, *Select British Documents*, 2, 32. Prevost to Procter, 7 May, 1813. Yeo's Royal Navy detachment was taking over from the largely moribund Provincial Marine, whose armed vessels were almost exclusively consigned to transport detail.

38. Harvey, *Journal.*

39. *Ibid.* "The possession of Sacketts Harbour necessarily involved the surrender of their whole Naval Establishment on Lake Ontario as the enemy had no other port on the shores of the Lake. The loss therefore was to them, what that of Kingston would be to us."

40. Prevost was born in New Jersey, 1767.

41. Wood, *Select British Documents*, 2, 130. Prevost to Bathurst, 1 June 1813.

## 5: "A flying enemy much less fatigued than his pursuers"

1. *New York Evening Post*, 3 December, 1816, Descent.

2. See *DCB* 5.

3. Bisshop.the aristocratic former MP and a Napoleonic war veteran commanded British defences on the Niagara River from Queenston in the north through Chippawa and Fort Erie to the Point Abino on the Lake Erie shore ; Cruikshank, *Battle of Fort George*, 51 ; *DocHis* 6, 193. Charles Askin to

John Askin, 2 June 1813.

4. *DCB 6.*

5. LAC, RG7, I, Vol 58, Nichol *Memorandum,* 10 Nov. 1817.

6. On the record Vincent is ambiguous. On 26 May he wrote Prevost "if I am overpowered I shall take up a central situation and wait there for the support I have every reason to expect from Kingston." Cruikshank, *Records of Niagara,* 44, 37.

7. Nichol *Memorandum, Trous de loup,* literally wolf holes, were conical pits with a pointed stake in the centre used to protect fortifications against cavalry. The ADC was Captain Henry Banks Oldenburgh Milnes, son of Sir Robert Milnes former lieutenant governor of Lower Canada.

8. Harvey, *Journal,* "the position at Queenston is not tenable without heavy ordnance to protect its right (which commanded from the Heights on the Enemy side (of) the river)". The site of Beaver Dams is now within the city of Thorold.

9. *DCB 8.* Captain John DeCew of the 2nd Lincoln was captured by the Americans on 29 May 1813. His house was used by the British as a depot and advanced picket throughout the war; Harvey, *Journal* ; Norton, *Journal,* 322.

10. Paul Shipman ran a tavern near a ford of the creek in what is now downtown St. Catharines. He would eventually lend his first name to St. Catharines' main street – St. Paul.

11. Norton, *Journal,* 325. "We heard that the army had reached the Depot of Ammunition on the Mountain about Three Miles from us; – I thought that as this was the only road by which the Enemy could pass – we might cut off their retreat & that to keep this position for the night would be rendering more service than to join our friends."

12. Lossing, *Pictorial Field-Book,* 600 ; *DocHis 6,* 251, Vincent to Prevost, 28 May 1813.

13. *DocHis 5,* 221, Glegg Memo, 3 May, 1813. *DocHis 6,* 271, Field Ordnance, 30 May 1813.

14. Now a neighborhood in northwest Buffalo.

15. *DocHis 5,* 274, Buffalo Gazette, 1 June 1813

16. British army regulations allowed twelve wives to accompany each company of a battalion on foreign posting and six wives per company when the battalion was on actual campaign. See Dianne Graves, *In the Midst of Alarms: The Untold Story of Women and the War of 1812.*

17. *DocHis 6,* 193-196, Askin to Askin, 2 June 1813. Captain John Askin of the 2nd Lincoln travelled as far as the Grand River, "But left the 41st behind me for they came on too slow. After a great deal of fatigue I arrived at the Forty Mile Creek on the 30th ulto. alone, for all my men had stopped at their homes."

18. *DCB 6.*

19. LAC, RG 7, G1, Vol 58. Bathurst to Smith, 10 November 1817.

20. *New York Evening Post,* 3 December, 1816, Descent.

21. Harvey, *Journal.*

22. *Ibid.*

23. Merritt, *A Desire of Serving,* 5, 6.

24. Cruikshank, *Battle of Fort George,* 40.

## 6: "The continual wavering of the commanding General"

1. Armstrong, *Notices,* 154. Van de Venter to Armstrong, 31 March 1813.

2. *Independent Chronicle,* 3 March 1817, Capture of York and Fort George ; Anonymous. *Sketch of the Life of Major Gen. Henry Dearborn,* 11, Campaign literature, 1817. The accounts, both part of Dearborn's campaign literature for governor of Massachusetts in 1817, are identical except for the manner in which Lewis was persuaded to go ashore. The *Independent Chronicle* said Dearborn "ordered him to land." The campaign sketch said, Dearborn "finding Gen Lewis still on board, repeated his suggestions for him to land."

3. *New York Evening Post,* 3-4 December 1816, Descent.

4. *Granite Monthly,* "Hon. John Chandler" 9, Dearborn to Wingate, 17 January 1817 ; Anonymous. *Sketch of the Life of Major Gen. Henry Dearborn,* 11.

5. Colonel Moses Porter had commanded the artillery during the 27 May invasion ; *New York Evening Post, Descent,* Beebe to Lewis, 28 May 1813.

6. *Nonsense Novels.*

7. The present-day city of Hamilton.

8. *New York Evening Post,* 3-4 December 1816, Descent. Memoranda from Major Christopher Van De Venter.

9. *New York Evening Post,* 3-4 December 1816, Descent.

10. *Ibid.* Lewis presumably knew something about logistics. Until March 13, 1813 he had been quartermaster general of the U.S. Army. During the Revolution he'd been deputy quartermaster general of the Northern Army.

11. *Ibid*

12. *Ibid.* Van De Venter Memoranda.

13. Just ten months earlier, while based in Albany, Dearborn had asked the secretary of war "Who is to have command of the operations in Upper Canada? I take it for granted that my command does not extend to that distant quarter." See Quimby, *The U.S. Army in the War of 1812,* 59.

14. *DocHis 5,* 275, army officer to Baltimore Whig, 30 May 1813. "When we marched to Queenston on the evening of the 28th we found (what intelligent men had told us at Newark) that the enemy was far advanced on his retreat by the back road towards the lower part of the Province with about 3,000 men."

15. Dearborn, *Letterbooks,* Dearborn to Armstrong, 29 May 1813.

16. NYSL, Gardner Papers, Scott to Gardner, 4 June 1813.

17. *DocHis 4,* 263, Noon to Tompkins, 28 May 1813.

18. *Macdonough Letters*, 84, 30 May 1813.
19. LAC, MG 24, F16, *Simonds Papers*, Walworth to Simonds, 29 May 1813.
20. Burn, *Letters*, 307.
21. Porter to Armstrong, 27 July 1813, cited in Coleman, *The American Capture of Fort George*, 32-33.
22. *Granite Monthly*, "Hon. John Chandler" 9, Dearborn to Wingate, 17 January 1817.
23. *Albany Argus*, 30 July, 1813, Fort George.
24. NYSL, Gardner Papers, Gardner to Scott, 30 June 1813 ; Myers, *Reminiscences*, 28. *Evening Post*, 4 June 1813, Buffaloe, May 25. Myers said Stanard was fatally wounded, the *Post* said the wound was not considered mortal and Heitman's *Historical Register* says Stanard lived until 1843. Bronaugh's second at the duel was future president Zachary Taylor, then a captain in the Seventh Infantry. NYSL, Gardner Papers, Scott to Gardner, 16 July 1813. "I called him a coward – he provoked me to say it & I believed what I spoke. He challenged me on 3rd June & I declined fighting him."
25. Wilder, *Battle of Sackett's Harbour*, 136. Macomb to Samuel Smith, 24 June 1813.
26. NYSL, Gardner Papers, Scott to Gardner, 16 July 1813.
27. Armstrong, *Notices*, 154. Van de Venter to Armstrong, 31 March 1813.
28. *Simonds Papers*, Walworth to Simonds, 29 May 1813.
29. Dearborn to Eustis, 11 December, 1813. Cited in Quimby, *U.S. Army*, 83. The secretary of war, until he resigned in December 1812, William Eustis had succeeded Dearborn in the position. Eustis was followed by Armstrong in January 1813.
30. Eustis to Dearborn, 18 December, 1812. Cited in Quimby, *U.S. Army*, 83 ; Dearborn to Madison, 13 March 1813. cited in Malcomson, *Capital in Flames*, 127.

### 7: "The total want of Enterprise"

1. Harvey, *Journal*.
2. Vincent's route likely followed Pelham Road in current day St. Catharines. *DocHis 5*, 220. Thomas McCrae diary, 4 May 1813.
3. Harvey, *Journal* ; The great road refers to the old Highway 8, now Niagara Regional Road 81.
4. *Ibid.*
5. *Ibid.*
6. *DocHis 5*, 237, Vincent to Prevost, 19 May 1813.
7. *DocHis 5*, 298, Vincent to Baynes, 4 June 1813. Vincent was forced to borrow 500 guineas from Lieuenant-Colonel Thomas Clark of the 2nd Lincoln to buy cattle for the British garrison at Malden because local farmers would not take army script. ; Merritt, *Desire of Serving*, 11. "There was a sort of prejudice against the inhabitants by Military men, getting to a great length."
8. *DocHis 5*, 301. Militia District General Order, 4 June 1813.
9. The Lincoln Militia, comprising five battalions,

numbered one through five, was drawn from the twenty townships of the Niagara Peninsula with a total strength of 1,500. The various battalions took part in virtually every action in Niagara during the war.
10. Merritt, *Desire of Serving*, 5.
11. Dwight, *Diary*, 18.
12. Mann, *Medical Sketches*, 63.
13. Dwight, *Diary*, 19.
14. McFeeley, *Journal*, 259.
15. *New York Evening Post*, 9 July 1813, Letter to the editor.

### 8: Disappointed & dispirited"[1]

1. NYSL, Gardner Papers, Scott to Gardner, 4 June 1813.
2. *New York Evening Post*, 3-4 December 1816, Descent.
3. *Ibid.*
4. *Ibid.*
5. *Ibid.*
6. *Ibid*
7. *Ibid.*
8. *Ibid*. NYSL, Gardner Papers, Scott to Gardner, 4 June 1813.
9. DocHis 5, 266. *Dearborn to Armstrong*, 29 May 1813 ; Van De Venter's memoranda, *New York Evening Post*, 4 Dec. 1816, is scathing in rebuttal. "Gen. Dearborn believed that he (the enemy) would patiently wait for the approach of the American army at Beaver Dams, make a show of resistance, and then surrender. No fact derived from the geography of that part of Canada, or its resources, or from the character of the British officers, could give a plausible appearance of a probability of such a result. The retreat of the British army to the head of the lake was certain."
10. *Ibid*
11. *Ibid*

### 9: "A scandalously managed affair"

1. LeCouteur, *Merry Hearts*, 117.
2. Thirty-seven Missisauga and Mohawk. See Wilder's *Battle of Sackett's Harbour*, 73
3. LeCouteur, *Merry Hearts*, 117. Dudley, *Naval War*, 473, Wingfield Memoir.
4. MHS, Taliaferro Papers, Orders, 2 June 1813. *Feu de joie*, literally fire of joy, is a musket salute whereby formed troops fire consecutively from one end of the line to the other.
5. *DocHis 5*, 153. The Buffalo Gazette, 13 April 1813.
6. *DocHis 5*, Chauncey to Jones, 19 May 1813 ; Dudley, *Naval War*, 480, Perry to Chauncey, 12 June 1813.
7. In a perilous voyage down the Lake Erie shoreline, Perry managed to evade the Royal Navy squadron twice, making port at Presque Isle, present day Erie PA, on June 18. Within three months the Black Rock vessels would prove their worth at the decisive Battle of Lake Erie. See Sandy Antal, *A

*Wampum Denied*, 244.

## 10: "The roads, they say, are very bad."

1. McDonough, *Letters*, 84.
2. Cruikshank, *Public Life and Services of Robert Nichol*, 29. The pond is now called Jordan Harbour. The former Henry farm, on Niagara Regional Road 81, one mile east of Vineland at Maplewood School, lies in the midst of the Beamsville Bench, a premium wine-growing area of the Niagara Peninsula. Nichol, *Memorial*. Harvey, *Journal*. "the rear Brigade (as it was called) & the whole of the Guns, with which I remained." Harvey halted at the present site of the village of Jordan.
3. *DocHis 5*, 288, Vincent to Baynes, 31 May 1813. *DocHis 6*, 91, Fulton to Prevost, 18 June, 1813. "I found the troops in great distress for necessaries, shirts, shoes and stockings. Most of the 49th are literally naked." *DocHis 6*, 74. Vincent to Baynes, 14 June, 1813.
4. Harvey, *Journal*.
5. *Ibid*.
6. *Ibid*.
7. Norton. *Journal*, 326.
8. *DocHis 5*, 265, Dearborn to Tompkins, 29 May 1813. "We may yet intercept him at York, though the prospect is unfavorable."
9. McDonough, *Letters*, 84 ; *DocHis 7*, 258, Chauncey to Jones, 2 June 1813.
10. McDonough, *Letters*, 84.

## 11: "They also talk of following us in force."

1. *DocHis 5*, 257, Harvey to Baynes, 29 May 1813.
2. Grimsby, known in 1813 as the Forty. Merritt, *Desire of Serving*, 5.
3. Norton, *Journal*, 327.
4. Harvey, *Journal*. "As however I had only recently arrived in this Country, my advice & opinions had not, at the time, all the weight & influence which subsequent events & circumstances concurred to give them."
5. Merritt, *Desire of Serving*, 5 "The greater part went to 40 Mile Creek, trusting a stand would be made there." *DocHis 6*, 193. Askin to Askin, 2 June 1813. Captain John Askin of the 2nd Lincoln walked from Fort Erie along the shoreline of Lake Erie to the Grand River. "After a great deal of fatigue I arrived at the Forty Mile Creek on the 30th ulto. alone, for all my men had stopped at their homes, and I knew that if I waited to bring them with me I should probably not be able to join the army myself, which I was very anxious to do. On my arrival at the Forty I was unfortunately taken with a fit of ague which detained me there for a day."
6. LAC, MG 19, F1, Claus Papers, 91.
7. Dundurn Park in Hamilton.
8. Merritt, *Desire of Serving*, 5. "The Militia had no encouragement to follow, as they were given to understand the Army would not stop, until they arrived at Kingston."

9. *DocHis 5*, 250, Vincent to Prevost, 28 May 1813.
10. *DocHis 5*, 257, Harvey to Baynes, 29 May 1813.
11. *DocHis 5*, 271. Troop returns 40 Mile Creek 30 May 1813. Fencibles, recruited in British North America for service in North America only, were trained, equipped and disciplined as regulars. *DocHis 5*, 300, Mcdouall to Procter, 4 June 1813. Recruited under the Militia Act 1813, the provincial units included dragoons, artillery drivers and artificers ; Sedentary militia included every able-bodied male between 16 and 60. Outside of the flank companies, training was very limited.
12. The American-born Beasley had established a substantial holding on the heights, including a large brick house, barn and warehouse on the bay. After the war he was awarded £1,500 compensation for rents, the loss of his orchard and crops and the burning of his fences as fuel. See *DHB 1*. The steep-sided peninsula is now occupied by Dundurn Castle and Hamilton Cemetery and crossed by York Boulevard. Little Lake is now Hamilton Harbour. Joseph Brant's imposing Georgian home, inhabited by his widow Catherine, stood on the north end of the Beach Strip that separates Hamilton Harbour and Lake Ontario on the site of what is now Burlington's Joseph Brant Memorial Hospital. At the time the only access between the lake and the harbour was a shallow outlet just north of the current ships' canal.
13. Simcoe, *Diary, 323*, 11 June 1796.
14. Cruikshank, *Records of Niagara*, 44, 78. Beasley to Board of Claims, 12 September 1815. Beasley said the army took "forcible possession" of his premises ; LAC Reel T1127 Vol 3740 #46. Beasley Loss Claims. Vincent paid Beasley a monthly rent of £8 for the house.
15. *DocHis 5*, 288, Vincent to Baynes, 31 May 1813.
16. The earthwork, which appears on neither of the two extant military maps of Burlington Heights, 1813 and 1823, was excavated in 1993 by archeologist John R. Triggs and turned up pewter buttons from the 8th Regiment and the 19th Light Dragoons as well as a small Jew's harp, a trade copper arrowhead and glass beads. See *AARO, 5*, 1994, McMaster University Field School at Dundurn Castle. *Hamilton Spectator*, 17 September, 1993, Dundurn's diamonds; The Corps of Artificers, recruited primarily in Niagara from black Loyalists, former servants and slaves, saw action at Queenston and Fort George but was used primarily as a labour company. Reflecting the high cost of skilled labour, they were paid four or five times as much as their milita counterparts. See Gray, *Soldiers of the King, OH 27* , Upper Canada's Black Defenders; RG 8, C2936, 103, Bruyeres to Prevost, 4 Sept, 1813. Lieutenant Colonel Ralph Henry Bruyeres, commanding Royal Engineer in Canada said the ground in front of position was "very much broken and would afford great shelter to an advancing enemy." The works had been completed

in haste by non-engineers "and in its present state cannot easily be improved. The situation is also very unhealthy owing to the exhalation of a stagnate swamp which contents the whole length of the Peninsula."; HPL, Thompson Papers, Frederick Snider's account of the Battle of Stoney Creek.

17. Built in 1794 as a rest stop for travelers and government warehouse by Lieutenant Governor John Graves Simcoe, in what is now Confederation Park in Hamilton, the inn, also known as Government House, stood at the junction of the Stoney Creek road and a road that ran south to the Queenston road, parallel to Red Hill Creek; Burlington Beach is now known as the Beach Strip and site of the Burlington Skyway Bridge that carries the QEW (Queen Elizabeth Way) over the entrance to Hamilton Harbour; *DocHis 7*, 249. Chauncey to Jones, 11 May 1813. The 6-gun *Governor Tompkins* under Lieutenant Thomas Brown and the 3-gun *Conquest* under Lieutenant John Pettigrew, had been ordered to "take or destroy" a British sloop believed to be a Forty Mile Creek. The King's Head may have been a target of opportunity; *Northern Post*, 27 May 1813. From the Buffalo Gazette Extra of May 16.

18. Wentworth Historical Society, *Journal*, 4, 7. Norton, *Journal*, 322. LAC, RG9, IB7, Vol. 24, 5th Lincoln 1812-1814. Abraham Markle would desert to the Americans in July to become an officer in Joseph Willcocks' Canadian Volunteers. Nineteen-year-old William Green would attain folk hero status in Stoney Creek after the war. See appendix A. Both Hatt and Land were veterans of Brock's Detroit campaign and the Battle of Queenston Heights. See *DHB* 1; A local story persists that the daughter-in-law of the proprietor who returned to find the inn in flames, rowed out to the ships and successfully demanded return of her personal belongings that had been looted. See Freeman, *A Mountain and a City; DocHis 5*, 236, Vincent to Prevost, 19 May 1813. *DocHis 5*, 239, Burwell to Talbot, 21 May, 1813.

19. *Quebec Gazette*, 7 July 1813. Letter of an Officer, 31 May 1813. A Tartar refers to an unexpectedly formidable foe.

**12: "Some extraordinary delusion"**
1. Armstrong, *Notices*, 158.
2. Fort Malden is in present-day Amherstburg at the mouth of the Detroit River on Lake Erie; The white flag of truce was a common means of communicating, and spying, between early 19th Century armies; Captain Horatio Gates Armstrong, Twenty-Third Infantry.
3. *Courier*, 9 July 1812, Oration.
4. *DocHis 4*, 242, Report on 14th Regiment by Captain William King, 24 October 1812. King's report damns everything – discipline, weapons, equipment, food and company officers.
5. Frenchmen's Creek is just north of Fort Erie. The

action occurred on November 28, 1812 ; Ingersoll, *Historical Sketch of the Second War*, 96 ; *DocHis 4*, 264, Winder to Smyth, 2 December 1812 ; Quimby, *The U.S. Army in the War of 1812*, 78; *Broome County Patriot*, 1 December 1812, Summary.

6. The fiasco architect was Brigadier General Alexander Smyth, whose performance on the Niagara was so abysmal that he was removed from the army list by Congress. According to one of his junior officers Smyth was notorious for his proclamations threatening the British Army. Roach, *Journal* 132 ; Ingersoll, *Historical Sketch of the Second War*, 98 ; *Buffalo Gazette*, 15 December 1813, Letter from Peter Porter, Black Rock, 14 December 1812 ; *Hagerstown Gazette*, 19 January 1813, Private Correspondence, Washington, Jan. 13 *Federal Republican*, 17 January 1814, Reflections and Strictures upon the Last Campaign.

7. Duane, *Letters*, 363, Duane to Jefferson, 26 September, 1813 ; *United States Gazette*, 8 July 1813, Letter from army officer, Fort George, 22 June 1813.

8. Burn, *Letters*, 307, Burn to Ingersoll, 16 July 1813; *New York Statesman*, 21 June 1813, Letter to editor Baltimore Whig dated Fort George, 5 June 1815. "Winder is enraged at the generalship displayed here on the 27th, I am confident he will repair the error"; Lossing, *Pictorial Field-Book*, 601.

9. *DocHis 5*, 266. Dearborn to Armstrong, 29 May 1813. The reinforcement comprised two companies of the King's, 150 men.

10. Chandler, *Autobiography*, 187.

11. Walworth, *Letters*. Walworth to Simonds, 13 May 1813, "Gen. Winder has command of the Second Brigade which is composed of a part of almost every Regiment of Infy. in service."; Hindman's, Nicholas' and Biddle's companies were acting as light infantry, Towson's battery had four field guns – three six-pdrs. and one six-inch howitzer; USNA, Registry of Enlistments. RG94 Army Muster Rolls 1812-1814.

12. Ten companies of ninety men, six corporals, five sergeants, one ensign, one third lieutenant, one second lieutenant, one first lieutenant and one captain. "An Act to raise an additional military force" 29 January 1813.

13. Based on figures reported in April- May 1813, the Thirteenth had 450 men and the Sixteenth approximately 340, less 158 or 20 per cent sick for a combined strength of 632 effectives. In June the Fourteenth Infantry mustered approximately 350 effectives and the Fifth Regiment, bolstered by two companies from the Twentieth, had 250 men on the ground bringing the total to 1,232 troops. Reckoning at least another 500 for the dragoon squadron, various companies of artillery, rifles and whatever piecemeal detachments Winder pressed into service, the final figure must top out somewhere in excess of 1,700. Dwight, *Diary*, 13 May 1813. The Thirteenth's casualties at Fort George,

if any, were light. Graves/Chartrand, *Army Hand Book*, 240. 244. At Beaver Dams on 24 June 1813 "16 officers and 316 other ranks, almost the total strength of the regiment on active service, became prisoners of war." The Sixteenth, 400 strong in April 1813, took 59 casualties at Fort York and Fort George; *Enquirer*, 2 July 1813, Extract of a Letter from an Intelligent Captain, 10 June 1813.

14. *Northern Post*, Salem NY, June 24, 1813. Letter from a gentleman, 19 June 1813. Myers, *Reminiscences*, 31. *New York Spectator*, 23 June 1813, Disastrous Intelligence from the North.

15. Fort Schlosser was originally Fort du Portage built in 1760 on the Niagara River just above the falls. Rebuilt and renamed by the British.; Pearce, *Historical Sketch*, 142. NWR, 12 June 1813, Letter to the Editor.

16. *New York Evening Post*, 4 December 1816. Extract 3d. In reference to Winder's command of the pursuit brigade: "Was the honor of capturing the British army too great for any but a favorite?"

17. *Ibid*, Beebe to Lewis, 1 June 1813; The Black Swamp road is the present day Niagara Stone Road, Regional Road 55. So named in 1813 because it crossed what was then extensive swamp land.

18. *New York Evening Post*, 4 December 1816, Lewis to Dearborn, 1 June 1813. It is notable that the name St. Catharine's for Shipman's Corners was already in wide usage.

19. Dwight, *Diary*, 1 June 1813; *DocHis 5*, 140. Armstrong to Dearborn, 29 March 1813.

20. Armstrong, *Notices*, 158.

21. Cochrane, *History Monmouth*, 68. "Dearborn was here seized with violent fever, and, for many days, not the slightest hope for his recovery.";Mann, *Medical Sketches*, 60; Cochrane, *History Monmouth*, 86. "General Dearborn's condition now became so critical that he was compelled to relinquish the immediate sight of the troops."

22. Roach *Journal*, 144.

23. *DocHis 7*, 263. Chauncey to Jones, 11 June 1813.

## 13: "'Tis the eye of childhood that fears a painted devil."

1. Shakespeare, *Macbeth*, Act II, scene II.

2. Fifteen Mile Creek flows through Vineland; Myers, *Reminiscences*, 31.

3. Armstrong, *Hints to Young Generals*, 48.

4. An American 6-pdr. field gun and carriage weighed 2,000 pounds. See Graves, *Field of Glory*, Appendix A.; Myers, *Reminiscences*, 31; Kearsely, *Memoirs*, 6

5. Mann, *Medical Sketches*, 64 "Excepting a few hot days in the first week of June, the remainder of that month and July following, were cold and unpleasant."

6. *DocHis 6*, 298. Vincent to Baynes, 4 June 1813.

7. Bulger, *Autobiographical Sketch*, 4.

8. Harvey, *Journal*.

9. Cruikshank, *Records of Niagara*, No 44, 12, Claus to Johnson, 7 January, 1813.

10. Johnston, *Valley of the Six Nations*, 195, Brock to Prevost, 3 July 1812. 197, Brock to Prevost, 7 September 1812

11. Howison, *Sketches of Upper Canada*, 166. For a discussion on native war philosophy see Benn, *Iroquois*, 53-54

12. Ingersoll, *Historical Sketch of the Second War*, 279.

13. *Enquirer*, 8 January 1814, Proctor's Letters, McDouall to Proctor, 29 April 1813.

14. *Ibid*. Myers to Procter, 29 April 1813. "What essential aid could be rendered to us by the timely arrival here of five hundred Indians."

15. Norton, *Journal*, 327; Major General John Sullivan led an army of 4,500 troops against the British-allied Iroquois Confederation in the summer of 1779. destroying 40 villages in the process. When he was done Sullivan reported to congress, "there is not a single town left in the Country of the five nations."

16. Nichol, *Memorandum*.

17. Benn, *Iroquois*, 109; *DocHis 5*, 292, Norton to Prevost, 1 June 1813.

18. Merritt, *Desire of Serving*, 6 .

19. Graves/Chartrand, *Army Hand Book* , 203, "The 2nd Regiment of Artillery was the best unit in the army during the war."; John Lyttle's Rifle Company was recruited and organized by the revered, and reviled, rifleman Benjamin Forsyth as a unit of the U.S. Voluntary Corps and was trained and equipped as regular riflemen. See Eric E. Johnson, *U.S. Army Regiments in the War of 1812.*

20. Highway 8 in Hamilton and Regional Road 81 in Niagara tracks the Iroquois Trail ; The Irish-born Willcocks, member of the legislature for Niagara and former newspaper editor, joined the American forces in July 1813, forming the infamous Canadian Volunteers. *OH, 25*, 196. Cruikshank says Willcocks was accused of leading the American army to Stoney Creek.; *Quebec Gazette*, 28 July 1813, Extract of a letter, Flamborough, Upper Canada, 20 June , 1813. "You will not be surprised when you learn that the Editor of the late Guardian, led the American army in pursuit of ours." From 1807 until the beginning of the war, Willocks edited and published the *Upper Canadian Guardian* or *Freeman's Journal* , the colony's first opposition newspaper.

21. Biggar, *Battle of Stoney Creek.*

22. *DocHis 5*, 295. Prevost to Bathurst, 3 June 1813.

23. William Crooks,was a captain in the 4th Lincoln and brother and business partner of James Crooks, whose property was the starting point for the Battle of Fort George.; *Hamilton Spectator*, An Oldest Inhabitant, 5 March 1890.

## 14: "Ensign No Coat"

1. Cochrane, *History of Monmouth*, 104.

2. *Ibid*, 112. Maine was part of Massachusetts until it acquired statehood in 1820; *Granite Monthly*,

"Hon. John Chandler", 6. Chandler, *Autobiography*, 178. Quimby, *U.S. Army*, 59.

3. Cochrane, *History of Monmouth*, 104. Chandler's entry in the Dictionary of American Biography said "he soon acquired a competence, shrewd practices, according to his neighbours, aiding his natural diligence and frugality."

4. *Ibid*, 106.

5. *American Advocate*, 9 July 1812, Independence – 4th July 1812; *American Advocate*, 3 August 1812, Public Tribute of Respect.

6. With an army of 3,500 regulars and 2,500 militia plus artillery and cavalry, Dearborn marched north from Plattsburgh to the Quebec border. His advanced guard crossed the border and was roughed up, his militia refused to follow and after waiting three days, he decided to call the invasion off. In the wake of this fiasco Dearborn offered to resign but the government chose not to accept.; Ingersoll, *Historical Sketch of the Second War*, 98, 102. The *Northern Whig* in Hudson, New York quipped "*Granny Dearborn with fifteen thousand men. March'd into Canada and then march'd out again.*"; Enquirer, 10 December 1812, News from the Frontiers; *Eastern Argus*, 14 January 1813, To the Printers of the N. England Palladium. The letter, by Hospital Surgeon Benjamin Waterhouse, referred to measles – for which the cause was unknown – as "a pestilence that walks in darkness."

7. *United States Gazette*, Letter from an officer, 22 June, 1813.

8. *Federal Republican*, 4 August 1813, Communication from the Baltimore Whig; *Portland Gazette*, 21 September 1813, Miscellaneous Selections.

9. *Portland Gazette*, 2 August 1813, By the Mails.

10. Minnesota Historical Society, Taliaferro Papers, General Orders 4 April 1813.

11. MHS, Vaughn Family Papers, Chandler to Warren, 14 April 1813.

12. Dwight, *Diary*, 11 April 1813.

13. Made brigadier general the same time as William Winder, Pike was one of the few bright lights appointed to high command in the first two years of the war. A career officer with a national reputation as an explorer, he was killed six weeks after his appointment at the taking of Fort York on April 27 1813, struck by flying rock when the fort's powder magazine exploded. See Malcolmson, *Capital in Flames.*

14. Wilder, *Battle of Sackett's Harbour*, 66.

15. *Ibid*, 66.

16. *Federal Republican*, 17 January 1814, Reflections and Strictures Upon the Last Campaign.

17. CHS, George Howard Letterbook. Letter to wife Sarah, 12 June 1813; *Eastern Argus*, 3 June 1813, Extract of a letter dated Sackett's harbor 30th April.

18. *NWR*, 19 October 1816, "Battle of Stoney Creek"; Chandler, *Autobiography*, 186.

19. *New York Evening Post*, 3 December 1816, Descent.

20. Chartrand, *Uniforms and Equipment*, 41-42; Harvey, *Journal.*

21. Graves/ Chartrand, *Hand Book*, 260; *New York Evening Post*, 3 December 1816, Descent.; *NWR*, 19 October 1816, Battle of Stoney Creek. *NWR* 4 January 1817, General Chandler and the affair of Stoney Creek; Auchinleck, *History of the War*, 169.

22. NYSL, Gardner Papers, Scott to Gardner, 4 June 1813.

**15: "The survivors were intensely excited."**

1. *Hamilton Spectator*, An Oldest Inhabitant, 5 March 1890.

2. Johnston, *Valley of the Six Nations*, 207, Vincent to Six Nations 22 October 1813; *Ibid*, 219. Seven months later fifteen Grand River chiefs would ask that 105 warriors, predominately Mohawk, be cut off from Indian Department presents because they "acted in an Unbecoming manner towards their Great Father."

3. *DocHis* 6, 196. Charles Askin to John Askin, 8 June 1813.

4. Norton, *Journal*, 327

5. *DocHis* 7, 254, Mcdouall to Freer, 29 May 1813.

6. Harvey, *Journal.*

7. *Ibid*; *DocHis* 6, 16, FitzGibbon to Somerville, 7 June 1813.

8. Harvey, *Journal.*

9. *Ibid.*

10. Myers, *Reminiscences*, 31. Myers said the officers breakfasted with "Mr Cook a wealthy gentleman." Since he had already identified the camp ground as being "at Crooks" it's unclear if Cook and William Crooks are one and the same. If they were, it raises the question whether Crooks was hedging his bets in the event of an American victory. James Bronaugh was surgeon for the Twelfth Infantry.

11. *DocHis* 5, 292, Norton to Prevost, 1 June 1813.

12. *Hamilton Spectator*, An Oldest Inhabitant, 5 March 1890.

13. Norton, *Journal*, 327.

14. John Smoke Johnson, *Sakayen'kwarahton*, godson of Sir William Johnson. See DCB 9.

15. Winona.

16. HPL, Thompson Papers, *Reminiscence of the Battle of Stoney Creek by a Living Witness*; USNA , RG 94 Muster Rolls United States Army 1812-1814.

17. *Hamilton Spectator*, An Oldest Inhabitant, 5 March 1890.

18. Hickman. *Sketch of the Life of General Towson*, 11; Shaler, *Memoirs*, 419.

19. *DocHis* 6, 196, Askin to Askin, 4 June 1813. Askin's reference to gentlemen taking protection from the enemy refers to the 1,193 militia who were paroled after the fall of Fort George. USNA, RG 98, Records of the United States Army Command, 1784 -1821, Vol 1, Entry 57.

20. *DocHis* 5, 298. 4 June 1813, Vincent to Baynes.

21. Captain Henry Milnes and Captain Robert McDouall

22. *DocHis 5*, 266, Dearborn to Armstrong, 4 June 1813.
23. *Baltimore Patriot*, 17 June 1813, Extract of a Letter from an Officer dated Fort George June 4th 1813.

### 16: "Laden with the furniture of death and destruction"

1. *New England Galaxy*, 18 August 1820, Miscellany from the Morning Chronicle.
2. *NWR*, 4 January 1817, General Chandler and the Affair of Stoney Creek; Armstrong, *Notices*, 133; LAC, MG 24, F16, *Simonds Papers*, Walworth to Simonds, 29 May 1813; *United States Gazette*, 8 July 1813, Letter from an officer ; If the figure of 6,000 is correct and 2,643 were at the Forty, then 3,400 troops were still at Fort George and posted south along the river to Fort Erie. Yet, according to one officer there were only two regiments left at Fort George after Winder and Chandler's brigades departed, not likely more than 1,000 troops maximum. The figure of 1,000 at Fort George is further supported by a report received by Commodore Isaac Chauncey that after Lewis and his 600-strong reinforcement left Fort George for the Forty there were no more than 400 men left in forts George and Niagara. Dudley, *Naval War*, 493, Chauncey to Jones, 11 June 1813 ; Allowing another 800 for the Fort Erie and Chippawa garrisons, that still leaves a shortfall of 1,600.
3. *DocHis 6*, 8, Vincent to Prevost, 6 June 1813 ; *Northern Post*, Salem, NY, 24 June 1813, A Letter from a Gentleman. *New York Spectator*, 23 June, 1813, Disastrous Intelligence from the North.
4. Although the numbers may seem small compared to the massive armies fielded in Europe during the same period, they should be viewed in the context of local population. There were perhaps 15,000 people living in the Niagara Peninsula in 1813 including Barton, Ancaster townships and the Grand River settlements. Chandler's army of 3,500 represents 22 per cent of the population. Based on the 2001 census figure of 1.275 million living in Hamilton-Niagara, a comparable army in modern terms would be 280,000 troops.
5. *New England Galaxy*, 18 August 1820, Miscellany from the Morning Chronicle.
6. A short military coat, cut to the waist in front with short tails.
7. Chartrand, *Uniforms and Equipment*, 24-35.
8. Chartrand, *Uniforms*, 113. The national standard was 6 by 7 feet on a 10-foot staff, the regimental standard was 5 by 6 feet on a 9-foot staff.
9. *St. Catharines Star*, Stoney Creek Reminiscences, 26 June 1889.
10. Graves, *Soldiers of 1814*, 37. According to drummer Jarvis Hanks , a total of nine men were shot while carrying the colours at the Eleventh Infantry at the Battle of Lundy's Lane.
11. *DocHis 6*, 142 , Roach Journal. NYSL ; Gardner Papers, Scott to Gardner, 4 June 1813; *Portico*,

March 1816, 42, Biographical Sketch of Colonel Jacob Hindman.
12. Smyth, *Infantry Regulations*, 165.
13. Barber was the son of Matthias Barber, born Sussex County, New Jersey 1779; HPL, Thompson Papers, Daniel Barber Reminiscence.
14. *Evening Star*, Stoney Creek Reminiscences, 26 June 1889.
15. *Portico*, March 1816, 42, Biographical Sketch of Colonel Jacob Hindman. *DocHis 6*, 23, Burn to Dearborn. Kearsley, *Memoirs*, 6
16. A billhook is a hook-bladed cutting tool, not unlike a machete. A mattock is similar to a pickaxe but with a broader blade rather than a narrow spike.
17. LAC, General Entry Book of American Prisoners of War at Quebec, C-3233; At Stoney Creek there were very few high-ranking field officers in the infantry. The highest rank in the Twenty-Fifth was a major, ditto the Twenty-Third, the Sixteenth was commanded by a captain, the Fifth alone had a lieutenant colonel; Burghardt, *The Origin and Development of the Road Network of the Niagara Peninsula*, n 420. The King's highroad was, by law, thirty feet wide, a byroad, twenty-four feet; Companies were divided into two platoons, one commanded by a captain and the other by a first lieutenant, assisted by a 2nd lieutenant, 3rd lieutenant and an ensign. The next command level consisted of five sergeants and six corporals. "An Act to raise an additional military force" 29 January 1813.
18. *DocHis 6*, 25, Chander to Dearborn, 18 June 1813.
19. Tin or canister filled with small iron balls approximating the effect of a giant shotgun.
20. HPL, Slater Diary. See Elliott, *Billy Green and the Battle of Stoney Creek.*
21. Shaler, *Memoirs*, 416; *City Gazette*, 31 August 1820, From the Baltimore Federal Republican. Cummin's account of Stoney Creek, published seven years after the battle is perhaps the most literary version and quite likely the only one that provides details of troop dispositions. It does, however, omit any mention of lost generals or artillery.
22. Chandler, *Autobiography*, 188 ; *DocHis 6*, 25, Chandler to Dearborn, 18 June 1813 ; *NWR*, Battle of Stoney Creek, 19 October 1816.
23. *DocHis 6*, 95, Armstrong to Dearborn 19 June 1813.

### 17: "His Light Troops were already on the skirts of our Camp."[1]

1. Harvey, Journal.
2. Aikman, a captain in the 5th Lincoln militia, had a farm at the present-day intersection of King Street East and Sanford Avenue in central Hamilton. See *DHB 1* and *Loyalist Ancestors*, 34; LAC loss claim, T1134, Vol. 3572 #163
3. Red Hill Creek and King Street East, now the site of the Red Hill Creek Expressway. William Davis Jr. was the son of a North Carolina planter who

harboured the army of Lord Charles Cornwallis during the Revolution. The family resettled in Barton Township in 1793 and Davis opened the Red Hill House on the west side of Big Creek. See *Loyalist Ancestors*, 76

4. Biggar, a respected author and journalist, wrote the first detailed account of the battle, an eight-page pamphlet, in 1873. Although he offers no documentation for incidents or characters, the narrative is convincingly detailed, and Biggar who had five great uncles in the 5th Lincoln during the war, certainly had access to people who were there. Biggar said the village's name derived from the rocky stream bed at the base of the escarpment.

5. Saltfleet Township. Gourlay, *Statistical Account*, 402.

6. The road was the present-day King Street West in Stoney Creek. The creek is now called Battlefield Creek.

7. Harvey, *Journal.*

8. Kearsley, *Memoirs*, 6; *Buffalo Gazette*, 22 June 1813, Battle at Stoney Creek.

9. Militia units accepted into federal service for one-year term. Trained and equipped as regulars, they were often the equal of their longer-term counter-parts. John Lyttle's Rifle Company was recruited and organized by Major Benjamin Forsyth of the First Regiment of U.S. Rifles and saw action at Ogdensburgh as well as in Upper Canada

10. *Buffalo Gazette*, 22 June 1813, Battle at Stoney Creek; *DocHis* 6, 25. Chandler to Dearborn, 18 June 1813; LAC, T1131, Vol 3749 #693, Davis loss claim.

11. *DocHis* 6, 12. FitzGibbon to Somerville, 7 June 1813; Kearsley, *Memoirs*, 6; *DocHis* 6, 23 Burn to Dearborn; *New York Statesman*, 24 June 1813, Letter from an Officer; Merritt, *A Desire of Serving*, n. 25; Biggar, *Battle of Stoney Creek.*

12. *Portico*, March 1816, 42, Biographical Sketch of Colonel Jacob Hindman; *National Advocate*, 2 July 1813, From the Buffalo Gazette of 22nd June.

13. Lossing, *Field-Book*, 601

14. The time is EST non-daylight saving; Travel time based on the author walking King Street from Sanford Avenue, the site of the original Aikman farm, to Red Hill Creek on 2 June 2004 in one hour and fifteen minutes.; *DocHis* 6, 25, Chandler to Dearborn, 18 June 1813; Burn, *Letters*, 306, 1 July 1813, Burn to Ingersoll. "We had a sharp skirmish in the afternoon of the 5th with the advance of the enemy which led us to pursue them farther than was intended by the Generals, and induced them to (I believe) encamp more advanced than they originally intended."

15. Lossing, *Field Book*, 602; Merritt, *A Desire of Serving*, 6. n. 25. Barn's tavern was near the current intersection of King and James in downtown Hamilton.

16. Harvey, *Journal.*

**18: "As sure as the morning dawn appears."**

1. Harvey, *Journal.*

2. The mouth of Stoney Creek in Hamilton's Confederation Park. Judging by Bates' 1812 Map of Grand River & Map of River Niagara (LAC G 3462, N 53, 1815 M 37) the road to the lakeshore probably followed at least part of the current Lake Avenue; *DocHis* 6, 25, Chandler to Dearborn, 18 June 1813; Armstrong, *Hints to Young Generals*, 46.

3. *City Gazette*, 31 August 1820, From the Baltimore Federal Republican; Irish-born James Gage was killed 6 October 1777 at the defence of Fort Clinton on the Hudson River near West Point. His wife, Mary Jones – ironically the daughter of a Loyalist, Ebenezer Jones – sought and received a war pension from the state of New York after his death. See Clyde Gage, *Gage Families*, 205.

4. *DCB 7, DHB 1.* The leading land surveyor in early Upper Canada, Augustus Jones surveyed the original town sites for Niagara-on-the-Lake and Toronto, Yonge Street north to Lake Simcoe, most of the land along the Grand River and the Detroit frontier. A friend of Brant's, he spoke Mohawk and Ojibwa and had families with two different native women, marrying the second and eventually becoming a devout Methodist. Cruikshank, *Records of Niagara*, 42, 117. In 1811 Jones resigned his commission in the 5th Lincoln. His commanding officer, Andrew Bradt, said it was because "he does not like to get the illwill of his Neighbours by making them do their duties in the Militia."

5. LAC, RG 9, IB 7, Vol 24, 425. Statement of Captain Durand's Flank Company of 5th Lincoln Militia on actual duty in 1812. Durand's named five men as of dubious loyalty – Absolom Summers , David Reynolds, Gilbert Shaw, Randal Butt and John Richards. Durand's suspicion of Richards, at least, was justified as he subsequently deserted to the enemy. Gage's substitute is listed only as deserted, meaning he probably just went home. Another private, Daniel Crosthwaite, was noted as "Mutinous & Cowardly."

6. *DHB 1.* William Gage served in the 2nd Ulster County Militia during the Revolution. *Hamilton Spectator*, 14 May 2007, Gaging History; He married Susannah Jones, 1751-1821.

7. Smyth, *Infantry Regulations*, 168.

8. Shaler, *Memoirs*, 414 ; *Hamilton Evening Times*, 9 June 1891, Interesting Details Made Public by a Veteran.

9. *Enquirer*, 2 July 1813, Extract of a Letter from an Intelligent Captain in the Army 10 June 1813.

10. *Statesman*, 24 June 1813, Letter from an officer.

11. *United States Gazette*, 8 July, 1813, Letter from an officer.

12. *City Gazette*, 31 August 1820, From the Baltimore Federal Republican. *Husteron proteron* – latter first or back-to-front.

13. *Ibid.*

14. Biggar, *Battle of Stony Creek*, 5; The distance from

Red Hill Creek to the battlefield is one mile ; Harvey, *Journal*. Harvey said he was "overjoyed to find that he had taken up his ground for the night."

15. Commins, *The War on the Canadian Frontier*, 206. Lieutenant Henry Banks Oldenburgh Milnes, son of baronet and former lieutenant governor of Quebec, Robert Milnes. Lieutenant Milnes was one of two of Prevost's aides-de-camp sent to the Head of the Lake to keep an eye on Vincent. The other was Captain Robert McDouall. There are six other different and differing accounts of this spy incident. Cruikshank said militiamen, under Harvey's direction, "passed through every part of their lines, under the pretence of selling supplies." Cruikshank, *Fight in the Beechwoods*, 5. Mary Agnes FitzGibbon claims it was her grandfather, Lieutenant James FitzGibbon of the 49th who sold butter and gave bogus information about the British while gathering authentic information about the American camp. FitzGibbon, *A Veteran of 1812*, 68.

    Young Jacob Cline said an unamed British soldier was dressed as a farmer and sent in with a sack of potatoes. *Hamilton Spectator*, 5 March 1890, An Oldest Inhabitant.

    In her celebrated drama, *Laura Secord, The Heroine of 1812*, which opens with a recounting of the Battle of Stony Creek, Sarah Anne Curzon confected a fifth contender, the Quaker John Penn, who not only sold potatoes to the Americans as a spy but also witnessed the battle from the top of an elm tree.

    An anonymous document in the Thompson Collection at Hamilton Public Library says Billy Green pretended to be a farmer selling provisions to obtain information about his brother-in-law, Isaac Corman. HPL, Thompson Collection, *How they came to meet*.

    Frederick Snyder, who lived near the battlefield, said it was Harvey himself who went in with a load of potatoes. HPL, Thompson Collection, *Account of the battle* ; Harvey, *Journal*.

16. Merritt, *A Desire of Serving*, 6; Norton, *Journal*, 327; Robert McDouall, *DCB* 7; FitzGibbon, *A Veteran of 1812*, 68

17. Harvey says that Milnes, "the gallant youth" actually wept when he delivered the news.

18. Harvey, *Journal*.

19. *Ibid*.

20. *DocHis 6*, 8. Vincent to Prevost, 6 June 1813.

## 19: "The art of blundering"

1. *NWR*, 4 January 1817, General Chandler and the affair of Stony Creek.

2. *NWR*, 19 October 1816, Battle of Stony Creek; The lane roughly tracked the current Faircourt Drive to Faircourt Place, through # 29 on Faircourt Place up the hill to # 61 Phyllori Court, the site of William Gage's house in 1813; Shaler, *Memoirs*, 416; LAC Reel T1129 Vol 3745 # 394, loss claim.

Parts of the original estate, still occupied by a Corman descendant in 2008, survive at #7 Placid Place between Gray's Road and Green Road.

3. *Hamilton Spectator*, 12 June 1889, What Little Elizabeth saw at Stony Creek.

4. *Ibid*.

5. *Ibid*.

6. *Ibid*.

7. Biggar, *Battle of Stony Creek*, 5. The cabin, according to Biggar, was owned by a man named Lappin. Biggar added: "All the settlers in the vicinity were taken and held as prisoners lest they should carry any information to Vincent." HPL, *Slater Diary*. HPL *Thompson Papers*, Career of a Country Clergyman.

8. Smyth, *Regulations for the Field Exercise, Manoeuvres, and Conduct of the Infantry*, 171.

9. *Ibid*, 172.

10. *Ibid*, 194.

11. *City Gazette*, 31 August 1820, From the Baltimore Federal Republican; Library of Congress, RG 107, L-110 (7), Map of Stoney Creek battlefield; *National Advocate*, 2 July 1813, "From the Buffalo Gazette of 22nd June."

12. *NWR*, 4 January 1817, General Chandler and the affair of Stony Creek.

13. Wilder, *Battle of Sackett's Harbour*, 65.

14. A captain of artillery, Jones was brevetted major for his conduct at Chippawa and Lundy's Lane, lieutenant colonel for gallantry at Fort Erie in 1814, appointed adjutant-general of army in 1825 and promoted to major general in 1848.

15. Kearsely, *Memoirs*, 6.

16. *Ibid*.

17. *Ibid*, 7; The church stood on the high ground in what is now Stoney Creek Cemetery on King Street just west of Highway 20; *New York Statesman*, 24 June 1813, Letter from an officer.

18. *NWR*, 4 January 1817, General Chandler and the affair of Stony Creek. If the stated disposition of the Ninth – three miles from the battlefield – is correct the rear guard would have been near Dewitt Road.

19. Chandler, *Autobiography*, 190. Beyond Chandler's claim, there is no evidence the orders were followed, or for that matter, that they were ever issued.

20. MHS, Dearborn Papers, Chandler to Dearborn, 13 June 1813; Chandler, *Autobiography*, 190.

21. *DocHis 6*, Armstrong to Dearborn, 15 May 1813.

## 20: "Our little band"

1. Harvey, *Journal*.

2. Norton, *Journal*, 327. "There only remained with me my young Cherokee Cousin, a few Delawares, some Chippawas, one Mohawk and a Cayugwa." The 2nd Lincoln Militia captain, Charles Askin said there were "only four or five Indians" in the engagement. *DocHis 6*, 196, Askin to Askin, 8 June 1813.; LAC, MG 19, F1, Claus Papers, 91. The

intentions of the Iroquois in the days leading up the Battle of Stoney Creek are not clear. Neither Norton nor Claus appears to have had much influence in the community at this point. Carl Benn in *The Iroquois in the War of 1812*, suggests the Iroquois were considering abandoning the British and cutting a deal with the Americans to save their Grand River lands. In the wake of American victories at York, Fort George and Sackett's Harbour he suggests, "the future of the province as a British colony never hung more precariously in the balance than it did when British troops left Burlington Heights to march on Stoney Creek on the night of 5-6 June."

3. Norton, *Journal*, 328.

4. Merritt, *Desire of Serving*, 6.

5. NA WO12/6044 muster book and pay lists of 49th Foot March-June 1813. WO25/1829 Casualty returns 49th Foot. WO97/631 49th Regt; NA WO 12/2575 Muster Book & Pay List 8th Foot, March-June 1813. WO25/1549 Casualty Roll 25 December 1812 – 24 June 1813.

6. Cannon, *Historical Record of the Eighth*, 86, 88, 89.

7. Myatt, *The Royal Berkshire Regiment*, 12.

8. *Ibid*, 19; Tupper, *Brock Correspondence*. Brock to brother Savery, 18 September 1812. The inspection report from 31 May 1811 conducted by Major General Gordon Drummond, NA WO27/102, noted the men of the 49th were "pretty well drilled, and attentive but far from sober, though well behaved."

9. NA WO27/104 Inspection returns 8th Foot, 14 October 1813.

10. Ogilvie was the son of Major General James Ogilvie, DCB 5. *Quebec Mercury*, 4 June 1816; *DocHis 5*, 250, Vincent to Prevost, 28 May 1813.

11. NA WO27/102. Inspection returns 49th Foot 31 May 1811.

12. Charles Plenderleath was born in Peebles in 1780. *East Gloucester Election*, 14 January, 1854, Colonel Plenderleath ; NA WO27/102 49th inspection returns 31 May 1811.

13. Claus, Norton, Merritt and the militia officer, Charles Askin all mention a single piece of artillery, Claus says it was a 6-pdr; Sutherland, *His Majesty's Gentlemen.*

14. Cochran, *The War in Canada 1812-1814*, 30. The militia officer, Charles Askin said the total British force that left the heights "was one thousand strong."

15. NA, WO 31/290, Maitland to Dundas, 21 December 1809.

16. NA WO 31/290, letter from R. Mathews, 12 December 1809. Sutherland, *His Majesty's Gentlemen*, 115.

17. *DCB 5.*

18. NA, WO 31/284, Walker to Torrens, 17 October 1809.

19. NA, WO 31/314 Craig to Torrens, 25 May 1810.

20. LAC RG 8, C 924, 30, Memorial of Thomas Nairne. *DCB 5*, John Nairne.

21. *Acadiensis*, 19 February, 1923.

22. Glover, *A Gentleman Volunteer*,[2]. During the Peninsular War, 4.5 per cent of all new officers began as gentlemen volunteers, 5.42 per cent were promoted from the ranks and 3.9 per cent earned commissions from the Royal Military College.

23. Grantham Township is the site of St. Catharines ; *OH 31*, pp114-34.

24. George Jarvis, *DCB 10. DocHis 4*, 116, Jarvis narrative; LAC RG8 C 21, General Orders Fort George 27 February 1813. Sutherland, *His Majesty's Gentlemen*, 329.

25. *DCB 10*. MacDonell was the son of Miles MacDonell (DCB 6) an officer in the King's Royal Regiment of New York and grandson of "Spanish" John MacDonell of Butler's Rangers; LAC RG 8 C 833, Young to Freer, 6 June 1813, Ogilvie to Freer, 29 March 1814.

**21: "We want experience in … the Art of War."**

1. LOC, Smith Family Papers, Macomb to Smith, 24 June 1813.

2. George Washington, in the first State of the Union message, delivered 8 January 1790.

3. Armstrong, *Hints to Young Generals*, 7.

4. Chartrand, Graves, *Army Hand Book*, 38.

5. Mann, *Medical Sketches*, 122.

6. *DocHis 4*, 241-242. 5 October 1812, Inspection Report of Fourteenth Infantry by Captain William King.

7. Chartrand, Graves, *Army Hand Book*, 44, 101; Scott, *Memoirs*, 35.

8. *DocHis 6*, 283, Porter to Tompkins, 27 July 1813.

9. *The Tickler*, 20 October 1812, Extract of a letter from an officer.

10. *DocHis 6*, 144, Roach Journal.

11. *NWR*, 19 December 1812, Events of the War.

12. LOC, Smith Family Papers, Macomb to Smith, 24 June 1813.

13. Johnson, *Birth of the Modern*, 64; Weller, *Wellington at Waterloo*, 24.

14. LAC, MG 24, F 16, 29 May 1813, Walworth to Simonds.

15. NA, WO27/102, 31 May 1811, 49th Foot Inspection Returns.

16. Powell, *List of Officers*, 65.

**22: "The victory they expected the next day."**

1. MHS, Charles E. French Papers, Johnson to Dearborn, 7 June 1813.

2. Numerous eyewitness accounts, including Shaler, Chandler, Johnson, Hindman, FitzGibbon and Norton mention the extreme darkness.

3. LAC Reel T1130 Vol 3746 #447. James Gage's loss claim indicates 500 fence rails were burned and three calves, one sheep and over 500 pounds of flour were taken by Chandler's army.

4. Shaler, *Memoirs*, 417.

5. Smith, *Incidents in the Life*, n 103.

6. *Ibid*, 111.

7. *Ibid*, 111; *NWR*, General Chandler, 4 January 1817.

8. Shaler, *Memoirs*, 417.

9. Smith, *Incidents in the Life*, 111.

10. Shaler, *Memoirs*, 417. Shaler's estimate of the distance between the advance line and main line – 88 yards – is not accurate. The actual distance was closer to 150 yards.

11. *DocHis 6*, 25-28, Chandler to Dearborn, 18 June, 1813.

12. *NWR*, 19 October 1816, Battle of Stoney Creek. Although unsigned, this 4,000 word apologia contains so many phrases and complete sentences that occur in other signed Chandler documents that he must be considered the author.

13. *Ibid*.

14. Chandler, *Journal*, 36-37. Chandler's 129-page, hand-written journal, undated but clearly written several years after the end of the war, now resides in the Folger Library at the University of Maine. Extracts were published as his autobiography in *Collections of the Maine Historical Society*, Vol. 9 in 1887.

15. USNA, RG 107, L-110 (7), Map of Stoney Creek battlefield; The artillery was centred in the parkette that houses the Lion's Monument on King Street just west of Battlefield Drive.

16. Livingston, *Sketches*, 391.

17. LAC C Series, 694A *General Entry Book of American Prisoners of War*. British POW records indicate a dozen or more Stoney Creek prisoners were New York State militia.

18. *NWR*, 4 January 1817, General Chandler.

19. Chandler, *Autobiography*, 191.

20. MHS, Charles E. French Papers, Johnson to Dearborn, 7 June 1813. This letter raises several questions. It was written at least 24 hours after the battle yet begins by "announcing" the loss of two general officers. Surely this was not news at Fort George. An express from the battlefield that reached the fort on the evening of June 6 would have broken that story. Johnston insists the two generals were expecting a night attack yet spent the evening planning the victory they expected the next day. Despite the loss of generals and artillery and a precipitate retreat that left their dead unburied on the battlefield, Johnson had the temerity to proclaim "never was a more compleat victory obtained." The timing of this missive and the fact that excerpts were widely reprinted in the press, suggest the intent was largely damage control.

21. Chandler, *Autobiography*, 190.

## 23: "Only the utmost daring."

1. *DocHis 6*, 12-15, FitzGibbon to Somerville, 7 June 1813.

2. WO27/102 Inspection Returns 49th Foot, 31 May 1811. Fourteen enlisted men in 1811 were 50 years or older, making them at least 17 years old in 1777.

3. Brandywine Creek was a solid British victory by Major General William Howe that cost the Americans 1,200 casualties and their *de facto* capital and pre-eminent city, Philadelphia. Howe was criticized subsequently however for not capitalizing on his victory by pursuing Washington's retreating army; "Mad Anthony" Wayne, was a hero of the American Revolution and the victor over the Indians of the northwest at the decisive Battle of Fallen Timbers in 1794.

4. During the 18th Century the British regularly formed the light companies from regiments of the line into elite light infantry battalions.

5. The charismatic young British officer is best known for his part in the defection of Benedict Arnold to the British side. Andre was captured in 1780 after negotiating a deal with Arnold to hand over the Hudson River strongpoint at West Point. Although he was convicted as a spy, his hanging engendered considerable regret on both sides.

6. McGuire, *Battle of Paoli*, 93. Boatner, *Encylopedia of the American Revolution*, 829.

7. McGuire, *Battle of Paoli*, 109. Col. Thomas Hartley, 1st Pennsylvania Brigade commander.

8. Boatner, *Encylopedia of the American Revolution*, 829; McGuire, *Battle of Paoli*, 132.

9. For Anthony Wayne, Paoli was the worst defeat of an otherwise distinguished career. Furious that some of his officers openly questioned his leadership after Paoli, he demanded a court martial which cleared him of all charges. The lesson of the bayonet would not be lost on him. At Stony Point, New York in 1779 he won a night battle with a bayonet charge, and two years later, at Green Spring Plantation in Virginia narrowly averted a major defeat by leading a desperate bayonet charge.

10. Myatt, *The Royal Berkshire Regiment*, 17.

11. *DocHis 6*, 12-15, FitzGibbon to Somerville, 7 June 1813. Case's house stood on the northwest corner of King Street and Lottridge Street in east Hamilton, on what is now a parking lot between two credit unions just west of New Westminster Presbyterian Church, 1025 King Street East.

12. Major James Glegg was Vincent's brigade major.

13. *DocHis 6*, 12-15, FitzGibbon to Somerville, 7 June 1813.

14. McGuire, *Battle of Paoli*, 93.

15. Grimsby Historical Society, *Annals of the Forty*, 57.

16. LAC RG 8, Vol 679 pp. 38-41, Harvey to Baynes, 6 June 1813; *Journals and Transactions of the Wentworth Historical Society*, Vol 1, 24. "The Battle of Stoney Creek," J. H. Land. 26.

17. *DocHis 6*, 12-15, FitzGibbon to Somerville, 7 June 1813.

18. *Ibid*, 325.

19. *Ibid*. 325.

20. *Ibid*, 326.

21. *Ibid*, 327.

22. *Ibid*, 328.

**24: "A burglarious assault."**

1. *ADC*, 207.
2. Grimsby Historical Society, *Annals of the Forty*, 57.
3. Merritt, *Desire of Serving*, 6. Merritt said "on our arrival at Davis', we heard a report of a gun from their picket." William Green's claim (see Appendix) that three sentries fired at the British at Red Hill Creek, seems highly unlikely given that three aroused sentries would have given the whole show away.
4. HPL, *Slater's Diary*. Green says he got the password from his brother-in-law, Isaac Corman who, after being released from custody by American troops, was given the password so he could return home. Even allowing for Chandler's slack security arrangements, this seems highly unlikely ; *DocHis* 6, 7. Harvey to Baynes, 6 June 1813.
5. HPL, Thompson Papers, *Snider's Account of the Battle of Stoney Creek*.
6. *Ibid.*
7. *NWR*, 12 June 1813, Letter to the Editor.
8. *Northern Post*, 24 June 1813, Letter from a Gentleman.
9. Lilly Library, Fraser to Stevenson, 13 June 1813.
10. *NWR*, 19 October 1816, Battle of Stoney Creek.
11. *DocHis* 6, 12-15, FitzGibbon to Somerville, 7 June 1813.
12. *Canadian Magazine*, 1, 387. "The Battle of Stony Creek" by E. B. Biggar.
13. Harvey, *Journal.*; Merritt, *A Desire of Serving*, 6.
14. Chandler, *Autobiography*, 190.
15. Kearsley, *Memoirs*, 6-7. Myers, *Reminiscences*, 32. *NWR*, 19 October, 1816 Battle of Stoney Creek
16. According the map drawn by Lieutenant Donald Fraser, the woods ended roughly along the line of the current Highway 20 and extended west approximately as far as Greenhill Avenue.
17. Grimsby Historical Society, *Annals of the Forty*, 57.
18. USNA, OW IF #15848. David and Jeremiah Legg depositions. Both were at Stoney Creek. Jeremiah said his brother returned from captivity in "poor health subject to pains in his left hip…a scrofulous running sore on his right leg…greatly disabling him and making labor painful."
19. USNA, OW IF #26763.
20. *ADC*, 5, 207.
21. Merritt, *Desire of Serving*, 6. *DocHis* 6, 30, FitzGibbon to Somerville, 7 June 1813. *NWR*, 12 June 1813, Letter to the Editor. Bonnycastle, *Canada, As It Was, Is, and May Be*, 73. Bonnycastle, citing "an officer of rank" at the battle, said the dying sentry made a noise "as a fowl would make" which alerted the picket to discharge his musket.
22. Norton, *Journal*, 328.

**25: "That night a child might understand / The De'il had business on his hand."**

1. Burn's *Tam O'Shanter*, the line was quoted by Captain Francis Cummins in his account of the Battle of Stoney Creek, *City Gazette*, 31 August 1820

2. For a detailed account of the battle see *A Wampum Denied* by Sandy Antal.
3. Shaler, *Memoirs*, 418. Shaler's recollections, with his Indian conviction still intact, were published in 1844, 31 years after the battle.
4. What the German military strategist actually said was "no plan of operations extends with any certainty beyond the first contact with the main hostile force." Keyes, *The Quote Verifier*, xi.
5. *DocHis* 6, 12-15, FitzGibbon to Somerville, 7 June 1813.
6. Part of the Charge Bayonet drill includes shouting huzza (probably pronounced huzzay) as the musket is thrust forward ; *DocHis* 6, 197, Askin to Askin, 8 June 1813. "Our troops, in order to alarm them, yelled as much like the Indians as they could. *Enquirer*, 2 July 1813, Extract of a Letter from an Intelligent Captain.
7. *DocHis* 6, 12-15, FitzGibbon to Somerville, 7 June 1813.
8. *Ibid.*
9. *Ibid.*
10. Shaler, *Memoirs*, 418.
11. *Buffalo Gazette*, 22 June 1813, Letter to the Editor ; Norton, *Journal*, 328; *Enquirer*, 2 July 1813, Extract of a Letter from an Intelligent Captain.
12. Lilly Library, Fraser to Stevenson, 13 June 1813.
13. *City Gazette*, 31 August 1820, From the Baltimore Federal Replulican.
14. *Hamilton Spectator*, 12 June 1889. What Little Elizabeth Gage saw at Stony Creek.
15. *NWR*, 10 July, 1813. Letter from Captain John Johnson, 7 June 1813.
16. Livingston, *Sketches of Eminent Americans*, 391. Towson believed the officer was Harvey, although Harvey recorded no mention of the incident and there are no other corroborating accounts.
17. The height and appearance of the ground that the Twenty-Fifth formed on can best be seen today from the parking lot behind Park Pharmacy at 72 King Street West. The high ground on the edge of the bank, that the Twenty-Fifth defended, is almost entirely covered by a large multi-storey red-brick apartment building called the Robinaire, at 4 Village Green Boulevard; Chandler, *Autobiography*, 191; The three regiments formed, overlooking what is now the northeastern boundary of Battlefield Park, extending south from King Street to the edge of the Gage House; Shaler, *Memoirs*, 417. See René Chartrand, *Uniforms and Equipment of the United States Forces in the War of 1812*, 94.
18. Shaler, *Memoirs*, 418.
19. *Ibid*, 418.
20. *Portico*, March 1816, 42, "Biographical Sketch of Colonel Jacob Hindman."
21. Kearsley, *Memoirs*, 7.
22. *Poulson's American Daily Advertiser*, 23 June 1813. Army of Upper Canada; *DocHis* 6, 166, To the Editor, Buffalo Gazette, 24 June 1813.
23. Livingston, *Sketches of Eminent Americans*, 392;

The easiest way to disable artillery was to drive a spike into the vent hole at the rear of the gun, making it impossible to ignite the main charge.

24. Livingston, *Sketches of Eminent Americans*, 392.
25. USNA, OW IF #28120.
26. *Statesman*, 24 June, Extract of a letter from an officer; USNA, OW IF #28138.
27. Merritt, *A Desire of Serving*, 6.
28. *DocHis* 6, 7. Harvey to Baynes, 6 June 1813
29. *NWR*, 19 October 1816, Battle of Stoney Creek; USNA OW IF #5571; USNA OW IF #7315.
30. The Fifth's commanding officer who bore the names of three famous poets, gained a measure of notoriety in 1812 by slaying a carriage horse with his sword because it came too close to his troops on the march. *Commerical Advertiser*, 21 September 1812, Gross Outrage; Scott made amends for the slur. "After the Stoney creek affair on the 6th I wrote him a very handsome note acknowledging that his conduct had disproved my former accusation." NYSL, Gardner Papers, Scott to Gardner, 16 July 1813. This was a rare occurrence, the imperious Scott rarely apologized to anybody for anything.; *Enquirer*, 2 July 1813, Extract of a Letter from an Intelligent Captain.
31. McFeely, *Journal*, 266.
32. Grimsby Historical Society, *Annals of the Forty*, 58.
33. Livingston, *Sketches of Eminent Americans*, 392.
34. *DocHis* 6, 13. FitzGibbon to Somerville, 7 June 1813.
35. Grimsby Historical Society, *Annals of the Forty*, 58.
36. *DocHis* 6, 13. FitzGibbon to Somerville, 7 June 1813.
37. HPL, Thompson Papers. *Snider's Account of the Battle of Stoney Creek*.
38. *Hamilton Spectator*, 12 June 1889, What Little Elizabeth saw at Stony Creek.
39. Kearsley, *Memoirs*, 7.
40. *DocHis* 6, 166, To the Editor of the Buffalo Gazette, Fort George 24 June 1813.
41. *Western Press*, 20 July, 1813. Extract of a letter.
42. *New England Galaxy*, 18 August 1820, Miscellany from the Morning Chronicle.

**26: "The Hill was a Continual sheet of fire."**
1. Merritt, *A Desire of Serving*, 6.
2. Chandler, *Autobiography*, 188; Canister was a tinned-iron can packed with musket balls which when fired, gave the artillery piece the effect of a giant shotgun.
3. Merritt, *A Desire of Serving*, 6.
4. *DocHis* 6, 23, Burn to Dearborn.
5. Smith, *Incidents in the Life*, 112.
6. Shaler, *Memoirs*, 418.
7. Graves/Chartrand, *Army Hand Book* , 357.
8. Dury's father, Alexander Dury, was a lieutenant colonel in the 1st Foot Guards and his grandfather, also Alexander Dury, was a major general.
9. *DocHis* 6, 16, FitzGibbon to Somerville, 7 June 1813; *Gentleman's Magazine*, August 1813, Plend-

erleath to Maitland, 18 June 1813; *DocHis* 6, 197, Askin to Askin, 8 June 1813.
10. *DocHis* 7, 257, McDouall to Freer, 29 May 1813. On the day of the invasion at Newark, Goldicutt was so ill with fever that the regimental surgeon, Willam Hacket ordered him to bed. Distraught when prevented from joining his men when the firing began, Goldicutt first tried to drown himself and then threw himself from the second-storey window of a house and died within minutes. Fellow-officer McDouall, in his anguish, wrote "My God! 'Was ever tale so sad as this!' I can dwell on it no longer."
11. *DocHis* 6, 13. FitzGibbon to Somerville, 7 June 1813
12. The west side of Centennial Parkway, north of King Street.
13. *DocHis* 6, 16. FitzGibbon memorial to Plenderleath; *DocHis* 6, 13. FitzGibbon to Somerville, 7 June 1813.

**27: "The enemy appeared to be completely broken."**
1. *DocHis* 6, 26, Chandler to Dearborn, 18 June 1813.
2. MHS, Dearborn Papers, Chandler to Dearborn, 13 June 1813.
3. *DocHis* 6, 26, Chandler to Dearborn, 18 June 1813.
4. *DocHis* 6, 74. Lewis to Armstrong, 14 June 1813. "The gallantry of the 5th…saved the army."
5. *Enquirer*, 2 July 1813, Extract of a Letter from an Intelligent Captain. The letter is from Captain John Thornton, whose company of the Twentieth Infantry was attached to the Fifth Infantry at Stoney Creek.
6. *NWR*, 19 October 1816, Battle of Stoney Creek. "Knowing this regiment to be new and undisciplined, he naturally concluded it might be broken and, thereby occasioned the confusion he had discovered."; MHS, Dearborn Papers, Chandler to Dearborn, 13 June 1813
7. Hickman. *Sketch of the Life of General Towson*, 11. Towson said "his men were not provided with small arms," but offers no explanation why.
8. *NWR*, 19 October 1816, Battle of Stoney Creek.
9. *Ibid.*
10. Chandler, *Autobiography*, 192, 193.
11. *NWR*, 19 October 1816, Battle of Stoney Creek.

**28: "The moment must be seized."**
1. *DocHis* 6, 22, Plenderleath to Vincent, 23 July 1813.
2. Keegan, *Face of Battle*, 173.
3. *DocHis* 6, 13. FitzGibbon to Somerville, 7 June 1813.
4. *DocHis* 6, 22, Plenderleath to Vincent, 23 July 1813.
5. *Ibid*; The number in this party is problematic. Plenderleath said fifteen to twenty, FitzGibbon said thirty and Fraser himself, forty-seven years after the battle, told Lossing that he began with forty-six but was down to twenty-five by the time they reached the guns. All information/vitals on the Fraser brothers from NA WO12/6043-6075,

Muster books and pay list, 49th Foot.

6. Kearsley, *Memoirs*, 7. *Enquirer*, 2 July 1813, Extract of a Letter from an Intelligent Captain.

7. Hickman. *Sketch of the Life of General Towson*, 11.

8. Burn, *Letters*, 306, Burn to Ingersoll, 1 July 1813.

9. Lossing, *Pictorial Field-Book*, 604. Joseph Brant – Thayendanegea, 1742-1807 – fought for the British during the American Revolution and resettled at the Head of the Lake after the war. That Fraser would brandish his name as a war cry, six years after his death, is a testament to Brant's fearsome reputation as a warrior during the Revolution; James, *A Full and Correct Account*, 205; *DocHis 6*, 13. FitzGibbon to Somerville, 7 June 1813; Livingston, *Sketches of Eminent Americans*, 392. Towson said the Twenty-Third "abandoned their positions at the commencement of the action." *DocHis 6*, 22-23, Plenderleath to Vincent, 23 July 1813. "The party afterwards charged and put to flight a body of infantry formed immediately in rear of the guns."

10. James, *A Full and Correct Account*, 205; *DocHis 6*, 13. FitzGibbon to Somerville, 7 June 1813. *Bathurst Courier*, 1 February 1842, To the Editor of the Bytown Gazette.

11. *NWR*, 19 October 1816, Battle of Stoney Creek.

12. *Ibid.*

13. *Bathurst Courier*, 1 February 1842, To the Editor of the Bytown Gazette; *DocHis 6*, 25. Chandler to Dearborn, 18 June 1813; *Weekly Messenger*, 16 July 1813, From the U.S. Gazette.

14. Chandler, *Autobiography*, 193-194.

15. Lossing, *Pictorial Field-Book*, 604.

16. *Ibid*. *Enquirer*, 2 June 1813, Extract of a Letter from an Intelligent Captain.

17. *DocHis 6*, 16-17. FitzGibbon Memorial to Plenderleath.

18. *Bathurst Courier*, 1 February 1842, To the Editor of the Bytown Gazette. James, *A Full and Correct Account*, 205.

19. *Bathurst Courier*, 1 February 1842, To the Editor of the Bytown Gazette.

20. McFeely, *Journal*, 266. *United States Gazette*, 8 July 1813. Letter from an officer; CHS, George Howard Letterbook. Letter to wife Sarah, 12 June 1813.

21. *Bathurst Courier*, 1 February 1842, To the Editor of the Bytown Gazette. The letter, signed "One of the Old 49th" was datelined Perth, a settlement in the Ottawa Valley where Alexander Fraser settled after the war, rising to prominence as a Justice of the Peace and a militia colonel.

22. *NWR*, 4 January 1817, General Chandler.

23. Lilly Library, Fraser to Stevenson, 13 June 1813. Fraser seemed to be making a habit of losing generals in battle, he was also ADC to Pike at Little York; *General Scott and His Staff*, 215. In initial press reports on the battle, Jones was named as captured with Chandler and Winder.

24. *DocHis 6*, 13. FitzGibbon to Somerville, 7 June 1813; USNA, Registry of Enlistments in the United States Army, 1798-1914, Vol. 1-2. RG 94 Muster

Rolls United States Army1812-1814. LAC C-3233. General Entry Book of American Prisoners of War at Quebec; *DocHis 6, 11*. Return of Ordnance Captured 6 June 1813; USNA OW IF #26610; USNA, Registry of Enlistments in the United States Army, 1798-1914, Vol 1-2. RG 94 Muster Rolls United States Army 1812-1814. Peters' arm was amputated and he died at the army hospital at Lewiston on 1 Sept 1813 from the effects of his wound.

25. Livingston, *Sketches of Eminent Americans*, 393.

26. Smith, *Incidents in the Life*, 112.

27. *Hamilton Evening Times*, 5 June 1909. Col. Cruikshank on the Battle of Stoney Creek. *DocHis 6*, 197, Askin to Askin, 8 June 1813.

**29: "None could conjecture what had happened to the Generals."**

1. *Enquirer*, 2 July 1813, Extract of a letter from an Intelligent Captain.

2. *NWR*, 4 January 1817, General Chandler. Chandler's ADC, Donald Fraser said "I ran and could not find General Winder; the general opinion was that he was taken."

3. *DocHis 6*, 23. Burn to Dearborn; Burn, *Letters*, 306. Burn to Ingersoll, 1 July 1813; *Portico*, March 1816, 43, Biographical Sketch of Colonel Jacob Hindman.

4. *NWR*, 10 July 1813. Letter from Captain John Johnson; *Enquirer*, 2 July 1813, Extract of a letter from an Intelligent Captain.

5. *Hamilton Evening Times*, 9 June 1891, Interesting Details Made Public by a Veteran; McFeely, *Chronicle of Valor*, 266.

6. Chandler, *Autobiography*, 193.

7. *DocHis 6*, 13. FitzGibbon to Somerville, 7 June 1813.

8. Burn, *Letters*, 306. Burn to Ingersoll, 1 July 1813.

9. Shaler, *Memoirs*, 419.

10. *City Gazette*, 31 August 1820, From the Baltimore Federal Republican.

11. Dwight, *Diary*, 18.

12. *United States Gazette*, 8 July 1813. Letter from an officer.

13. *DocHis 6*, 16-17. FitzGibbon Memorial to Plenderleath.

14. *DocHis 6*, 13. FitzGibbon to Somerville, 7 June 1813.

15. *Ibid.*

16. *DocHis 6*, 16-17. FitzGibbon Memorial to Plenderleath.

17. *DocHis 6*, 13. FitzGibbon to Somerville, 7 June 1813.

18. *Ibid.*

19. Merritt, *A Desire of Serving*, 6.

20. Burn, *Letters*, 306. Burn to Ingersoll, 1 July 1813; *United States Gazette*, 8 July 1813, Letter from an Officer; Dwight, *Diary*, 18.

21. *City Gazette*, 31 August 1820, From the Baltimore Federal Republican; Enquirer, 2 July 1813, Extract of a letter from an Intelligent Captain.

22. *American Mercury*, 6 July 1813, Extract of a letter

from an officer. The letter is not signed but is accompanied by a copy of regimental orders issued 6 June 1813 that is signed by Smith. One of his company commanders, Captain Henry Leavenworth, said Smith wrote a report on Stoney Creek "in which he has distinguished Capt Batty and Lieut Watson." CHS, *Howard Letterbook*, Leavenworth to Howard, 26 June 1813. The letter in the *American Mercury* singles Batty and Watson out for "particular mention."

23. *Connecticut Mirror*, 12 July 1813, From the Albany Gazette.

24. *DocHis 6*, 23. Burn to Dearborn. Several newspaper accounts – *NWR* 12 June 1813 – had the dragoons carving their way through American and British units in the dark, but Burn and Chandler both say they were not engaged and contemporary British historian William James said "no dragoons were encountered or seen by any of our troops." *A Full and Correct Account*, 210.

25. *AO MS 842*, Harvey, *Journal*.

26. *DocHis 6*, 16-17. FitzGibbon Memorial to Plenderleath. *DocHis 6*, 11. Return of Ordnance Captured 6 June 1813; Spiking was a fast and effective way of temporarily disabling a gun. In order to get the piece back in service the venthole had to be drilled out.

27. Hickman. *Sketch of the Life of General Towson*, 12.

28. Shaler, *Memoirs*, 306; Kearsley, *Memoirs*, 7; *Salem Gazette*, 20 July 1813, Private Correspondence; Thomson, *History of the War*, 170; Kearsley, *Memoirs*, 7. *Sketch of the Life of Major Gen Henry Dearborn*, campaign literature 1817, 5. *American Advocate*, 15 March 1817, Political Miscellany.

29. Harvey said three quarters of an hour, Burn said one hour. Their estimates seems feasible in that Chandler's adjutant marked the beginning of the action at 2:20 a.m. On 6 June 1813, nautical twilight, during which the general outline of ground objects become distinguishable, began at 3:20 a.m.

## 30: "The awful dream of the night"

1. *New England Galaxy*, 18 August 1820, Miscellany from the Morning Chronicle.

2. *Ibid.*

3. *Western Press*, 20 July 1813, Extract of a letter; USNA OW Widow #1015. Captain Thomas Read deposition.

4. *Hamilton Spectator*, 12 June 1889. What Little Elizabeth Gage saw at Stony Creek. Interviewed in 1899 when she was 85, Elizabeth Birely scotched a long-standing rumour. "There was a story told for many years after the battle that my father found the paymaster's saddle bags in the well after the battle, but this was all nonsense, The soldiers drank our well dry, though."

5. Merritt, *A Desire of Serving*, 7.

6. Hickman, *Sketch of the Life of General Towson*, 12.

7. *Inter nos* – Between us; Burn, *Letters*, Burn to Ingersoll, 16 July 1813.

8. Library of Congress, RG 107, L-110 (7), Map of Stoney Creek battlefield. In neither of the of two post-battle positions is there any sign of the Sixteenth Infantry.

9. Kearsley, *Journal*, 8. "The army fell back a mile or two."; Library of Congress, RG 107, L-110 (7) Map of Stoney Creek battlefield; Ingersoll, *Historical Sketch of the Second War*, 287

10. Kearsley, *Memoirs*, 8.

11. *DocHis 6*, 23. Burn to Dearborn.

12. Current day Crescent Beach in Confederation Park.

13. Dwight, *Diary*, 19. Myers, *Reminiscences*, 29.

14. Myers, *Reminiscences*, 29. *United States Gazette*, 8 July 1813, Extract of a letter.

15. Dwight, *Diary*, 19.

16. USNA, OW IF # 28120, Mills deposition, 22 December 1817.

17. Ibid, Malcolm and Dwight deposition, 29 November 1813, Ingersoll deposition, 19 November 1817.

18. Myers, *Reminiscences*, 29.

19. *DocHis 6*, 12-15, FitzGibbon to Somerville, 7 June 1813.

20. *Northern Post*, Salem NY, June 24, 1813. Letter from a gentleman, 19 June 1813.

21. Land, *Address*, 26.

22. Myers, *Reminiscences*, 29.

23. Armstrong, *Notices*, 139; *DocHis 6*, 23. Burn to Dearborn.

24. *Ibid.*

25. Kearsley, *Memoirs*, 8.

26. Hickman, *Sketch of the Life*, 12; *Enquirer*, 2 July 1813, Extract of a Letter from an Intelligent Captain; *Albany Register*, 22 June 1813, From the Baltimore Whig – June 17.

27. Dwight, *Diary*, 19. Myers, *Reminiscences*, 29.

28. *DocHis 6*, 12-15, FitzGibbon to Somerville, 7 June 1813.

29. *Ibid.*

30. Chandler, *Autobiography*, 194.

31. *DocHis 6*, 196-198. Charles Askin to John Askin, 8 June 1813.

32. Myers, *Reminiscences*, 32; Kearsley, *Memoirs*, 8.

33. *ADC*, 5, 208.

34. MTRL, Anne Powell Letters, Powell to Powell, 10 June 1813.

35. Van Wagner, *Reminiscences of the Battle of Stoney Creek*.

36. AO, MS-MU 2095, item 26. War of 1812 pension applications. Downs received his $20 but left some confusion over who ran away from whom. The *Hamilton Spectator*, 4 October 1875, recorded "He served as orderly to Gen Vincent at Stony Creek, but he ran away from him."

37. Livingston, *Sketches*, 391.

38. A widespread search of church and civil records of Upper and Lower Canada turned up no records of Page's marriage. The best probable source, the 49th regimental records, were lost when Fort George fell.

**31: "You will be surprised to find our loss so small."**

1. *DocHis* 6, 23. Burn to Dearborn.
2. *DocHis* 6, 7. Harvey to Baynes , 6 June 1813.
3. Lossing, *Pictorial Field-Book*, 604.
4. *DocHis* 6, 15, FitzGibbon to Somerville, 7 June 1813.
5. *Ibid.*
6. *DocHis* 6, 25. Report of Killed, Wounded and Missing.
7. *Carisle Gazette*, 18 June 1813, Carisle, June 18, 1813. Chambers, a major in the Fifth Infantry, was like Johnson, an assistant adjutant general.
8. *American Mercury*, 6 July 1813, Extract of a letter from an officer The letter, almost certainly written by Smith, said "the killed and wounded of the 25th…was finally found to be forty-five, tho' on the morning of the battle it was supposed to be only 42."
9. CHS, *Howard Letterbook*, Leavenworth to Howard, 26 June 1813; Eight units – Second Artillery, Fifth, Sixteenth, Twentieth, Twenty-Second, Twenty-Third, Twenty-Fifth, First Rifles – plus company-size or less detachments of the Twenty-First and Lytle's Rifle Company of U.S. Volunteers were involved in the action.
10. *New York Statesman*, 24 June 1813. Letter from an officer, June 9 1813. The letter says the advance at Fort George on May 27 included "our battalion of artillery, acting as infantry, consisting of the same companies that left Philadelphia under col. Scott." The three companies at Fort George were Hindman's, Biddle's and Nicholas'. The same Second Artillery companies, plus Towson's company were in action at Stoney Creek.
11. Cruikshank, *Stoney Creek and the Blockade of Fort George*, 16. *United States Gazette*, 8 July 1813, Letter from an officer at Fort George, 22 June 1813; *New England Galaxy*, 18 August 1820, Miscellany from the Morning Chronicle.
12. USNA, RG 94 *Returns of the Killed and Wounded of American Troops*, Compiled by Col. J. H. Eaton.
13. USNA, *Registry of Enlistments in the United States Army, 1798-1914*, Vol 1-2. RG 94 *Muster Rolls United States Army 1812-1814*; *Enquirer*, 2 July 1813, Extract of a Letter from an Intelligent Captain.
14. *NWR*, 12 June 1813. Dearborn to Armstrong, 6 June 1813.
15. *DocHis* 6, 23. Burn to Dearborn.
16. *NWR*, 19 October 1816. Battle of Stoney Creek.
17. Shaler, *Memoirs*, 419.
18. *DocHis* 6, 11. Return of American Prisoners of War Captured near Stoney Creek.
19. *NWR*, 19 October 1816. Battle of Stoney Creek; Cochrane, *History of Monmouth and Wales*, 195.
20. *NWR*, 12 June, 1813. Letter to the Editors. CHS, *Howard Letterbook*. 12 June 1813. Howard to Sarah Howard.
21. *DocHis* 6, 10. General Return of Killed, Wounded and Missing, 6th June 1813. Based on muster and payroll archives, the figures appear reasonably accurate. American returns for prisoners list 56 regulars, one of whom is a deserter from 5 June. NYSL, Gardner Papers, List of British Prisoners brought to Fort Niagara, June 8 1813.

**32: "Never was a more compleat victory obtained."**

1. MHS, Charles E. French Papers, Johnson to Dearborn, 7 June 1813.
2. *ADC*, 5, 207. A barber's block is a wig stand.
3. *DocHis* 6, 23, Burn to Dearborn.
4. *Carisle Gazette*, 18 June 1813, Carisle, June 18 1813.
5. *Albany Register*, 22 June 1813, From the Baltimore Whig – June 17.
6. *Ibid.*
7. MHS, Charles E. French Papers, Johnson to Dearborn, 7 June 1813; The letter was reprinted in at least six prominent newspapers including *Niles' Weekly Register* and the *Boston Patriot*.
8. *DocHis* 6, 4, Armstrong to Dearborn, 15 May 1813.
9. *DocHis* 6, 6, Dearborn to Armstrong, 6 June 1813. *NWR*, Dearborn to Armstrong, 12 June 1813.
10. *Ibid.*
11. *DocHis* 6, 77, Dearborn to Lewis, 6 June 1813; *DocHis* 5, 254, Lewis to Dearborn, 27 May 1813.
12. Cochrane, *History of Monmouth and Wales*, 83. Cruikshank, *Stoney Creek and the Blockade of Fort George*, 17. *Sketch of the Life of Major Gen Henry Dearborn*, campaign literature 1817, 12.
13. *ADC*, 6, 278.

**33: "An action … has quite altered the face of affairs."**

1. *DocHis* 6, 196, Charles Askin to John Askin, 8 June 1813.
2. *NWR*, 19 October 1816. Battle of Stoney Creek.
3. Norton, *Journal*, 329.
4. *DocHis* 6, 196, Charles Askin to John Askin, 8 June 1813.
5. *Hamilton Spectator*, 12 June 1889, What Little Elizabeth saw at Stony Creek. "Months afterwards they brought some of them back when they found they were ours."
6. Biggar, *Battle of Stony Creek*.
7. Canniff, *Medical Profession in Upper Canada*, 286. Case's house, which stood on the northwest corner of Lottridge and King Street East, would become a military hospital for the next two years; Pension petition, 11 November, 1854, McFall family collection; *DocHis* 5, 305, Diary of Col Claus.
8. *Hamilton Spectator*, 12 June 1889, What Little Elizabeth saw at Stony Creek.
9. LAC, War Loss Claims, T1139 Vol 3757 #1851. Gage claimed £5 "Hallfax coranc" for the damage and was allowed the full amount.
10. James. *A Full and Correct Account*. 207; LAC T1130 Vol 3746 #497, William Gage Loss Claim. Unlike his neighbours and relatives who received at least partial compensation for claimed losses, William Gage received nothing.
11. LAC T1136 Vol 3755 #1455. Statement of Losses

sustained by Samuel Nash of Saltfleet. Nash claimed £6 for damage to the house and bedding and was awarded £4; OHS, *Billy Green the Scout*.

12. Biggar, *Battle of Stony Creek*, 8; *Ibid*. HPL. *The Battle of Stoney Creek as related by an Eye-Witness*, *The Battle of Stoney Creek*, *The Old Burial Ground where the Battle was Fought*. OHS, *Billy Green the Scout*.

13. Chandler, *Autobiography*, 197; Bloodletting dates back at least as far as ancient Egypt and was predicated on the theory illness resulted from an imbalance in body humors. Virtually every known medical condition has, at one time or another, been treated by bloodletting. The American army surgeon, James Mann, treated pneumonia by drawing off as much as two quarts of blood over two days. See Mann, *Medical Sketches*, 25; The remnants of Beasley's wharf have been found at the bottom of Burlington Heights on what was originally the shoreline of Hamilton Harbour but now adjoins the rail lines built on reclaimed land. See *Hamilton Spectator*, 6 October 2000, "Finding the birthplace of our city" by James Elliott; Bulger, *An Autobiographical Sketch*, 5; *DocHis 6*, 67. Harvey to Baynes, 11 June 1813; Dudley, *Naval War*, 495, Chauncey to Jones, 18 June 1813; *Northern Post*, 8 July 1813, Latest from Montreal. Lieutenant Colonel James Cuthbert, 3rd Battalion, Select Embodied Militia of Lower Canada.

14. LAC Reel T1127 Vol 3740 # 46, Loss Claims, deposition from Richard Beasley taken by Titus Simons.

## 34: "The enemy's fleet have an intention on this place."

1. *DocHis 6*, 77, No. 7. Dearborn to Lewis, no date.
2. *DocHis 6*, 6, Dearborn to Armstrong, 6 June 1813.
3. *Sketch of the Life of Major Gen Henry Dearborn*, campaign literature 1817, 13.
4. *DocHis 6*, 77, Dearborn to Lewis. No. 5. Cruikshank's date of 6 June on the order is an error, it should be 7 June.
5. *DocHis 6*, 77. No. 6. Dearborn to Lewis. Again, the date should be 7 June.
6. Lossing, *Pictorial Field Book*, 604.
7. *DocHis 6*, 77, No. 7. Dearborn to Lewis, no date.
8. Cruikshank, *Stoney Creek and the Blockade of Fort George*, 19.
9. *Ibid*.

## 35: "We're going back to fetch a bigger army."

1. HPL, Thompson Papers, Daniel Barber Reminiscence.
2. Mann, *Medical Sketches*, 63. "Typhous fever and diarrhea pervaded the army after their retrograde march from Stony Creek."
3. HPL, Thompson Papers, Daniel Barber Reminiscence.
4. *Hamilton Spectator*, 5 March 1890, An Oldest Inhabitant.
5. *New England Galaxy*, 18 August 1820, Miscellany

from the Morning Chronicle.
6. Dwight, *Diary*, 19.
7. *American Mercury*, 6 July 1813, Camp 40 Mile Creek June 6 1813, Regimental Orders!

## 36: "With all possible despatch"

1. *DocHis 6*, 74. Lewis to Armstrong, 14 June 1813.
2. LAC, MG 24, F18. Wingfield, Four Years on the Lakes.
3. *DocHis 6*, 178-181, Hamilton to Henderson, 4 July 1813. Alexander Hamilton was a captain in the Niagara Light Dragoons.
4. *ADC*, No 6, 282; LAC, MG 24, F18. Wingfield, Four Years on the Lakes.
5. Francis Spilsbury, DCB 6; Dudley, *Naval War*, 498, Yeo to Croker, 29 June 1813. Harvey, *Journal*. *DocHis 6*, 76. Lewis to Armstrong,14 June 1813. Cruikshank, *Stoney Creek and the Blockade of Fort George*, 19. Hickman, *Sketch of the Life of General Nathan Towson*, 12.
6. Heated or hot shot was a process where a solid iron ball was heated red-hot while the gun was loaded with a powder charge topped with a tight-fitting wooden plug followed by wet rags and oakum for insulation. The ball, when red-hot was loaded down the barrel and the gun was discharged. A highly dangerous procedure, its use was restricted to wooden targets such as ships and buildings which could be set afire by the ball; Dudley, *Naval War*, 498. Yeo to Croker, 29 June 1813; *DocHis 6*, 76. Lewis to Armstrong,14 June 1813.
7. *NWR*, 12 June 1813. Letter to the editors from Fort George, 8 June 1813.
8. Norton, *Journal*, 329. Norton writes cryptically of "cabals" and suggestions "from a certain Quarter" which Carl Benn interprets as evidence the Iroquois – despite British success at Stoney Creek – were still equivocating.
9. Nelles' store was on the west side of Forty Mile Creek in Grimsby where Highway 8 crosses the creek; Norton, *Journal*, 330. Shaler, *Memoirs*, 416.
10. Eldridge's eagerness to engage native warriors would cost him dearly a month later when he was killed after being taken prisoner in a skirmish near Fort George. Merritt said Eldridge "forfeited his Life by firing at an Indians while a Prisoner." ; *ADC*, No 6, 282.
11. Norton, *Journal*, 330; Yeo's cheeky demand echoes Brock's spectacularly successful bluff at Detroit and is in some ways a dress rehearsal for FitzGibbon's similarly audacious ultimatum to follow shortly at Beaver Dams. In his report to the first secretary of the Navy, however, Yeo mentions nothing of the exchange with Lewis.
12. *DocHis 6*, 74. Lewis to Armstrong, 14 June 1813.
13. *Ibid*.
14. *Ibid*.
15. Cruikshank, *Stoney Creek and the Blockade of Fort George*, 19. *DocHis 6*, 62. Evans to Harvey, 10 June 1813.

16. *DocHis* 6, 64, Return of camp equipage, 10 June 1813. Within two days only 200 of the 500 tents remained, the militia quartermaster Robert Nichol reported Indians made off with 180 and local settlers another 120.
17. *DocHis* 6, 62. Evans to Harvey, 10 June 1813.
18. *DocHis* 6, 63. Robert Nichol, Returns of camp equipage, provisions, arms, ammunition and ordnance stores belonging to the enemy, 10 June 1813.
19. *DocHis* 6, 74. Lewis to Armstrong, 14 June 1813.
20. Harvey, *Journal.*
21. Merritt, *A Desire of Serving,* 7.
22. Norton, *Journal,* 330; Grimsby Historical Society, *Annals of the Forty,* 64; *Argus,* Albany, NY. 13 June 1813, Letter from a gentleman at Newark.
23. USNA, OW IF # 3017. Boyd was part of Winder's Fourteenth Infantry that briefly visited the Canadian shore of 28 November 1812.
24. USNA, OW IF # 200226.
25. *ADC,* No 6, 285.
26. *Ibid;* The Queenston road ravine is on Regional Road 81 just west of St. Catharines, most likely either Fifteen-Mile Creek or Sixteen-Mile Creek.
27. *Ibid.*
28. *Ibid.*
29. Norton, *Journal,* 330.
30. McFeely. *Journal,* 266.
31. *Enquirer,* 2 July 1813, Extract of a Letter from an Intelligent Captain.
32. *Ibid.*
33. *DocHis* 6, 204. Charles Askin to John Askin, 8 July 1813.
34. Ford, *Soldiers of 1814,* 52.
35. Kearsley, *Memoirs,* 52.
36. Dwight, *Diary,* 19.
37. Von Clausewitz, *On War,* 250.
38. Smith, *A Geographical View,* 10; *DocHis* 6, 74, Lewis to Armstrong, 14 June 1813; *Baltimore Whig,* Letter to the editors, 8 June 1813, reprinted in DocHis 6, 46; *Albany Gazette,* 19 June 1813, Events of the War.
39. *NWR,* 26 June 1813, The Army in Canada.
40. *Federal Republican,* 5 January 1814, Reflections and Strictures upon the last Campaign.
41. Cruikshank, *Stoney Creek and the Blockade of Fort George,* 21; Myers, *Reminiscences,* 33.
42. *DocHis* 6, 11, Return of American Prisoners, 7 June 1813. *DocHis* 6, 64, Return of prisoners from Forty Mile Creek, 8, 9, 10 June 1813.
43. *DocHis* 6, 62. Evans to Harvey 10 June 1813 ; *Albany Gazette,* 19 June 1813, Events of the War.
44. *ADC* 7, 173.
45. Myers, *Reminiscences,* 33
46. *ADC* 7, 175.

**37: "More contradictory statements we have never seen."**

1. *Columbian,* 17 June 1813, From the Northern Army.
2. *Albany Argus,* 15 June 1813, From the Frontiers. Extract of a letter from the post-Master at Niagara.
3. Plattsburgh *Republican,* 25 June 1813, Burlington Bay; *Evening Post,* 16 June 1813. Canandaigua, Thursday Evening, June 10 1813.
4. *Albany Register,* 15 June 1813, Communicated by the Editor of the Geneva Gazette; *Boston Patriot,* 19 June 1813, N. York, Albany, June 15, From the Frontiers.
5. *Pittsfield Sun,* 17 June 1813, From the Frontiers, 9th June 1813.
6. *Albany Register,* 15 June 1813, Communicated by the editor of the Geneva Gazette June 11.
7. *Evening Post,* 18 June 1813, Extract of a letter to a gentleman in Albany dated Little Falls, June 15; *War,* 15 June 1813, Latest From The Army.
8. *Weekly Messenger,* 18 June 1813, Latest from the Frontiers.
9. *Albany Argus,* 18 June 1813, The Western Mail.
10. *Columbian,* 17 June 1813, From the Northern Army.

**38: "That approval which valor and discipline must ever receive."**

1. *DocHis* 3, 2 , Duke of York to Prevost, 10 August 1813.
2. *DocHis* 6, 62, Evans to Harvey, 10 June 1813. *DocHis* 6, 67, Harvey to Baynes, 11 June 1813. *DocHis* 6, 59, Vincent to Prevost, 9 June 1813. *DocHis* 6, 74, Vincent to Baynes, 14 June 1813; Harvey, *Journal.*
3. *DocHis* 6, 15, FitzGibbon to Somerville, 7 June 1813.
4. Norton, *Journal,* 328; *DocHis* 6, 196, Askin to Askin 8 June 1813; *Chronicle,* 26 June 1813, Extract – Dated. Camp near Fort George, July 3, 1813 The extract was reprinted from William Duane's *Aurora* in Philadelphia; *DocHis* 6, Glegg to Jarvis, 15 June 1813; *DocHis* 6, 7, Harvey to Baynes, 15 June 1813.
5. *DocHis* 6, 8, Vincent to Prevost 6 June 1813; *DocHis* 6, 66-67, District General Orders, Burlington, 7 June 1813.
6. *DocHis* 6, 54, Vincent to Prevost, 8 June 1813; *DocHis* 6, 74, Vincent to Baynes 14 June 1813.
7. *DocHis* 6, 53, General Orders, Kingston, 8 June 1813.
8. *DocHis* 6, 65, General Orders, Kingston, 11 June 1813; *DocHis* 6, 83, Proclamation, 14 June 1813; *Canadian Courant,* 10 July 1813, To Brigadier General John Vincent.
9. *DocHis* 6, 79, Prevost to Bathurst, 14 June 1813.
10. *The Times,* 26 July 1813, London Gazette Extraordinary; *DocHis* 6, 330, Bathurst to Prevost, 10 August 1813.
11. *DocHis* 3, 2 , Duke of York to Prevost, 10 August 1813.
12. *DocHis* 6, 74, Vincent to Baynes, 14 June 1813.
13. Cruikshank, *Records of Niagara* 44, 46, Prevost to Vincent, 18 June 1813.
14. Cruikshank, *Records of Niagara,* 44, 28. Sheaffe to Prevost, April 1813. Believing only 200 men defended Fort Niagara, Vincent proposed an assault

by 400 troops. The plan was rejected by Major General Sir Roger Sheaffe as contrary to Prevost's strictly defensive policy.

### 39: "Poor victims to fear"

1. McFarland, *Papers*, 115.
2. *DocHis* 6, 12, Glegg Memo. The accuser was most likely Archibald McDonald, a lifer who in 1813 had already been in the army 29 years; PA, WO 12/2383-2385, Muster books and pay list, 6th Foot 1799-1803. Hunt, and his accuser MacDonald, were part of a draft of 590 men taken into the 6th and 41st when the 2nd Battalion of the 60th Foot was disbanded in October 1799.
3. *DocHis* 6, Baynes, General Order 29 June 1813.
4. LAC, C1170 pp 287-8, Vincent to Prevost 22 June 1813.
5. *DocHis* 6, 199, de Rottenburg to Prevost, 7 July 1813. "Desertion is a growing evil in this army. I am trying today a man of the 41st. If he is sentenced to suffer death the same shall be put into execution 24 hours later."; LAC, C65, 141, de Rottenburg to Brenton, 9 July 1813; Public Archives, WO12/2575, Muster and pay rolls 8th Foot, March-June 1813.
6. *DocHis* 6, 161, Baynes, General Order 29 June 1813.
7. *Ibid.*
8. McFarland, *Papers*, 115.
9. *DCB* 7, The Canadian-built *Swiftsure* made the trip to Quebec in 24 hours.
10. Hamilton, *The Life and Dying Confessions*, 10; Myers, *A Life Before the Mast*, 101; USNA, OW IF #26763. Story deposition.
11. Myers, *A Life Before the Mast*, 105 ; Unable to transport convicts to America during the Revolution – the British took to storing them in prison hulks on the Thames which literally overflowed until a new destination, Australia, was found in 1787. Hulks continued to be used during the Napoleonic Wars for POWs; LAC, C690, roll 3233 50, General Entry Book for American Prisoners of War at Quebec.
12. LAC, C690, roll 3233 114, General Entry Book for American Prisoners of War at Quebec. Weekly sick return, August 22-28 1813.
13. Already a prison for French and Spanish sailors taken during the Napoleonic Wars, Melville Island housed more than 8,000 American prisoners during the War of 1812. Ned Myer's *Life Before the Mast* provides a insider's view of prison life. Confinement from a militia officer's standpoint is covered in Samuel White's *History of the American Troops during the Late War under the command of Colonels Fenton and Campbell.*
14. USNA, HOR-27AG 24, Petition of Bernard Hoy.
15. SCHS, Whitridge Papers, Sturtevant to West, 7 April 1814. Presumably Sturtevant is referring to vermin.
16. LAC, RG 8 I , vol 691 93-96. Stewart and Lyford Deposition, 3 October 1813.

17. *American Watchman*, 11 August 1813, Albany, August 3.
18. LAC, RG 8 I , vol 691 93-96. Stewart and Lyford Deposition, 3 October 1813.
19. Ibid, Delaney Deposition 4 October 1813. Delaney, Stewart and Lyford all escaped from Greenbush and made their way to Montreal.

### 40: "Canada will not be conquered this year."

1. LOC, Samuel Smith Family Papers, Macomb to Smith, 24 June 1813.
2. Coleman, *The American Capture of Fort George*, 36. "By 23 June there were still over 500 in the hospital."; Mann, *Medical Sketches*, 122; *DocHis* 6, 6. Dearborn to Armstrong, 6 June 1813. "I never so severely felt the want of health as at present, a time when my services might perhaps be most useful."
3. Armstrong, *Notices*, 150. "My ill state of health renders it extremely painful to attend to current duties, and unless it improves soon, I fear I shall be compelled to retire to some place where my mind may be more at ease."
4. Adams, *War of 1812*, 85.
5. *Ibid.*
6. Cochrane, *History Monmouth*, 86
7. *Federal Republican*, 25 June 1813, Copy of a Letter from Maj. Gen Lewis. The letter, almost certainly released to the Washington press by Armstrong, spread like wildfire and within two weeks had been reprinted in Virginia, New York, New Jersey, Massachusetts, West Virginia, Pennsylvania, New Hampshire and Vermont.
8. Steiner, *The Life and Correspondence of James McHenry*, 600, Tallmadge to McHenry, 16 June 1813.
9. In 1813 Winfield Scott said Dearborn "saw more hard fighting during the revolutionary war than any three men now alive.". NYSL, Gardner Papers, Scott to Gardner, 16 July 1813; *DocHis* 6, 95. *Armstrong to Dearborn* 19 June 1813
10. *Federal Republican*, 21 June 1813, Gen. Dearborn.
11. *DocHis* 6, 95. Dearborn to Armstrong, 20 June 1813.
12. Merritt, *Desire of Serving*, 7. FitzGibbon, *A Veteran of 1812*, 72. *DocHis* 5, 154, Memoirs of Col. John Clark. *DCB* 9.
13. Cruikshank, *Fight in the Beechwoods*, 9-10 ; Quimby, *US Army in the War of 1812*, 248, *DocHis* 6, 130-131, Narrative of the Expedition.
14. Benn, *Iroquois in the War of 1812*, 115; See Dominique Duchame, DCB 8.
15. The battlefield site is now within the city of Thorold. *DocHis* 6, 140, Boerstler to Dearborn, 25 June 1813 ; *DocHis* 6, 120, FitzGibbon to Kerr, 30 March 1818 ; *DocHis* 6, 141, Colonel Boerstler to his father, 25 June 1813. Boerstler was exonerated by a court of enquiry after the war, the real culprit, Boyd, who championed this foolish expedition, was never called to account.
16. *ASPMA*, 1, 449, Dearborn to Armstrong, 25 June 1813.

17. *New York Evening Post*, 13 July 1813, Letter from a gentleman.
18. USNA, RG107, Letters received, V 7, D153, Dearborn to Armstrong 6 July 1813.
19. Ingersoll, *Historical Sketch of the Second War*, 287-288. Republican Charles Jared Ingersoll, chair of the judiciary committee said the defeat at Beaver Dams was "the climax to continual tidings of mismanagement and misfortune. On the 6th of July, therefore, after a short accidental communion of regret and impatience in the lobby with the speaker, (Henry Clay) and General (Samuel) Ringgold of Maryland, I was deputed a volunteer to wait on the President and request General Dearborn's removal…The president was ill abed when I called but promised me an early answer, which soon followed me to the capital…that General Dearborn should be removed : the order went at once."; *DocHis 6*, 187. Armstrong to Dearborn 6 June 1813. "I have the President's orders to express to you his decision that you retire from the Command of District No. 9 and of the troops with the same until your health be re-established and until farther orders."
20. Burn, *Letters*, 307, Burn to Ingersoll, 16 July 1813; *NWR*, August 7, 1813, Retirement of General Dearborn; Scott, *Memoirs*, 93.
21. Burn, *Letters*, 307, Burn to Ingersoll, 16 July 1813.
22. NYSL, Gardner Papers, Scott to Gardner, 16 July 1813.
23. Lewis appears to have been in cahoots with his brother-in-law, John Armstrong to effect Dearborn's removal. The letter in which Lewis doubted his fitness to command was widely published. Dearborn believed Armstrong wanted him removed so that he could take field command of the army "and thus secure to him the presidential chair." Armstrong did get rid of Dearborn but his subsequent involvement in the disastrous St. Lawrence campaign and the equally-disastrous defence of Washington scuttled his political career. See *Sketch of the Life of Major Gen. Henry Dearborn*, 22; *ADC*, No 7, 182.
24. *Baltimore Patriot*, 31 July 1813, General Dearborn; *Ibid.*
25. *Portland Gazette*, 9 August 1813, Miscellany. The article was reprinted from the *Federal Republican*.
26. Duane, *Letters*, 362. Duane to Jefferson, 26 September 1813.
27. *DocHis 6*, 201, Armstrong to Boyd, 7 July 1813.
28. *ASPMA 1, 450*, Boyd to Armstrong, 27 July 1813.
29. Today's Hamilton Harbour.
30. Malcomson, *Lords of the Lake*, 164.
31. Dudley, *Naval War*, 356, Unknown Midshipman to J. Jones, 13 August 1813.
32. *ASPMA 1, 450*, Scott to Boyd, 3 August 1813.
33. Harvey, *Journal*.
34. Known variously as "Jupiter Williams", "Thunderbolt Williams" and "Thunder and Lightning Williams", because of his swaggering pro-war rhetoric

as a politician, Williams resigned his commission in April 1814 after eight months of unremarkable service; *ASPMA 1*, 451, Boyd to Armstrong, 8 August 1813; Dudley, *Naval War*, 538, Chauncey to Jones, 13 August 1813.
35. One of Chauncey's midshipmen suggested Chauncey was intimidated by Yeo's bold approach. "Never again will we have the opportunity we have this day had, of settling the contest with so small a sacrifice." Dudley, *Naval War*, 357, Unknown Midshipman to J. Jones, 13 August 1813.
36. Battle of Moraviantown, 5 October 1813, see Antal, *A Wampum Denied*; *DocHis 8*, 244, General Order, Newark 30 November 1813, *New York Gazette*, 11 October, 1813, Extract of a Letter. *Albany Register*, 7 December 1813, Extract of a Letter. *New York Spectator*, 1 December 1813, Extracts of a Letter. *Columbian*, 3 December 1813, Editor's Correspondence. Benn, *Iroquois in the War of 1812*, 144. *DocHis 8*, 222, McClure to Tompkins, 21 November 1813, Bacon to Tompkins, 21 November 1813.
37. LOC, Samuel Smith Family Papers, Macomb to Samuel Smith, 24 June 1813.
38. The October-November St. Lawrence Campaign ended the 1813 campaign. See Graves' *Field of Glory*; Ingersoll, *Historical Sketch of the Second War*, 300.
39. SCHS, Whitridge Papers, Whitridge to Whitridge, 19 December 1813.
40. *Portland Gazette*, 12 July 1813, General Dearborn has resigned. The article was reprinted from the *Connecticut Mirror*.

**41: A time for peace.**
1. *Portland Gazette*, 12 July 1813, General Dearborn.
2. *Ibid*, Independence.
3. *American Advocate*, 9 July 1812. Hallowell. Chandler's toast was to the American army and mentioned neither wine nor Quebec. One year later on 10 July 1813, the *American Advocate* reprinted the toast "to correct a base and malicious lie."
4. *Proceedings of the American Antiquarian Society*, 19, 33 Matthews, "Uncle Sam". Cochrane, *History of Monmouth*, 108.
5. *Portland Gazette*, 12 July 1813, North-Yarmouth.
6. *Portland Gazette*, 2 August 1813, Gen. Chandler – an Anecdote.
7. *Portland Gazette*, 9 August 1813, Miscellany.
8. Imprisoned officers could sign a parole – effectively a promise not to attempt escape – which permitted them limited freedom of movement; LAC, Series C 690, roll 3233, p 50, Chandler to Glasgow, 27 July 1813. *Malabar* and *Hydra*.
9. See "Retaliation for the Treatment of Prisoners in the War of 1812" by Ralph Robinson, *American Historical Review*, 49, 1, pp 65-70.
10. Maine was part of Massachusetts until it gained statehood in 1820.
11. The first newspaper appears to be the *Eastern Argus*, 25 September 1816, Brig. Gen John Chandler;

John Chandler Journal, Folger Library, University of Maine; *Eastern Argus,* 25 September 1816, Brig. Gen John Chandler.

12. *Granite Monthly,* 6, 1884, Hon. John Chandler, Dearborn to Wingate, 17 January 1817.

13. *New Hampshire Patriot,* 7 October 1841, Gen. Chandler.

14. Robinson, *Organization of the Army,* 146.

15. http://bioguide.congress.gov/scripts/biodisplay.pl?index=C000291.

16. *Federal Republican,* 3 April 1813, General Winder; *DocHis 6,* 67. Harvey to Baynes, 11 June 1813.

17. Maryland Historical Society, Winder Papers, Winder to Armstrong, 19 June 1813.

18. Maryland Historical Society, Winder Papers, Winder to Prevost, 8 July 1813; The hostage situation began in October 1812 when twenty-three of the American prisoners taken at Queenston Height were found to be British subjects and shipped to England to face treason charges. In retaliation the Americans put an equal number of British prisoners in close confinement as hostages and the British responded by putting forty-six American prisoners in close confinement. From there it escalated to more confinements and death threats. See *American Historical Review,* 49, 1, Robinson, "Retaliation for the Treatment of Prisoners in the War of 1812."

19. Stanley, *Land Operations,* 341.

20. Adams, *War of 1812,* 229.

21. Scott, *Memoirs,* 1 n 92.

22. *Baltimore Patriot,* 26 May 1824, Baltimore." *Portsmouth Journal of Literature and Politics,* 26 June 1824, Miscellaneous.

23. *DAB. Village Register,* 11 June 1829, General Henry Dearborn. *Connecticut Mirror,* 13 June 1829, General Henry Dearborn.

24. Kearsley, *Memoirs,* 5.

25. Scott, *Memoirs,* 2, 342. Scott said the two often exchanged salutes on the field and that he once deflected the weapon of a rifleman who had Harvey in his sights. As chiefs of staff of their respective armies they negotiated terms of parole for prisoners; The so-called Aroostook War in 1839 was averted by the Webster-Ashburton Treaty.

26. *DCB 8.*

27. *Globe,* 1 April 1852, The Late Sir John Harvey. *North American Semi-Weekly,* 2 April 1852, The Late Sir John Harvey.

28. *DocHis 6,* 12-16, FitzGibbon to Somerville, 7 June 1813.

29. See Dominique Duchame, DCB 8.

30. *DocHis 6,* 296, Left Division Orders, 31 July 1813.

31. Perth is the seat of Lanark County, fifty miles SW of Ottawa; Fraser family records compiled by Irene Spence of Perth, ON. Brewster, *Descendants of Simon Fraser of Laggan, Inverness-Shire, Scotland.* 165.

32. *Bathurst Courier,* 12 January 1847, The Bathurst Courier, Fraser was found guilty and fined £25.

33. *Bathurst Courier,* 2 November 1847, Bathurst District Council.

34. *Perth Courier,* 12 July 1872, Decease of Colonel Alexander Fraser. The *Bathurst Courier* became the *Perth Courier* in 1858. Fraser's obituary and his tombstone both incorrectly list his age as 78

35. NA WO12/6043-6075, Muster books and pay list, 49th Foot.

36. RG 8 C 17, 108-109, Fulton to Prevost, 18 June 1813.

37. RG8 C 17 684 125-127, Vincent to Baynes, 6 May 1814.

38. *Gentleman's Magazine,* 6 April 1815, "Gazette Promotion." *East Gloucester Election,* 14 January 1854, Colonel Plenderleath

39. *DocHis 6,* 17, From a Memorandum; *Columbia Electronic Encyclopedia* 6th Edition. Cimitero 'Degli Inglesi' Elenco. http://www.florin.ms/cemetery3.html

40. Prevost to de Rottenburg, 22 October 1813, cited in *Field of Glory,* 72; *DHB* 1. *DCB* 7 ; FitzGibbon, *A Veteran of 1812,* 319.

41. Canniff, *The Medical Profession in Upper Canada,* 286.

42. Hobbs, *Thomas Taylor's War.*

43. *Hamilton Herald,* 11 May 1910, The Lion on the Monument.

44. *Oxford DNB. DCB 9.*

45. *Oxford DNB. DCB 5.*

## Appendix A: Billy Green: The Scout and the Rout

1. Kezia Green, born 1781.

2. Lareine Ballantyne, *The Scout who led an army,* Toronto: Macmillan, 1963. James Elliott, *Billy Green and the Battle of the Stoney Creek,* Stoney Creek Historical Society 1994; Woody Lambe, *The Battle of Stoney Creek, 1960.* Lois Fletcher and Gord Bailey *The Ballad of Billy Green,* CHCH TV 1965. Stan Rogers, *Billy Green the Scout,* Fogerty's Cove Music, 1977; *OHS 44,* "Billy Green the Scout". *Cuesta,* Spring 1981 "The Mystery & Legend of Billy Green the Scout." ; George F. Stanley, *The War of 1812: Land Operations,* Ottawa: National Museums of Canada, 1983; Pierre Berton, *Flames Across the Border,* Toronto, McClelland and Stewart, 1981; Hansard 173, 22 April 2002, Tony Valeri, Lib. Stoney Creek "It is time for the national government to fund the production of stories like Billy Green's. It is time to embrace our unknown past."

3. LAC, RG 9, IB 7, Vol 24, 5th Regiment, Lincoln Militia, 25 May – 24 June 1813; USNA, RG 98, Records of the United States Army Command, 1784 -1821, Vol 1, Entry 57, List of Prisoners Paroled (exclusive of regulars) after the taking of Fort George May 27th 1813. Although only 507 militia were captured at Fort George, a total of 1,193 were paroled on May 28-29-30, a figure that represents the bulk of the militia in Niagara; Robert Land was the son of Hamilton pioneer Robert Land, 1736-1818. See James Elliott, *If Ponies Rode Men:*

*The Journeys of Robert Land.* Stoney Creek Historical Society, 1999; *Journals and Transactions of the
Wentworth Historical Society,* Vol 1, 24. "The Battle
of Stoney Creek," J. H. Land.

4. *Journals and Transactions of the Wentworth Historical Society* Vol. 5, "An Old Diary: Entries from D.
Slater's Diary, Stoney Creek."

5. Guthrie, *A New Geographical, Historical, and Commercial Grammar; and present state of the several
Kingdoms of the world,* Dublin, John Exshaw, 1794.
William E. Corman had given the text to the Hamilton Scientific Association who in turn gave it to
the Dundurn Museum in 1938, it eventually ended
up in Special Collections at the Hamilton Public
Library.

6. *Hamilton Spectator,* 12 March 1938, Descendants
of Billy the Scout Recall His Deeds. The statement
was in possession of John W. Green's widow, Sarah.

7. Shaler, *Memoirs,* 416; Green's sister-in-law was
Christina Cook, 1780-1882.

8. Harrison, the 9th president of the Unites States
in 1841 and the oldest until Ronald Reagan, also
served the shortest term, dying of pneumonia a
month after taking office.

9. Now known as Red Hill Creek.

10. *OHS, 44,* "Billy Green the Scout" Billy Green's
statement, 174-178.

11. *DocHis* 6, 7. Harvey to Baynes 6 June 1813.

12. LAC, C-2035, RG 1 L3, Vol 213 G, bundle 20, petition 88.

13. Durand's Company. LAC RH 9, IB7, Vol 24, p 425.
5th Regiment, Lincoln Militia

14. LAC 2-2035 RG1, L3, Vol 212 G bundle 20, petition 14a. The name of Freeman's first wife is not
known although the couple had two children.
After the war, Green moved to Howard County
near Ridgetown, Ontario, where he remarried and
had four more children.

15. HPL, Special Collections. Nisbet, "The Battle of
Stoney Creek" *Souvenir Book and Programme for
Military Encampment,* 1895. pp 34-36

16. Lossing, *Pictorial Field Book,* 602-603.

17. E. B. Biggar 1853-1921, see DHB, 2. Biggar's donation of several hundred volumes of early Canadian
works to the Hamilton Public Library in 1905
formed the basis of the library's fledgling Canadi-
ana collection; *Hamilton Spectator,* 6 June 1873, E.
B. Biggar "The Story of the Battle of Stoney Creek".

18. Amos, James and William Biggar. LAC, RG9. 1B7,
Vol 24, 5th Regiment, Lincoln Militia, 1812-1814.

19. *Hamilton Spectator,* 4 October 1875, The Veterans
of 1812-15.

20. *Laura Secord, the Heroine of 1812,* Toronto: 1887;
*Hamilton Evening Times,* 6 June 1889, The Pioneer
Picnic.

21. *Journals and Transactions of the Wentworth Historical Society* Vol 1, 24. "The Battle of Stoney Creek" J.
H. Land.

22. *Canadian Magazine,* Vol 1, 387, "The Battle of
Stony Creek" by E. B. Biggar.

23. *Hamilton Evening Times,* 5 June 1909. Col. Cruikshank on the Battle of Stoney Creek.

24. *Paper and Records, Wentworth Historical Society,*
Vol 7 26-34, "An Account of the Battle of Stoney
Creek" by Hazel Corman.

25. *Hamilton Spectator,* 15 July 1926, Stoney Creek was
Decisive Battle.

26. Robert McCullough, 1865-1947, was a founding
member of the Canadian Club in 1893 ; *Hamilton
Spectator,* 26 December 1932. Stories of Stoney
Creek.

27. *Mail and Empire,* 6 June 1935. The Boy Hero of
Stoney Creek.

28. Refers to Tina (Christina) Green, wife of Levi.
Hannah was their daughter.

29. Dezi is Keziah, wife of Isaac Corman and sister of
William Green. Alph and Becky are her children.

**Appendix B: Bones of Contention**

1. Myers, *Reminiscences,* 32. *ADC* 5, 108. Myer's
account, published 87 years after the battle,
confuses events at the Forty with Stoney Creek.
ADC's account is secondhand; Dwight, *Diary* 19,
*DocHis* 6, 12-16, Fiztgibbon to Somerville, 7 June
1813, *Hamilton Spectator,* 12 June 1889, What
Little Elizabeth Gage saw at Stony Creek. Lossing,
*Pictorial Field Book,* 604. *OHS* 44 4. Billy Green the
Scout; Biggar, *Battle of Stoney Creek.*

2. Smith's Knoll, site of the current Lion's monument
parkette on King Street; Biggar, *Battle of Stoney
Creek*; The church occupied the high ground in
what is now Stoney Creek cemetery on King Street,
just west of the Highway 20 intersection.

3. HPL, Thompson Papers, The Battle of Stoney
Creek as related at by an Eye Witness; United
Church Archives, Journal of Reverend George Fer-
guson. *Hamilton Spectator,* 2 January 1932, Charles
McCulloch, Stories of Stoney Creek.

4. *Hamilton Spectator,* 6 June 1889, How We Did
Them Up. The article said Blachford unearthed
"relics" the previous summer; The original grant
was Lot 26, Concession 3, Saltfleet Township; Allen
Ernest Smith, 1878-1932. Two of Smith's granddaughters, Bernice Ott of Hamilton and Helen
Crichton of Winona, say he made the initial discovery when he was a boy.

5. *Ye Olde Tyme Entertainment,* souvenir book and
programme, April 1900. "Reminiscences of the
Battle of Stoney Creek" by Peter Van Wagner.

6. *Hamilton Evening Times,* 6 June 1889, The Pioneer
Picnic; *Journals and Transactions, Wentworth His-
torical Society,* Vol 3, 33, "Historic Value of Smith's
Knoll," George H. Mills. *Hamilton Spectator,* 2
January 1932, Charles R. McCullough, Stories of
Stoney Creek.

7. Louise Wilson, great granddaughter of Hiram
Smith, letter to the author, 7 June 1999. Wilson,
who grew up on the farm said: "Two acres near
the Smith Knoll site remained untouched and not
tilled, by instructions handed down from grand-

parents to grandparents." Wilson said her grandfather, Dilly Coleman campaigned unsuccessfully for a museum in Stoney Creek. The artifacts were lost after his death. *Journals and Transactions, Wentworth Historical Society,* Vol 3, 33, "Historic Value of Smith's Knoll," George H. Mills. "Mr. Smith, the owner of the knoll, had a considerable collection of relics of the battle, all taken from the knoll. These may be seen by calling upon him."

8. *HPL,* Archives File, Wentworth Historical Society, 13 June 1894. Kingsford, *The History of Canada,* 8 277. Visiting the knoll in 1895, Kingsford reported : "Many human remains have been found there, with old buttons and belt-plates of the 8th or King's and of the 49th regiment, as well as those of the artillery of both services."; *Hamilton Spectator,* 10 May 1908. Consecration of Soldiers' Plot. The ceremony was conducted by Bishop John Phillip DuMoulin and witnessed by a crowd of 1,000, including 600 members of the militia; The abstract for the knoll transfer at the Hamilton Land Registry Office incorrectly lists the consideration as $4,000. The correct figure, as per the deed, is $400.

9. Hamilton, Grimsby and Beamsville Electric Railway Company, 1896-1931; Rita Griffin-Short, the archeologist who excavated the knoll in 1998 and 1999 confirmed such a possibility in a 13 January 2006 address to the Head-of-the-Lake Historical Society in Hamilton. "In the late 19th Century the electric railway was built and I'm sure that in excavating all that area they probably found other human bones. Either it was reported and nobody has it, or it was just ignored."

10. *HPL,* WHS Archives File, Gardner to WHS, 1 October 1907.

11. The stone lion was created by Ottawa sculptor Hamilton MacCarthy. creator of South African War monuments in Halifax and Charlottetown, the Ottawa and Quebec Champlain statues and the Annapolis Royal de Monts memorial; Plaque inscription from Lion's Monument celebrates the "23 good and true". In 1926 the American Daughters of 1812 presented a small bronze plaque commemorating the US dead that was embedded at ground level on the monument site; The Wentworth County Veterans' Association evolved into Her Majesty's Army and Navy Veterans' Society of Hamilton which ceded ownership of the Knoll to the City of Stoney Creek in 1995. In 2001 Stoney Creek was amalgamated as part of greater Hamilton.

12. *Hamilton Spectator,* 4 June 1999, Dig finds desecrated bones of 1812 troops by James Elliott. Interview notes taken 3 June 1999 by the author. Casual regard for human remains from the War of 1812 was by no means restricted to Stoney Creek. In 1853 following demolition of the original damaged Brock's Monument at Queeenston, the *Niagara Mail* reported that upon entering Brock's tomb "the clownish and ignorant workmen proceeded, without ceremony, to shovel up the bones, dust and dirt, all together." Malcomson, *Brilliant Affair,* 217

13. *Ibid.*

14. Formed the 1758, the 66th was amalgamated in 1881 with the 49th to form the The Princess Charlotte of Wales's (Berkshire Regiment); *Hamilton Spectator,* 28 September 1999, Troops' bones hint at life in the 19th century.

15. Griffin-Short, 1999 Field Work at Smith's Knoll Cemetery. Recommendations, 2-4. June 2000

16. The Village Green apartment complex occupies nearly every square foot of the northeast section of the battlefield.

17. Interview with the author, 20 December 2005.

18. *Ibid.*

19. Interview with the author, 20 December 2005, 5 January 2006.

20. Dilly Coleman, 1871-1956, married Nellie Victoria Smith, second child of Hiram and Louisa . The Colemans inherited the 12-acre, fruit and flower farm adjacent to Smith's Knoll. Coleman served as a Justice of the Peace in Stoney Creek; Letter to the author, 7 June 1999.

21. *Ibid.*

22. *Ibid.* Interview with the author, 9 January 2006.

23. *Human Skeletal Remains, Smith's Knoll Historic Cemetery,* Maria A. Liston, May 2000. Interview notes, Maria Liston, 6 April 2000, author's collection. See also *Hamilton Spectator,* 13 April 2000, James Elliott, Old bones give up their secrets.

24. Interview with the author, 11 March 2004.

25. The shooting took place at an outdoor trap range in Niagara Falls, Crowland Gun Club; *Human Skeletal Remains, Smith's Knoll Historic Cemetery,* Maria A. Liston, May 2000; The Canadian 25 cent coin is 23.88 mm or slightly less than an inch and the $1 loonie, at 26.5 mm is slightly more.

26. *Journals and Transactions, Wentworth Historical Society,* Vol 3, 33, "Historic Value of Smith's Knoll," George H. Mills.

27. Interview notes, Donald E. Graves, 6 April 2000, author's collection.

28. Interview notes, Maria Liston, 6 April 2000, author's collection.

29. Officially the 3rd U.S. Infantry Regiment, the Old Guard is a largely ceremonial unit based in Fort Myer, VA. best known as the guard of the Tomb of the Unknown Soldier. In reference to its distinguished service in the Mexican War, 1846-1848, it is the only American infantry unit to parade with fixed bayonets.; *The Hamilton Spectator,* 5 June 2000, Final rest for dead of crucial battle. Anne Bain, mayor of Stoney Creek,said "We thought this very befitting to have a proper burial. We wanted to make sure there was a memory of the soldiers who helped Canada and were never really buried properly."; Anna Bradford, manager of culture and recreation for the city of Hamilton said in 2006 there were no immediate plans to follow through

on Griffin-Short's recommendations. "We've got some other priority projects right now going on at Battlefield (Park) and there's only so much money."

## Appendix C: The Second Battle of Stoney Creek

1. Sarah Anne Curzon, 1833-1898, see *DCB* 12; The Pioneer and Historical Association of Ontario – formed on 4 September 1888 – evolved ten years later into the Ontario Historical Society. This era, Carl Berger wrote in *The Sense of Power*, was "truly the golden age of local history and the local historical society became the chief instrument for popularizing the past."; The founders of the WHS were John H. Land, grandson of Hamilton pioneer, Robert Land, George Barton, an Irish-born lawyer and politician, George H. Mills, a lawyer and former mayor who was a staunch Canadian nationalist, Frederick W. Fearman, a pioneer meatpacker, and Sir John Gibson, a lawyer and politician who would become attorney general and lieutenant governor of Ontario. See *DHB* 1 and 2. By 1894 the society had dropped pioneer from its name ; The picnic was held on the William Nash estate, directly across King Street from the current Stoney Creek Cemetery ; Both the *Hamilton Spectator* and the *Hamilton Times* of 6 June 1889 estimated the crowd at 500, three years later the WHS in Vol. 1 of its Journals and Transactions put the figure at 1,000 ; Curzon would only live another nine years but her influence was considerable. When she died in 1898 the Wentworth Historical Society mourned a woman who "left an indelible impress upon our national life." ; *Hamilton Spectator,* 6 June 1899. How We Did Them Up.

2. *Hamilton Evening Times,* 6 June 1899. The Pioneer Picnic.

3. *Ibid.*

4. See *DHB* 2. Freed, who was born in Beamsville, worked on the *New York Tribune* under its legendary editor Horace Greeley and fought in the American Civil War with the 27th Connecticut before returning to Hamilton as editor of the *Hamilton Spectator* for 12 years; *Hamilton Evening Times,* 6 June 1899. The Pioneer Picnic.

5. *Ibid.*

6. *Ibid* ; See *DHB* 2, *DCB* 14, Sara Galbraith Beemer.

7. MacCuaig, *Women's Art Association of Hamilton,* 8; *Hamilton Spectator,* 14 October 1914, Honored Memory of Noble Woman.

8. HPL, WHS archives, Mills to Caron, 20 March 1890. In his correspondence at least, Mills would continue to spell Stoney Creek as Stony Creek for ten years; LAC, RG 24 v 6559 HQ-899-11 v 2, 8 Dec 1899 Calder to Benoit; The gracious design of Charles Mulligan, the main court room featured a 30-foot ceiling with a dome skylight in the centre. Completed in 1879, it was torn down in 1957 amid considerable regret.

9. The Calder banner, for many years a fixture in the

Hamilton Public Library has been restored and is now on permanent loan to Battlefield House Museum in Stoney Creek from the Head-of-the-Lake Historical Society.

10. *WHS,* Journal and Transaction, v. 2 152.

11. Calder said her great-grandfather was killed fighting under the old flag in the revolutionary war, whereas subsequent genealogical research has revealed that while James Gage was indeed killed fighting in the Revolution, he was not on the British side. *Gage Families* by Clyde V. Gage cites New York State pension records indicating Mary Gage, widow of James Gage, a private in the Ulster County Militia, drew a pension "due to me on the death of my late husband who was slain on 6th of October 1777 in the defence of Fort Clinton." Murray Killman, in *Stoney Creek: The Skeletons in its Closet,* is more blunt. "Contrary to the propaganda that has proliferated over the years, they were not United Empire Loyalists." Calder could claim UE status through her maternal grandfather Ebenezer Jones, but not through the Gage line.

12. *WHS,* Journal and Transactions, v. 2 153-4.

13. *Ibid,* v. 3 92

14. *WHS,* Journal and Transactions, v. 3, 92; Maslin, *High Tea*; MacCuaig, *Women's Art Association of Hamilton,* 8.

15. The original Ladies' Committee executive included Harriet Sanford, wife of Senator William Sanford, Priscilla Grace Teetzel, wife of Hamilton city councilor James Teetzel who would become mayor in 1899, Emma Francis Pratt, wife of retailer Thomas Henry Pratt, Marianam Martin, wife of lawyer Edward Martin, Janet Legatt, wife of hardware magnate Matthew Leggat, Caroline Papps, wife of lawyer George Papps and Frances Gates, widow of Arthur Robert Gates and daughter of WHS president George Mills; *Hamilton Spectator,* 21 May 1895. An Historic Auxiliary.

16. *Hamilton Spectator,* 23 November 1895.

17. Maslin, *High Tea.*

18. MacCuaig, *Women's Art Association of Hamilton,* 7.

19. *DCB* 2, 14, Beemer, Sara Galbraith.

20. *WHS,* Journal and Transactions, 3, 94.

21. The society appears to have been somewhat unrealistic about how much money was available. Early in 1898, one member of the executive told Borden, "we hope to hear a sum of ten to fifteen thousand dollars shall be set aside by your government this year." LAC RG24 v 6559, HQ 899-11, 29 Jan 1898; The seven ministers were Adolphe-Philippe Caron, Mackenzie Bowell, James Patterson, Arthur Rupert Dickey, Alphonse Desjardin, David Tisdale and Frederick Borden; *HPL,* WHS Archives File, Mills to Wood, 5 February 1898.

22. See Colin S. Macdonald's *A Dictionary of Canadian Artists,* v 4 954. Sir John A. stands outside the provincial legislature in Toronto less than a mile from where the Ryerson statue overlooks Gould Street at Ryerson University; Thomas Taylor, *DHB* 1; *HPL,*

WHS Archives File, MacCarthy to Mills, 2 August 1899.

23. *Hamilton Spectator*, 6 June 1899, Women's Historical Society.

24. The other trustees were businessman William Hendrie and Calder's husband, John; LAC, RG24 v 6559, HQ 899 v 2, Calder to Borden 21 June 1899.

25. The petition reads like a Who's Who of early Stoney Creek and includes Greens, Cormans, Lottridges, Speras, Smiths, Lees, Glovers, Springsteads and Nashs; *DCB* 2, 14. *HPL*, WHS Archives File, Benoit to Mills, 23 June 1899.

26. HPL, WHS Archives File, Mills to Bain, 29 June 1899, Mills to Grant 30 June 1899, Mills to Bain 4 July 1899.

27. *Toronto Globe, Ottawa Times*; HPL, WHS Archives File, Bain to Mills, 15 July 1899.

28. *Ibid*, Benoit to Mills, 15 July 1899

29. Judging by the WHS correspondence the mail service of 1899, between Hamilton and Ottawa at least, appears to have been excellent. Two days was the norm and next-day service was not unheard of; *WHS Archives File*, Mills to Borden, 17 July 1899.

30. *Ibid*, Mills to Borden, 17 July 1899.

31. *Ibid* p 71, fragmentary letter from Mills; Mills to Bain, 17 July 1899.

32. *Ibid*, Benoit to Mills, 19 July 1899.

33. *Ibid*, Mills to Borden, 21 July 1899.

34. *Ibid*, Benoit to Mills, 22 July 1899.

35. *LAC*, RG24 v 6559 HW899-11, Woods to Pinault, 26 July 1899. Wood's presumption of superior knowledge derives from his first marriage to Mary Freeman, also a granddaughter of James Gage, who died in 1860.

36. *HPL*, WHS Archives File, Mills to Fearman, 8 August 1899.

37. *BHM*, WWHS Papers, Calder to Suilt, 25 July 1899.

38. *Ibid*. Which Mr. Corman is not clear, there were dozens of Isaac Corman's descendants living in Stoney Creek including seven who signed the petition supporting Smith's Knoll. The Stoney Creek Historical Society, a branch of the Wentworth Historical Society, officially supported Calder's site.

39. *Wentworth Landmarks*, 130.

40. *Hamilton Herald*, 23 October 1899, Now a Public Park. *DHB* 1, 171, Roach, Mary Emily.

41. HPL, WHS Archives File, MacCarthy to WHS, 21 November 1899.

42. *Ibid*, Benoit to Fearman 22 November 1899.

43. WHS, *Journal and Transactions*, 3, 100, Griffin to Benoit 27 November 1899.

44. LAC, RG 24 v 6559 HQ 899-11, Calder to Benoit, 8 December 1899.

45. Ibid.

46. See DCB 12, Frederick James Rastrick died in 1897 but the firm was carried on by two of his sons, Edward Llewellyn and Francis Reginald.

47. The Boer War, 1899-1902. Canada sent more than 7,000 volunteer troops to South Africa, 267 were killed including, Lieutenant Harold Borden of the Canadian Mounted Rifles, the only son of militia minister Frederick Borden. A monument to the 24-year-old McGill medical student, sculpted by Hamilton MacCarthy, was unveiled in 1903 in Canning, NS.

48. The Gore Park Queen Victoria statue by sculptor Louis-Philippe Hébert, was unveiled by Governor General Earl Grey before 22,000 people on 25 May 1908.

49. HPL, WHS Archives File, MacCarthy to WHS, 16 January 1905.

50. *Ibid*, Gardner to WHS, 1 October 1907, Land to Gardner, 18 October 1907; LAC, RG24 v 6559 HQ 899-11, Griffin to Borden, 15 February 1908.

51. *DHB* 2 15.

52. LAC, RG 24, v 6559 HQ 899-11, Calder to Benoit 8 December 1899.

53. *Hamilton Spectator*, 1 August 1908, Grant of $5,000.

54. LAC, RG24 v 6559 HQ 8999-11 Gardner to Borden, 22 July 1908.

55. Ibid, Calder to Borden, 4 August 1908.

56. Ibid, Pinault to Zimmerman, 6 August 1908.

57. *Hamilton Evening Times*, 29 August 1908, Minto Subscribes.

58. LAC, RG 24, v 6559 HQ 899-11 Seely to Pinault, 31 August 1908.

59. Ibid, Calder to Borden, 31 August 1908.

60. Ibid, Jarvis to Martin, 10 September 1908.

61. Ibid, Martin to Jarvis, 22 September 1908.

62. Ibid, Gardner to Zimmerman, 20 October 1908.

63. Kirwan Martin, *DHB* 4; WHS Archives File, Martin to Jarvis, 21 November 1908.

64. Ibid, Fiset to Calder, 30 November 1908.

65. *DHB* 2.

66. *Ibid*. minutes of meeting, 6 January 1909. Samuel Barker told the meeting it "was the intention of the government to give the money to the Women's Wentworth Historical Society."

67. Although Frederick James Rastrick had been dead for 16 years, the firm carried only his name. His sons, Edward and Francis remained largely anonymous. All transactions and correspondence regarding the Stoney Creek monument were signed F. J. Rastrick & Sons although the design work is credited to Edward. See *DHB* 3; A veteran of the Sudan and the Boer War, French was the first commander of the British Expeditionary Force in the First World War. In his address at the ceremony, French paid a backhanded compliment to one of the heroes of Stoney Creek, Major Charles Plenderleath. "An officer, whose name I cannot remember, went and silenced several of the enemy's guns, captured two or three generals and turned the whole tide of the war." *Hamilton Herald*, 27 May 1910, Corner Stone Laid Under Distinguished Auspices.

68. Edward Rastrick, *DHB* 3; Hucker, *Stoney Creek Monument*, 6.

69. *Hamilton Spectator*, 17 June 1911, "Women's Wentworth Historical Society"; Beemer, *DCB* 15.

70. LAC, RG 24, v 6559, HQ 899-11, Fiset to Hughes, 2 December 1911.

71. *Ibid*, Calder to Hughes, 18 December 1911.

72. *Ibid*, Rastrick to Fiset, 4 March 1912. Dickenson to Militia Counil, 21 March 1912. Labourers on the job were paid 20 cents an hour, a team and driver cost $6 a day and a horse alone, cost $2 a day or the same as a labourer earned in a 10-hour day.

73. *Ibid*, Rastrick to Calder, 29 January 1912.

74. Dickenson to Militia Council, 21 March 1912.

75. *Ibid*, Specifications for the several Trades to be required and materials to be used in erecting a Monument, 12 June 1912.

76. Ibid, Boudreau Memo, 3 July 1919.

77. *Hamilton Herald*, 7 June 1913. Great and Glorious Victory Honored. *Toronto Daily Star*, 6 June 1913, 15,000 People saw unveiling of Monument; Five hundred boy scouts drawn from all over the region camped on the grounds overnight as a guard of honour; Mary Agnes FitzGibbon was also grand-daughter of Susanna Moodie. A pair of wreaths from the King's Regiment and the Princess Charlotte of Wale's (Royal Berkshire Regiment) the successor of the 49th Foot, were laid at the base of the monument. Both had been prepared in England and carried to Canada on the White Star liner *RMS Teutonic*. *Manitoba Free Press*, 5 June 1913, Anniversary of Stoney Creek Victory.

78. *Hamilton Evening Times*, 7 June 1913, Stoney Creek Function. Ethel McIntosh interview, family collection. McIntosh, who died in 1998 at the age of 94, was one of the last surviving witnesses of the monument unveiling. The ceremony made a lasting impression on McIntosh but was largely lost on her younger brother, Ransom Lounsbury who was more interested in rolling down the hill and catching tadpoles in the creek.

79. Queen Mary's brief and remote involvement with the unveiling of the Stoney Creek monument is entirely in keeping with her public persona. Intensely shy she made only two official speeches in her entire public life and her only broadcast contact with her subjects consisted of the twenty-eight words with which she christened the Cunard liner that bore her name.

80. McIntosh interview.

81. *Hamilton Spectator*, 15 June 1910, Annual Meeting.; *Hamilton Evening Times*, 7 June 1913, Stoney Creek Function.

82. LAC, RG 24 6559, HQ 899-11, Calder to Hughes, 12 January 1914.

83. *Hamilton Spectator*, 16 March 1914, Mrs. Calder Claimed by Death.

84. *Hamilton Spectator*, 19 October 1914, Honored Memory of Noble Woman.

85. LAC, RG 24 V 6559, HQ 899-11, Lynch-Staunton to Macdonald, 1 April 1925.

86. In the late 50s and early 60s with commercial development booming in Stoney Creek, proposals for Battlefield Park included high-rise apartments and a swimming pool complex. In 1971 the site attracted only 1,500 paying visitors. *Hamilton Spectator*, 17 June 1972, Boost battlefield, tourism plea.

# Bibliography

PRIMARY SOURCES – ARCHIVAL

Archives of Ontario
    MS 842, Journal of a Staff Officer
    MS MU2095, The Veterans of 1812
Battlefield House Museum
    WWHS Papers
Connecticut Historical Society
    George Howard Letterbook
Folger Library, University of Maine
    John Chandler Journal
Hamilton Public Library, Local History & Archives
    Battle of Stoney Creek Scrapbook
    Mabel Thompson Collection/Papers
    Diary of D. Slater
    Wentworth Historical Society, Archives File
    Women's Wentworth Historical Society Scrapbooks
Library and Archives Canada
    Record Group 1, land grand petitions
    Record Group 8, C-2936, Bruyeres' inspection reports
    Record Group 8, C-3233, General Entry Book of American Prisoners of War at Quebec
    Record Group 8, Memorial of Thomas Nairne
    Record Group 9, 1B7. vol. 24, 5th Regiment, Lincoln Militia
    Record Group 24, vol. 6559, correspondence
    Manuscript Group 19, F1, Claus Papers
    Manuscript Group 19, E5, Board of Claims for War Losses
    Manuscript Group 24, F16, Simonds Papers
    Manuscript Group 24, F18, Four Years on the Lakes of Canada by David Wingfield
Library of Congress, Washington, D.C.
    Samuel Smith Family Papers
Lily Library, Indiana University
    War of 1812 Manuscripts
Massachusetts Historical Society
    Henry Dearborn Papers
    Charles E. French Papers
    Vaughan Family Papers
Maryland Historical Society
    MS 919 William H. Winder Papers
Mercer County Historical Society
    Mercer County Estate # 126 OS, James Crawford will
Minnesota Historical Society
    Taliaferro Papers, vol. 1, Order Book
National Archives, Kew, Surrey
    War Office 12, Muster books and pay lists
    War Office 25, Casualty returns
    War Office 27, Inspection returns
National Archives of the United States
    RG 94, M1832 Returns of the Killed and Wounded of American Troops, Compiled by Col. J. H. Eaton

Registry of Enlistments in the United States Army, 1798-1914, vol. 1-2

Muster Rolls United States Army 1812-1814

List of British Prisoners of War at Fort Niagara, 8 June 1813

Descriptive list of British prisoners at Greenbush 6 September 1813

RG 98, List of Prisoners Paroled after taking of Fort George 27 May 1813

Old War Invalid Files

New York State Historical Society

Henry Dearborn Letterbooks

New York State Library

Gardner papers

South Carolina Historical Society

Whitridge Papers

Syracuse University Library

Osborne Family Papers

Toronto Reference Library

Ann Powell Letters

United Church Archives, Toronto

Journal of Reverend George Ferguson

Welch Regiment Museum, Cardiff

The War in Canada 1812-1814 by James Cochran

## PRIMARY SOURCES – PUBLISHED

**Newspapers and Periodicals**

*Acadiensis,* 1923

*Albany Argus,* 1813

*Albany Gazette,* 1813

*Albany Register,* 1813

*American Advocate,* Hallowell, Maine, 1812, 1817

*American Mercury,* Hartford, 1813

*American Watchman,* 1813

*Baltimore American and Commercial Daily Advertiser,* 1824

*Baltimore Patriot,* 1813, 1824

*Baltimore Whig,* 1813

*Bathurst Courier,* 1842, 1847

*Buffalo Gazette,* 1813

*Boston Daily Advertiser,* 1813

*Boston Patriot,* 1811, 1812, 1813.

*Broome County Patriot,* 1812

*Canada Constellation,* 1800

*Canadian Courant,* 1813

*Canadian Magazine,* 1893

*Carolina Federal Republican,* 1813

*Chronicle,* Harrisburg, Penn., 1813

*City Gazette,* Charlotte, 1820

*Columbian,* New York, 1812

*Columbian Centinel,* Boston, 1813

*Columbian Phenix,* 1813

*Commercial Advertiser,* New York, 1813

*Connecticut Mirror,* 1813

*Courier,* Washington, 1812

*East Gloucester Election,* 1854

*Enquirer,* Richmond, 1813

*Evening Star,* St. Catharines, 1889

*Federal Republican,* Georgetown, 1812, 1814
*Gentleman's Magazine,* 1813
*Globe,* Toronto, 1852
*Hagers-town Gazette,* Halifax, Maryland, 1813
*Hamilton Evening Times,* 1875, 1889
*Hamilton Herald,* 1889
*Hamilton Spectator,* 1873, 1875, 1889, 1890, 1893, 1894, 1899, 1908, 1909, 1910, 1911, 1912, 1913, 1931,
    1932 1938, 1957, 1999, 2000
*Independent Chronicle,* Boston, 1817
*Mail and Empire,* 1913, 1935
*Mercantile Advertiser,* New York 1812, 1813
*National Advocate,* Burlington, 1813
*New England Galaxy,* Boston, 1820
*New York Evening Post,* 1813
*New York Spectator,* 1813
*Niagara Herald,* 1801
*Niles Weekly Register,* 1813-1817
*North American Semi-Weekly,* Toronto, 1852
*Northern Post,* Salem, N.Y., 1813
*Northern Whig,* Hudson, N.Y., 1813
*Portico,* 1816
*Portland Gazette,* 1813
*Portsmouth Journal of Literature and Politics,* 1824
*Poulson's American Daily Advertiser,* 1813
*Republican Star,* Easton, Md., 1813
*Quebec Gazette,* 1813
*Quebec Mercury,* 1816
*Repertory,* Boston, 1813
*Republican,* Plattsburgh, 1813
*Statesman,* New York 1813
*The Times,* 1813
*Toronto Daily Star,* 1913
*United States Gazette,* 1813
*Village Register,* Dedham, 1829

**Published Documents**

Brannan, John, ed. *Official Letters of the Military and Naval Officers of the United States during the War
    with Great Britain in the Years 1812, 13, 14 & 15.* Washington: Way and Gideon, 1823
Cruikshank, Ernest A., ed. *Documentary History of the Campaigns upon the Niagara Frontier in 1812-1814.*
    Welland: Tribune Press, 1896-1908, 9 vols.
Cruikshank, Ernest A., ed. *Records of Niagara,* 44. Niagara-on-the-Lake: Niagara Historical Society, 1939.
Dudley, William S., ed. *The Naval War of 1812: A Documentary History,* vol. 2. Washington: Naval
    Historical Center, 1992.
Johnston, Charles M., ed. *The Valley of the Six Nations: A Collection of Documents on Indian Lands of the
    Grand River.* Toronto: The Champlain Society, 1964
Powell, R. Janet, ed. *Annals of the Forty: 1783–1818.* Grimsby: The Grimsby Historical Society, 1955
United States Congress. *American State Papers: Class V, Military Affairs,* vol. 1. Washington: Gales &
    Seaton, 1832
Wood, William C., ed. *Selection British Documents of the Canadian War of 1812.* 4 vols. Toronto,
    Champlain Society, 1920-1928

**Published Memoirs, Diaries, Journals and Correspondence**

*American*

Anonymous. "First Campaign of An A.D.C.," *Military and Naval Magazine of the United States,* 1834. 3: 10-20, 4: 73-82, 5: 200-210, 6: 278-288, 7: 172-182, 8: 258-266

Anonymous. *Sketch of the Life of Major Gen. Henry Dearborn,* campaign literature, 1817.

Armstrong, John. *Notices Of the War of 1812.* New York: George Dearborn, 1836

Boyd, John Parker. *Documents and Facts Relative to Military Events During the Late War.* Washington: n.p. 1816

Burn, James. "Colonel James Burn and the War of 1812: The Letters of a South Carolina Officer," ed. John C. Fredriksen, *South Carolina Historical Magazine,* 90 (October 1989), 299- 312

Chandler, John. "General John Chandler of Monmouth Maine, with extracts from his Autobiography," ed George Foster Talbot, *Collections of the Maine Historical Society Vol. 9,* Portland, 1887.

Duane, William, "The Letters of William Duane," ed. Worthington C. Ford, *Proceedings of the Massachusetts Historical Society,* 20, Boston: 1906-1907.

Dunlop, William [89th Regiment of Foot]. *Recollections of the American War 1812-1814.* Toronto: Historical Publishing Company, 1905.

Dwight, Joseph [Thirteenth Infantry]. "Plow-Joggers for Generals: The Experience of a New York Ensign in the War 1812," ed. John C. Fredriksen, *Indiana Military History Journal,* 11 (1986) 16-27

Ford, Amasiah [Twenty-Third Infantry]. *Soldiers of 1814.* ed. Donald E. Graves, Lewiston, N.Y.: Old Fort Niagara Press, 1996

Hamilton, James [Rifles]. *The Life and Dying Confessions of James Hamilton.* ed. Calvin Pepper, Albany: 1818.

Kearsley, Jonathan [Artillery]. "The Memoirs of Jonathan Kearsley: A Michigan Hero from the War of 1812," ed. John C. Fredriksen, *Indiana Military History Journal,* vol. 10, 2 (May 1985), 4-16.

Mann, James [Surgeon]. *Medical Sketches of the Campaigns of 1812, 1813, and 1814.* Dedham, Mass.: H. Mann, 1816

Macdonough, Patrick [Artillery]. *Copy of Letters written by Patrick McDonogh of Philadelphia, Lieutenant in the Second Regiment of U.S. Artillery, during the War of 1812.* Buffalo Historical Society Publications, Vol. V. Buffalo: 1911.

McFeely, George [Twenty-Second Infantry]. "Chronicle of Valor: The Journal of a Pennsylvania Office in the War of 1812" ed. John C. Fredriksen. *The Western Pennsylvania Historical Magazine,* vol. 67, July 1984, 243-284

Melish, John. *Travels in the United States of America,* vol. II, Philadelphia, 1812.

Myers, Mordecai [Thirteenth Infantry]. *Reminiscences 1780-1814. Including Incidents in the War of 1812-1814.* Washington: Crane, 1900.

Myers, Ned [U.S. Navy]. *A Life Before the Mast.* ed J. Fenimore Cooper. Annapolis: United States Naval Institute, 1989

Patterson, John [Twenty-Second Infantry]. "The Letters and John Patterson, 1812-1813," ed. Florence and Mary Howard, *Pennsylvania Historical Magazine, 23, June 1940*

Pearce, Cromwell [Sixteenth Infantry]. "A Poor But Honest War Sodger': Colonel Cromwell Pearce, the 16th U.S. Infantry and, the War of 1812," ed. John C. Fredriksen, *Pennsylvania History* 52 (1985), 131-161.

Roach, Isaac. "Journal of Major Isaac Roach, 1812-1824," ed. Mary Roach Archer, *The Pennsylvania Magazine of History and Biography, 17 (1893) 129-158.*

Scott, Winfield. *Memoirs of Lieut-General Scott, LL.D: Written by Himself.* New York: Sheldon & Company, 1864.

Shaler, Ephraim [Twenty-Fifth Infantry]. "Memoirs of Captain Ephraim Shaler: A Connecticut Yankee in the War of 1812," 3, ed. John C. Fredriksen. *The New England Quarterly,* vol. 57, no. Sept. 1984, pp 411-420.

Shepard, Elihu Hotchkiss, *The Autobiography of Elihu H. Shepard,* St. Louis, G. Knapp & Co., 1869

Simcoe, Elizabeth. *The Diary of Mrs. John Graves Simcoe,* ed. J. Ross Robertson. Toronto: Ontario Publishing, 1934

Smith, Joseph Lee [Twenty-Fifth Infantry]. "Lawyer, Soldier, Judge: Incidents in the Life of Joseph Lee

Smith of New Britain, Connecticut," ed John C. Fredriksen, *The Connecticut Historical Society Bulletin*, 51 (1986) 103-121.

Wilkinson, James. Memoirs *of my own times.* Philadelphia: Abraham Small, 1816

**British and Canadian**

Commins, James [8th Foot]. "Letters Written by Sergt. James Commins, 8th Foot," ed. Norman C. Lord, *Journal of the Society of Army Historical Research, 18 (1939) 199-211.*

Hennell, George. *A Gentleman Volunteer. The Letters of George Hennell from the Peninsular War, 1812-1813.* ed. Michael Glover. London: Heineman, 1979.

Merritt, William Hamilton. [Provincial Light Dragoons]. *A Desire of Serving and Defending My Country: The War of 1812 Journals of William Hamilton Merritt.* ed Stuart Sutherland. Toronto: Iser, 2001

Norton, John [Indian Department]. *The Journal of Major John Norton 1816,* eds., J.J. Talman & C.F. Klinck. Toronto: The Champlain Society, 1970.

Tupper, Ferdinand Brock. *The Life and Correspondence of Major-General Sir Isaac Brock.* London: Simpkin, Marshall & Co. 1845; ebook, Project Gutenberg, 2004

**Biographical Encyclopedias, Registers, Dictionaries and Military Units**

*American Statesman's Kalendar and Register for 1813.* New York: D. Langworth, Shakespeare Gallery, 1813.

Boatner, Mark Mayo. *Encyclopedia of the American Revolution.* New York: David McKay Company, 1966.

*Dictionary of American Biography.* New York: Charles Scribner's Sons. 1928-1936. 20 vols.

*Dictionary of American Biography.* New York: Scribner, 1958-1964. 22 vols.

*Dictionary of Canadian Biography.* vols. 5-9. Toronto: University of Toronto, 1976-1988

Dodge, Prentiss C. *Encyclopedia Vermont Biography: A Series of Authentic Biographical Sketches.* Burlington: Ullery Publishing, 1912.

Heitman, Francis B. *Historical Register and Dictionary of the U.S. Army* 2 vols. Washington: Government Printing Office, 1903.

Homfray, Irving L. *Officers of the British Forces in Canada during the War of 1912-15.* Welland: Canadian Military Institute, 1908.

Powell, William H. *List of Officers of the Army of the United States from 1779 to 1900.* New York: L. R. Hamersly, 1900.

Sutherland, Stuart. *His Majesty's Gentlemen. A Directory of British Regular Army Officers of the War of 1812.* Toronto: Iser, 2000.

Smy, William A. and Alan Holden. *Casualties of the Militia of Lincoln County in the War of 1812.* St. Catharines: Colonel John Butler Branch United Empire Loyalists' Association of Canada, 2002

Winearls, Joan. *Mapping Upper Canada, 1780-1867: An Annotated Bibliography of Manuscript and Printed Maps.* Toronto: University of Toronto, 1991

**Period Military Regulations, Treatises and Technical Literature**

Clausewitz, Carl, *On War,* ed. translated Michael Howard, Peter Paret. London: David Campbell, 1993

Clausewitz, Carl, *On War,* translated J. J. Graham. London: Kegan Paul, Trench, Trubner, 1911

Smyth, Alexander. *Regulations for the Field Exercise, Manoeuvres, and Conduct of the Infantry of the United States.* Philadelphia: Anthony Finley, 1812

## SECONDARY SOURCES

**Books**

Adams, Henry. *The War of 1812,* ed. H.A. DeWeerd. New York: Cooper Square, 1999.

Agar, Herbert. *The Price of Union.* Boston: Houghton Mifflin, 1950.

Anonymous. *General Scott and his Staff.* Philadelphia: Grigg, Elliot & Co., 1848

Anonymous. *Taylor and his Generals.* Philadelphia: E.H. Butler & Co., 1847.

Antal, Sandy. *A Wampum Denied.* Ottawa: Carleton University Press, 1997.

Armstrong, John. *Hints to Young Generals by an Old Soldier.* Kingston: J. Buel, 1812.

Auchinleck, Gilbert. *A History of the War between Great Britain and the United States.* Toronto: Mclear & Company, 1855.

Benn, Carl. *The Iroquois in the War of 1812.* Toronto: University of Toronto, 1998.

Berger, Carl. *The Sense of Power.* Toronto: University of Toronto, 1970.

Biggar, E.B. "The Battle of Stony Creek". *Canadian Magazine, Vol. 1.* Toronto: Ontario Publishing Company, 1893.

Bonnycastle, Richard Henry, and James Edward Alexander. *Canada, as It Was, Is, and May Be.* London: Colburn, 1852, 2 vols.

Brackenridge, H. M. *History of the Late War between the United States and Great Britain.* Philadelphia: James Kay, 1839.

Brewster, Margaret Isabel Fraser. *Descendants of Simon Fraser of Laggan, Inverness-Shire, Scotland.* Bradenton, Fl.: 1956.

Cain, Emily. *Ghost Ships: Hamilton and Scourge.* Toronto: Musson, 1983.

Campbell, Marjorie Freeman. *A Mountain and a City.* Toronto: McClelland and Stewart, Toronto, 1966.

Canniff, William. *The Medical Profession in Upper Canada 1783-1850.* Toronto: William Briggs, 1894.

Cannon, Richard. *Historical Record of the Eighth or the King's Regiment of Foot.* London: Parker, 1844.

Chartrand, René. *Uniforms and Equipment of the United States Forces in the War of 1812.* Youngstown: Old Fort Niagara Association, 1992.

Coleman, Margaret. *The American Capture of Fort George, Ontario.* Ottawa: Parks Canada, 1977.

Corman, Hazel. "An Account of the Battle of Stoney Creek." *Papers and Records of the Wentworth Historical Society, Vol. 7.* Hamilton: 1916.

Christie, Robert. *The Military and Naval Operations in the Canadas during the Late War with the United States.* New York: Oram & Mott, 1818.

Cruikshank, Ernest. *The Battle of Fort George.* Niagara-on-the-Lake: Niagara Historical Society, 1990.

Cruikshank, Earnest. *Fight in the Beechwoods.* Welland: Lundy's Lane Historical Society, 1895.

Cruikshank, Ernest. "Public Life and Services of Robert Nichol." *Papers and Records/Ontario Historical Society, Vol. 19.* Toronto: Ontario Historical Society, 1922.

Durant, Samuel W. and Henry B. Peirce. *History of St. Lawrence Co., New York, with illustrations and biographical sketches of some of its prominent men and pioneers, 1749-1878.* Philadelphia: L.H. Everts & Co., 1878.

Elting, John. *Amateurs to Arms! A Military History of the War of 1812.* Chapel Hill, N.C.: Algonquin, 1991

FitzGibbon, Mary Ages. *A Veteran of 1812.* Toronto: William Briggs, 1894.

Gage, Clyde V. *Gage Families.* Worcester, N.Y.: 1965.

Gates, Curtis. *Our County and its People: A Memorial Record of St. Lawrence County,* New York. Syracuse: D. Mason & Company, 1894.

Gillett, M.C. *The Army Medical Department, 1775-1818.* Washington: The Government Printing Office, 1981.

Gourlay, Robert. *Statistical Account of Upper Canada Compiled with a View to a Grand System of Emigration.* London: Simpkin & Marshalll, 1822, 2 vols.

Graves, Donald E. *Field of Glory: The Battle of Crysler's Farm, 1813.* Toronto: Robin Brass Studio, 1999.

Graves, Donald E. *Where Right and Glory Lead! The Battle of Lundy's Lane, 1814.* Toronto: Robin Brass Studio, 1997

Griffin-Short, Rita. *1999 Field Work At Smith's Knoll Historic Cemetery for the City of Stoney Creek.* Stoney Creek: June 2000.

Hamilton Branch United Empire Loyalists' Association of Canada. *Loyalist Ancestors: Some Families of the Hamilton Area.* Toronto: Pro Familia, 1986.

Hitsman, J.M. *The Incredible War of 1812: A Military History.* Toronto: Robin Brass Studio, 1999.

Holden, Alan and William Smy. *Casualties of the Militia of Lincoln County in the War of 1812.* St. Catharines: Colonel John Butler Branch, United Empire Loyalists' Association of Canada, 2002.

Howison, John. *Sketches of Upper Canada.* Edinburgh: Oliver & Boyd, 1822

Ingersoll, Charles J. *Historical Sketch of the Second War Between the United States and Great Britain,* vol. 1. Philadelphia: Lea & Blanchard, 1845.

James, William. *A Full and Correct Account of the Military Occurrences of the Late War between Great Britain and the United States.* London: Black, 1818, 2 vols.

Johnston, Charles M. *A Battle for the Heartland.* Hamilton: 1965.

Johnston, Charles M. *The Head of the Lake: A History of Wentworth County.* Hamilton: Wentworth County Council, 1958.

Johnson, Paul. *Birth of the Modern: World Society 1815-1830.* New York: Harper Collins, 1991.

Keyes, Ralph. *The Quote Verifier.* New York: St. Martin's Griffin, 2006.

Kingsford, William. *The History of Canada,* vol. 8. Toronto: Rowsell & Hutchinson, 1895.

Kirby, William. *Annals of Niagara.* Niagara Falls: Lundy's Lane Historical Society, 1896, 1972.

Land, John H. "Address to the Wentworth Historical Society, 21 March, 1889." *Journal and Transactions of the Wentworth Historical Society,* vol. 1. Hamilton: Spectator Printing, 1892.

Landon, Fred. *Western Ontario and the American Frontier.* Toronto: McClelland and Stewart, 1967.

Lossing, Benson J. *Pictorial Field-Book of the War of 1812.* New York: Harpers, 1868.

MacCuaig, Stuart. *Women's Art Association of Hamilton: The First 100 Years.* Hamilton: Art Gallery of Hamilton, 1996.

McGuire, Thomas J. *Battle of Paoli.* Mechanicsburg: Stackpole Books, 2000.

Malcomson, Robert. *Lords of the Lake: The Naval War on Lake Ontario, 1812-1814.* Toronto: Robin Brass Studio, 1998.

Mansfield, Edward, *The Life of General Winfield Scott.* New York: A.S. Barnes & Co., 1846

Matthews, Albert. "Uncle Sam." *Proceedings of the American Antiquarian Society,* vol. 19. Worcester: Davis Press, 1908.

Myatt, Frederick, *The Royal Berkshire Regiment (the 49th/66th Regiment of Foot).* London: Hamish Hamilton, 1968 (Famous Regiments).

Ord-Hulme, Arthur. *Perpetual Motion: The History of an Obsession,* London: George Allen & Unwin, 1977.

Petre, Francis Loraine. *The Royal Berkshire Regiment, v.1 1743-1914.* Reading: The Barracks, 1925.

Pratt, Julius W. *Expansionists of 1812.* New York: Peter Smith, 1949.

Quimby, Robert S. *The U.S. Army in the War of 1812. An Operational and Command Study.* East Lansing: Michigan State University, 1997, 2 vols.

Robinson, Fayette. *An Account of the Organization of the Army of the United States.* Philadelphia: E.H. Butler, 1848.

Smith, David William. *A short topographical description of His Majesty's province of Upper Canada in North America: to which annexed a provincial gazetteer.* London: W. Faden, 1813

Smith, John Henry. *Historical Sketch of the County of Wentworth and the Head of the Lake.* Hamilton: Wentworth County Council, 1897.

Smith, Michael. *Geographical View of the Province of Upper Canada and Promiscuous Remarks on the Government.* Trenton: Moore and Lake, 1813.

Smith, Michael. *Geographical View of the British Possessions in North America.* Baltimore: 1814.

Steiner, Bernard Christian. *The Life and Correspondence of James McHenry.* Cleveland: Burrows Brothers, 1907.

Thomson, John Lewis. *History of the War of the United States with Great Britain in 1812.* Philadelphia: J. B. Lippincott Company, 1887. (Originally published 1818 as *Historical Sketches of the late War between the United States and Great Britain* by Thomas Desilver, Philadelphia).

Tucker, Glenn. *Poltroons and Patriots.* New York: Bobbs-Merrill, 1954, 2 vols.

Wentworth Historical Society. *Journal and Transactions of the Wentworth Historical Society, Vol. 4.* Hamilton: 1905.

*Wentworth Landmarks.* Hamilton: Spectator Printing Company, 1897.

Wilder, Patrick. *The Battle of Sackett's Harbour: 1813.* Baltimore: The Nautical & Aviation Publishing Company, 1994.

### Articles

Biggar, E.B. "The Battle of Stony Creek." *Canadian Magazine,* vol. 1 (1893) 378-393.

Burghardt, Andrew F. "The Origin and Development of the Road Network of the Niagara Peninsula, Ontario, 1770-1851." *Annals of the Association of American Geographers,* 59, 3 (September 1969) 417-440.

Graves, Donald E. "American Ordnance in the War of 1812: A Preliminary Investigation." *Arms Collecting,* 31, 4 (November 1993) 111-120.

Hobbs, Raymond. *Thomas Taylor's War.* <http:fortyfirst.org/writings/taylor.htm> 2004.

Riddell, William R. "The First Canadian War-Time Prohibition Measure" *Canadian Historical Review,* vol. 1. (1920) 187-190.

Robinson, Ralph. "Retaliation for the Treatment of Prisoners in the War of 1812." *The American Historical Review,* 49, 1 (Oct. 1943) 65-70.

Roland, Charles. "War Amputations in Upper Canada." *Archivaria,* 10, (Summer 1980) 73-84.

Scripture, E.W. "Arithmatical Prodigies." *The American Journal of Psychology,* 4, 1 (April 1891) 11-17.

Singla, Rohit K. *Missed Opportunites: The Vaccine Act of 1813,* Cambridge, Harvard Law School, 1998.

Smith, William H. "Hon. John Chandler," *Granite Monthly, A New Hampshire Magazine,* 6, 1, (October 1883) 5-11.

Thompson, Mabel W. "Billy Green The Scout" *Ontario Historical Society, Papers and Records, Vol. 44,* Toronto, Ontario Historical Society, 1952.

Triggs, John R. "McMaster University Field School at Dundurn Castle, Hamilton: Fortifying the Beasley Homestead" *Annual Archeological Reports Ontario, Vol.,* 1994, 100-106.

Willegal, Michael J. *The Accuracy of Black Powder Muskets.* <http://www.willegal.net/iron_brigade/musket.pdf>, 199.

### Secondary Sources – Unpublished

Chartrand, René and Donald E. Graves. *The United States Army and the War of 1812: A Hand Book.* Unpublished manuscript, 1986

Couture, Paul. *The Non-Regular Military Forces on the Niagara Frontier: 1812-1814.* Ottawa: Parks Canada, Microfiche Report Series No. 193, 1985.

Hucker, Jacqueline. *Stoney Creek Monument, Battlefield Park, Stoney Creek, Ontario.* Historic Sites and Monuments Board of Canada Agenda Paper, 1992.

Liston, Maria A. *Human Skeletal Remains, Smith's Knoll Historic Cemetery, AhGw-132.* Unpublished preliminary report, 2000.

McAllister, Michael Fitzpatrick. *A Very Pretty Object: The Socially Constructed Landscape of Burlington Heights 1780- 1815.* M.A. thesis, McMaster University, 2002.

Maslin, Marnie. *High Tea and High Hopes: Sara Calder and her Battle for Stoney Creek.* Paper presented to the Friends of Battlefield House Museum, 8 April 2003.

# Index

## ABOUT THE AUTHOR

Photo by Irene Reinhold

**James Elliott** is a Canadian journalist and author with a keen and abiding interest in early North American history. With the *Hamilton Spectator* he wrote widely on the War of 1812 on subjects ranging from the Bloody Assizes to the Burlington Races. He worked on several episodes of the CBC's Gemini Award–winning *Canada: A People's History* both as a consultant and a special-skills extra. He is the author of the critically acclaimed *If Ponies Rode Men,* which should have been made into a major motion picture. James Elliott lives in Hamilton, Ontario, with his wife, Irene, four miles from the Stoney Creek battlefield.